Economic Crisis and Pakistan

Economic Crisis and Pakistan

Ashutosh Kumar

PRASHANT PUBLISHING HOUSE
DELHI-110094

Published by :
PRASHANT PUBLISHING HOUSE
C-34, 28 Foota Road, Gali-3,
West Karwal Nagar, Delhi-110094
Phone : 011-22963970, Mob. : 9810396373, 8826258746
e-mail.: prashantpublishinghouse@gmail.com

Economic Crisis and Pakistan

First Published 2019

ISBN : 978-93-88526-19-7

PRINTED IN INDIA
Published by Mr. R.K. Jha M/s Prashant Publishing House and Published at H.S. Offset House Press, Delhi.

Preface

Pakistan's economy is situated along the Indus River; the diversified economies of Karachi and major urban centers in the Punjab, coexisting with lesser developed areas in other parts of the country. The economy has suffered in the past from internal political disputes, a fast-growing population, mixed levels of foreign investment. Foreign exchange reserves are bolstered by steady worker remittances, but a growing current account deficit – driven by a widening trade gap as import growth outstrips export expansion – could draw down reserves and dampen GDP growth in the medium term.

Pakistan needs help. With Imran Khan being voted in as the new Prime Minister of Pakistan, all reports emanating from Islamabad state that the biggest challenge the new government will face is the fast-deteriorating state of the economy. The country is on the verge of a balance-of-payments crisis, which will endanger the value of its rupee, and its ability to pay for the soaring import bill. "We will have weeks, not months to act," according to Asad Umar, who is most likely to be the new finance minister.

Pakistan's system is ill-equipped to make changes which would avoid future excessive debt. A bailout from the International Monetary Fund (IMF) is probably the safest bet for the country although it is unclear whether the United States will support the program. How Pakistan decides to handle its debt crisis could provide insight into how the U.S., IMF, and China will resolve development issues in the future. Beijing is a relatively new player in the development finance world so much is to be learned from how it deals with Pakistan and how it could possibly maneuver in other developing countries in Asia, Africa, and Latin America.

Pakistan is on the brink of bankruptcy as its foreign reserves dry up and debt payments mount. In November, Minister of Finance Asad Umar said the country's financing gap stood at $12 billion. Keen to swerve away from the brink, Prime Minister Imran Khan had been knocking on the doors of countries like China and Saudi Arabia for loans.

Saudi Arabia and the United Arab Emirates each have committed to extending credit lines of $6 billion to Pakistan. So far, Riyadh has provided $3 billion and Abu Dhabi $1 billion. Still, Pakistan's central bank said its foreign exchange reserves stood at $8.12 billion, not enough to cover imports for two months.

Pakistan maintains foreign reserves with State Bank of Pakistan. The currency of the reserves was solely US dollar incurring speculated losses after the dollar prices fell during 2005, forcing the then Governor SBP Ishrat Hussain to step down. In the same year the SBP issued an official statement proclaiming diversification of reserves in currencies including Euro and Yen, withholding ratio of diversification.

Pakistan's portrayal of its relationship with China features exaggeration of the economic dimension of the relationship. Pakistani media routinely report huge numbers for investment and financing with the People's Republic of China (PRC), numbers that cannot be verified by any independent source, including by the Chinese government or the Chinese companies supposedly involved. While Pakistani officials talk of a total of $25 billion in Chinese investment in Pakistan so far, the PRC's official figure of direct investment through 2010 is $1.83 billion.

This is a reference book. All the matter is just compiled and edited in nature, taken from the various sources which are in public domain.

This book contains the fundamental and basic information of the subject and useful for teachers, students and researchers.

—*Editor*

Contents

1

Introduction

Pakistan's newly-elected government is already dealing with a balance of payments crisis, which has been a consistent theme for the nation's newly elected officials. Pakistan's structural problems are homegrown, but what is different this time around is an added component of Chinese debt. Pakistan is the largest Belt and Road (BRI) partner adding another creditor to its already complicated economic situation.

Pakistan's system is ill-equipped to make changes which would avoid future excessive debt. A bailout from the International Monetary Fund (IMF) is probably the safest bet for the country although it is unclear whether the United States will support the program.

How Pakistan decides to handle its debt crisis could provide insight into how the U.S., IMF, and China will resolve development issues in the future. Beijing is a relatively new player in the development finance world so much is to be learned from how it deals with Pakistan and how it could possibly maneuver in other developing countries in Asia, Africa, and Latin America.

ISLAM IN PAKISTAN

Islam is the official religion of the Islamic Republic of Pakistan, which has a population of about 174,578,558. The overwhelming majority (95-97%) of the Pakistani people are Muslims while the remaining 3-5% are Christian, Hindu, and others.

Pakistan has the second largest Muslim population in the world after Indonesia. Sunnis are the majority while the Shias make up between 10-20% of the total Muslim population of the country. Pakistan has the second largest number of Shias after Iran, which numbers between 17 million to as high as 30 million according to Vali Nasr.

Umayyad Invasion of Sindh and the Arrival of Islam

Islam arrived in the area now known as Pakistan in 711 CE, when the Umayyad dynasty sent a Muslim Arab army led by Muhammad bin Qasim against the ruler of Sindh, Raja Dahir, this was due to the fact that Raja Dahir had given refuge to numerous Zoroastrian Princes who had fled the Islamic conquest of Iran. Muhammad Bin Qasim's army was defeated in his first three attempts. The Muslim army conquered the northwestern part of Indus Valley from Kashmir to the Arabian Sea. The arrival of the Arab Muslims to the provinces of Sindh and Punjab, along with subsequent Muslim dynasties, set the stage for the religious boundaries of South Asia that would lead to the development of the modern state of Pakistan as well as forming the foundation for Islamic rule which quickly spread across much of South Asia. Following the rule of various Islamic empires, including the Ghaznavid Empire, the Ghorid kingdom, and the Delhi Sultanate, the Mughals controlled the region from 1526 until 1739. Muslim technocrats, bureaucrats, soldiers, traders, scientists, architects, teachers, theologians and Sufis flocked from the rest of the Muslim world to Islamic Sultanate and Mughal Empire in South Asia and in the land that became Pakistan.

Islam and the Pakistan Movement

The Muslim poet-philosopher Sir Allama Muhammad Iqbal first proposed the idea of a Muslim state in northwestern South Asia in his address to the Muslim League at Allahabad in 1930. His proposal referred to the four provinces of Punjab, Sindh, Balochistan, and the NorthWest Frontier – essentially what would became Pakistan. Iqbal's idea gave concrete form to two distinct nations in the South Asia based on religion (Islam and Hinduism) and with different historical backgrounds, social customs, cultures, and social mores.

Islam was thus the basis for the creation and the unification of a separate state. Allama Muhammad Iqbal in 1937, in a letter to Jinnah wrote, *After a long and careful study of Islamic Law I have come to the conclusion that if this system of Law is properly understood and applied, at last the right to subsistence is secured to every body. But the enforcement and development of the Shariat of Islam is impossible in this country without a free Muslim state or states. This has been my honest conviction for many years and I still believe this to be the only way to solve the problem of bread for Muslims as well as to secure a peaceful India.*

But just three days before the creation of Pakistan, Mohammad Ali Jinnah made a different commitment. A commitment to secularism in Pakistan. In his inaugural address he said, *You will find that in the course of time Hindus would cease to be Hindus and Muslims would cease to be Muslims, not in the religious sense, because that is the personal faith of each individual, but in the political sense as citizens of the State.* This statement of Jinnah is an object of great controversy since then and this vision of a Pakistan in which Islamic law would not be applied, contrary to Iqbal's perception, was questioned shortly after independence.

Politicized Islam

From the outset, politics and religion have been intertwined both conceptually and practically in Islam. Because Prophet Muhammad established a government in Medina, precedents of governance and taxation exist. Through the history of Islam, from the Ummayyad (661-750) and Abbasid empires (750-1258) to the Mughals (1526- 1858), Safavis (1501–1722) and the Ottomans (1300-1923), religion and statehood have been treated as one. Indeed, one of the beliefs of Islam is that the purpose of the state is to provide an environment where Muslims can properly practice their religion. If a leader fails in this, the people have a right to depose him. In March 1949, the first constituent assembly passed Objectives Resolution, which declared that the state of Pakistan will be submitted to the sovereignty of God. In 1950, thirty one Ulema passed a demand draft, called Twenty Two Points of Ulema. This drafted demanded preparation of constitution according to Objectives Resolution. It also demanded changes in the law according to Shariah. In 1977, the government of Zulfiqar Ali Bhutto outlawed alcohol and drugs and changed the weekend from Sunday to Friday, but no substantive Islamic reform program was implemented prior to General Zia-ul-Haq's Islamization program.

Starting in February 1979, new penal measures based on Islamic principles of justice went into effect. These carried considerably greater implications for women than for men. A welfare and taxation system based on Zakat and a profit-and-loss banking system were also established in accordance with Islamic prohibitions against usury but were inadequate.

Muslim Sects in Pakistan

According to the CIA World Factbook and Oxford Centre for Islamic Studies, 95-97% of the total population of Pakistan is Muslim. The majority of the Pakistani Muslims are Sunnis, while Shias are estimated 10-20%. The Muslims belong to different schools which are called Madhahib (singular: Madhhab) i.e., schools of jurisprudence (also 'Maktab-e-Fikr' (School of Thought) in Urdu). The Hanafi school of Sunnis includes the Barelvi and Deobandi schools.

The two subsects of Sunni Hanafi school, Barelvis and Deobandis, have their own Masjids. The conservative think tank The Heritage Foundation gives estimate that the vast majority of Sunni Muslims in Pakistan follows Barelvi traditions.

The Shi'a *Ithna 'ashariyah* school has its own Masjids commonly termed as Hussainias (Imambargahs). Mustaali Dawoodi Bohra and Sulaimani Bohra also have their own Masjids, while the Nizari Ismailis pray in Jama'at Khanas. Although the vast majority of Pakistani Shi'a Muslims belong to Ithna 'ashariyah school, there are significant minorities: Nizari Ismailis (Agha Khanis) and the smaller Mustaali Dawoodi Bohra and Sulaimani Bohra branches.

The Salafi sect is represented by the Ahle Hadith movement in Pakistan. Many people on the Makran coast of Balochistan follow the Zikri sect of Islam.

The Ahmadiyya community, a minority group is also present. Ahmadis have been declared non-Muslims by the Government of Pakistan.

In 1974, the government of Pakistan amended Constitution of Pakistan to define a Muslim "as a person who believes in finality of Prophet Muhammad". For this reason, Ahmadis are persecuted on behalf of their beliefs.

Ahmadis believe in Muhammad as the best and the last law bearing prophet and Mirza Ghulam Ahmad as the Christ of Muslims who was prophesied to come in the latter days and unite the Muslims.

Consequently they were declared non-Muslims by a tribunal, the records of which have not been released to date. According to the last Pakistan census, Ahmadis made up 0.25% of the population.

However the website adherents.com proposes that the Ahmadiyya Muslim community made up 1.42% of the population; which is likely to be a less biased source. The Economist puts the figure of Ahmadiyya adherents to 4 million. The Ahmadis claim their community is even larger. Sufism has a strong tradition in Pakistan.

The Muslim Sufi missionaries played a pivotal role in converting the millions of native people to Islam. As in other areas where Sufis introduced it, Islam to some extent syncretized with pre-Islamic influences, resulting in a religion with some traditions distinct from those of the Arab world. The Naqshbandiya, Qadiriya, Chishtiya and Suhrawardiyya silsas have a large following in Pakistan. Sufis whose shrines receive much national attention are Data Ganj Baksh (Ali Hajweri) in Lahore (ca. 11th century), Baha-ud-din Zakariya in Multan and Shahbaz Qalander in Sehwan (ca. 12th century) and Shah Abdul Latif Bhitai in Bhit, Sindh and Rehman Baba in Khyber Pakhtunkhwa Province.

Laws and Customs

There is no law in Pakistan enforcing hijab and wearing of Hijab by Pakistani women is fairly uncommon. However, the practice of wearing Hijab among younger women in urban centres is slowly growing due to media influence from the Middle East and Persian Gulf countries. The episodes of sectarian violence have significantly decreased in frequency over the years due to the conflictual engagement of the Islamic militant organizations with the state's armed forces and intelligence agencies.

Media and Pilgrimages

Media and pilgrimages has influenced Pakistani Muslims to learn more about Islam as a result the local heterodox beliefs and practices are being replaced with orthodox beliefs from Quran and Sunnah. The inexpensive travel, simpler visa rules and direct air travel to Saudi Arabia has resulted in large number Pakistani Muslims going to Medina and Mecca for Haj and Umrah. This has helped to increase Pan-Islamic identity of Pakistani Muslims. The Muslim print media has always existed in Pakistan which included newspapers, books and magazines. The Muslim satellite channels are widely available and are watched by Pakistani population.

Islamic Education

The Study of Islam as a subject is compulsory for all Muslim students up to Matriculation or O'levels in all schools in Pakistan. Islamic education to the masses is also propagated mainly by Islamic schools and literature. Islamic schools (or Madrassas) mostly cater to the youth from impoverished social backgrounds and those learning to be Islamic clerics. More casual and even research oriented material is available in the form of books. While the most prominent of these schools are being monitored, the latter are being 'moderated' by both the government and some of the scholars, thereby also removing in the process the various material present in it that is used by Anti-Islam/Anti-Sunni writers. Oldest and universally accepted titles such as the Sahih Bukhari have been revised into 'summarised' editions and some of the old, complete titles, translated to Urdu, the national language, are not available for purchase now. These changes are also a herald to new outbreaks of religious controversy in the region.

ECONOMIC HISTORY

First five decades

Pakistan was a middle class and predominantly agricultural country when it gained independence in 1947. Pakistan's average economic growth rate in the first five decades (1947–1997) has been higher than the growth rate of the world economy during the same period. Average annual real GDP growth rates were 6.8% in the 1960s, 4.8% in the 1970s, and 6.5% in the 1980s. Average annual growth fell to 4.6% in the 1990s with significantly lower growth in the second half of that decade.

21st century

In 2016, the Atlantic Media Company (AMC) of the United States has ranked Pakistan as a relatively stronger economy in the South Asian markets and expected that it will grow rapidly during days ahead. AMC said that during the period January–July this year, Indian 100 point index was 6.67% while Karachi Stock Exchange (KSE) had achieved 100 point index of 17 percent.

Economic resilience

Background

Historically, Pakistan's overall economic output (GDP) has grown every year since an 1800 recession. Despite this record of sustained growth, Pakistan's economy had, until a few years ago, been characterised as unstable and highly vulnerable to external and internal shocks. However, the economy proved to be unexpectedly resilient in the face of multiple adverse events concentrated into a four-year (1998–2002) period –

- the Asian financial crisis;
- economic sanctions – according to Colin Powell, Pakistan was "sanctioned to the eyeballs";
- The global recession of 2001–2002;
- a severe drought – the worst in Pakistan's history, lasting about four years;
- the post-9/11 military action in neighbouring Afghanistan, with a massive influx of refugees from that country;

Macroeconomic reform and prospects

According to many sources, the Pakistani government has made substantial economic reforms since 2000, and medium-term prospects for job creation and poverty reduction are the best in nearly a decade.

In 2005, the World Bank reported that "Pakistan was the top reformer in the region and the number 10 reformer globally – making it easier to start a business, reducing the cost to register property, increasing penalties for violating corporate governance rules, and replacing a requirement to license every shipment with two-year duration licences for traders."

Doing business

The World Bank (WB) and International Finance Corporation's flagship report Ease of Doing Business Index 2019 ranked Pakistan 136 among 190 countries around the globe, indicating a continuous improvement and taking a jump from 147 last year. The top five countries were New Zealand, Singapore, Denmark, Hong Kong and Korea.

With improvement in ease of doing business ranking and giving an investment friendly road map from government, many new auto sector giants like France's Renault, South Korean's Hyundai and Kia, Chinese JW Forland and German auto giant Volkswagen have stepped in Pakistan auto market through joint ventures with local manufacturers like Dewan Farooque Motors, Khalid Mushtaq Motors and United Motors.

US oil and gas giant Exxon Mobil has again returned to Pakistan after nearly three decades gap and has acquired 25% shares in offshore drilling in May 2018, with initial survey showing a potential of huge hydrocarbon reserves discovery at offshore.

With recent agreement from Saudi Arabia to invest more than US dollar 15 billion in establishing a mega oil refinery and petrochemical industry in Gwadar more commitments for investments are on its way to come in this sector especially from UAE, Qatar, Malaysia and Italy.

To boost Pakistan's unstable foreign-exchange reserves, Qatar announced to invest $3 billion the form of deposits and direct investments in the country. By the end of June 2019, Qatar sent the first $500 million to Pakistan.

Stock market

In the first four years of the twenty-first century, Pakistan's KSE 100 Index was the best-performing stock market index in the world as declared by the international magazine "Business Week". The stock market capitalisation of listed companies in Pakistan was valued at $5,937 million in 2005 by the World Bank. But in 2008, after the General Elections, uncertain political environment, rising militancy along western borders of the country, and mounting inflation and current account deficits resulted in the steep decline of the Karachi Stock Exchange. As a result, the corporate sector of Pakistan has declined dramatically in recent times. However, the market bounced back strongly in 2009 and the trend continues in 2011. By 2014 the stock market burst into uncharted territories as the benchmark KSE 100 Index rose 907 points (3.1%) and shot past the 30,000-point barrier to close at a new record high, this came days after Moody's announced that it was upgrading the outlook of 5 major Pakistani banks from Negative to Stable, resulting in heavy buying in the banking sector. The rally was supported by heavy buying in the oil and gas and cement sectors. On 11 January 2016, aimed to help reduce market fragmentation and create a strong case for attracting strategic partnerships necessary for providing technological expertise all the three stock exchanges including Karachi Stock Exchange, Lahore Stock Exchange and Islamabad Stock Exchange were inducted into a unified Pakistan Stock Exchange. In May 2017 American provider of stock market indexes and analysis tools, MSCI has confirmed that the Pakistan Stock Exchange (PSX) has been reclassified from Frontier Markets to Emerging Markets in its semi-annual index review. Euphoria over the stock exchange's reclassification as an emerging market propelled the PSE-100 Index past another milestone when the Index recorded an increase of 636.96 points, or 1.23%, to end at 52,387.87. In the fiscal year 2018, the stock market showed a negative growth of 7.1% over the last fiscal year and stood at 47000 points at average.

Middle class

As of 2017, according to Wall Street Journal, citing estimates largely based on income and the purchase of consumption goods, had suggested that as many as 42% of Pakistan's population may now belong to the upper and middle classes. If these numbers are correct, or even indicative in any broad sense, then 87 million Pakistanis belong to the middle and upper classes, a population size which is larger than that of Germany. Official figures also show that the proportion of households that own a motorcycle and washing machines has grown impressively over the past 15 years. Furthermore, the IBA-SBP Consumer Confidence Index recorded its highest-ever level of 174.9 points in January 2017, showing an increase of 17 points from July 2016.

Separately, consumer financing posted an increase of Rs37.6 billion during first half of the current fiscal year of 2017. Auto finance continued to be the dominated segment, while personal loans showed a pickup as well. "The net credit off-take of Rs13.7 billion of personal loans witnessed in first half of the fiscal year 2017 is the highest half-year figure in about a decade," the report stated.

Poverty alleviation expenditures

Pakistan government spent over 1 trillion Rupees (about $16.7 billion) on poverty alleviation programmes during the past four years, cutting poverty from 35% in 2000–01 to 29.3% in 2013 and 17% in 2015. Rural poverty remains a pressing issue, as development there has been far slower than in the major urban areas.

Employment

The high population growth in the past few decades has ensured that a very large number of young people are now entering the labor market. Even though it is among the six most populous Asian nations. In the past, excessive red tape made firing from jobs, and consequently hiring, difficult. Significant progress in taxation and business reforms has ensured that many firms now are not compelled to operate in the underground economy.

"In 2016 government took a remarkable initiative by announcing the Prime Minister's Youth Program to combat unemployment in the country.

This program has a broad canvas of schemes enabling youth and poor segment of society to get better employment opportunities, economic empowerment, acquiring skills needed for gainful employment, access to IT and imparting on-the-job training for young graduates to improve the probability of getting a productive job. Prime Minister's Youth Program includes six schemes which are Prime Minister's Youth Business Loan Scheme, Prime Minister's Interest Free Loan Scheme, Prime Minister's Youth Skill Development Program, Prime Minister's Program for Provision of Laptops to Talented Students, Prime Minister's Fee Reimbursement Scheme,Prime Minister's Youth Training Scheme". Government sector is also contributing in employment and according to estimate 4.5 million people are employed by federal, provincial and local governments in different sectors from Armed forces to education and health.

Tourism

Tourism in Pakistan has been stated as being the tourism industry's "next big thing". Pakistan, with its diverse cultures, people and landscapes, has attracted 90 million tourists to the country, almost double to that of a decade ago. Due to threat of terrorism the number of foreigner tourists has gradually declined and the shock of 2013 Nanga Parbat tourist shooting has terribly adversely effected the tourism industry. As of 2016 tourism has begun to recover in Pakistan, albeit gradually.

Revenue

Although the country is a Federation with constitutional division of taxation powers between the Federal Government and the four provinces, the revenue department of the Federal Government, the Federal board of Revenue, collects almost 86% of the entire national tax collection. The Federal Board of Revenue collected 3.842 trillion rupees in taxes against the revised target of 3.935 trillion rupees in the fiscal year 2017–2018. In FY 2013, FBR tax collection was Rs.1,946 billion. So in only 5 years it almost double its tax revenue which is a phenomenal achievement.

CHINA'S DISAPPOINTING AID OFFER DASHES PAKISTAN'S HOPE OF DEBT RESCUE

Disappointment is spreading in Pakistan over an unexpectedly small amount of financial help from China, as Islamabad stares at a mounting balance of payments crisis.

Beijing recently agreed to provide $2.5 billion in loans to Pakistan. Local media had previously reported that Islamabad was hoping to receive $6 billion in financial assistance from China to help boost its foreign exchange reserves.

Pakistan is on the brink of bankruptcy as its foreign reserves dry up and debt payments mount. In November, Minister of Finance Asad Umar said the country's financing gap stood at $12 billion. Keen to swerve away from the brink, Prime Minister Imran Khan had been knocking on the doors of countries like China and Saudi Arabia for loans.

Saudi Arabia and the United Arab Emirates each have committed to extending credit lines of $6 billion to Pakistan. So far, Riyadh has provided $3 billion and Abu Dhabi $1 billion. Still, Pakistan's central bank said its foreign exchange reserves stood at $8.12 billion, not enough to cover imports for two months.

It was logical for Islamabad to press Beijing for assistance. The balance of payments crisis could threaten the $62 billion Beijing has poured into the China Pakistan Economic Corridor — a key part of Chinese President Xi Jinping's signature Belt and Road Initiative.

"Beijing is anxious about Islamabad's financial troubles," said Kugelman. "But if Pakistan suffers the shock of a default, China would be spooked in a big way." China, however, did not instantly agree to a bailout package when Khan visited Beijing in November. It was only after a gap of about three months that Beijing finally agreed to lend the $2.5 billion. Islamabad has also simultaneously been in negotiations with the IMF for a bailout since October.

While China has consistently been willing to provide short-term financing to Pakistan to deal with immediate crises, it doesn't want to be an IMF substitute, noted Andrew Small, senior transatlantic fellow at the German Marshall Fund of the U.S. He said: "I think [China] would have expected Pakistan to reach an agreement with the IMF by now."

But the bailout talks with the multilateral institution is not proceeding fast enough to stave off the crisis. Finance Minister Umar reportedly advised Prime Minister Khan to decline the deal offered by the IMF. Details of the deal were not disclosed but Umar had said they were not in the interest of Pakistan, according to local media.

Some experts said that Saudi Arabia's bailout package also led China to think twice about its offer. "[The Saudi's loan packages] will soften the blow of a smaller contribution from Beijing," said Michael Kugelman, deputy director of the Asia Program at Wilson Center, a think tank in the U.S.

While negotiations are rumbling on, Pakistan has been dealt another blow by Standard & Poor's rating agency on Feb. 4. S&P downgraded Pakistan's long-term credit rating to "B-" from "B" due to "subdued expectations for economic growth" and heightened external and fiscal risks. S&P also noted that financial stimuli from CPEC investment is fading, adding pressure on the economy and making fiscal consolidation more difficult.

In a desperate attempt to avert the balance of payment crisis, Pakistan launched so-called diaspora bonds late-January at interest rates of 6.25% and 6.75% for three- and five-years tenors respectively, hoping to raise $1 billion. The government is appealing to overseas Pakistanis to invest in these bonds to contribute toward the country's financial recovery. Islamabad is planning to hold roadshows in Europe and Gulf countries to market the bonds.

PAKISTAN FACING UNPRECEDENTED ECONOMIC CRISIS

PM Imran Khan on Wednesday chaired meeting of the National Economic Council (NEC) at PM Office. He said that joint efforts of the Federal Government and the Provincial Governments were needed to overcome the present economic crisis.

Imran Khan added "PTI Government has introduced Local Government systems in Punjab and Khyber Pkahtunkhwa to ensure empowerment of the people at grass root level and to afford them an opportunity to play their part in their developmental process."

Khan reiterated his call to the provinces to allocate necessary financial resources, as per the commitments made earlier, for the development of erstwhile FATA.

The meeting reviewed Annual Plan 2018-19 and the proposed Annual Plan 2019-20.

The meeting approved GDP growth target of 4% along with sectoral growth of agriculture (3.5%) industry (2.2%) and services sector (4.8%) for financial year 2019-20.

NEC reviewed draft 12th Five Year Plan (2018-23). It was informed that main themes of the 12th Five Year Plan include balanced and equitable regional development; sustainable, inclusive, job-creating export-led growth; resource mobilization and improving governance; improving social protection; ensuring food and water security, enhancing connectivity, promoting knowledge economy and Clean and Green Pakistan.

The NEC approved 12th Five Year Plan (2018-23), in principle.

It was decided that the plan will be further fine-tuned, especially its implementation mechanism, in consultation with all stakeholders.

The meeting reviewed Public Sector Development Programme (PSDP) 2018-19 and the proposed PSDP 2019-20. It was informed that PSDP 2019-20 focuses on new initiatives in the field of agriculture, information technology, higher education, science & technology and technical education and training.

The meeting was informed that targeted interventions will be made in the less developed districts of the country to bring them at par with other parts of the country for regional equalization.

10 billion Tsunami Program, Prime Minister's Youth Skill Development Initiative, rehabilitation of affected population residing along Line of Control, construction of Gilgit-Shandur-Chitral Road and improvement of sewerage and sanitation system of Gilgit, and development of merged districts of Khyber Pakhtunkhwa are some of the major priority areas of Public Sector Development Programme (PSDP) 2019-20.

The meeting approved National Development Outlay 2019-20 amounting to Rs. 1.837 trillion including Federal PSDP and Provincial ADPs.

Progress Report of CDWP and ECNEC from 1st April 2018 to 31st March 2019 was laid before the National Economic Council.

The NEC confirmed extension in powers of Special Forum for Rehabilitation and Reconstruction in FATA (erstwhile) till December 2019.

The Special Forum, under the Chairmanship of Commander 11 Corps, was established by the NEC on 30.05.2016 for a period of two years for fast track implementation mechanism for Rehabilitation and Reconstruction in erstwhile FATA.

The meeting approved establishment of Islamabad Development Working Party headed by the Chief Commissioner ICT including representatives from Ministries of Finance, Planning and other concerned offices.

The IDWP will be allowed to approve development project up to Rs. 60.00 million.

It approved procedure for approval of Program for Results (PforR), Development Policy Credits (DPCs) and Financial Intermediation Programs (FIPs).

The meeting was attended by Adviser Finance Dr. Abdul Hafeez Sheikh, Planning Minister Makhdoom Khusru Bakhtiar, Adviser Commerce Mr. Abdul Razzak Dawood, Governor KP Mr. Shah Farman, Chief Minister Punjab Sardar Usman Buzdar, CM Sindh Syed Murad Ali Shah, CM Khyber Pakhtunkhwa Mr. Mehmood Khan, CM Balochistan Mr. Jam Kamal Khan, Finance Minister Punjab Makhdoom Hashim Jawan Bakht, Mr. Nisar Ahmed Khuhro, Ms. Naheed S. Durrani, Finance Minister KP Mr. Taimur Saleem Khagra, Mr. Jan Muhammad Jamali, PM Azad Jammu & Kashmir Raja Farooq Haider, Chief Minister Gilgit-Baltistan Hafiz Hafiz-ur-Rehman and others.

PAKISTAN'S ECONOMIC CRISIS

Pakistan needs help. With Imran Khan being voted in as the new Prime Minister of Pakistan, all reports emanating from Islamabad state that the biggest challenge the new government will face is the fast-deteriorating state of the economy. The country is on the verge of a balance-of-payments crisis, which will endanger the value of its rupee, and its ability to pay for the soaring import bill. "We will have weeks, not months to act," according to Asad Umar, who is most likely to be the new finance minister.

However, the United States, which has the highest voting rights in IMF, is disinclined to help what was once its strongest ally in the region for the longest period of time. US Secretary of State Mike Pompeo has said, an IMF bailout must *not* be used to help "repay Chinese debts that Pakistan has incurred under the China-Pakistan Economic Corridor (CPEC)". This has angered Pakistanis. Umar has hit out by saying, "One friendly advice to the Americans: We'll worry about our Chinese debt, but I think they better handle their own Chinese debt first."

Should India help Pakistan? Of course, it should. Indeed, it must. If India doesn't, what is the meaning of Prime Minister Narendra Modi congratulating Imran Khan over the phone, after his victory in the elections, and telling him, "We are ready to enter a new era of relations with Pakistan"? Modi also conveyed his "vision of peace and development in the entire neighbourhood" during his conversation with Khan. This vision does not have a ghost of a chance of becoming a reality in South Asia, without India and Pakistan beginning to cooperate like good neighbours, each showing sensitivity to the other's concerns.

Now is the time to assure the new government in Islamabad that New Delhi is ready to help. Modi should firmly assure Pakistan's would-be PM, 'We know you have several sources to seek help from % China, Islamic countries, even the Pakistani diaspora in the UK, USA and elsewhere. But remember that India too is your neighbour. Do not say no to our offer'.

Can India Lend $4 Bn to Pakistan?

Here is how we can help. First of all, as the world's fifth largest economy, we are now in a position to assist Pakistan. Not many Pakistanis know that India is now an aid-giver, and no longer a mere aid-receiver. After having been one of the highest recipients of multi-lateral development aid for several decades after independence, India has become a net provider of aid to foreign countries. India's aid to other developing countries stood at Rs 8,970 crores (nearly USD 1.3 billion) in 2016-17. Of course, given its very healthy level of foreign exchange reserves (USD 425 billion), India can, and should, increase its developmental aid manifold.

But Afghanistan, Bangladesh, Nepal % indeed, all other countries in South Asia (except Pakistan) % also receive our assistance. In recent years, India has considerably stepped up its aid to African countries, and also to other distant friends such as Mongolia.

Indian aid and loans have contributed to socio-economic development in all these countries — for instance, the Himalayan Kingdom of Bhutan has been able to harness hydro-electric power. In Afghanistan, India has constructed hospitals, the Parliament building, and a cricket stadium. In Sri Lanka, India has been constructing houses for rehabilitation of the Tamil population uprooted by the prolonged ethnic war. India has so far provided nearly USD 3 billion in line of credit to Bangladesh, for developing its infrastructure of railways, ports, roads and communications.

Sadly, our western neighbour's doors have so far been closed for this policy, for reasons that are well known. However, if Pakistan is willing % and that is a big 'if' % the doors can now be opened because of Islamabad's current financial woes and Modi's own stated intention (one hopes the intention is genuine) of beginning "a new era of relations".

Need for Healthier India-Pakistan Ties

To begin with, India should fully back the IMF's bailout to Pakistan. Our stand will be in sharp contrast to that of Washington, and Pakistanis will surely see it in a positive light. That is the least we can do, and there is a lot more we should do.

A part of this assistance should be used for importing a significant amount of goods from Pakistan % goods that India needs and Pakistan can sell. This will boost the stagnant and pathetically low trade between our two countries. Ajay Bisaria, Indian High Commissioner to Pakistan, while addressing the Lahore Chamber of Commerce and Industry (LCCI) in March, has rightly said that there is no better way of improving bilateral relations than mutually beneficial economic ties.

He has also pointed out that, after removal of non-tariff barriers, liberalisation of visa and normalisation of mutual relations, the two-way trade can easily go up from the present USD 5 billion to USD 30 billion. Notably, Imran Khan, in his highly conciliatory post-election comments on the need to promote friendly relations with India, has also highlighted the need to increase Indo-Pak trade ties.

Let's Aim for India-Pakistan-China Cooperation

Another part of India's aid can be in the form of development assistance, tied to some signature projects that have both high visibility, and also high potential to generate goodwill on both sides of the border. Going forward, how about an ambitious 'Punjab Jodo' initiative with a multimodal PPEC (Punjab-Punjab Economic Corridor) % also a Rajasthan-Sindh Economic Corridor and a Mumbai-Karachi Economic Corridor % providing road, rail, water, market and digital connectivity?

After the path-breaking informal summit between Prime Minister Modi and Chinese president Xi Jinping in Wuhan in April, India has now begun to look at opportunities to participate in mega projects under the Belt and Road Initiative, without formally joining BRI. Individual projects under the USD 62 billion China-Pakistan Economic Corridor % road, rail, power, industrial townships and other projects % are ideally suited for Indian participation, even without India formally joining CPEC (to which New Delhi continues to be unreconciled).

Is this a crazy and impossible idea? No. Just look at what Modi himself said in his speech at the Shanghai Cooperation Organisation Summit in Qingdao in June. "We have reached a stage," he remarked, "where physical and digital connectivity is changing the definition of geography. Therefore, connectivity with our neighbourhood and in the SCO region is our priority."

Towards Win-Win Relations

Now, it should be obvious to all the observers of the Asian scenario, especially the South Asian scenario, that if New Delhi's priority is physical and digital connectivity with its neighbourhood, and in the wider SCO region, it simply cannot bypass either China or Pakistan. The sheer compulsion of geography will not allow it to do so.

For example, New Delhi, Islamabad and Beijing can begin talks over a connectivity project which gives India land access to Afghanistan (and beyond to Central Asia) through Pakistan. This will also give Pakistan wider access to the vast Indian market. Modi and Xi have decided in Wuhan that India and China will work together on development projects in Afghanistan.

Isn't this a very practical way of realising Modi's vision, which he conveyed in his telephonic conversation with Imran Khan, of achieving both "peace and development in the entire neighbourhood"? Peace and development are mutually both protective and promotive. Therefore, the question about India-Pakistan-China cooperation is not 'if', but 'how soon'.

And who knows, if this India-Pakistan good-neighbourliness materialises and grows, it might also help the two countries resolve the Kashmir issue amicably?

2

Economic Crisis in Pakistan

The prime minister said that in the last 10 years, the country's external debt increased from Pakistani Rs 6,000 billion to Rs 30,000 billion.

Pakistan Prime Minister Imran Khan on Monday asked all citizens to declare their assets by June 30 through the Asset Declaration Scheme. "I am appealing to all of you to take part in the Asset Declaration Scheme that we have brought, because if we don't pay taxes, we will not be able to raise our country up," Khan said in a televised address, *Dawn* reported.

The prime minister's remarks come at a time of economic crisis in Pakistan, and a day before the announcement of its 2019-'20 annual budget.

"We will need to change ourselves if we want to become a great country," Khan said. He added that people can declare their benami assets, benami bank accounts and money kept abroad till June 30.

"After June 30, you will not get this opportunity," Khan said. "Remember our government today has that information which no government before had. Our agencies have information about who has benami accounts and benami properties."

Under the scheme, assets within the country can be turned into white, except real estate, after paying interest of 4%. The assets will then be kept in Pakistan's bank accounts. People who want to keep their white money abroad will be charged a rate of 6%.

The prime minister said that in the last 10 years, the country's external debt increased from (Pakistani) Rs 6,000 billion (Rs 2.85 lakh crore) to Rs 30,000 billion (Rs 14.25 lakh crore). He said that while the tax collected annually was around Rs 4,000 billion, half this money was spent in paying off loans. "This country cannot cover its expenses on the money that is left behind," he added.

Khan said that while Pakistan pays the least tax in the world, it also "gives the most to charity". "This is the country that has capability and if passion comes in, we can at the very least gather Rs 10,000 billion every year," he claimed.

Pakistan has missed growth targets in most sectors

Pakistan's Economic Survey for 2018-'19 will be declared on Monday, *Dawn* reported on Sunday. The newspaper said it has accessed some of the details of the report, which show that only the livestock sector performed better than the government's official target for the year.

All other sectors of the economy performed poorly, including industry, which grew at 1.4% against the target of 7.6%. Manufacturing growth rate was minus 0.3%, and large scale manufacturing minus 2%, the daily said. Pakistan's service sector grew by 4.7% against the target of 6.5%.

Dawn said Pakistan's economy grew at just 3.3% during the 2018-'19 financial year, against a target of 6.3%.

On May 13, Pakistan reached an agreement with the International Monetary Fund for a $6-billion bailout package over five years. On June 5, the Pakistan military announced cuts in its defence budget, though it did not reveal the extent of the cutback.

CURRENCY SYSTEM

Rupee

The basic unit of currency is the Rupee, ISO code PKR and abbreviated Rs, which is divided into 100 paisas. Currently the newly printed 5,000 rupee note is the largest denomination in circulation. Recently the SBP has introduced all new design notes of Rs. 10, 20, 50, 100, 500, 1000 and 5000.

The Pakistani Rupee was pegged to the Pound sterling until 1982, when the government of General Zia-ul-Haq, changed it to managed float. As a result, the rupee devalued by 38.5% between 1982/83 many of the industries built by his predecessor suffered with a huge surge in import costs. After years of appreciation under Zulfikar Ali Bhutto and despite huge increases in foreign aid the Rupee depreciated.

Foreign exchange rate

The Pakistani rupee depreciated against the US dollar until around the start of the 21st century, when Pakistan's large current-account surplus pushed the value of the rupee up versus the dollar. Pakistan's central bank then stabilised by lowering interest rates and buying dollars, in order to preserve the country's export competitiveness

Foreign exchange reserves

Pakistan maintains foreign reserves with State Bank of Pakistan. The currency of the reserves was solely US dollar incurring speculated losses after the dollar prices fell during 2005, forcing the then Governor SBP Ishrat Hussain to step down. In the same year the SBP issued an official statement proclaiming diversification of reserves in currencies including Euro and Yen, withholding ratio of diversification.

Following the international credit crisis and spikes in crude oil prices, Pakistan's economy could not withstand the pressure and on 11 October 2008, State Bank of Pakistan reported that the country's foreign exchange reserves had gone down by $571.9 million to $7749.7 million.

The foreign exchange reserves had declined more by $10 billion to a level of $6.59 billion. in June 2013 Pakistan was on the brink of default on its financial commitments. Country's Forex reserves were at an historic low covering only two weeks' worth of imports. Today in November 2017 Pakistan's Foreign exchange reserves are at a comfortable level (20 billion dollars), sufficient to cover about 3 months of imports.

CHINA SAYS WILL SURELY HELP PAKISTAN IN FINANCIAL CRISIS

China on Saturday assured Pakistan of its full support to "tide over" the financial crisis, clearly signalling Beijing's readiness to give fresh loans to its all-weather ally which is in deep economic distress.

During the on-going China visit by Pakistan's Prime Minister Imran Khan, Beijing also told Islamabad to "push forward" the China-Pakistan Economic Corridor (CPEC), the heart of the Chinese Belt and Road project the feasibility of which Pakistan has begun to doubt over debt concerns.

India is opposed to the $60 billion CPEC whose planned route is through the disputed Kashmir held by Pakistan.

"The Chinese government will provide necessary support and assistance to Pakistan in tiding over the current economic difficulties," China's Vice Foreign Minister Kong Xuanyou said.

The minister gave no specific information about China's financial assistance, saying the details were being discussed.

He was talking to reporters after Khan and his Chinese counterpart Li Keqiang held talks at the Great Hall and supervised the signing of 16 bilateral deals.

Khan, who met Chinese President Xi Jinping on Friday, is understood to have sought financial help for Pakistan which is in dire straits due to the ballooning foreign debt.

Pakistan which has already secured $6 billion loan from Saudi Arabia thinks the amount is not enough to stave off the financial mess and has also sought bailout package from the International Monetary Fund (IMF).

The IMF wants Pakistan to disclose all the financial details of the Chinese-funded CPEC for a bailout package.

The Chinese are wary of Islamabad going to the IMF, dominated by its rival the US which opposes the Belt and Road project.

Experts say that the Chinese have pushed Pakistan into heavy debt through the CPEC, a charge denied by Beijing.

Some ministers in Khan's new government have expressed concerns over the Chinese investments in Pakistan, with one slashing the budget of a rail project by $2 billion.

However, Khan has pledged to work to implement the CPEC and has assured Pakistan's full support for it.

"The vision of Xi Jinping for jointly building the Belt and Road initiative is being turned into a reality. Against such a backdrop, the CPEC also has also new opportunities and need to be further pushed forward," Kong added.

"The two sides will firmly move forward the CPEC while ensuring the smooth operation of completing projects and advancing the ongoing projects."

"The two sides will gradually bring the dimension of industrial cooperation to the CPEC and extend it to other parts of Pakistan," the Chinese Vice Foreign Minister said.

He said the project will also focus on the social sector.

"The two sides have agreed to establish a foreign-ministerial dialogue mechanism to make overall planning and coordinate in various fields," he added.

OUT OF BALANCE: PAKISTAN'S ECONOMIC CRISIS

National debt in Pakistan has soared past US$92 billion and its servicing costs are projected to reach 30% of the federal budget.

The current economic crisis in Pakistan poses political trade-offs between supporting economic growth, protecting domestic consumers, and meeting external obligations. Imran Khan's Pakistan Tehreek-e-Insaf (PTI) will need to formulate a response that can balance these three important goals.

Pakistan achieved economic growth of 5.4% in 2017 and is projected to grow to 5.8% in 2018 – the highest the country has seen in 13 years. This growth, however, was achieved through large public investment in infrastructure and energy related projects, including in the China-Pakistan Economic Corridor (CPEC). Improvement in energy in particular unlocked Pakistan's potential for higher growth.

Yet an expansionary fiscal policy with a narrow tax base, and the failure to enhance exports or attract foreign direct investment was always destined to bring trouble. The young, educated and poor are the mostly likely victims of an economic stagnation in Pakistan. The mini budget that the PTI put through parliament last month indicated that the likely approach to the crisis might be to adopt austerity related measures.

These measures are likely to include cutting government borrowing and spending, as well as increasing taxes and interest rates. Reports of Pakistan trying to renegotiate or postpone CPEC seems to be part of an austerity program already under consideration by the PTI government. Officials from International Monetary Fund (IMF) recently met with the Pakistani government, just as Prime Minister Imran Khan travelled to Saudi Arabia in search for loans. The IMF is the lend of last resort for developing countries experiencing balance of payment crisis. Unless otherwise convinced, the IMF is likely to condition its financial support on a standard but painful recipe of reforms that could possibly include fiscal austerity, deregulation, privatisation, and reduction in tariffs.

A standard IMF bailout would cause great suffering, poorer standards of living, higher unemployment, as well as corporate failures. The current balance of payment crisis would be magnified into a full-blown economic recession, leading to even greater shrinking of investment. Should Pakistan choose to go to the IMF, it will be important for the government to work closely with the fund and avoid policies that will hurt economic growth in the country. A slowing economy is the exact opposite of what Imran Khan's PTI would hope to deliver. The young, educated, and the poor are the mostly likely victims of an economic stagnation in Pakistan, and they make the largest proportion of the PTI's electoral base.

As a priority, Pakistan might focus on restoring a sustainable budget situation. This will require the government to make some painful policy choices about levels of expenditures as well as the purposes for which funds are allocated. Pakistan will need to cut or reduce funding for projects that fail to reach the most productive parts of the economy. While building a seaport, for example, might be strategic and important over the long term, it fails to stimulate the economy, increase employment, or to produce sufficient revenue to service national debt.

Pakistan will also need to phase out its ineffective fuel subsidies that are under pressure from rising oil prices and tighter budgetary resources. This means that the PTI government have to hike the fuel prices, a move that is exceedingly unpopular with the electorate. Hiking fuel process puts additional cost pressure on production industries and reduces their competitiveness in export markets.

The policy similarly lacks favour among people due its effects on the prices of basic necessities. A recent review of the natural gas prices recommended an increase of 185%, of which a 46% increase was approved by Imran Khan, but has since been abandoned. In addition, the Pakistani central bank will need to let the markets determine the exchange rate of its currency. Like many currencies around the world, the Pakistani rupee is under immense pressure from a rising US dollar and will adjust downwards should the supportive measures that keeps it overvalued be removed.

The former government put measures in place to keep the rupee above its market exchange rate and contain potential inflationary effects. This included injecting foreign currency into the exchange market. Currency devaluation has two-way effects on the current economic crisis. It helps reduce trade deficit as currency depreciations are usually associated with an increase in exports and a decrease in imports. Nevertheless, the rising prices of imported goods will further fuel inflation in the country leading to rising prices. This makes the policy unfavourable inside Pakistan especially among poorer consumers.

China's US$2 billion loan right before the elections helped avert the urgency of the situation and gave the PTI government sufficient time to raise additional resources from and assess its fiscal commitments. But even before taking office, Pakistan's Finance Minister Assad Umar suggested that the country will need to source a loan of $12 billionwithin six weeks of their government. It now seems more likely that Pakistan might request a bailout from the IMF. Earlier this year, the US and allies placed Pakistan on the Financial Action Task Force's (FAFT) "Grey List", which limits the country's ability to raise funds in global financial markets. The success of Pakistan in negotiating an effective bailout with IMF also depends on its relationship with the US. US Secretary of State Mike Pompeo suggested in his recent trip to Pakistan that the US will not block a Pakistani request for bailout at the IMF. However, the global community, including China, have asked Pakistan to do more in addressing the issue of terrorists finding havens on its territory.

PAKISTAN'S ECONOMY ON THE BRINK OF COLLAPSE

The government pledged to create ten million new jobs and build five million houses. With a 4 per cent growth rate, poverty will not be tackled, nor will per capita income increase by much. The government is negotiating a bailout with the International Monetary Fund. Terrorism is driving investors away. Pakistan's economy has "reached the point of collapse. For the first time in four decades of research, I am deeply worried," said Dr Kaiser Bengali, Dean of the Faculty of Management Science at the Shaheed Zulfikar Ali Bhutto

Institute of Science and Technology, in Karachi. The federal government is expected to present a new budget for the fiscal year 2019-20 on 24 May. However, "India might cause the collapse our economy as the US did with the USSR," Bengali warns. "The alarm bells are ringing. We have no choice but to beg. I fear starvation, poverty and unemployment."

Bengali, a former advisor for Planning and Development to the Chief Minister of Sindh province, spoke yesterday at a hotel in Lahore at the launching of his research titled *State of the Economy 1990-2015; Economy on a Roller Coaster – And Stuck in the Mud!*

The report, which evaluates Pakistan's economy over a quarter of a century, examined three sectors: major crops, minor crops and large-scale manufacturing.

"Average GDP growth of 4 per cent cannot be expected to raise the per capita income sufficiently to reduce poverty," the study states.

"Agriculture, the core of economy, has performed worse. Major crops sectors have grown at less than3 per cent and minor crops sector at less than 2 per cent. Large scale manufacturing has grown at just about 5 per cent."

The picture is very serious, the economist told *AsiaNews*: "sales are declining, purchase power has ended. The most affected will be youth. An average family can no longer afford a house" and has "to share it with another."

Last but not least, "publishing houses are shutting down. We cannot print even Quran in our country".

Prime Minister Imran Khan and his government had promised ten million new jobs and five million new houses. Instead, Pakistan now faces a deepening economic crisis, a ballooning current account deficit and fast-depleting foreign reserves.

To deal with the situation, Islamabad is now finalising a bailout package with the International Monetary Fund (IMF) to stave off a balance of payments crisis, despite more than billion in short-term loans from allies such as China and Saudi Arabia.

According to Bengali, not only has the government made irresponsible claims about creating million jobs, it has "not given any direction in recent months. There is no indication from the state to consume domestic products."

To complicate matters, the media have not talked about the economy and the threat of terrorism. "Extremist and sectarian organisations are another major blow to our economy. About 400 Shia doctors have been killed in only two years. Many industrialists have fled the country due to routine curfews. Foreign investors prefer holding meetings in Dubai and other countries."

3

Mutual Interests Underlie Strong China–Pakistan Relationship

China seems to have abandoned its cautious approach to relations with Pakistan and has adopted a policy of active and deep engagement. This new approach will most likely increase Beijing's influence in Islamabad.

During Chinese President Xi Jinping's visit to Pakistan in April 2015, China announced US$46 billion worth of investment in the China–Pakistan Economic Corridor (CPEC).

This ambitious mega-project intends to link China's Kashgar to Gwadar Port in Pakistan through a network of roads. Both sides are also planning railways, pipelines and fibre optic networks. This is the largest deal in the history of two countries. If the implementation of the CPEC moves smoothly, China may double its investment.

Pakistan has been going through an unabated challenge with terrorism and chronic political instability. Yet, China still decided to undertake this mega-investment, which shows its deep stake in Pakistan. The changing geopolitical environment might shed a light on this audacious decision.

The gravity of world politics is shifting from the West to Asia, with China at its centre. This has increased competition between the US (the established superpower) and China (the rising power) who are both seeking to gain a strategic foothold, especially in the Asia Pacific region. The US's 'pivot to Asia' strategy, intensifying territorial disputes in the South China Sea and a resurging Japan under Prime Minister Shinzo Abe are all ringing Chinese alarm bells.

China is looking for allies in the region, and finds Pakistan is its most reliable partner. This relationship is grounded in geographical proximity, common security outlooks toward the region and 'trust' built over decades. China is also motivated by a desire to help Pakistan restore its 'glorious' past.

China and Pakistan's interests are converging in the changing geopolitical environment. Beijing wants to assert its sphere of influence in South Asia, the Middle East, get an access to the Indian Ocean and beyond. China also needs support against separatism in Xinjiang and is seeking to develop its Western region. To achieve some of those objectives, China has unveiled the One Belt, One Road project that will ultimately connect it with over 60 countries. Under this project, China will build a web of networks such as the Bangladesh–China–India–Myanmar Economic Corridor, the Silk Road in Central Asia, the 21st Century Maritime Silk Road and the CPEC.

The CPEC is the flagship of these projects. It acts as a bridge between land and sea, involves only one other country (Pakistan), and gives China the quickest route to the Indian Ocean and beyond. The CPEC will complement China's desire to modernise its Western region and deal with separatists in Xinjiang. For the terrorism-hit Pakistan, the CPEC could bring huge investment, infrastructural development, China's political and diplomatic support at international fronts.

China's economic assistance is also backed by strong defence ties. Within days of Xi's visit, China announced the supply of 50 JF-17 aircraft, jointly produced by China and Pakistan. The two sides have also finalised the largest defence deal for either side: six Chinese nuclear-capable submarines worth US$4–6 billion. China has already become Pakistan's largest arms suppliers and meets over 50 per cent Pakistan's weapons needs.

China's renewed engagement with Pakistan is not directed against India as is generally perceived. That might be Pakistan's wish, and the concern of some Indian and Western spectators, but it does not seem to be China's intention. Since the late 1980s, Beijing has separated its relationship with Pakistan from its relationship with India. China deals with each country independently. China looks at South Asia from a long-term perspective, and is not focused on the Indo–Pakistan rivalry. A stable South Asia and improved India–Pakistan relations will also serve China's interest more than any other big power.

Based on its geo-strategic location, Pakistan has acquired a new importance in Beijing's long-term strategy. This can be seen in China's bold investment in mega projects and burgeoning defence ties between the two nations. Given the high stakes, this will likely increase China's influence in Pakistan. Unlike in the past, Beijing may now take stand on issues affecting its interests.

At the same time Islamabad is cognisant that in the wake of a partial withdrawal from Afghanistan, relations with the US may enter into another phase of uncertainty. Islamabad has thus shown alacrity in intensifying ties with China, especially through a commitment to the early implementation of the CPEC. This deep congruence of mutual interests guarantees a durable Sino–Pakistani relationship into the future.

THE ECONOMIC RELATIONSHIP: SURPRISINGLY LIMITED

Pakistan's portrayal of its relationship with China features exaggeration of the economic dimension of the relationship. Pakistani media routinely report huge numbers for investment and financing with the People's Republic of China (PRC), numbers that cannot be verified by any independent source, including by the Chinese government or the Chinese companies supposedly involved. While Pakistani officials talk of a total of $25 billion in Chinese investment in Pakistan so far, the PRC's official figure of direct investment through 2010 is $1.83 billion.

The Heritage Foundation's China Global Tracker documents investments as well as engineering and construction contracts of $100 million or more since the beginning of 2005, as reported by the companies. The China Tracker shows only $1.2 billion in such investment and contracts combined through 2010. These are dominated by telecommunications, with China Mobile acquiring Paktel and investing in improvements in Pakistan's telecommunications system, such as paying the Chinese engineering company Great Wall to launch a satellite.

The Heritage Foundation figure precludes transactions initiated before 2005 and is therefore too low for a country like Pakistan, where Chinese involvement is long-standing. But it also does not include road and port projects that have not begun and are unlikely to look anything like the gigantic endeavors advertised by Pakistan. While Pakistan touts the expansion of Gwadar and other ports as multibillion dollar projects, the leading enterprise China Communications Construction notes only a modest project to expand facilities in Karachi. In sum, Chinese investment activity in Pakistan is quite modest. It is a negligible fraction of total Chinese outward investment of more than $250 billion since 2005 and dwarfed by Chinese activity in Indonesia, for example. This should not be a surprise. Chinese outward investment is motivated more by domestic economic needs than by foreign policy goals. What the PRC deems to be strategic sectors — iron, copper, oil, coal, and gas — are materials needed to keep domestic industry humming and hundreds of millions of people employed. Farmland is similar, though it has proven more difficult to acquire. Pakistan has comparatively little in the way of any of these resources.

Chinese private investors, which are far smaller than their state-controlled counterparts, seek either an asset that will considerably strengthen their position in the home market, or a new market they can sell to because they are hampered at home. Textiles might be attractive now that Chinese costs are rising, but most of the textile investment moving out of the PRC to this point is foreign-funded. Pakistan again has fairly little to offer commercially and the political connection has proven inadequate to spur exchange.

While China is not spending much money itself in Pakistan, it might be financing Pakistani spending. Here the evidence is not clear because the principal vehicle for Chinese financing, the China Development Bank (CDB), does not provide information of the same quality or quantity as many Chinese enterprises investing overseas. The CDB's foreign loan portfolio has been stated as more than $140 billion, but the many claims made around the world about its loans add up to far more than that. One important reason for the gap is that countries boast about lines of credit, not actual loans made.

In this somewhat unclear environment, it does not appear that realized Chinese lending to Pakistan is large or even moderate. Scattered claims of large loans are again unverified by independent sources and tied to projects or shipments that have not yet been made. The PRC typically lends large amounts in barter — such as loans for oil — or to fund sizable engineering projects, and neither is frequent among Chinese-Pakistani economic transactions. Indirect evidence comes from the Pakistan-China Investment Company (PCIC). The PCIC is an alliance between the China Development Bank and the Pakistani government. Elsewhere, the China Development Bank uses such entities extensively.

The China-Africa Development Fund, for instance, was set up about the same time as PCIC but is 25 times larger in terms of capital, and far more active. According to the public record, PCIC does not seem to be doing much of anything.

Chinese humanitarian aid to Pakistan also has been modest, especially when compared to that provided by the U.S. After massive flooding in Pakistan in the summer of 2010, for instance, the U.S. provided nearly $700 million in flood relief and in-kind assistance. China eventually committed to providing $250 million, after a meagre initial contribution of $18 million.

While U.S. humanitarian aid outstripped that from China, Beijing has provided much-needed reconstruction aid for the worst-hit flood areas. U.S. media reports claimed in September 2010 that 7,000 to 10,000 People's Liberation Army (PLA) troops were deployed to Gilgit-Baltistan in northern Pakistan to help rebuild areas devastated by the 2010 floods.

Indian analysts also noted the presence of PLA logistics and engineering corps in the region to provide flood relief and to build infrastructure projects, such as roads, railways, and dams. In early October, Indian army chief General V. K. Singh noted that about 3,000 to 4,000 Chinese troops were stationed in northern Pakistan focusing on construction projects. The final, and perhaps most important, indication of the limits of the China-Pakistan financial relationship is the PRC's not-so-gentle shunting of Pakistani aid requests to the International Monetary Fund (IMF).

The IMF denied large-scale aid requests made by Pakistan immediately after the September 2008 financial shock, forcing Islamabad to accept a multi-billion-dollar IMF program with stringent economic conditions. In the end, China did agree to provide around $500 million in concessionary lending to Pakistan, but its refusal to provide large-scale loans indicates clear limits on China's willingness to take primary responsibility for Pakistan's financial woes.

CHINA-PAKISTAN RELATIONSHIP

For China, Pakistan is essentially a surrogate army. Owing to traditional military rivalry, India has for decades maintained a Pakistan centric strategic policy which keeps its military tied up and limits its options against China. According to Husain Haqqani, of Carnegie Endowment for International Peace, "For China, Pakistan is a low-cost secondary deterrent to India". "For Pakistan, China is a high-value guarantor of security against India." In this mutually beneficial friendship however, owing to Pakistan's limited strategic capability against India, China is essentially a needed ally, while China does not necessarily rely on Pakistan.

China-Pakistan relations are diverse, and the Chinese have a strong investment presence in Pakistan. According to Jing Huang, senior fellow in Asia Studies at the Brookings Institution, "Pakistan would welcome investments from China more than anywhere else because Chinese are our brothers and time-tested friends". The two countries have cooperated on a variety of large-scale infrastructure projects in Pakistan, including highways, gold and copper mines, major electricity complexes and power plants, and numerous nuclear power projects. Pakistan helps China on a range of issues, including "providing intelligence, fighting terrorism, and repairing relations with the Muslim world".

However, this strategic relationship has adopted a sinister dimension of proliferation of sensitive nuclear and missile technology to Pakistan. Commercially, as China began its economic reform and opening up in the early 1980s, defence industries and arms exporting companies were under tremendous pressure to tap into the lucrative international arms market. Pakistan became a valued customer for Chinese arms. Finally, given US concern about and emphasis on missile proliferation issues, Beijing has also found it useful to exploit them as bargaining leverage in dealing with Washington on issues important to China: US arms sales to Taiwan, TMD deployment in East

Asia, among others. American intelligence reports have alleged that China has transferred complete M-11 missiles, missile related technology, and manufacturing assistance to Pakistan.

The M-11 is a single stage, solid fuelled missile with a reported range of 290 km and a payload of 800 kg. While technically the M-11 missile does not fall within the MTCR parameter, they have the inherent capability of being able to deliver a 500 kg payload over 300 km. The fact that China has resisted joining the MTCR as a formal member, coupled with its ambiguous interpretation and implementation of its bilateral commitments with the United States, raises questions as to the seriousness of Chinese commitment to arms control and nonproliferation.

Significantly, some news reports suggest Chinese security agencies knew about Pakistani transfers of nuclear technology to Iran, North Korea, and Libya. China also had longstanding ties with Abdul Qadeer Khan, known as the father of the Pakistani nuclear program, and head of an international black market nuclear network. "The Pakistani nuclear program is largely the result of Sino-Pakistani relations" says Huang.

China-Pakistan nuclear cooperation began in the early 1980s. The United States government and many Western analysts believe that China assisted Pakistan in developing nuclear explosives prior to its accession to the NPT in 1992. In 1983, US intelligence agencies reported that China had transferred a complete nuclear weapon design to Pakistan, along with enough weapons-grade uranium for two nuclear weapons. China also reportedly helped Pakistan operate its Kahuta uranium-enrichment plant. According to media reports the amount transferred was enough for making 10 nuclear weapons China also provided assistance and transferred dual-use materials that could be applied in the development of nuclear weapons. Beijing insists that China's assistance involved the provisions of peaceful technical information rather than weapons-related technologies or materials. According to Chinese Foreign Ministry spokesman Qin Gang, nuclear energy cooperation between China and Pakistan is "absolutely for peaceful purpose."

China allegedly involved Pakistani scientists in a nuclear test at its Lop Nur test site in 1989. On December 31, 1991, China signed a contract to build the Chashma 300-MW nuclear power reactor for Pakistan, and has agreed to build an additional three more reactors Chasma II (which is already under construction) and Chasma III and Chasma IV (III and IV are to be contractually agreed upon).

Beijing has adopted a number of measures to improve its proliferation image including publicly adopting responsible nuclear export policies after joining the International Atomic Energy Agency (IAEA) in 1984 and furthered its commitment by acceding to the Nonproliferation Treaty (NPT) in 1992. In addition, Beijing has formally enunciated three principles governing its nuclear exports: (1) acceptance of IAEA safeguards; (2) peaceful use only; and (3) no re-transfers to a third country without China's prior consent.

In 1993 China and the International Atomic Energy Agency (IAEA) signed an agreement to apply IAEA safeguards to a Chinese nuclear power station sold to Pakistan (INFCIRC/418). In 1994, China reportedly turned down a Pakistani request to "correct" Pakistan's nuclear weapons and to use the Chinese Lop Nur testing range.

In recent years, China has also promulgated domestic laws regulating nuclear and dual-use exports. It has also played a highly constructive role in the six party talks in restricting the North Korean nuclear weapons program and also international efforts in curbing the Iranian nuclear program. Beijing, while advocating a nuclear deal for Pakistan, has indicated that a more detailed study of the Pakistani request would be needed by the Chinese leadership.

However, significant concerns continue to emanate out of Chinese exports, particularly to Pakistan. In 1995, a major controversy erupted over suspected sales of 5,000 specially designed ring magnets from the China Nuclear Energy Industry Corporation (CNEIC) to a non-safeguarded Pakistani nuclear laboratory, which was allegedly involved in nuclear weapons work. China initially denied that the sale had taken place; a Chinese Foreign Ministry spokesman called the reports "groundless" and warned the United States not to impose sanctions based on "rumours."

Pakistan also denied that any transfer of sensitive nuclear technology had taken place. However, in talks with US officials, China eventually privately admitted that the sale had taken place, but argued that China should not be penalized for two reasons.

First, China insisted that CNEIC had arranged the sale without the knowledge or consent of the central government. Second, China argued that the ring magnets were not magnetized, and the Nuclear Suppliers Group (NSG) Trigger List only covers ring magnets magnetized at a specific tolerance. Suspicions of sensitive technological transfers resurfaced in August-September 1996, when reports indicated that China had agreed to sell a special industrial furnace and high-technology diagnostic equipment to a Pakistani nuclear facility, equipment which reportedly can be used in the construction of nuclear bombs. The reports were dismissed by the Chinese and investigators could not find sufficient evidence against China.

The May 1998 tests by Pakistan in response to similar tests by India, further fuelled suspicions over Pakistan's nuclear program. While scientists claimed it to be an indigenous test, many commentators allege that the tests could not have been possible without the explicit help of China. In response to Pakistan testing its nuclear weapons, China practically laid all blame on India. According to a statement from the foreign office "The present situation in South Asia has been caused solely by India. India conducted nuclear tests in disregard of strong opposition by the international community." In February 2001, the press reported that China's Seventh Research and Design Institute, which is overseen by the China National Nuclear Corporation, supplied 50 ceramic capacitors to Pakistan's New Labs plutonium reprocessing plant. The Institute was reportedly paid through a bank account maintained by an official at the Pakistani embassy in Beijing. The Chinese-supplied Khushab reactor can generate enough plutonium for at least one nuclear weapon per year, and probably more. According to US think tank Institute for Science and International Security (ISIS), Pakistan is close to increasing several-fold its ability to make weapon-grade plutonium through developments at Khushab. The Khushab nuclear site in Punjab province originally consisted of one heavy-water reactor with a power of about 50 MW and a heavy water production facility. Details about the construction of the second and third reactors emerged in 2006 and 2007. "No electricity production equipment is seen in the (satellite) images. This is consistent with the purpose of the reactors being to produce plutonium for nuclear weapons," the report said. Chinese proliferation activities during the eight years of the Clinton administration resulted in Chinese entities subject to sanctions 17 times. In four years of the Bush administration, Chinese entities have been sanctioned a total of 50 times. In 2004 alone, 14 Chinese entities were sanctioned a total of 23 times.

Five companies—China Great Wall Industry Corporation, China Precision Machinery Import/Export Corporation, China North Industries Corporation (NORINCO), Wha Cheong Tai Company, Ltd., and Zibo Chemical Equipment Plant—and one Chinese national, Q.C. Chen, have all been sanctioned at least four times by the United States and are often referred to as "serial proliferators" by U.S. officials. For some entities, such as the China Great Wall Industry Corporation and China Precision Machinery Import/Export Corporation, the sanctions have been spread out over more than a decade. But for NORINCO and Zibo Chemical Equipment Plant, the sanctions have all occurred since 2003 and 2002, respectively.

Wider Proliferation Circle

Chinese proliferation to Pakistan has indirectly fuelled weapons activities across the world, especially owing to the role of disgraced Pakistan nuclear scientist Abdul Qadeer Khan. In 2004, as a result of on-site investigations into Libya's nuclear weapons program new details of the Pakistan-China collaboration were studied. As part of disarmament inspections, early Chinese nuclear weapons designs were handed over to IAEA inspectors by Libyan scientists, wrapped in plastic bags bearing an address in Islamabad.

Several recent developments have once again highlighted not only the central role that Beijing in developing Pakistan's nuclear arsenal, but also Dr. Khan's intimate links with China's nuclear establishment. According to Professor Mohan Malik of Security Studies at the Asia-Pacific Centre for Security Studies, Honolulu, "the Chinese seem to have been thoroughly beaten in the proliferation game by their own clients and allies-Pakistan and North Korea". Reacting to reports about the Khan nuclear network, the Chinese Foreign Ministry spokesperson urged Islamabad to undertake the investigations "properly" and bring them to a conclusion "quickly." Professor Malik, draws attention to the Chinese preference for conducting investigations "properly" and ending them "quickly". This, he argues, reveals Beijing's apprehensions over exposing the Chinese nuclear establishment's long standing ties with Khan. Mallik argues that Khan's numerous visits to China's nuclear installations over the last three decades and gains accrued to China's weapons program from the Dutch centrifuge technology stolen by him in the mid-1970s are particularly sensitive issues for Beijing. A senior member of the Pakistan Muslim League (Quaid-e-Azam) told a Pakistani journalist that "Chinese officials had expressed a desire for the proliferation inquiry to end quickly as they feared that Dr. Khan would publicly detail his network's 'China connection,' thereby embarrassing a crucial ally that Pakistan considers a strategic counterweight to India."

Although the bomb designs sold to Libya were of a 1960s Chinese vintage, an analysis of Pakistan's May 1998 nuclear tests reveals that China may have supplied more advanced nuclear weapons designs of the late 1980s and early 1990s to Pakistan, which may have been shared with other countries. The close cooperation between Chinese and Pakistani military agencies also leaves little doubt that the Chinese had greater knowledge about Khan's proliferation activities than is publicly reported.

PAKISTAN-CHINA RELATIONS AND ITS PHASE

Pakistan's relations with China have always been the most important of its relationships with other countries. It is based on trust, respect, and mutual benefit. Over the past 55 years, since the two countries established their diplomatic relations, this relationship has evolved in a manner to serve the interests of both countries. To understand the evolution of this relationship from a correct perspective, it is important to have a brief overview of the relationship between the two countries.

Pakistan was the first Islamic country and third noncommunist state to accord recognition to the People's Republic of China. Although Pakistan established diplomatic relations with China in 1951, the actual consolidation of relations started in the early 1960s, when Pakistan changed its previous stance and supported China's seating in the UN in 1961. In the 1962 Sino-Indian border war, the US rushed military assistance to India, which Pakistan, being an allay of the West, considered detrimental to its security concerns and moved out of the Western orbit (SEATO and CENTO). At that point in time, a commonality of interests seemed to be emerging between Pakistan and China. It was the shared sense of an evolving geostrategic environment in which the two countries amicably negotiated and signed an agreement on the demarcation of their common border in March 1963.

In the following years, Pakistan on its part sincerely helped China to end the isolation that both the superpowers wished to impose on China, by signing an air-transport agreement and trade agreement and helping China maintain contact with a number of countries, especially the Islamic world. Similarly, China played a commendable role in its support of Pakistan in achieving a ceasefire in the 1965 Indo-Pakistan war by issuing stern warnings to India. Following the war, China, also in an attempt to compensate for war losses, supported Pakistan with military equipment including tanks and aircraft. In the 1960s, Pakistan-China relations evolved on firm foundations of mutual trust and confidence.

In the early 1970s, Pakistan played an important role in facilitating secret communications between the US and China that resulted in Henry Kissinger's secret visit to China followed by President Richard Nixon's historic visit. Sino-US normalization of relations was perceived in Indian strategic thinking as the emergence of a US-Pakistan-China strategic triangle, which prompted India to sign a treaty of peace, friendship and cooperation with the Soviet Union. It could be termed as a kind of a security treaty because Article IX of the treaty stipulated that in "the event of either party being subject to an attack or threat thereof, the high contracting parties shall immediately enter into mutual consultations in order to remove such threat and to take appropriate effective measures to ensure peace and security of their countries." 1 This development introduced a new dimension to the region, especially if seen in the context of the Cold War, and also created more space for further consolidation of Pak-China relations. The other development, which had profoundly influenced Sino-Pak relations, was the Indo-Pakistan war in 1971, followed by the Chinese military and economic assistance to Pakistan. Later, on the issue of Bangladesh's application for membership to the UN, China, on Pakistan's request, exercised its veto power for the first time to stall the move, which helped Pakistan to secure in a bargain the release of its POWs and the return of troops to their prewar positions. The Indian nuclear explosion of 1974 introduced a new dimension to the strategic balance in the region and gave fresh impetus to expanding Pak-China defence cooperation. Between 1971 and 1978, China assisted Pakistan in building two defence-related mega projects, first, the Heavy Rebuild Factory for T–59 tanks, and second, the F-6 Aircraft Rebuild Factory. Chinese intent to make Pakistan self-reliant in the production of a conventional weapons system, without attaching any political strings to its assistance, cultivated deep-rooted respect and goodwill for China in Pakistan.

The end of the 1970s witnessed international developments of immense consequences that continued to impact on the entire region throughout the following decades and even today. These were the Iranian Islamic Revolution in February 1979, the declared hostility of the new Iranian leadership towards the US, and in the later part of the year, the invasion of Afghanistan by the Soviet Union. Invasion of Afghanistan created a situation of two hostile fronts for Pakistan—India and Afghanistan—threatening peace and stability in the region. At this crucial juncture, China stood firmly by Pakistan and condemned the invasion of Afghanistan as a "hegemonic action" that posed a threat to peace and stability not only for the region but for the entire world. Pakistan and China had a shared perspective and developed coordinated strategies to deal with the Afghan situation. China provided covertly, in the following years, military supplies worth $200 million annually to the Afghan resistance groups, and extended political support to Pakistan at all international fora.

Throughout the 1980s, Pakistan-China relations continued to develop into a comprehensive relationship. While China improved its relations with India towards the end of the 1980s, Pakistan did not feel that China's improving relations with India were at the cost of China's relations with Pakistan. Although there was a visible shift in the Chinese stance on Kashmir, Pakistani policy makers believed that China's improved relations with India would act as a restraining factor on Indian belligerency towards Pakistan. Pakistan always supported China on all issues important to Chinese national interests such as sovereignty over Hong Kong, Taiwan, and Tibet and issues relating to human rights and democracy. China always appreciated and counted on Pakistan's strong support as a trusted friend over all these issues at international fora. Following the withdrawal of Soviet forces from Afghanistan in 1988–1989, the regional strategic dynamics changed once again. The US, after having achieved its strategic interest of rolling back communist aggression, claimed victory over the former Soviet Union and abandoned Afghanistan. Pakistan's support was no longer required by the US, so it came under US sanctions for secretly developing nuclear weapons; an issue to which the US turned a blind eye for a decade during the Afghan War. Throughout the 1990s,

Pakistan remained under US sanctions and China was the primary source of Pakistan's military hardware procurements. During this period, Pakistan-China defence-related cooperation also substantially increased. China's support for Pakistan's nuclear and missile programs became a constant irritant in Sino-US and Sino-Indian relations, especially the issue of supply of M-11 missiles and 500 ring magnets to an "unsafeguarded" nuclear facility. China, on its part, despite tremendous US pressure to cut off high-technology links with Pakistan, remained steadfast in its commitment to strengthen Pakistan's defence capability.

In May 1998, Indian nuclear tests destabilized the strategic balance in South Asia. As a prelude to these tests, the Indian defence minister and prime minister described China as a long-term security threat. While commenting on the Indian assertion, the official Chinese media reported that "India's explosions have sabotaged the fragile trust built up with Beijing over the past decade." Following the Indian nuclear tests, Sino-Indian relations suffered a severe setback. Deterioration in Sino-Indian relations reinforced Pakistan's importance in China's South Asia policy. Pakistan and China held high-level consultations on the situation in South Asia. China expressed its understanding of Pakistan's compulsion to go nuclear. It gave Pakistan the confidence to reestablish the strategic balance in South Asia by conducting its own nuclear tests. The depth of Pakistan-China relations was reflected from the fact that it was after Pakistan had acquired demonstrable nuclear weapons capability that the Chinese leadership gave assurance to the visiting US president Bill Clinton in June 1998 of cooperating with the US on the issue of nuclear proliferation. In 1999, during the Kargil conflict between the two nuclear states, India and Pakistan, China adhered to a strict neutral position. China was concerned over the possibility of escalation of the conflict, and asked both countries to defuse tensions. The Chinese position of neutrality was duly acknowledged by India, and provided both countries with an opportunity to mend their fences and once again improve their bilateral relations. Pakistan also had a complete understanding of China's interest to improve bilateral relations with India, especially in the context of evolving Indo-US strategic partnership.

After the events of 9/11, Pakistan and China consulted each other on the unfolding situation in the region. On September 18, 2001, a special envoy of the then Chinese president, Jiang Zemin, arrived in Islamabad to meet General Pervez Musharraf and other officials and discussed the situation emerging as a consequence of the 9/11 attacks. Pakistan's decision to side with the US and to provide use of its airspace and base facilities had initially raised some concerns in Chinese policy-making circles. However, the exchange of high-level visits clarified the Pakistani position that under no circumstances would Pakistan allow its cooperation with the US to undermine Chinese strategic interests.

During the India-Pakistan military standoff in 2001–2002, China continued with its position of neutrality and played an important role in defusing tensions between India and Pakistan through telephone diplomacy. Since India escalated the tensions, despite Pakistan's repeated requests for negotiation, China's role to pacify the situation was considered more favorably by the Pakistani authorities and people. The Chinese leadership stated that "it is in the interests of both countries and the expectation of the international community for both Pakistan and India to maintain the utmost restraint and safeguard the peace and stability of South Asia." China's proactive diplomacy to engage the US and India in the volatile South Asian situation was received well in Pakistan and indeed helped to ease tensions. There was complete understanding between Pakistan and China, and the Chinese leadership appreciated Musharraf government's policies on antiterrorism and peaceful resolution of contentious issues with India.

President Musharraf, in his December 2001 visit to China, explicitly expressed support of the Chinese campaign against Muslim separatists in Xinjiang. He urged the Chinese Muslims to be very patriotic and to work for the betterment of their country. He declared that Pakistan would extend full support to China to fight against East Turkestan terrorist forces. This was the first time that a Pakistani leader went public in support of Chinese policies to curtail Muslim separatists in Xinjiang. In view of Chinese concerns that there is a link between the separatist forces in Xinjiang and the jihad organizations in Pakistan and Afghanistan, Pakistan has also institutionalized antiterrorism dialogue with China and the two sides have agreed to share intelligence on terrorism. In December 2003, the Pakistan Army in a military operation near the Pak-Afghan border killed Hahsan Mahsum, the leader of the East Turkestan Islamic Movement, while extraditing a number of alleged terrorists to China. In recent years, antiterrorism-related cooperation between the two countries has constantly been expanding. On August 6, 2004, China and Pakistan conducted their first joint antiterrorism military exercise named "Friendship 2004," in Xinjiang.

In April 2005, during Premier Wen Jiabao's visit to Islamabad, the two sides signed a treaty of friendship, cooperation and good neighborly relations as well as an agreement on combating terrorism, separatism and extremism. The comprehensive antiterrorism cooperation from Pakistan has effectively removed the apprehensions of the Chinese side, holding in regard the support of the Uighur Muslim separatists from some of Pakistan's religious groups.

Pakistan-China defence-related cooperation has always been the most important component of their overall bilateral relations.

The tradition of high-level exchange of visits for consultations between the armed forces of the two countries has provided sustenance to the bilateral relations, as the institution of the armed forces plays a special role in political decision making in both countries. In recent years, a mechanism of defence and security consultation has been institutionalized between the two countries. Since March 2002, three rounds of consultations have taken place. In order to enhance military-to-military cooperation, China and Pakistan, in October 2003, conducted a joint maritime search-and-rescue exercise near Shanghai. That was the first time for the navy of the People's Liberation Army (PLA) to conduct an exercise with a foreign country.

Similarly, in November 2005, during their visit to Pakistan, Chinese naval ships conducted a second joint maritime search-and-rescue exercise with the Pakistan Navy. That was again the first time for the PLA Navy to conduct a joint exercise in waters abroad.

Pakistan and China share a common interest in the security of the sea lanes of communication, and both support a multilateral framework for guarding energy and trade sea routes. Defence production-related cooperation has also expanded in recent years between the two countries. Pakistan and China have jointly developed JF–17 Thunder—a multi-role fighter aircraft. Pakistan and China finalized a deal in April 2005, under which China Dockyard in Shanghai will build four F–22P frigates for the Pakistan Navy and transfer the technology as well. Cooperation on other ongoing defence projects is continuing to the satisfaction of both.

At the political level, Pakistan and China have unanimity of views on issues like the war on terrorism, Iraq, Afghanistan, and the Iranian nuclear program. Both countries wish to strengthen the authority of the UN and oppose unilateralism and concepts such as "coalition of the willing" or "concert of democracies" outside the UN ambit to deal with international security issues.

PAKISTAN RELATIONS WITH CENTRAL ASIAN STATES

The Changing Dynamics of Pakistan's Relations with Central Asia

Background: The relations between Pakistan and Central Asia are an intricate blend of economic interdependence and mistrust. They share a common history and culture, and in contemporary politics face common threat perceptions and economic problems. A common strategy to deal with these problems would be significant for the economic wellbeing of the entire region. This gives Central Asia a place of prominence in Pakistan's foreign policy, something that the local states have amply realized, as is evident in the high level exchanges taking place lately.

Pakistan is an ideal route for Central Asia's international trade. However, this route remained disrupted for long because of turmoil in Afghanistan. Pakistan's Gwadar and Karachi seaports can provide ideal port and transit facilities for the Central Asian republics to establish their trade links with the outer world for the benefit of entire region. The Central Asian states, in particular Tajikistan and Kyrgyzstan, also have an immense potential for the production of hydroelectric power, which is badly needed in Pakistan.

So far, Pakistan has established Joint Economic Commissions (JECs) with all the Central Asian States. The JECs take important decisions to promote cooperation in the economic and commercial spheres and other avenues of cooperation. Under a Special Technical Assistance Program (STAP) initiated in 1992-93, Pakistan provides fully funded training facilities to Central Asian states.

The program includes courses ranging from English language, banking and accounting to diplomacy. In the energy sector, Turkmenistan, Afghanistan and Pakistan signed an agreement in December 2002 for a gas pipeline from Turkmenistan via Afghanistan to Pakistan, whose estimated cost is US$2 billion. The Asian Development Bank is the lead coordinating partner. It has, in addition to financial and technical assistance, played an important role in integrating efforts to realize the project.

Tajikistan has a potential to be a substantial producer of hydroelectric power. Being the closest geographically to Pakistan of the Central Asian Republics, Pakistan stands to benefit from Tajikistan's hydroelectric potential. An intergovernmental agreement to that effect has already been signed. Pakistan has also signed an agreement to import electricity from Kyrgyzstan through Tajikistan and Afghanistan. Terrain and weather conditions are a clear impediment for this project, yet both states appear determined to pursue it.

The Economic Cooperation Organization comprising Afghanistan, Azerbaijan, Iran, Kazakhstan, Kyrgyzstan, Pakistan, Tajikistan, Turkey, Turkmenistan, and Uzbekistan provides another common platform to generate economic activity in the region. As Pakistan's Prime Minister Shaukat Aziz has recently emphasized, the organization needs to be used in result-oriented policies instead of mere lip service. ECO can be an effective organization if the ECO Trade Agreement, Transit Transport Agreement and the Trade and Development Bank are operationalized swiftly.

Implications: Pakistan and Kyrgyzstan have a long history of ties, being linked by the historic Silk Road. On January 17, 2005, Kyrgyzstan's President

Askar Akaev visited Pakistan on the invitation of President General Pervez Musharraf. It was his third visit, the earlier being in 1994 and 1995, a decade ago. Kyrgyzstan and Pakistan are signatories to the Quadrilateral Agreement along with China and Kazakhstan, effective since May 2004, which aims at promoting regional trade through Pakistan's Karakoram Highway and onward road links through China to Kazakhstan. Both countries are keen to increase trade and economic relations, a fact that President Akaev stressed during the visit.

Cooperation in the fields of education and culture is an important aspect of Pakistan-Kyrgyz relations. Kyrgyz students have been pursing studies in Pakistani educational institutions in various fields such as engineering, business administration, information technology and the English language. Kyrgyz civil servants also attend training programs in Pakistan. Conversely, over 350 Pakistani students are currently pursuing studies, mainly in medical colleges, in the Kyrgyz Republic. The expansion of bilateral ties are set to further increase with the reopening of the historic Silk Road, allowing transportation between Kyrgyzstan and Pakistan via China.

Pakistan's relations with the Central Asian Republics have progressed in the past few years, inspiring hope for brighter prospects ahead. The completion of the Gwadar Port is a milestone in this context. When it comes online alongside Karachi shortly, it will provide the shortest access to the Sea for large parts of Central Asia. Pakistan is also giving priority to road and rail links and related facilities for more effective and mutually beneficial access to Central Asia. Air services to Tashkent and Almaty have already been resumed. Similar services to other parts of the region are under active consideration. This process of closer ties is set to receive a significant boost from the ongoing improvement of the political and economic situation in Afghanistan. The laying of railway tracks from Turkmenistan to Pakistan via Afghanistan is an important part of this program. Pakistan's Ministry of Railways has completed a feasibility study for a Chaman-Kandahar rail project. The Pakistan-Afghanistan Joint Economic Commission, which will be held in Islamabad shortly. The quadrilateral agreement is also gradually being implemented, with a first caravan from Pakistan using this route last year. The completion of Murghab-Kulma road from Tajikistan to China linking to the Karakoram highway to Pakistan is also a significant development. Once operationalized, it will boost the transit trade between Pakistan and the Central Asia. Pakistan has no gas needs of its own at this moment although this may become a future issue, but it can facilitate the export of Central Asian oil and gas to South Asia, Southeast Asia and beyond. The oil and gas pipeline from Turkmenistan to Pakistan and onward to India would indeed be a sound investment in the future of the region.

The exchange of high-level visits has been an important aspect of relations between Pakistan and the Central Asian Republics. These have contributed to better understanding and closer cooperation, and the momentum in these visits is continuously growing. In the meantime, peace and stability in Afghanistan remains a sine qua non for the developing relations. Pakistan can contribute, albeit modestly, in construction and rehabilitation of Afghanistan, especially in housing, trade, transportation and infrastructure sectors. Radical Islam has destabilized the societies of both Pakistan and Central Asia, and further mutual cooperation is required in dealing with this problem. But beyond security concerns, mutual economic stakes are likely to play a more pivotal role in mutually beneficial relations in the future. Economic interests have always been and will continue to be the foundation for the relations between Pakistan and Central Asian states.

CHINA: A RISKY BUSINESS PROPOSITION

With a largely untapped market of 1.2 billion people, China has had a magical allure for international capital. In 1995, Canada was China's 5th largest trade partner, and that level of trade is expected to increase with the Chinese takeover of Hong Kong in 1997. However, investment in China is a high-risk proposition. In 1994, the Chinese national government decided that foreigners could not have a majority ownership of power projects. China has also apparently decided to limit the rate of return for foreign companies investing in power projects ~ limits ranging from 12 to 15% have been discussed. Even well-known power project developers such as Gordon Wu have abandoned China for deals in Pakistan and India that are presumably safer and more lucrative. This is extremely revealing, since through Hopewell Holdings, Wu pioneered power investments in China. There are a number of other danger signs ~ Chinese state enterprises have defaulted on $600 million in loans from Japanese, German and Italian banks; the China International Trust & Investment Corp. (CITIC) refused to pay a $40 million debt to the London Metal Exchange; and two other state companies are refused to pay $100 million in trading losses to Lehman Brothers Inc. In a survey of Canadian businesses with an interest in China, the Conference Board of Canada found that less than half of businesses surveyed that invested in China in the last five years had made money on their investments.

For several years, a serious trade disagreement has been simmering between the USA and China over the copyright protection of intellectual property rights in Chain ~ in particular Chinese pirating of western video's, music recordings and computer software. A trade war was narrowly averted in February 1995. However, the reconciliation was short-lived, as a new trade disagreement was triggered when China failed to live up to a 1992

Memorandum of Understanding to lift import controls, licence requirements and quotas on a variety of products. By May 1996, the US government was again threatening to place 100% tariffs on $2 billion worth of Chinese imports, such as textiles and electronics, to the US. China for its part threatened to place retaliatory tariffs on US exports to China. The US imported about $46 billion worth the US of goods from China in 1995, and exported about $12 billion to China. However, on June 17 1996, the US pulled back from the brink of a trade war, when it announced that sanctions would not be placed on China, since it was taking steps towards cracking down on illegal compact disk manufacturers. Given past history, it seems unlikely that we have seen the last of the "intellectual property" issue. This will remain a concern for potential investors in China, who may see their interests affected by international trade problems with the US.

Adding to the economic and political uncertainty of China's future is the impending death of national leader Deng Xiaoping. The 90 year-old Communist Party leader has been in control since 1978, and has been the architect of China's recent mix of brutal repression and market liberalization. A recent Pentagon report has given only even odds for the maintenance of stability following Deng's demise.

Corruption in China remains an endemic problem. In 1995, almost 100,000 people in China were charged with corruption ~ an increase of 8% from 1994. The German organization Transparency International, has ranked China as the second-most corrupt country, behind Indonesia, among the world's 41 major trading nations. In December 1995, a guide book published by Canada's Foreign Affairs Department warned that Canadian business people "may receive requests for agency fees or kickbacks" in China. The guidebook notes that kickbacks are illegal in China.

CPEC: THE BUMPY NEW TRADE ROUTE BETWEEN CHINA AND PAKISTAN

A new international trade route in Southwest Pakistan opened up on Sunday by a Chinese ship exporting goods to the Middle East and Africa. The route that is being developed by the Chinese in Pakistan is expected to make huge amount of economic gains for the country. When China decided to develop the China Pakistan Economic Corridor (CPEC) in 2015, the idea was to deepen economic ties with Pakistan and ensure security for China's larger 'One belt, one road' project. Involving an investment of $46 billion, the project is the means by which China can ensure the quickest availability of energy resources from the Middle East by avoiding the Malacca straits and the South China sea.

Over the year, however, the project has witnessed a large number of obstacles, especially resulting from the poor economic conditions in Balochistan which forms the bulk of the area in which the CPEC is being developed and the opposition to the project meted out by the locals.

What is the CPEC?

The CPEC is one of the most important projects of the 'one belt, one road' project initiated by China that aims to connect the Asian economic giant with Europe and Africa, thereby making the country a bigger player in world economic affairs. Consisting of a number of road, rail and pipeline ventures, the CPEC connects Xinjiang in Northwestern region of China with Pakistan's Gwadar port on the Arabian sea, going over the Pakistan occupied Kashmir territory of Gilgit-Baltistan and the disputed region of Balochistan.

Reportedly, the port at Gwadar will have the capacity to manage 19 million tons of crude oil which will be directly transferred to China.

The project had been conceived much earlier in the 1950s, but failed to achieve completion over the years due to political instability in Pakistan. Its present form was announced by the Chinese government in November 2014 and work started off in April 2015. As a multi-million dollar project, the CPEC is reported to have brought Pakistan twice the amount of foreign investments the country received since 2008.

How does it benefit Pakistan?

In the words of Pakistani leaders, their relationship with China is "higher than the mountains, deeper than the oceans, stronger than steel and sweeter than honey". For Pakistan, the Chinese investment in the south-western region of the country is a game-changer for the economy, especially considering the fact that despite the high concentration of mineral resources in the region it has remained the poorest district.

The $46 billion promised by China will be used in generating close to 17,000 megawatts of electricity at a cost of $34 billion through coal, nuclear and other renewable energy projects. The rest of the money would be utilised in building up transport infrastructure. According to Pakistani Prime Minister Nawaz Sharif the development of the Balochistan province could make Pakistan a regional hub of economic activities.

Why is it opposed by Balochistan?

All of Pakistan is not unanimous in its claims of high gains being made from the Chinese initiated project. The strongest opposition to the investment comes from the disputed territory of Balochistan that has historically had strained relations with the government of Pakistan.

The province of Balochistan is the largest district in the country and its importance lies in the high concentration of natural resource. Despite this, it has remained the poorest province in Pakistan.

The conflict with the Pakistani government is rooted in a feeling of nationalism that stretches back to the 1948 when the province was allegedly made a part of Pakistan on unfair terms. That apart, there is also a feeling of political and economic isolation that the government of Pakistan has not been able to erase in all these years.

The strongest grievance of the Baloch nationalist groups against CPEC is that benefits from developmental projects like these are almost always, unfairly distributed, majority of the employment opportunities and profits going to non-Balochs, especially Punjabis.

The Baloch Republican Party, a separatist group, recently made its opposition to the CPEC very clear, stating that an economic pact between China and Pakistan would lead to both countries utilising the resources of Balochistan that belong to the locals. They further believe that an increase in military operations and abductions are a direct result of the pact between Pakistan and China. There is also the fear that the initiation of the project would lead to the influx of a large number of non-Balochs, thereby demographically outnumbering the Balochs in the region.

Abductions of activists and even civilians have for long been a problem in Balochistan. Allegedly, they are carried out by Pakistan's military forces in order to subjugate the separatist movement. As per the International Voice for Baloch Missing Persons (IIVBMP), a protest group formed by families of missing people in Balochistan, between 2001 and 2013, about 18,000 people have gone missing in the area, out of which around 2000 have been killed.

In the wake of the thriving separatist movement in Balochistan, the Pakistan government has vowed to increase military surveillance in the area in order to quell Chinese fears. Reportedly, a sum of $250 million has been promised by the Pakistani government for the sake of building a new security force in the region.

A result of these new arrangement has been a strengthening opposition to the project by the Baloch nationalist groups. Protest movements are being held outside Balochistan as well. In August this year, separatist groups staged a protest outside the Chinese embassy in London. Baloch activists have been particularly reaching out to India, asking the country's media and bureaucracy to raise the issue of atrocities against Baloch nationalists onto the international stage. In September, a group of Balochis along with Indians held a joint protest outside the United Nations headquarters in New York asking for UN intervention in order to protect the Balochis.

What are the challenges being faced by China?

For the Chinese, security in the province of Balochistan has been the biggest concern. Reportedly, Baloch separatists, especially those from the Baloch Liberation Army, have been abducting and killing foreigners, particularly the Chinese. In May 2014, a Chinese tourist had been kidnapped from Dera Islmail Khan, close to the balochistan border.

In March 2015, five oil tankers carrying fuel from Karachi, reportedly for a Chinese company was set on fire. The Balochistan Liberation Army was accused for the attack. Further disruptions to the infrastructural projects are being anticipated by other Islamist groups and splinter factions of the Pakistani Taliban. The prime motive of these acts is to make the Pakistan government appear incapable of providing adequate security measures.

However, the Pakistani government has been continuously assuring the Chinese state of security to their personnel and assets in the region. Although the CPEC is being funded by China, at the initial stage of the project, only Pakistani personnel would be involved in the construction. Chinese personnel are expected to come in after the first stage, by which time the Pakistani government has promised to take requisite measures to curb militancy.

How is India responding?

India is not exactly welcoming towards the Chinese funded project, mainly because of the fact that it crosses through the Pakistan occupied part of Kashmir. Earlier in September, PM Modi expressed his concerns over CPEC to President Xi Jinping of China at a bilateral meeting between the two leaders. He is reported to have told the Chinese president that both countries need to be 'sensitive' towards their respective strategic interests. A response to the Chinese development of Gwadar is the bilateral agreement between India and Iran to develop the Chabahar port.

In the recent past though experts on South Asian politics have been ringing alarm bells that any act on the part of India that explicitly opposes CPEC might lead to strained relations between India and China.

CHINA'S ECONOMIC INTERESTS WITH AFGHANISTAN AND PAKISTAN

China's economic interests in both countries are also substantial. In Afghanistan, the China Metallurgical Construction Group's $3.2 billion Aynak copper mine investment, in the eastern province of Logar, is the country's largest, with the mine holding as much as the equivalent of a third of China's total copper reserves. Chinese companies have interests in mineral deposits elsewhere in the country and are also active in the irrigation, infrastructure, telecommunications, and power sectors. China has an even wider-ranging set of investments in Pakistan. In addition to large-scale projects in telecommunications and hydropower, the Chinese-built port at Gwadar in Baluchistan potentially provides both an energy transshipment route_once connected to the expanded Karakoram Highway (KKH)_and a future naval facility. Not only does rising extremism in the region threaten these projects, it also puts Chinese nationals at risk, and calls into question the very viability of China's most important ally in the region, Pakistan.

The theoretical result, therefore, should be a China willing to find ways to support international efforts to combat militancy and bring stability to both states. But the reality is different, even if Sino-U.S. cooperation on Afghanistan and Pakistan is not itself new. In fact, few regions have played as prominent a role in the Sino-U.S. relationship in recent decades. Islamabad was the conduit for the normalization of relations between the United States and China in the 1970s. It was the Soviet invasion of Afghanistan that provided the final catalyst for establishing joint Sino-U.S. signal intelligence bases in Xinjiang to monitor Soviet military activities. China, in close conjunction with the Central Intelligence Agency and Pakistan's Inter-Services Intelligence (ISI), became the leading weapons supplier to the mujahideen in the first years of the Afghan campaign, while Chinese arms, mules, and military training were an integral part of the mujahideen's war throughout its duration.

Recent examples of Sino-U.S. coordination during crises in the region have underscored the necessity of bilateral cooperation. Officials from both sides have described close bilateral liaisons over issues ranging from the Kargil conflict of 1999 to the financial turbulence in Pakistan in 2008 as well as the Mumbai attacks of the same year. China played a supportive role in the immediate aftermath of the September 11, 2001 attacks, backing Pakistan's decision to withdraw its support for the Taliban, and developing a limited program of cooperation on counterterrorism issues with the United States, which included the establishment of a Federal Bureau of Investigation office in Beijing.

Formal bilateral consultation mechanisms were expanded under George W. Bush's administration, which launched a South Asia dialogue at the assistant secretary of state level as part of a package of new exchanges on regional issues established under the U.S.-China Senior Dialogue. Without necessarily translating into immediate outcomes, these dialogues set down broad markers for both sides, established a basic tradition of coordination, and brought into regular contact parts of the U.S. and Chinese bureaucracies that would otherwise have had little interaction. The prospects for upgraded cooperation with China under the Obama administration seemed good. Aside from Beijing's own concerns about the worsening situation in the region, China has traditionally felt under pressure to appear cooperative on the top tier of U.S. security priorities and Afghanistan and Pakistan were set to occupy a higher status for President Barack Obama than for Bush. Officials in the Obama administration were less ambivalent than those in the previous administration about the virtues of greater Chinese involvement in Afghanistan, particularly on the security side where limited offers from Beijing had been rebuffed in the past. The greater prominence given to Pakistan in U.S. strategy exemplified by the "AfPak" coinage also placed China toward the top of any possible list of countries whose cooperation could have a major impact. And the promise of a broader regional engagement strategy meant that a more extensive and systematic U.S. diplomatic effort to solicit that involvement was anticipated.

This was reinforced by Special Representative for Afghanistan and Pakistan Richard Holbrooke's early initiatives, which included visiting Beijing in March 2009 and attending the U.S.-China Strategic and Economic Dialogue (SED) in Washington in July 2009, which featured discussions on Afghanistan and Pakistan under the strategic track. capacity, investment, trainers for police, peacekeepers, and allowing its territory to be used as a part of the Northern Distribution Network for the NATO-led International Security Assistance Force.

Even more importantly, some think that China could use its leverage over the Pakistani military to press it to rein in the Afghan-focused groups operating out of Pakistan, such as the Haqqani network and the Afghan Taliban itself, as well as refocusing its "India-centric" doctrine toward a more effective set of counterinsurgency capabilities. It is hoped that some of these steps can be coaxed out by a more sustained U.S. effort to engage China on regional policy and to draw Beijing into an active role in the various multilateral groupings that deal with Afghanistan and Pakistan.

CHINA'S FALTERING STRATEGY IN AFGHANISTAN AND PAKISTAN

The approach China has been taking in Afghanistan and Pakistan is not devoid of successes. Indeed, it has served Beijing well for many years. To date, China has avoided becoming a focus of militant efforts on a scale remotely comparable to that of the West, despite an approach to sections of its own Muslim population, which would attract fierce condemnation were it carried out by any Western state. It has maintained its close relationship with Pakistan military, political parties, and public alike while developing good relations with the Afghan government. Its access to economic projects in both states is also second-tonone. Yet, in many other respects, things are not going according to plan.

The direct threat to China is growing. This year has seen the first kidnappings in Afghanistan of Chinese workers by Taliban guerillas in the Fayrab province. Rocket attacks on the Aynak facility have cooled Chinese willingness to move forward with the project itself as well as with future prospects, such as the Hajigak iron ore deposit, where Chinese companies were again prominently placed in the bidding. But Pakistan has been an even greater concern. The situation there certainly posed difficulties in the past. In the 1990s, until Beijing exerted considerable pressure, Pakistan was viewed as a haven for Uighur refugees, a number of whom were given training by an array of jihadi groups. Chinese workers have been targeted directly by insurgents in Baluchistan, where several have been killed in recent years, as well as by local groups in the FATA. China has also been prompted to close the border and move troops to its vicinity on different occasions. But the events since 2007 have taken a more dangerous turn.

The June 2007 Lal Masjid incident, in which Chinese "massage workers" were kidnapped and held in the heart of Pakistan's capital, was a watershed. While they were eventually released, the subsequent Pakistani military assault on the mosque complex was seen to have taken place at Beijing's instigation. As an immediate reprisal in the North-West Frontier Province (now known as Khyber Pukhtoonkhwa), three Chinese engineers were executed in July 2007,26 along with a suicide attack on a convoy of Chinese workers in the same month in a market town near Karachi, indicating a more systematic targeting of China throughout Pakistan. Pakistani politicians have expressed concerns that militant groups will look to "drive a wedge" between Beijing and Islamabad. An extensive set of security measures have since been put in place, with a joint task force established in August 2007 at the national and provincial levels to address the threat to the 10,000 Chinese in Pakistan, including providing direct military protection.

But subsequent attacks and kidnappings have led to continued tension in the relationship. At the time of President Asif Ali Zardari's maiden visit to China in 2008, the failure to gain the release of Chinese telecommunications workers in Swat resulted in threats to withdraw all Chinese personnel from the country. While these have been made before, and are seen by some on the Pakistani side as a bluff to extract concessions, the personal involvement of President Hu Jintao and other senior Chinese leaders in statements about the kidnapping incidents have added a level of seriousness to the Chinese threats.

This focus on personnel security has been coupled with Chinese political pressure, as one former Pakistani military officer put it "of a kind that there has not been before," on Islamabad to crack down on Uighurs based in the country. At points, this has leaked into the press when Chinese behind-the-scenes lobbying has not delivered results, such as 2009 pressure ahead of supposed threats to the 60th anniversary celebrations for the People's Republic. Despite a number of high-profile extraditions, Chinese analysts have described counterterrorism cooperation as falling short of expectations, criticizing ISI warnings to Uighur groups to disperse ahead of some of their operations and questioning their motivation to eliminate the threat.

The strength of the TTP has also been a concern to China. While initially sanguine about the Pakistani government's deals in Swat and Buner, they became increasingly worried that the writ of the Pakistani state was running out in a territory that runs dangerously close to the principal Sino-Pakistani trade route, the KKH. While never as worried about the "Talibanization" of Pakistan as some of the more alarmist accounts suggested they should be, the Chinese ultimately took a clear position encouraging the Pakistani government not just to mount the operation, but to bring it to a decisive conclusion. Since the campaign started, China has provided aid to assist with massive numbers of internally displaced persons as well as counterterrorism equipment, ranging from scanners to night-vision goggles, to the Pakistani army. The army, in turn, has provided additional security for the KKH, placing troops along its length to protect it from being used as an escape route for militants fleeing the Pakistani army's campaign.

The deterioration in the general security situation and the fracturing of the Pakistani military's relationship with various militant groups has posed broader problems for Beijing. China is particularly exposed when it comes to groups seen to operate under the authority of elements of the Pakistani state itself, such as the LeT and the Jaish-e-Mohammed (JeM), which have the capacity to precipitate conflict in the event of another major attack on Indian territory.

China will inevitably be pulled into any potential Indian-Pakistani crisis diplomatically, and has even attempted to send signals which convince few that it could be engaged militarily in the event of any Indian retaliation. Since China bears significant historic responsibility for Pakistan's nuclear program, it is also notably culpable in the event of any diversion of nuclear materials, a scenario most likely to occur in just such a conflict situation.

Managed tension has been in China's interests, but Pakistan's capacity to maintain control is essential. While China continues to express faith in Islamabad, doubts have inevitably been creeping in as militant groups have become stronger and the lines between them have become less cleanly delineated. The capacity of the jihadi groups to hijack policy is a major risk to Chinese strategy in the region, not least because the ramifications are so unpredictable.

Many of these problems escalated under General Pervez Musharraf, but China is far more skeptical about the political direction in which Pakistan has been headed since his fall in September 2008. As a general principle, Beijing is more comfortable with Pakistani military than civilian rule. Although it can work with Pakistan People's Party governments, it sees them as the most pro-Western of the possible political constellations. Zardari's relationship with Beijing has been particularly poor from the very start, when he bypassed the traditional practice of paying the first presidential visit to China, and instead took trips (albeit classified as private) to the United Arab Emirates, the United Kingdom, and the United States.

Zardari's quarterly visits to China since then have not notably remedied this, and Chinese officials have been privately disparaging about the weakness of the civilian government. While any problems on the civilian side are traditionally trumped by the Sino-Pak military relationship, China has also been uncomfortable with what it sees as closer U.S.-Pakistani military-to-military ties. Chinese officials have sought assurances that their interests will remain a protected class.

The common thread across all of these issues is that the principal guarantor of China's interests, the Pakistani military, is growing less capable of securing them. But Beijing at present lacks a Plan B. The People's Liberation Army is resistant to rethinking the level of Chinese reliance on Rawalpindi, and as a group they are unusually influential over this bilateral relationship. Even among the Chinese military though, while the basic tenets of the Sino-Pakistani relationship are not in doubt, there is reportedly a broader debate about the competing imperatives of geopolitics and the more pragmatic desire to improve the stability of China's Western periphery.

The first school of thought sees the overriding regional objectives as keeping India down and the United States down or out. The latter position sees greater strategic advantage in being able to minimize the risk of major contingencies in Pakistan, weaken the external support base for Uighur militants, and embed Xinjiang in a secure and economically thriving environment. This stance still does not inherently result in any greater cooperation with the West per se, but it does imply a more active and nuanced set of Chinese policies, especially in a context where Beijing increasingly expects Washington to draw down its presence in the coming years and is starting to feel the need to prepare for the aftermath.

There have certainly been some modest tweaks to China's approach. The weakening of the military channel in dealing with militants has led China to seek more direct methods. The most potent recent successes against Chinese targets have come not from the Pakistani military which was responsible for the 2003 operation against ETIM's leader but from U.S. drone strikes, which have killed numerous TIP militants in the province of Baghdis in Western Afghanistan, along with its leader, Abdul Haq al-Turkistani, in North Waziristan. China has also courted parties with their own routes to extremist groups, the MMA as well as the Jamaat-e-Islami (JI) in particular, being wooed in the past two years. Various members of the MMA have been invited on public relations visits to China, with one of the most recent culminating in a memorandum of understanding between the JI and the Communist Party of China's international department, in which JI "fully backed China's stance on Taiwan, Tibet and Xinjiang issues," and pledged cooperation on "justice, development, security and solidarity," as well as stating that the agreement "makes us accept finally and formally that China's internal affairs are not our business."

Crisis-management scenarios for Pakistan, along the lines of those for North Korea, have even been drawn up by groups affiliated with Chinese military intelligence, even though these are not part of any formal contingency planning process. Looking at case studies such as nuclear weapons falling into the hands of terrorists, another potential conflict between India and Pakistan, and the failure of efforts to contain militancy in the region they suggest that in various worst-case scenarios, Chinese interests can only effectively be secured through closer coordination with other major powers, principally the United States.

THE TRADE IMPLICATIONS OF CHINA'S EMERGENCE

China's economic development has hardly been mono-dimensional. It is not simply a creation of Western capitalists seeking to outsource labour to the lowest bidder; nor is China any longer simply a manufacturing centre of cheap plastic and simple electronic products. Chinese industry has moved rapidly up the production chain and is now producing a very large share of the world's office equipment, DVD players, digital cameras, personal computers as well as clothing and shoes and other simpler manufactured goods.

China's swift development has rerouted global supply chains forged over the last thirty years. It now runs large trade deficits with Eastern Asia while enjoying inexorably expanding trade surpluses with North America and Europe. It has become a trading nation par excellence and currently generates 70% of its national income through foreign trade. China's overall share of world trade has increased from 5% in 2000 to 10% today. (Rossi)

China is also exerting trade pressures on a range of developing and transition countries with which it is directly competing. Mexico and Turkey, for example, are losing market share in textiles to the Chinese without the kind of offsetting compensation that has proven so beneficial to much of Asia. Central and Eastern Europe now find themselves engaged in a global battle to win new investments. Hungary won important investments for basic assembly manufacturing in the mid-1990s; yet some of those plants have subsequently relocated to China. The Hungarians now recognize that in the face of serious Chinese competition, their best option is to move into ever more sophisticated production if they are to flourish in the emerging global division of labour (Visit to Budapest 2004, NATO PA Secretariat Report).

The net effect of China's rapid growth on the global economy has been highly positive, despite the inevitable dislocation suffered in certain sectors. Its booming economy is generating wealth worldwide. Those benefits accrue through countless channels. Yet, mercantilists and protectionists falsely argue that rising Chinese imports are invariably a bad thing and are simply sparking plant closures and job losses.

Trade economists counter that this is a misleading and partial economic interpretation of what transpires when a large country undergoes economic take-off and emerges as a major global commercial player. First of all, trading with that low cost producer invariably lowers prices for consumers as well as producers, who, as a result, are able to purchase lower cost capital goods. Price falls, in turn, check inflationary pressures in the importing economy, raise consumer welfare, and lower exporters' production costs. The resulting productivity gains help certain domestic industries win market share both domestically and internationally while rewarding workers employed in those sectors. It must also be noted that non-Chinese companies are currently generating over half of China's export earnings and 60% of import revenue. In 2000 alone, U.S corporate earnings generated in China reached $7.2 billion. (Hale and Hale) Western firms are also selling value added inputs to Chinese producers and are thus benefiting from China's place in the international division of labour. These are the winners in the game.

The losers are both the producers of import competing industries that cannot match the price/quality of imported Chinese goods and workers in those industries. Yet, those domestic import competing firms that manage to compete are likely to emerge even stronger. Most empirical work on the broad effects of expanding trade suggests that the gains of the winners in open trading systems significantly outweigh the losses of those suffering from new competition. In this process, moreover, trading countries are likely to grow more specialized in their production, leading to further productivity gains and wealth generation.

Empirical evidence tends to confirm that precisely such processes are at work in those developed and developing countries with growing trade links to China. The Economist recently estimated that if China continues to develop, and if parts of the developing world respond to its competitive challenge by adopting liberal commercial policies, the developed world could enjoy an additional 1% of growth a year, while the developing world would undergo a substantially larger rate of growth despite the dislocation which some economies would obviously undergo. (The Economist, October 2, 2004) The capacity of a single non-oil exporting developing country to have such a broad global economic impact represents an undeniable revolution in international financial and trading systems. As suggested above, it is an economic shift laden with political, diplomatic and strategic significance. Yet, in order to capture the potential gains, Western governments must ensure their economies are ever more agile and flexible. They should increase their respective capacities to shift both capital and labour into those sectors in which they are most competitive and out of those in which they are least productive.

The McKinsey Global Institute recently examined the fate of western workers who lost jobs because of firms moving production facilities to China or India. According to this study, 70% of such American workers find new work within six months, while in Germany only 40% do. This suggests that labour market rigidities can gravely complicate efforts to adapt to changing international market conditions.

China is also having a strong effect on global demand. While many casual observers see its most substantial economic impact largely in terms of its enormous exports, China is also a large and growing capital and consumer goods market. It is estimated that if current growth and income distribution were sustained until 2020, China would offer the world 100 million consumers with an average income equivalent to the current income average of Western Europe. (The Economist, October 2, 2004.) Already it has almost single-handedly revived the previously flagging economies of East Asia through high demand for a range of manufacturing inputs, high technology components and consumer goods. Australia - like a range of other commodity exporters - is enjoying a veritable economic boom thanks to burgeoning Chinese demand.

China's imports are growing at a very rapid rate - 40% in 2003 alone. Since 2001, it has accounted for one third of the increase in global import volume. China is the world's third largest importer, and in 2004 accounted for 17% of Japan's exports, 16% of the European Union's, 8.5% of the United States', 38.5% of the rest of Asia's, and 20% for the rest of the World. (Rossi) It is now Japan's leading trade partner and the second largest trade partner of the European Union behind only the United States. EU-China Trade doubled between 1999 and 2003. (Eurostat, 14/6/2004, Kihara and Takeuchi) China is also providing an important market for developing countries; 45% of China's

$400 billion in annual imports comes from developing countries, and these rose by $55 billion in 2003. It is, in fact, running a significant trade deficit with the developing world. (Kharas) Some optimistic forecasts suggest that if China continues down the reform path it could be the world's largest exporter and importer within ten years.

The US trade with China deficit has reached the enormous sum of $162 billion. (Teather) Yet, imports from China do not explain the explosive growth of the US current account deficit, now at 7% of GDP and rising, partly because China has, in fact, simply replaced other suppliers to the US market. In 1988, for example, only 2% of US shoe imports came from China, while 60% came from Taiwan and South Korea. Today China has 70% of the US shoe import market, having all but displaced South Korea and Taiwan from the US market, although the Koreans and Taiwanese effectively own many of the Chinese plants selling to the United States. Many of Taiwan's electronics companies have also relocated to the Chinese mainland and are playing a pivotal role in China's electronics exports to the United States. By the end of 2003, China's deficit with Taiwan stood at $31.5 billion; $13.1 billion with South Korea; $7.6 billion with ASEAN; $5 billion with Japan; and $1.3 billion with Australia. (Hale and Hale) A similar trend can be traced in other goods markets including personal computers. While Asian countries are losing market share in the United States to China, they are being compensated by a massive increase in exports to China in higher end and more valuable products.

The Chinese economy is far more open than the Korean or Japanese economies were at similar points in their economic take-off, and the state seems to have rejected the more dirigiste model of development employed by the Japanese. China's general tariff rates have fallen precipitously from 40% in the early 1990s to 10.4% in 2004. (Beattie) It entered the WTO under highly stringent conditions that have helped to open its market even further. In 2004, exports and imports together accounted for nearly 75% of China's total GDP. This is an extraordinarily high share for such a large country, and more than double that of the United States. Part of the reason is that China's domestic non-tradable economy remains very underdeveloped. China has also implemented exceedingly open investment rules, although foreign investors still complain about serious administrative burdens and creeping non-tariff barriers in areas like financial services and investment rules. Still, foreign investment in China accounts for some 35% of its GDP. (The Economist, October 2, 2004) It is now the world's fifth largest recipient of foreign direct investment (FDI) and is moving quickly up the list. FDI in the first ten months of 2004 reached $54 billion. These funds are fundamentally transforming China's manufacturing and transport infrastructure.

PAKISTAN, CHINA AGREE TO PROPEL LEVEL OF ECONOMIC COOPERATION

Pakistan and China Thursday agreed to propel level of economic cooperation in diverse sectors on fast trajectory as an important plank of comprehensive strategic partnership. The two countries also agreed to make continuous efforts to strengthen good-neighbourly relations and friendship, develop mutually beneficial cooperation and deepen strategic partnership of cooperation which serves the fundamental interests of the two peoples and contributes to peace and development in the region, said a Joint Statement issued on the first state visit of Pakistan's President Asif Ali Zardari to China. Both sides opposed to all forms of terrorism, extremism and separatism, resolved to cooperation with each other to fight the above-mentioned three forces, said the Statement adding, China conveyed its complete support to Pakistan's commitment and efforts to fight terrorism and appreciated the sacrifices made by the government and people of Pakistan in this regard. The two sides agreed that economic cooperation is an important part of strategic partnership and both sides enjoy great economic complementarity and should fully tap the potential and comprehensively deepen mutually beneficial cooperation in the economic field. The two countries agreed to fast track the implementation of the Five Year Development Programme on Economic Cooperation and make full use of the Free Trade Agreement in Goods and Investment and Pakistan-China Joint Investment Company.

In this regard, the statement said, they agreed to convene a meeting of Pakistan-China Economic Cooperation Group under the Five Development Programme on Economic Cooperation at an early date. Both sides agreed that the Treaty of Friendship, Cooperation and Good-neighbourly Relations between the People's Republic of China and the Islamic Republic of Pakistan (Treaty) signed in April 2005 is of great historic and immediate significance, laying a solid legal foundation for the long-term stable and health growth of China-Pakistan relations.

Both sides decided to abide by the policies and principles enshrined in the Treaty, earnestly implement the bilateral legal documents signed since the two countries established diplomatic ties and further intensify cooperation in the areas of economy, defense, science and technology, people to people contact, thus constantly advancing the China-Pakistan strategic partnership of cooperation. China stressed that Pakistan is China's good neighbour, close friend, dear brother and trusted partner. China will continue to view China-Pakistan relations from a strategic and long-term perspective, and make joint efforts with Pakistan to lift China-Pakistan Strategic partnership of cooperation to a new height, the statement said. Pakistan stressed that Pak-China relationship is the cornerstone of its foreign policy, and friendship with China represents the common desire of all Pakistani people, the statement observed continuing, Pakistan appreciated the strong support and assistance provided by the government and people of China to Pakistan in its economic development. Pakistan remained committed to continuing its policy of friendship towards China and making unremitting efforts to promote the healthy and steady growth of relations between the two countries.

According to the statement, President Asif Ali Zardari extended invitation to President Hu Jintao to visit Pakistan once again at his convenience and President Hu Jintao thanked President Zardari for his kind invitation. The statement said Pakistan unequivocally upheld the one-China policy and considers Taiwan as an inseparable part of the Peoples Republic of China and supports all efforts made by the Chinese government to realize national reunification. China, the statement added, appreciated Pakistan's long term and staunch support to China on issues concerning China's sovereignty and territorial integrity, reaffirmed its support for Pakistan's efforts to uphold its sovereignty, independence and territorial integrity and appreciated Pakistan's important role in promoting regional peace, stability and security and strengthening international counter-terrorism efforts.

The two sides agreed to enhance cooperation to further develop and boost Pakistan's Mineral and Energy sector as well as broaden financial and banking sector cooperation.

They agreed to further enhance "connectivity" by developing new communication and links including fiber optic links and also agreed to explore the concept of Integrated Border Management, overland trade and development of trans-border economic zones. Both sides agreed to maintain communication and coordination on major international and regional issues to safeguard their common interests besides continuing to cooperate closely on issues such as the reform of the United Nations, climate change and energy and food security to promote world peace and development. President Asif Zardari offered congratulation to the Chinese government and people on the successful hosting of the Beijing Olympic Games and the successful completion of Shenzhou VII's mission. According to the Statement, President HU Jintao congratulated President Zardari on his election as the President of Pakistan and thanked Pakistan for its valuable assistance in the wake of the devastating earthquake in Wenchuan, China. He also appreciated Pakistan's support to ensure the success of the Beijing Olympics and Paralympics Games.

Pakistan applauded the outstanding achievements China has made in the 30 years of reform and opening-up and believes that China's development will contribute to world peace and prosperity. On the invitation of President Hu

Jintao, President Asif Ali Zardari paid four-day long state visit and during the stay held talks with his Chinese counterpart. Mr Wu Bangguo, Chairman Standing Committee of the National Peoples Congress, Mr Wen Jiabao, Premier of the State Council, and Mr Jia Qinglin, Chairman of the Chinese Peoples Political Consultative Conference met the visiting president. Talks between the two Presidents and President Zardari's meetings with other Chinese state leaders were characterized by traditional warmth, friendship and mutual understanding. The two leaders reached broad agreement on strengthening China-Pakistan strategic partnership of cooperation and on international and regional issues of mutual interest under the new circumstances. The president of Pakistan also held wide ranging discussions with the leaders of the Chinese corporations and financial institutions.

The leaders of the two countries reviewed with satisfaction the growth of China-Pakistan relations over the past 57 years since the two countries established diplomatic ties. They agreed the friendship between China and Pakistan has withstood the test of time and practice, notwithstanding changes in the international, regional and domestic environments. The all-weather friendship and all-round cooperation have become the distinctive features of China-Pakistan relations. Both sides inked twelve agreements/MOUs during the visit in the fields of economic and technical cooperation, free trade, minerals, petroleum and natural resources, environmental protection, radio and television, space technology, agriculture sector, properties exchange between foreign ministries of the two countries, museum of natural history, cricket field and project of X-Ray container/vehicle inspection system.

CHINA'S BIG PLANS FOR PAKISTAN

On November 29, Pakistani prime minister Nawaz Sharif broke ground on a section of the Hazara Motorway, which will connect the outskirts of the capital city of Islamabad to China through the Karakoram Highway. The four-lane, fenced road in mountainous Khyber Pakhtunkhwa province will, according to current projections, take two years to complete and cost $297 million.

The groundbreaking move, China's Xinhua News Agency proclaims, "signal[s] the implementation of the China-Pakistan Economic Corridor agreement." When the Corridor is completed at the turn of the decade, China will have effectively cut Pakistan in two. At the same time, Beijing will be able to use the Corridor's new transportation links to faster deploy its forces to areas disputed by Pakistan and India.

In early November in Beijing, Sharif signed Corridor pacts authorizing $45.6 billion in projects in his country. Of that total, $33.8 billion is allocated for electricity generation—the addition of 16,520 megawatts by 2021—and $11.8 billion for transportation infrastructure.

The November pacts follow those signed this February, when the two countries inked deals to improve the Karakoram Highway and build an airport in Gwadar, a port on the Arabian Sea near the Iran border. The February agreements in turn came on the heels of one signed last year, when China and Pakistan agreed to build a fibre-optic cable from the Chinese border to the city of Rawalpindi, next to Pakistan's capital.

Chinese premier Li Keqiang called the Corridor, during his visit to Pakistan in May of last year, a "flagship," and the ambitious undertaking is indeed a wonder to behold. The transport and communication links—roads, railways, cable, and oil and gas pipelines—will stretch 2,700 kilometers from Gwadar to the Khunjerab Pass, where the Karakoram Highway leaves Kashmir and enters China, not far from the Chinese city of Kashgar.

Moreover, Islamabad will establish special economic zones in the Corridor where Chinese companies will locate operations. Beijing, as Tarique Niazi of the University of Wisconsin observed, is trying to "integrate Pakistan into the Chinese economy by outsourcing low-tech, labor-absorbing, resource-intensive industrial production," and the Corridor initiative makes it easier to transform the client state "into a giant factory floor for China."

Beijing has obviously gone all-in on Pakistan. Sharif's government will provide 15 percent of the financing for the cable to Rawalpindi, but almost all the rest of the Corridor projects will be on China's tab. Pakistan does not have the money to pay for the large projects, and according to Khawaja Asif, Pakistan's minister for water and power, Pakistan will not be incurring debt.

Beijing, it appears, will be providing almost all the funding, which means it will, one way or another, own resulting cash flows as the projects are supposed to be profit-making. Chinese companies will participate in the building of the infrastructure, and Chinese banks, especially the China Development Bank and Industrial and Commercial Bank of China, will be providing financing. The Beijing-sponsored Asian Infrastructure Investment Bank, when it opens its doors for business next year, will probably support Corridor projects as well. Sharif, therefore, should be worried that the tide of Chinese cash will effectively turn his country into Beijing's newest colony.

All the prime minister has to do is look at Gwadar to see Beijing's designs for Pakistan. China last decade provided about 75 percent of the funding for the strategic port's first phase of development. In February of last year, Islamabad transferred operations of the port to China, specifically state-run China Overseas Port Holding Co. Many believe the Chinese navy will use the facility, eventually turning it into a formal base.

For now, Beijing's strategy is to build additional facilities in the port area so that it can then offload oil there and send it across the Himalayas to Xinjiang. On paper, the overland route eliminates the need to ship crude through the easily blocked Malacca Strait, but the Gwadar-Kashgar plan has its own vulnerabilities, especially at both ends.

At the southern end, Gwadar is cut off from the rest of Pakistan by the separatist insurgency in Balochistan province, which has caused turmoil there since the 1960s. In the middle of last decade, Baloch separatists kidnapped and killed Chinese engineers in highly publicized incidents. As a result of the deteriorating situation, Beijing in 2009 decided not to go forward with a multibillion-dollar refinery planned for Gwadar.

Sharif, as part of the just-signed Economic Corridor deal, promised to provide security for China's projects, but his ability to honor the pledge is dubious. Baloch leaders have already expressed opposition to Beijing's increased involvement in Gwadar. "We have not invited them," says Amir Ahmed Suleman Daud, referring to the Chinese. His people, he states, have no choice but to "defend our land."

At the route's northern end, in what Beijing calls the Xinjiang Uyghur Autonomous Region and local Uyghurs claim is the East Turkestan Republic, the security situation is rapidly deteriorating. So far, the Chinese have been able to put down resistance to their increasingly harsh rule, but Beijing's policies look unsustainable. Transport links through Uyghur lands, therefore, are vulnerable to attack.

Despite everything, Chinese leaders think they can, through money, solve the security problems at both ends of the Economic Corridor. That, however, is unrealistic as their policies have in fact only made matters worse, both in Balochistan and Xinjiang. As Syed Fazl-e-Haider, a Pakistani expert on development, perceptively wrote this year, "One should keep in mind that development does not bring peace, rather it is peace that brings development." Pakistan, therefore, can end up a sinkhole for Chinese cash, which only exacerbates the insurgency problems in South Asia—and inside China's borders as well.

Beijing is not only creating militants and then taking them on. To make matters even worse, the Corridor enters China through an area India claims as its own.

Beijing says it does not take sides in the territorial dispute over Kashmir, but at the beginning of this month, it abandoned its asserted neutrality.

In a December 2 release, Xinhua News Agency stated that the Khunjerab Pass was "on the China-Pakistan border." "The pass," China's official media outlet stated, "is a strategic point on the Karakoram Highway, which links

China's Xinjiang with Pakistan's Gilgit-Baltistan region." New Delhi, however, maintains Gilgit-Baltistan is part of India.

In 2010, the Chinese government issued a similar statement, but withdrew it after New Delhi's protest. The risk for Beijing this time is that militant Pakistan launches still another attack, which India counters with a drive of its own, thereby threatening to cut the Corridor in two.

Pakistan has proven to be uncompetitive in the matchup with India: despite being led by military governments, the Islamic Republic has not been able to win wars against its large rival. So China is violating Oscar Wilde's first rule of successful international relations: "A man cannot be too careful in the choice of his enemies," he told us.

To Indian analysts, the Economic Corridor looks like part of a "pincer strategy" of China and Pakistan closing ranks to confront their country.

Moreover, it does not ease Indian concerns that in recent months there has been a growing Chinese military presence in the disputed region.

Beijing, despite everything, looks like it is absolutely determined to do whatever it takes to first build and then secure its corridor running through the heart of Pakistan. Its plan, however, is almost certainly misconceived, bound to cause more turmoil in already troubled areas.

THE ECONOMICS OF THE SILK ROAD ECONOMIC BELT

Making up for lost time with some old posting again now that we are surrounding Christmas, and first up is a short report withSarah from a workshop we did in Almaty taking a gander at the Silk Road Economic Belt's financial measurement. Part of a greater undertaking we are taking a shot at RUSI which will be a noteworthy need in the coming year.

The Economics of the Silk Road Economic Belt

On 20 October 2015, RUSI held a day-long workshop in Almaty, Kazakhstan, in collaboration with KIMEP University and the Friedrich Ebert Stiftung (FES). The focus of the workshop was the economics behind the Chinese Silk Road Economic Belt (SREB) and its impact in Central Asia. The key areas of discussion examined the potential benefits that the SREB could bring to participating countries, the integration of the SREB with other economic projects and the various funding mechanisms through which the SREB will be financed. The workshop brought together participants from Almaty, Astana, London, Beijing, Shanghai, New Delhi and Russia, including representatives from academia, the private sector and think tanks.

The first session discussed the real benefits of the SREB to both China and participating countries along the road. There is a risk that the SREB will simply turn Eurasia into a set of transport routes emanating from China, aimed at increasing the volume of Chinese goods going to Europe.

Other than transit fees, China has not made it explicitly clear as to what other value participating in the SREB can add to economic development. Special economic and free-trade zones are one opportunity, such as that of Khorgos on the border of Kazakhstan and China, or those planned for Pakistan.

However, the extent to which these are benefitting Central Asia is still unclear, and those for Pakistan are still under discussion. Kazakhstan's side of this free-trade zone is noticeably less developed than that of China's, highlighting that not all of these projects are implemented to meet maximum potential.

Furthermore, China's emphasis on connectivity as a key goal of the SREB runs the risk of over-emphasising railway development as an end goal, since not all goods are cost-effective to transport by rail.

High-value goods are the ideal product: one participant from Kazakhstan noted that Kazakhstan Temir Zholy, the national railway operator, had begun transporting Apple products from China, cutting down delivery time from sixty days (by sea) to eighteen days (by rail). For the SREB project to be successful, therefore, both Xinjiang, the northwestern Chinese province, and the countries along the Silk Road route need to increase their high-tech manufacturing capacity to produce these high-value goods for transport, neither of which are currently visible.

Understanding of the project has been limited by Beijing's vagueness on practical implementation. The Chinese government's 'Visions and Actions on Jointly Building Silk Road Economic Belt and 21st Century Maritime Silk Road' strategy paper, published by the National Development and Reform Commission (NDRC), emphasises the objectives of the SREB, such as connectivity and greater financial integration. However, it does not give practical detail on how this will be achieved. This approach of laying out a grand vision without detail is typical of the Chinese government. So far there is not even a formally government-endorsed map of the exact routes of the SREB.

The workshop discussion highlighted a potential explanation for this. China's goal may not be to unpack the details itself but instead to seek ideas and engagement from SREB countries to determine where participation can provide most benefit to them. China does not want to limit its options or jeopardise the project's 'inclusivity' by over-defining its approach.

There is an opportunity, therefore, for countries along the SREB to provide proposals back to China. However, there are some practical questions that China will need to address. Although its openended encouragement of connectivity is central to the SREB, certain political and geographical difficulties in implementing this are so far unresolved. Anyone who has travelled within Central Asia knows the difficulty of flying direct between most regional capitals, while land travel between the countries in the region is hindered by longstanding border disputes.

Although the SREB has broadly been received with enthusiasm by Central and South Asia, the lack of clarity around its planned implementation has led to some suspicion.

India stands out as the country in the region most apprehensive of China's plans. As one workshop participant said, 'there is no Indian perspective at the moment', in part due to a perceived lack of information from Beijing. The suspicions relate to whether there is a broader Chinese geopolitical strategy behind the SREB and whether political strings will become attached to China's infrastructure investment.

India's concerns over a geopolitical strategy are mainly due to the maritime element of the '21st Century Maritime Silk Road', which runs through the Indian Ocean. It covers ports in countries located around India, such as Sri Lanka, Maldives and Pakistan, but not India itself. This has raised alarm bells in New Delhi, who perceive China as encroaching on India's waterways. China's investment into the China–Pakistan Economic Corridor (CPEC), which cuts through the disputed areas of Kashmir as well as highlighting China's strong connection with Pakistan, is also a challenge for India. There are areas where India and China can co-operate on this SREB project, such as the Bangladesh–China–India–Burma corridor or areas where both have interests, like Iran. However, India requires more detail and reassurances regarding China's intentions.

A large part of the day's discussion focused on the issue of integrating the SREB with other economic projects. Russia has recently voiced its desire to integrate the SREB with the Eurasian Economic Union (EEU) and Kazakhstan has proposed something similar with its 'Bright Road' (Nurly Zhol) policy.

Although the Bright Road policy, which focuses on infrastructure development, is consistent with the aims of the Chinese project, SREB integration with the EEU is somewhat more complex. As one workshop participant pointed out, the EEU is an organisation with an institutional and regulatory framework, whereas the SREB is more of a 'vision' covering a variety of concrete projects.

'Integrating' these in practice may be difficult. A special economic zone may once again be an answer to this, and the EEU and China are currently exploring this idea. The EEU's external tariffs may present an immediate barrier to increased trade with China, although one benefit is that once this barrier is overcome countries gain access to a significant economic space consisting of five countries. However, to facilitate trade, China and Russia will need to address a number of bilateral trade issues. For example, the Russian–Chinese border currently suffers from excessive bureaucracy that, in particular, prevents cross-border travel and trade.

The third key aspect of the discussions examined the means by which the SREB will be funded. A major tool will be multilateral and national institutions driven by Beijing. China has allocated $29.8 billion to the Asian Infrastructure Investment Bank's (AIIB) overall $100 billion capitalisation and $40 billion to the national Silk Road Fund.

Furthermore, the China Development Bank (CDB) is the lead financial body for the SREB, investing $890 billion into over 900 projects. There are also bilateral funding relations between SREB countries and Chinese provinces. For example, the recent Tbilisi Silk Road Forum held in Georgia was the first event on the SREB co-sponsored by the Chinese state held outside of China. The principals on the Chinese side were the provincial governments of Xinjiang and Shaanxi. On top of this, China is seeking to stimulate public–private partnerships to help progress the project finance, as well as exploring opportunities of collaboration with other international financial institutions like the Asian Development Bank (ADB), the European Bank for Reconstruction and Development (EBRD) and the European Investment Bank (EIB).

Most participants agreed, however, that the predominant mechanism for SREB co-operation will continue to be bilateral agreements. As one workshop participant mentioned, China recently pledged $46 billion for the China–Pakistan Economic Corridor alone, a number that puts China's commitment into context when it is compared to the total $100 billion capitalisation of the AIIB. This highlights the degree to which China is likely to continue to prioritise bilateral agreements over its multilateral financial vehicles. A note of caution was made regarding the enormity of some of the SREB deals announced. As one participant pointed out, it seems in reality that the CPEC deal included a repackaging – or at least a reinvigoration – of some historical agreements between China and Pakistan, such as the development of Gwadar port and the Karakorum Highway, projects that have been underway for years. This demonstrates a lack of clarity in the detail behind some of these enormous declarations of financial support.

A repeated theme that came up during this discussion related to the broader transparency and governance of the SREB, particularly in participating countries outside of China. One workshop participant highlighted the need for SREB countries to ensure necessary reforms are conducted in the domestic markets to provide a degree of security and flexibility and to avoid an over-reliance on Chinese investment. The slow-down in the Chinese economy may produce constraints on China's ability to meet its ambitious investment programme. A lack of transparency as regards the relevant information has led to questions over China's asset quality. One workshop participant stated that a 'sudden large injection of external cash could exacerbate existing problems [in the domestic economy] rather than help'. Thus, SREB participants should ensure they protect and reform their own markets in preparation for any large investments from China to maximise returns and protect against a lack of transparency in the deals.

Another question mark surrounding China's funding of the SREB projects is the value this produces for China itself. The divestment opportunities or returns China makes on its infrastructure development projects in, for example, Central Asia, remain unclear. Much of the historical bilateral projects have been funded through linked loans, where China provides the funding through loans that have stipulations attached to them, such as the requirement that Chinese companies implement the projects on the ground. In other cases where China's Eximbank or CDB has provided loans to fund projects, it is unclear whether there are any short- or medium-term returns or even security on the investment. One workshop participant pointed out that given the dominance of the state in China's economic policy and the government's long-term vision of investments, China can afford more time to sit on these investments without requiring immediate returns. Moreover, another participant noted that some projects, such as when Eximbank loaned the money for the high-voltage power line recently unveiled in Kyrgyzstan, provide the Chinese government with foreign investment legitimacy and thus material return is not necessarily the priority.

It is clear that no one wants to be left out of China's SREB initiative. However, questions remain over the implementation plan of the project. For some SREB countries, there are significant concerns over the project's ultimate geostrategic goal as well as the detail of the various routes, both of which need more clarification from Beijing. However, it is clear that while China has ideas for how the SREB should develop, it is also seeking proposals from other countries about its development. This presents an opportunity for SREB countries to take ownership over the direction of their participation and to determine how best to maximise the benefits nationally.

CHINA'S NEW SILK ROAD: TACTICS, OVERSTRETCH OR GRAND STRATEGY?

Outside arrangement has generally been a bit of hindsight for China's pioneers for a great part of the nation's present day history. With the attention on the usage of socialism and communism involving the Mao period, resulting rulers have concentrated on the nation's monetary opening and what has been esteemed its "quiet ascent". Since accepting force in 2013, Xi Jinping has started to lead a more emphatic remote strategy, while seeking after a "purging" of the socialist party in what might be history's biggest against debasement battle and as yet concentrating on advancing, yet gradually, financial changes. As of late however, China seems to have made the jump to planning what seems, by all accounts, to be an amazing system, of sorts: the making of the "Silk Road Economic Belt" and the "21st-Century Maritime Silk Road", named the "One Belt, One Road" methodology. This activity apparently means to support availability and business amongst China and 65 nations in Eurasia and Northern Africa, which has an aggregate populace of 4.4bn. The arrangement is tobuild systems of streets, railroads, pipelines, ports and other foundation crosswise over Asia associating China to Europe, the Middle East, South-and Southeast Asia. Along the way China would like to work out vital, monetary and exchanging associations with the nations on the course, while securing genuinely necessary characteristic assets.

This yearning venture has been relevantly named: The New Silk Road. The verifiable Silk Road, which existed in different structures from ancient history through the start of the current age, was a noteworthy element in the improvement of China, India, Persia, the Levant and Europe, making political and financial linkages between these far flung civic establishments. All the more vitally maybe, the Silk Road was the methods by which China's Han administration broadened power and impact from the 3.4m sq km of domain acquired from the Qin to more than 6m sq km 2000 years back. In a nation, for example, China, with 5,000 years of constant civilisation, recollections are long and these names matter.

China's Marshall Plan or the British Empire's Railways Project?

The scope and scale of China's New Silk Road initiative is perhaps unrivalled in history and has been called China's Marshall Plan by Western commentators. Indeed, there are a number of similarities with the $120bn (in current terms) post WW II program that sought to rebuild Europe through kick-starting infrastructure and heavy industry as the basis for growth. But while the U.S. Marshall Plan sought to rebuild and stabilise Europe in the context of the imminent Cold War, the New Silk Road strategy is interesting since it comes in peace time and crosses continents. Its scale also poses the question as to whether it is more akin to the railways that the British Empire built across the colonies. Railways were the infrastructure used to cement its control over its own colonies. This was particularly the case not just in India, where a huge network of lines was created partly for military purposes, but also in Egypt where rail lines allowed the British to reclaim control over Sudan.

The evident primary purpose of The New Silk Road from public statements appears to be the generation of economic benefits to China itself. The initial focus of the strategy is on the financing and build-out of hard infrastructure, and most of the projects initiated or envisaged to date include a major role for Chinese companies, either as suppliers of equipment and materials or in construction and execution. The building of transport and trade linkages benefits China but also its neighbours for the trade they will facilitate. Further, Central Asia, in particular, is rich in resources that China needs for its continued development, including oil, gas, coal, gold, copper and uranium, and the build-out of sea links to the Middle East and the Mediterranean is critical to securing China's sea lines of communication on a route through which 80% of it is oil imports pass. Economically speaking, China's increased westward focus clearly makes sense: the region the strategy covers contains 65% of the world's population but accounts for only 26% of China's foreign trade, representing a significant growth opportunity.

The primary focus of the New Silk Road initiative, at least initially, appears to be infrastructure build-out, and the majority of commitments announced to date have been on scaled cross-border transportation linkages focusing on six geographic segments, or corridors, creating trade routes along which further economic activity is expected to develop. The map highlights the key corridors and routes of the New Silk Road. Projects initiated or currently under consideration include new highways and rail-lines connecting China to Central Asia, high-speed railway networks in Europe, including a Hungary-Serbia link, the build-out of a network of port facilities stretching from Athens to Malaysia and a canal through the Isthmus of Kraa in Thailand that would dwarf the Panama Canal.

China's play to build-out regional infrastructure is highly ambitious, the annual "gap" between the supply and demand for infrastructure spending in Asia being estimated at $800bn. With existing international institutions such as the World Bank, the Asian Development Bank and the IMF currently not positioned to adequately address this gap, China has emerged as a welcome financier to countries requiring infrastructure investment, particularly given its traditional policy of granting loans without imposing the reform and governance requirements set by other lending institutions. Given the massive geographic scale of the New Silk Road initiative, the scope of China's required financing activities is equally large. The countries defined as being part of the strategy are already capturing over 75% of the overseas loan commitments made by Beijing's largest policy lenders, the China Development Bank and the China Export-Import Bank, making obvious the need for significant additional financing to execute the strategy. Estimates of the total investment vary, but China has committed to finance the build-out through multiple pools of capital, including the US$100bn Asian Infrastructure Investment Bank (AIIB), a dedicated US$40bn Silk Road Fund, and the injection of US$62bn of fresh capital into the state-owned policy banks, as well as a number of funding commitments at the bilateral level, such as the $45bn funding of the China-Pakistan Economic Corridor. China's total investment (and its partners' in the AIIB) in its master plan could exceed US$1.4 trillion by some estimates, making it 12 times larger than the Marshall Plan, or approximately 15% of China's GDP

The scale of its funding requirement aside, China's New Silk Road is ambitious in that it touches on virtually every important issue facing the country today, although in certain cases it appears to be set to exacerbate rather than resolve many of these issues.

The relationships with key powers appears to be one of the most significant shortfalls of the New Silk Road initiative or at the least it is a factor for which China's aims and strategy have not been declared. For all of its focus on immediate economic benefits for China, very little is said about the New Silk Road's long-term political implications, particularly with regards to the countries that are not, or are only marginal beneficiaries of the initiative, but are impacted by its implications nonetheless. The list of these includes some of the world's most important countries and the initiative could easily lead to uniting them in opposition to China on a far wider front.

There are four significant potential geopolitical implications of a successful implementation of the initiative.

- The United States: Outpivoting the Pivot. The US, China's largest trading partner by a significant margin, is wholly outside of the scope and spirit of the New Silk Road strategy, which is a geographic counterpoint to America's own pivot westward into the Pacific. In parallel to building links westward, China appears to be drawing increasingly hard borders eastward, both in terms of defence and economics, with increasing territorial tensions with its Eastern and South-eastern neighbours, the extension of China's own air defence identification zone into those of Korea and Japan and a build-up of naval power, while progress on the proposed China–Japan-South Korea Free Trade Agreement appears to have stalled China has refused to take part in the 12 country, US led, Tran-Pacific Partnership (while the US, conversely, is not supporting the 51 country, China led, AIIB). With the US seeking to set the next generation of trade and investment rules for the Asian Pacific, China is increasingly looking to the Eurasian continent for economic growth and presumably long-term influence.

- Japan: Out in the Cold. The US's closest regional ally Japan, China's second largest sovereign trading partner, is similarly shut out of the New Silk Road initiative. With Sino-Japanese foreign policy relations already a casualty of both country's increasing nationalism, Japan stands to be one of the key losers of the New Silk Road strategy, with trade and investment shifting away from it. While Japan certainly does not require further infrastructure build-out, the Abe government has called for foreign direct investment into the country to double by 2020 to $280bn, with China currently investing less than US$500m in Japan annually, representing a significant lost opportunity for both Japanese and Chinese companies. More importantly, given Japan has historically been one of top three providers of FDI to China, this initiative potentially puts at risk a key source of foreign capital for the country.
- India: Encirclement Risk. Although technically, India is part of the New Silk Road strategy by virtue of the Bangladesh-China-India-Myanmar Economic Corridor, this is not at all how India views this part of the initiative. India very clearly sees encirclement by China. The Maritime Road passes through the Indian Ocean to the country's south, establishing ports and potentially naval bases in places that India considers within its sphere of influence, such Sri Lanka, or strategically sensitive, such as Pakistan. Similarly, the overland silk route bypasses the country's northern border to India's exclusion and to the benefit of its regional rival Pakistan.
- Russia: Security Encroachment. A full [5,000] km of the New Silk Road skirt Russia's southern borders, running through countries that until recently were part of or satellites of the Soviet Union. China has already eclipsed Russia as the largest trading partner of the five post-Soviet central Asian states, all of which the latter considers security buffer states. For the time being it appears that Russia and China have come to an agreement with regards to sharing regional power, with Russia recognising China's de facto economic dominance while remaining the sole military powerbase when it comes to hard security in the region. It remains to be seen, however, how stress-resistant this arrangement turns out to be, with both countries continuing to nurturing competing economic and security institutions as a potential back-up.

Clearly, it is hard to imagine that a country that plans as thoroughly as China would develop a mega-scaled project with a highly complex cross-border strategic thrust unfolding over decades without having planned out its political dimensions, too. However, if the New Silk Road truly lacks the political dimension, it highlights a key difference between it and the Marshall Plan and the British Empire's railways programme, both of which were part of a grand strategy driven by a set of long-term geopolitical foreign policy or military goals; the New Silk Road would be exclusively focused on economic issues and seemingly tactical ones at that. Supporting that idea, China's foreign affairs institutions do not appear to be directly involved with the initiative, it being under the remit of Zhang Gaoli, a ranking member of the standing committee of the politburo and the second-in-charge of China's government and economic sector. The key question this prompts is whether the lack of an evident political dimension is an oversight or a carefully weighed and determined geo-political move? The supplementary question is whether this is an economic initiative or a political one? If it is an economic one, then is it a tactical one or a strategic one? This in turn raises the question for others to determine what it means for them. In the absence of clarity on China's aims, they will need to form strategies under various scenarios. There are three distinct possibilities regarding the underlying nature of China's engagement on the New Silk Road.things. However, while China's current level of planning is unclear, a political strategic New Silk Road is certainly within its capabilities, and even a purely economic initiative today provides it with options to develop complementary political strategies.

Political Strategic Initiative. The New Silk Road, under this scenario, would be the play out of a long and patient game around the country's political position and the build-out of its power, under the cover of an initiative ostensibly run by the country's economic leaders. In support of this view, is the evidence that China in other areas has proven to be both highly strategic, willing to play long-term games patiently and has been shifting to a more muscular foreign policy in recent years. In this scenario, China's political non-engagement to date is a strategic tool that helps to obscure the country's end game. Having made a conscious decision to obscure, it make sense to de-politicise the initial stages of the strategy and thereby build credibility and trust as well as economic momentum while setting the pieces for later political moves. For example, the protection of economic interests in foreign countries have historically provided justifications for subsequent strategic and even military interventions, as Britain's expansion in India through the East India Company demonstrates. The key argument against this view is that such a strategy would represent a premature shift in the country's priorities: Chinese leaders since Deng Xiaoping have focused on economic development and the creation of a "moderately well off" society, a transformation process that remains difficult and is on-going. In this interpretation, China's more active foreign policy is a natural consequence of its growing importance and increasing global integration, rather than a necessary active choice. If it were indeed a political strategic initiative, the New Silk Road, given its scope, would be a major play in "great power" politics, which is something that countries can only afford when they are otherwise highly stable or desperate. China today is neither of these things. However, while China's current level of planning is unclear, a political strategic New Silk Road is certainly within its capabilities, and even a purely economic initiative today provides it with options to develop complementary political strategies.

Economic Strategic Initiative. Alternatively, the New Silk Road's primary objective might be economic and strategic because it has the potential to own the trade corridor linking the Middle East to East Asia, one of the world's most energy dependent regions. China currently imports 60% of its oil from overseas. Although oil contributes less than 20% of its primary energy consumption, China's demand makes it the largest net importer of petroleum globally. While China has sought to diversify its sources of oil by purchasing from places such as South America and Africa, two-thirds of its oil imports today come from the Middle East and the former Soviet Union. Locking in supply and controlling transportation infrastructure in the region is clearly highly strategic for China, given energy security is crucial for further economic development and stability. Per capita energy consumption in China today is only a quarter of that of advanced industrial economies such as a Japan and Germany, pointing a massive increase in China's medium to long-term energy requirements. Additionally, securing petroleum access is also highly strategic for many of its neighbours, who are even more dependent on foreign oil than China is, with imported oil representing approximately 25% of India's and 40% of Japan and Korea's total primary energy consumption. Owning key access routes for is neighbour's essential resources would provide China with significant future strategic leverage in trade negotiations. Executing the New Silk Road as an economic strategic initiative that ties into China's long-term development is significantly more complex than executing one focused on boosting trade and investment but the strategic value to China is commensurately greater, too.

Economic Tactical Initiative. While at first glance unlikely, it does remain possible that the New Silk Road, at least initially, is tactical, in that it is predominantly about utilising excess capacity in construction and related finance. Under this view, it would be argued that the New Silk Road is not a strategy at all, but a convenient label to group together a series of initiatives China has already been pursuing for over a decade, kicked off when former President Jiang Zemin told Chinese businesses to "go out". The various funding mechanisms and the vagueness of official language, which for examples waivers between calling the China-Pakistan corridor a part of the strategy or a closely related initiative, points to a lack of top level coordination. The "vision" of the New Silk Road espoused by Xi Jinping has been back-solved, adding the illusion of grand strategy to an ongoing series of tactical moves. However, the lack of an upfront long-term strategy does not preclude its development over time to something more strategic.

From the perspective of foreign policy makers, one of the lessons of history is how trade and infrastructure lead to ownership and control. So, whatever might be the initial objectives of The New Silk Road, policy makers would need to focus on the natural development of a political dimension over time: building out trade links provides influence over the movement of people, trade and information between two or more points and therefore virtually guarantees the accrual of political clout over time. History is full examples of infrastructure both enabling and requiring the use of political power. Egypt for example became a de-facto Anglo-French protectorate following the establishment of the Suez Canal and US intervention triggered by its interests in the Panama Canal drove the separation of Panama from Colombia.Especially poignant for the East is the story of the East India Company and how its trade linked sowed the seeds of the British Empire in India. From China's perspective, the issues being addressed by the New Silk Road are well understood and have been areas of focus of its leadership for some time. If there is a indeed a masterplan that was drawn up in Zhongnanhai it will have drawn upon the inputs from diverse sources and will have been drafted in a way that makes it acceptable to the various factions in China's leadership today, which means supporting multiple and differing views and providing flexibility in terms of future execution and focus. Regardless of China's current level of thinking on the New Silk Road, it is clear that unless thwarted, this initiative has long-term potential of a strategic and political nature.

Executing a Long-Term Strategy: The Long Road

Looking ahead, a successful New Silk Road will need to encompass a number of additional policy areas, both economic and political, which still appear to be missing today, including credibility, sustainability accountability and the parallel execution of domestic reform.

- Strategic Partnership. In terms of building credibility, China today has failed to build a base of soft power in the world today commensurate with its economic power and growing political clout. The New Silk Road in some ways represents a major soft power push, promising Chinese capital, expertise, good and services to countries along the route, along with closer relationships with Beijing, with its success depending on China being accepted as a credible partner. As currently envisaged though, the New Silk Road also represents a liability to

China's credibility, in that it comes at the expense of the countries outside of the routes, many of which have been its long standing economic partners. By turning its back on the countries that played an important part in its development until today, such as Japan and to a lesser degree South Korea and Vietnam, China risks sending signals that it is not a long-term strategic and economic partner. More importantly, China's increasing focus on the New Silk Road is allowing it to leave a growing number of issues with these countries unresolved. If China wants to be credible as a partner to the countries on the New Silk Road it will need to demonstrate both the long-term nature of the partnerships it is seeking to establish as well as its ability to constructively resolve the differences that surely will arise over time. If and once the New Silk Road is successful, China is very capable of using it of course to bring others to participate in it and thereby further enhance its power and influence.

- Sustainable Financing. Equally as important as credibility in winning acceptance as a strategic partner is sustainability and financial viability. China's policy in the past has often focused on providing soft loans with little or no financial accountability. The scaled infrastructure projects of the New Silk Road will need to pay for themselves however, at least over the long term. If the New Silk Road projects do not generate sustainable benefits to local economies however, China risks suffering political backlash from local electorates, as it has done in parts of Africa. This financial sustainability requirement creates a potentially high bar for projects on the route: China's own infrastructure investments in its sparsely populated western regions have seen much lower returns than its earlier coastal investments. China and its partners will need to build solid business cases for scaled projects even further afield for these to succeed over the long term.
- Security and Military Exposure. The New Silk Road passes through a number of global hotspots suffering from political instability that threaten the safety of traffic on the route and China's investments. Afghanistan, Iran, Sudan and Syria are all along or next to major proposed arteries of the road, and China's policy of non-intervention in other countries' affairs is not attuned to the needs of the New Silk Road strategy. As the architect and financier of the road, China will need to assume security accountability for its infrastructure and traffic. Once the precedent is set, it, one can envisage China playing a more active role in international affairs, contributing to international peacekeeping and disaster relief efforts generally as well as a as a

proactive mediator helping to solve specific regional issues. This would initially be seen as China becoming a broader responsible stakeholder. It is also one of the first step in China learning how the international conflict system works as a participant rather than an observer and as the world has seen in the sphere of trade, what begins as a participant ends with China becoming a force to reckon with.

- Domestic Reform. Most importantly, perhaps, China will also need to execute comprehensive domestic reforms. As currently formulated, the New Silk Road is a rear-guard action protecting China's investment led economic model, allowing it export overcapacity in sectors whose productive contribution to the Chinese economy is declining. Given that the country's economic restructuring is progressing only slowly, the New Silk Road initiative is one way of sustaining otherwise declining industries and making up for their contribution shortfalls to domestic growth. China's key long-term strategic objective needs to be the reshaping of its economy, and the New Silk Road initiative must clearly be recognised for what it is: one tool that affords China the opportunity to do so.

Ensuring the success of the New Silk Road, even if defined in a narrow economic fashion will therefore require expanding its scope significantly, from trade and investment today to foreign and security policy as well as governance and development, while also expanding its geographic scale to integrate or at least accommodate important constituents currently left outside the initiative. This suggests that it is irrelevant where the initiative began, even if that were tactical and economic, it has to end up as strategic and to some extent political in the end if it is to be successful.

For the New Silk Road to deliver its true potential to China, it will need to simultaneously execute a wide range of ambitious initiatives covering development, security, engagement in multi-lateral institutions and foreign policy that unpin its strategic nature.

Foreign policy implications and actions aside, it is also important for its leaders to consider the potential socio-political consequences of the New Silk Road at home. If China is able to achieve only a fraction of the potential vision for the New Silk Road, the domestic impact will be significant, and not just from an economic development perspective. The past 30 years of China's rise have created a mind-set in its leadership that is focused on hard assets: hard currency, hard trade, and hard power. Much like the original, the New Silk Road will also be a cultural transmission route for the exchange of ideas, and one runs in both directions. The original Silk Road, in addition to exporting China's goods to the world, also imported Buddhism, which became the state religion for centuries, and later Islam, which also had a major impact on Chinese history and culture. This transmission will certainly happen again and China's ability to absorb and successfully integrate new ideas will be a function of its openness. In the absence of openness and flexibility, new ideas can disrupt society rather than providing stimulus for further growth and development., and China's leadership's current categorical dismissal of Western "cultures and values" calls in question its receptiveness to the powerful new influences that that New Silk Road will bring.

Conclusion: Foreign Policy Considerations for the Rest of the World

Given the long-term strategic execution requirements of such a far-reaching initiative, the New Silk Road has the potential to be one of the defining economic and political constructs of the first half of the 21st Century, driving development, integrating and promoting trade and providing stability across the world's largest landmass and beyond as well as cementing China's position as a regional and global superpower. Foreign countries, whether in or outside of the scope of the New Silk Road, will need to formulate a response to China's moves, based on both their own strategic priorities and their views on the plan, its risks and benefits and its chances of success. These views and priorities can give rise to three distinct responses:

Accommodate and Influence. Countries seeking to benefit from the New Silk Road are the most likely candidates to be accommodating, welcoming engagement with China and with its trade and investment. This list includes both countries with pressing needs and limited alternatives to China's plans, such as the Central Asian countries, and mature developed countries that believe engagement creates win-win situations, such as the UK. PM David Cameron's red carpet roll-out to President Xi Jinping in London last month and its willingness to sign up to the AIIB speaks loudly to the UK government's conviction that an early submission to China's plans will reap greater benefits than a later one. Whether this will be the case remains to be seen.

Counterbalance and Contain. Countries potentially threatened by China's New Silk Road or by its rise to superpower status will more likely seek to counterbalance its actions and policies, containing China's expansion and influence. Japan and the US may well adopt this position; most of the US's presidential candidates appear to be adopting a more hawkish stance on China. The actions of these countries will be built on the view that constructive engagement with China is not and is unlikely to bear fruit and so measures are required to counteract the growth of China's power and influence. The US alone today has the experience to galvanise the array of chess pieces required to execute such a strategy in East Asia. This will also require the US to undertake a series of initiatives in Central and South Asia, the Middle East and Southeast Europe too that have the scope to counterbalance the New Silk Road. This will require the US to leapfrog the initiative through its ingenuity and resources while undermining it directly. This is by no means an easy task.

Wait and See. A standing option is of course to do nothing for the time being and wait and see. The challenges facing China today, whether domestically or internationally are significant and the country has recently proven itself to be unable to address these effectively.

The scope and scale of the New Silk Road would require China to solve all of these problems as well as a number of additional issues simultaneously and in a coordinated fashion, a scenario which many believe is highly unlikely.

If the New Silk Road represents a classic example of overextension, a studied policy of limited engagement is an effective option for China's rivals on both sides of the road's fence.

In this view, China will likely muddle through a series of economic reforms that keep the country creeping forward but not leaping ahead, while a carefully chosen mix of accommodating and counterbalancing responses to the New Silk Road will result in a patchwork of initiatives and investments that are never fully integrated. Countries that adopt this position can respond to events flexibly, accommodating China in areas where it needs them and counterbalancing it in those where China's interests run up against its own, getting the benefits of both strategies in areas where they are most effective and relevant.

Of course some countries may effectively default to the third option simply by lacking a coherent strategy for engaging with China. India today could fall into this category, having alternated between viewing China as a competitor for resources and as a partner for development. Whatever the view of world leaders, the New Silk Road is clearly a move with serious geo-political consequence and one only to be ignored at their own, if not the international order's, peril.

4

Pakistan's Current Financial and Economic Crisis

Pakistan held its most recent elections in July 2018. The Pakistan Tehreek-e-Insaf party gained over 100 seats in the parliament, and its founder Imran Khan, a famous cricket team captain, was installed as prime minister. Prime Minister Khan has inherited a balance of payments crisis, the third one in the last 10 years. By the end of June 2018, Pakistan had a current account deficit of $18 billion, nearly a 45 percent increase from an account deficit of $12.4 billion in 2017. Exorbitant imports (including those related to the China-Pakistan Economic Corridor (CPEC)) and less-than-projected inflows (export revenues and remittances) have led to a current account deficit widening, with foreign currency reserves levels covering less than two months of imports—pushing Pakistan towards a difficult economic situation.

Part of Pakistan's financial crisis stems from the fact that 2018 was a poor year for emerging markets. Global monetary tightening, increased oil prices, and reduced investor confidence have negatively impacted the country's already precarious economic situation. But the country's deep structural problems and weak macroeconomic policies have further exposed the economy to an array of debt vulnerabilities.

Pakistan has had an overvalued exchange rate, low interest rates, and subdued inflation over the last few years. This loose monetary policy has led to high domestic demand, with two-thirds of Pakistan's economic growth stemming from domestic consumption. An overvalued exchange rate has led to a very high level of imports and low level of exports. Pakistan's high fiscal deficit was accelerated even further in 2017 and 2018 because elections have historically caused spending to rise (both of the most recent fiscal crises followed elections). Perhaps the greatest financial issues facing Pakistan are its pervasive tax evasion and chronically low level of domestic resource mobilization. Taxes in Pakistan comprise less than 10 percent of GDP, a far cry from the 35 percent of countries that are part of the Organisation for Economic Co-operation and Development (OECD). Pakistan also suffers from impediments in the energy sector through frequent and widespread power outages that hurt its competitiveness.

In Western media, Chinese investment is often cited as the main driver of Pakistan's debt crisis. This is somewhat true as China's BRI makes Pakistan a key partner through the shared CPEC. The CPEC is a $60 billion program of infrastructure, energy and communication projects that aims to improve connectivity in the region. CPEC infrastructure costs have certainly placed a greater debt burden on Pakistan, but the current structural problems are homegrown; the root cause of the energy shortages is now less a matter of power generation, and more of fiscal mismanagement of the power sector.

Pakistan's options

Pakistan appears to be in perpetual crisis-mode, and for too long the Pakistani government has been overly reliant on U.S. bilateral assistance. While it may not be the first choice of the Pakistani government, an IMF bailout is the most likely outcome of this financial crisis because it is probably the only path for Pakistan to regain its macroeconomic stability. Any "bailout" from a bilateral donor (meaning China or Pakistan's Gulf State friends, including Saudi Arabia which has recently provided Pakistan $3 billion for a period of one year as balance-of-payment support) will not get at the root issues that Pakistan faces—its loose macroeconomic, fiscal, and monetary policies. Pakistan needs to get its house in order and remedy many of its domestic economic issues. 18 out of Pakistan's 21 IMF programs over the last 60 years have not been completed despite obtaining over $30 billion in financial support across those programs. Just like today's current financial crisis, Pakistan's last two IMF packages (in 2008 and 2013) were also negotiated by incoming governments.

U.S. support a new IMF Pakistan program

The current U.S. administration and Congress would not be supportive of additional bilateral funding to Pakistan—meaning money coming directly from the United States. Since 2001, Pakistan has been the beneficiary of the U.S. Coalition Support Fund (CSF), which reimburses allies for costs incurred by war on terrorism. The CSF is used to reimburse Pakistan for U.S. military use of its network infrastructure (e.g., ports, railways, roads, airspace) so that the United States can prosecute the war in neighboring Afghanistan, as well as certain Pakistani military counter-terrorism operations. The CSF for Pakistan has been as high as $1.2 billion per year, and, in recent years, $900 million per year. With nearly $1 billion in CSF distributed every year, along with $335 million in humanitarian assistance, it will be difficult to convince Congress to appropriate more funds for a Pakistan bailout yet. However, due to inaction on the part of Pakistan to expel or arrest Taliban insurgents operating from Pakistani territory, the United States has recently cut another $300 million from the CSF, bringing the total to $850 million in U.S. assistance withheld from Pakistan this year. In fact, all security assistance to Pakistan, whether it is international military education and training, foreign military financing, or the CSF, has been suspended for this year according to one State Department official.

An IMF program for Pakistan faces resistance from some members of Congress. A group of 16 senators has already signed a letter to President Trump that outlines their opposition to bailing out Pakistan because the IMF package would, in effect, be bailing out Chinese banks.

The Trump administration has also taken a hardline stance towards assisting Pakistan with its financial crisis. Secretary of State Pompeo stated this past July that he would not support an IMF bailout that went towards paying off Chinese loans. In September, Secretary Pompeo visited Pakistan, and there were indications that the United States would not block an IMF program. If an IMF program is enacted, there is no doubt that it would have stronger conditionality and a greater insistence on full transparency of Pakistan's debt obligations.

PAKISTAN SECURES FURTHER US$2B IN FUNDING FROM CHINA TO 'AVOID ECONOMIC CRISIS'

China has pledged to lend an additional US$2 billion to Pakistan to increase the foreign exchange reserves of its South Asian ally, according to a government official in Islamabad.

On Wednesday, an official who is not authorised to speak publicly on the matter said: "As Pakistan's financial position is weak and to further avoid economic crisis, the government is preparing to take appropriate measures to fix the economy through financial help from China."

Pakistan is trying to overcome its looming currency crisis – in the past year the rupee has lost more than a fifth of its value against the US dollar.

The latest financial assistance was not announced by Islamabad or Beijing. Pakistan finance minister Asad Umar did not respond to a request for comment.

Zhao Lijian, the Deputy Chief of Mission at the Chinese Embassy in Islamabad, said: "We don't have the actual amount of loans and CPEC [China–

Pakistan Economic Corridor] investment given to Pakistan but China will continue to provide grants for economic development."

The latest US$2 billion injection follows Beijing reportedly pledging US$2 billion in July last year to help Pakistan weather the economic crisis. There was no confirmation of the earlier amount, which was reported by the country's *Express Tribune* newspaper, citing unnamed finance ministry officials.

Pakistani Prime Minister Imran Khan, who came to power in August 2018, has been desperately seeking finances to fix Pakistan's dwindling foreign exchange reserves, high debt repayments and poor fiscal position.

Its allies from the Middle East have helped: Saudi Arabia has agreed to lend US$6 billion for the financial year to June 2019 and United Arab Emirates offered to lend US$3 billion during the same time period with negotiations going on deferred oil payments.

The Pakistani government is in the middle of negotiations with the International Monetary Fund (IMF) for a possible US$7 billion bailout package.

Miftah Ismail, Pakistan's former finance minister, said: "It is a welcome move from Beijing – China always helped Pakistan in difficult times and this financial help will help boost the foreign exchange reserves."

China always helped Pakistan in difficult times and this financial help will help boost the foreign exchange reserves

After three weeks of meetings in November, Pakistan's finance minister and the IMF are due to resume talks on January 15, to finalise the IMF's financial assistance under tough conditions including job cuts and increasing tariffs.

But the United States has expressed concerns the IMF money will be used to help Pakistan pay back its Chinese loans, as indicated by US Secretary of State Mike Pompeo in July.

The country's foreign reserves of US$7.3 billion are critically low and may not cover imports for the coming months. Fitch has cut Islamabad's debt rating to junk level – another alarm bell for the deteriorating economy, although Asad said early last month the country's economic crisis was over.

"The Chinese financial help will strengthen Pakistan's economy, and could win the trust of foreign investors and it will improve the overall situation of Pakistan's foreign exchange reserves," said Muhammad Sohail, an economic expert heading Topline Securities, a brokerage house.

"Imran Khan's government may think to delay the IMF bailout after help from its Chinese and Middle East friends but an IMF bailout is necessary to bring economy on the right track through structural reforms."

Beijing, through the CPEC, has committed US$62 billion to a series of infrastructure and transportation projects, primarily in the Baluchistan province, including a Chinese-operated port in Gwadar. Last weekend, just before the new year, the Chinese embassy in Islamabad issued a clarification to local media explaining that to date, 22 projects had been completed with a total investment from Beijing of US$18.9 billion.

The bulk of this was investment from Chinese companies and their partners in energy projects so the Pakistan government would only be liable for loans of US$6.02 billion plus interest.

Baluchistan is a mineral-rich region of key significance for Chinese strategic projects. The greater Chinese interest in Gwadar is to take advantage of reduced shipping costs and time for Chinese products. It could provide a cheap alternative in the event of any naval obstruction from the US and its Asian partners.

STRUCTURE OF ECONOMY

Agriculture accounted for about 53% of GDP in 1947. While per-capita agricultural output has grown since then, it has been outpaced by the growth of the non-agricultural sectors, and the share of agriculture has dropped to roughly one-fifth of Pakistan's economy. In recent years, the country has seen rapid growth in industries (such as apparel, textiles, and cement) and services (such as telecommunications, transportation, advertising, and finance).

Major sectors

Agriculture

The most important crops are wheat, sugarcane, cotton, and rice, which together account for more than 75% of the value of total crop output. Pakistan's largest food crop is wheat. In 2017, Pakistan produced 26,674,000 tonnes of wheat, almost equal to all of Africa (27.1 million tonnes) and more than all of South America (25.9 million tonnes), according to the FAOSTAT. In the current year of 2018/19 Pakistan has exported 1.7 million tonnes of wheat and 4.0 million tonnes of rice so far.Pakistan has also cut the use of dangerous pesticides dramatically.

Pakistan is a net food exporter, except in occasional years when its harvest is adversely affected by droughts. Pakistan exports rice, cotton, fish, fruits (especially Oranges and Mangoes), and vegetables and imports vegetable oil, wheat, pulses and consumer foods. The country is Asia's largest camel market, second-largest apricot and ghee market and third-largest cotton, onion and milk market. The economic importance of agriculture has declined since independence, when its share of GDP was around 53%. Following the poor harvest of 1993, the government introduced agriculture assistance policies, including increased support prices for many agricultural commodities and expanded availability of agricultural credit. From 1993 to 1997, real growth in the agricultural sector averaged 5.7% but has since declined to about 4%. Agricultural reforms, including increased wheat and oil seed production, play a central role in the government's economic reform package.

Majority of the population, directly or indirectly, dependent on this sector. It contributes about 18.9% percent of Gross Domestic Product (GDP) and accounts for 42.3% of employed labor force and is the largest source of foreign exchange earnings.During 2017–18, agriculture sector recorded a remarkable growth of 3.70 percent and surpassed its targeted growth of 3.5 percent and last year's growth of 2.18 percent. All the major crops showed a positive trend in their production except maize. Sugarcane and rice production surpassed their historic level with 82.1 and 7.4 million tons respectively. Pakistan Bureau of Statistics provisionally valued this sector at Rs. 7,764,218 million for the year 2018 thus registering the growth of 6.1% over the last year. Pakistan's Top commodities productions in 2017 and provisionally in 2018 are:

Pakistan's principal natural resources are arable land and water. About 25% of Pakistan's total land area is under cultivation and is watered by one of the largest irrigation systems in the world. Pakistan irrigates three times more acres than Russia. Pakistan agriculture also benefits from year round warmth. Agriculture accounts for about 18.9% of GDP and employs about 42.3% of the labour force. Zarai Taraqiati Bank Limited is the largest financial institution geared towards the development of agriculture sector through provision of financial services and technical expertise.

Mining

Pakistan is endowed with significant mineral resources and is emerging as a very promising area for prospecting/exploration for mineral deposits. Based on available information, the country's more than 6,00,000 km^2 of outcrops area demonstrates varied geological potential for metallic and non-metallic mineral deposits. In the wake of 18th amendment to the constitution all the provinces are free to exploit and explore the mineral resources which are in their jurisdiction. Mining and quarrying contributes 13.19% in industrial sector and its share in GDP is 2.8%. Pakistan mining and quarrying sector grew by 3.04% in 2018 against the negative growth of -0.38% last year.

In the recent past, exploration by government agencies as well as by multinational mining companies presents ample evidence of the occurrences of sizeable minerals deposits. Recent discoveries of a thick oxidised zone underlain by sulphide zones in the shield area of the Punjab province, covered by thick alluvial cover have opened new vistas for metallic minerals exploration.

Pakistan has a large base for industrial minerals. The discovery of coal deposits having over 175 billion tonnes of reserves at Thar in the Sindh province has given an impetus to develop it as an alternative source of energy. There is vast potential for precious and dimension stones.

Industry

Pakistan's industrial sector accounts for about 20.9% of GDP. In 2018 it recorded a growth of 5.80% as compared to the growth of 5.43% last year. Manufacturing is the most vibrant sub sector of the industrial sector having 64.8% contribution in the industrial sector and in GDP it accounts for 13.6%. Manufacturing sub-sector is further divided in three components including large-scale manufacturing (LSM) with the share of 79.6% percent in manufacturing sector, small scale manufacturing share is 13.8 percent in manufacturing sector, while slaughtering contributes 6.5 percent in the manufacturing. Major sectors in industries include cement, fertiliser, edible oil, sugar, steel, tobacco, chemicals, machinery, food processing and medical instruments, primarily surgical. Pakistan is one of the largest manufacturers and exporters of surgical instruments.

The government is privatizing large-scale industrial units, and the public sector accounts for a shrinking proportion of industrial output, while growth in overall industrial output (including the private sector) has accelerated. Government policies aim to diversify the country's industrial base and bolster export industries. Large Scale Manufacturing is the fastest-growing sector in Pakistani economy. Major Industries include textiles, fertiliser, cement, oil refineries, dairy products, food processing, beverages, construction materials, clothing, paper products and shrimp.

In Pakistan SMEs have a significant contribution in the total GDP of Pakistan, according to SMEDA and Economic survey reports, the share in the annual GDP is 40% likewise SMEs generating significant employment opportunities for skilled workers and entrepreneurs. Small and medium scale firms represent nearly 90% of all the enterprises in Pakistan and employ 80% of the non-agricultural labor force. These figures indicate the potential and further growth in this sector.

Construction material

In 1947, Pakistan had inherited four cement plants with a total capacity of 0.5 million tons. Some expansion took place in 1956–66 but could not keep pace with the economic development and the country had to resort to imports of cement in 1976–77 and continued to do so until 1994–95. The cement sector consisting of 27 plants is contributing above Rs 30 billion to the national exchequer in the form of taxes. However, by 2013, Pakistan's cement is fast-growing mainly because of demand from Afghanistan and countries boosting real estate sector, In 2013 Pakistan exported 7,708,557 metric tons of cement. Pakistan has installed capacity of 44,768,250 metric tons of cement and 42,636,428 metric tons of clinker. In the 2012–2013 cement industry in Pakistan became the most profitable sector of economy.

Information communication technology industry

The information communication technology (ICT) industry grossed over $4.8 billion in 2013. It is expected to exceed the $13 billion mark by 2018. A marked increase in software export figures are an indication of this booming industry's potential. The total number of IT companies increased to 1306 and the total estimated size of IT industry is $2.8 billion. In 2007, Pakistan was for the first time featured in the Global Services Location Index by A.T. Kearney and was rated as the 30th best location for offshoring. By 2009, Pakistan had improved its rank by ten places to reach 20th. According to Pakistan Startup report, there are about 1 million freelancers working from Pakistan mainly via Elance, Upwork, Fiverr, Guru, and freelancer – world's famous online marketplaces that count Pakistan among top 5 freelancing nations. An annual report that updated by State bank of Pakistan shows Pakistan cross 1 Billion($) IT Export which is a good achievement of Pakistan IT Industry. Also, an official said that Pakistan Freelance community generate 1 billion($) revenue this year. Overall Pakistan makes 2 Billion($) IT export worldwide.

Defence industry

The defence industry of Pakistan, under the Ministry of Defence Production, was created in September 1951 to promote and coordinate the patchwork of military production facilities that have developed since independence.It is currently actively participating in many joint production projects such as Al Khalid 2, advance trainer aircraft, combat aircraft, navy ships and submarines. Pakistan is manufacturing and selling weapons to over 40 countries, bringing in $20 million annually.The country's arms imports increased by 119 percent between the 2004–2008 and 2009–13, with China providing 54pc and the USA 27pc of Pakistan's imports.

Textiles

Most of the Textile Industry is established in Punjab. Before 1990, the situation was different; most of the industry was in Karachi. Textile industry in Pakistan is traditional and conservative, producing and exporting most of low cost raw articles e.g. Raw Cotton, Yarn, fabric etc. Share of finished goods and branded articles is nominal. Pakistan has a potential to quadruple its textile production and export, due to emerging Chinese markets and with its existing infrastructure. 10% of United States imports regarding clothing and other form of textiles is covered by Pakistan.

The textile sector accounts for 70% of Pakistan's exports, but the working conditions of workers are deplorable. Small manufacturing workshops generally do not sign employment contracts, do not respect the minimum wage and sometimes employ children. Violations of labour law also occur among major subcontractors of international brands, where workers may be beaten, insulted by their superiors or paid below the minimum wage. Factories do not comply with safety standards, leading to accidents: in 2012, 255 workers died in a fire at a Karachi factory. With 547 labour inspectors in Pakistan supervising the country's 300,000 factories, the textile industry is out of control. Nor are workers protected by trade unions, which are prohibited in industrial export zones. Elsewhere, "workers involved in the creation of trade unions are victims of violence, intimidation, threats or dismissals".

Other

As of 2010, Pakistan is one of the largest users of CNG (compressed natural gas) in the world. Presently, more than 3,000 CNG stations are operating in the country in 99 cities and towns, and 1000 more would be set up in the next two years. It has provided employment to over 50,000 people in Pakistan, but the CNG industry is struggling to survive the 2013 energy crisis.

Services

Pakistan's service sector accounts for about 60.2% of GDP. Transport, storage, communications, finance, and insurance account for 24% of this sector, and wholesale and retail trade about 30%. Pakistan is trying to promote the information industryand other modern service industries through incentives such as long-term tax holidays.

Telecommunication

After the deregulation of the telecommunication industry, the sector has seen an exponential growth. Pakistan Telecommunication Company Ltd has emerged as a successful Forbes 2000 conglomerate with over US $1 billion in sales in 2005. The mobile telephone market has exploded many-fold since 2003 to reach a subscriber base of 140 million users in July 2017, one of the highest mobile teledensities in the entire world. In addition, there are over 6 million landlines in the country with 100% fibre-optic network and coverage via WLL in even the remotest areas. As a result, Pakistan won the prestigious Government Leadership award of GSM Association in 2006.

The World Bank estimates that it takes about 3 days to get a phone connection in Pakistan.

In Pakistan, the following are the top mobile phone operators:

1. Jazz Pakistan (Parent: VEON, Netherland)
2. Ufone (Parent: PTCL (Etisalat), Pakistan/UAE)
3. Telenor (Parent: Telenor, Norway)
4. Zong (Parent: China Mobile, China)

By March 2009, Pakistan had 91 million mobile subscribers – 25 million more subscribers than reported in the same period in 2008. In addition to the 3.1 million fixed lines, while as many as 2.4 million are using Wireless Local Loop connections. Sony Ericsson, Nokia and Motorola along with Samsung and LG remain the most popular brands among customers.

Since liberalisation, over the past four years, the Pakistani telecom sector has attracted more than $9 billion in foreign investments. During 2007–08, the Pakistani communication sector alone received $1.62 billion in Foreign Direct Investment (FDI) – about 30% of the country's total foreign direct investment.

Present growth of state-of-the-art infrastructures in the telecoms sector during the last four years has been the result of the PTA's vision and implementation of the deregulation policy. Paging and mobile (cellular) telephones were adopted early and freely. Cellular phones and the Internet were adopted through a rather laissez-fairepolicy with a proliferation of private service providers that led to the fast adoption. With a rapid increase in the number of Internet users and ISPs, and a large English-speaking population, Pakistani society has seen an unparalleled revolution in communications.

According to the PC World, a total of 6.37 billion text messages were sent through Acision messaging systems across Asia Pacific over the 2008/2009 Christmas and New Year period. Pakistan was amongst the top five ranker with one of the highest SMS traffic with 763 million messages. On 14 August 2010, Pakistan became the first country in the world to experience EVDO's RevB 3G technology that offers maximum speeds of 9.3 Mbit/s. 3G and 4G was simultaneously launched in Pakistan on 23 April 2014 through a SMRA Auction.

Three out of Five Companies got a 3G licence i.e. Ufone, Mobilink and Telenor while China Mobile's Zong got 3G as well as a 4G licence. Whereas fifth company, Warid Pakistan did not participate in the auction procedure, But they launched 4G LTE services on their existing 2G 1800 MHz spectrum due to Technology neutral terms and became world's first Telecom Company to transform directly from 2G to 4G. With that Pakistan joined the 3G and 4G world. In December 2017, 3G and 4G subscribers in Pakistan reached to 46 millions.

Pakistan is ranked 4th in terms of broadband Internet growth in the world, as the subscriber base of broadband Internet has been increasing rapidly. The rankings are released by Point Topic Global broadband analysis, a global research centre.

- Pakistan has more than 20 million Internet users in 2009. The country is said to have a potential to absorb up to 50 million mobile phone Internet users in the next 5 years thus a potential of nearly 1 million connections per month.
- Almost all of the main government departments, organisations and institutions have their own websites.
- The use of search engines and instant messaging services is also booming. Pakistanis are some of the most ardent chatters on the Internet, communicating with users all over the world. Recent years have seen a huge increase in the use of online marriage services, for example, leading to a major re-alignment of the tradition of arranged marriages.
- Biometric reverification of SIMs in 2015 had an adverse impact on the cellular subscriber base when subscribers count dropped from 139.9 million to 114.6 million. However, the industry has survived through the tough period and continues to regain subscribers at a fast pace.

According to the report released by PTA for the FY 2017–18 :-

- Total teledensity of Pakistan reached at 74.4%.
- Telecom revenues were reached to Rs. 488.8 billion.
- Total contribution of telecom sector to the national exchequre was RS. 147.2 billion.
- Investment came to the telecom sector was US$ 670.3 million.

as of June 2018 there were four cell phone companies including PMCL(Jazz), Telenor, Ufone and Zong operating in the country with nearly 150.2 million mobile phone subscribers.

Pakistan Telecommunication Authority released the figures in June 2018 that Broadband subscribers in the country reached to approximately 56.1 millions thus gaining the growth of over 18 fold since 2006.

Transportation

Pakistan International Airlines, the flagship airline of Pakistan's civil aviation industry, has turnover exceeding $25 billion in 2015. The government announced a new shipping policy in 2006 permitting banks and financial institutions to mortgage ships. Private sector airlines in Pakistan include Airblue, which serves the main cities within Pakistan in addition to destinations in the Persian Gulf and Manchester in the United Kingdom. The other private carrier is Shaheen Air International whose network covers the main cities of Pakistan and the Persian Gulf.

A massive rehabilitation plan worth $1 billion over five years for Pakistan Railways has been announced by the government in 2005. A new rail link trial has been established from Islamabad to Istanbul, via the Iranian cities of Zahedan, Kerman and Tehran. It is expected to promote trade, tourism, especially for exports destined for Europe (as Turkey is part of Europe and Asia).

Finance

Pakistan has a large and diverse banking system. In 1974, a nationalization program led to the creation of six government-owned banks. A privatization program in the 1990s lead to the entry of foreign-owned and local banks into the industry. As of 2010, there were five public-owned commercial banks in Pakistan, as well as 25 domestic private banks, six multi-national banks and four specialized banks.

Since 2000 Pakistani banks have begun aggressive marketing of consumer finance to the emerging middle class, allowing for a consumption boom (more than a 7-month waiting list for certain car models) as well as a construction bonanza. Pakistan's banking sector remained remarkably strong and resilient during the world financial crisis in 2008–09, a feature which has served to attract a substantial amount of FDI in the sector. Stress tests conducted on June 2008 data indicate that the large banks are relatively robust, with the medium and small-sized banks positioning themselves in niche markets.

The Pakistan Bureau of Statistics provisionally valued this sector at Rs.807,807 million in 2012 thus registering over 510% growth since 2000.

An article published in Journal of the Asia Pacific Economy by Mete Feridun of University of Greenwich in London with his Pakistani colleague Abdul Jalil presents strong econometric evidence that financial development fosters economic growth in Pakistan.

Housing

The property sector has expanded twenty-threefold since 2001, particularly in metropolises like Lahore. Nevertheless, the Karachi Chamber of Commerce and Industry estimated in late 2006 that the overall production of housing units in Pakistan has to be increased to 0.5 million units annually to address 6.1 million backlog of housing in Pakistan for meeting the housing shortfall in next 20 years. The report noted that the present housing stock is also rapidly aging and an estimate suggests that more than 50% of stock is over 50 years old. It is also estimated that 50% of the urban population now lives in slums and squatter settlements. The report said that meeting the backlog in housing, besides replacement of out-lived housing units, is beyond the financial resources of the government. This necessitates putting in place a framework to facilitate financing in the formal private sector and mobilise non-government resources for a market-based housing finance system.

The Pakistan Bureau of Statistics provisionally valued this sector at Rs.459,829 million in 2012 thus registering over 149% growth since 2006.

Minor sectors

The Pakistan Bureau of Statistics provisionally valued this sector at Rs.389,545 million in 2005 thus registering over 65% growth since 2000. The Pakistan Bureau of Statistics provisionally valued this sector at Rs.631,229 million in 2005 thus registering over 78% growth since 2000. The Pakistan Bureau of Statisticsprovisionally valued this sector at Rs.1,358,309 million in 2005 thus registering over 96% growth since 2000. The wholesale and retail trade is the largest sub-sector of the services. Its share in the overall services sector is estimated at 31.5 percent. The wholesale and retail trade sector is based on the margins taken by traders on the transaction of commodities traded. In 2012–13, this sector grew at 2.5 percent as compared to 1.7 percent in the previous year.

Energy

For years, the matter of balancing Pakistan's supply against the demand for electricity has remained a largely unresolved matter. Pakistan faces a significant challenge in revamping its network responsible for the supply of electricity. While the government claims credit for overseeing a turnaround in the economy through a comprehensive recovery, it has just failed to oversee a similar improvement in the quality of the network for electricity supply. Most cities in Pakistan receive substantial sunlight throughout the year, which would suggest good conditions for investment in solar energy. If the rich people in Pakistan are shifted to solar energy that they should be forced to purchase solar panels, the shortfall can be controlled. this will make the economy boost again as before 2007. According to an econometric analysis published in Quality & Quantity by Mete Feridun of University of Greenwich and his colleague Muhammad Shahbaz, economic growth in Pakistan leads to electricity consumption but not vice versa.

IMF PACKAGE BE A BAILOUT OF THE CHINESE

The terms of Pakistan's loans with China are currently unclear and multiple news outlets have reported that Pakistan has refused to share CPEC information with the IMF. However, it is not unreasonable to presume that the terms in those contracts would be more demanding than terms typically asked by the

IMF. Unless the terms between Pakistan and China and its state-owned enterprises (SOEs) are disclosed and made clear to the IMF, then it is unwise for the IMF to proceed with a bailout package.

The IMF's focus is not in projecting power and influence; rather it seeks to help struggling nations get back on their feet. The same cannot be said for China. China appears to be most interested in spreading its influence and gaining valuable assets for its military and expanding economy, while at the same time exporting its surplus capacity for infrastructure building. In its annual report to Congress, the Department of Defense reiterated this concern, "countries participating in BRI [such as Pakistan] could develop economic dependence on Chinese capital, which China could leverage to achieve its interests."

Of Pakistan's nearly $30 billion trade deficit, 30 percent is directly attributable to China. If China were concerned about the economic crisis in Pakistan, it would make immediate concessions which Pakistan Finance Minister Asad Umar says China is working on. To help with the crisis, China could readjust its trade surplus with Pakistan in different ways. For example, China could buy Pakistani cement and other purchases in the short term to illustrate that they are aware of and swiftly responding to the economic turmoil in Pakistan. Other nations have struggled with debt obligations to China. For instance, in July 2017, Sri Lanka signed over a 99-year lease for Hambantota Port to a Chinese SOE because of Sri Lanka's inability to pay for BRI costs. Malaysia took a different path and decided to cancel major infrastructure projects with China in August 2018 due to worries that they would increase its debt burden.

The consequences if there is no IMF package

It is likely that China will provide even more assistance to broaden Pakistan's dependency. Chinese banks and SOEs have already invested heavily into Pakistan, so much so that state bank loans have not been fully disclosed to the global community. In fact, Pakistan's Status Report for July 2017 through June 2018 shows that Chinese commercial banks hold 53 percent of Pakistan's outstanding commercial debt. However, that percentage may be even higher than the report depicts. While China and Pakistan have agreed to make all CPEC projects readily available to the public, the information is scattered and often left blank on essential financial reports, and so it is difficult to obtain a full sense of the degree of Pakistan's indebtedness to China. Again, much of the loan information provided by the Pakistani government, especially concerning China, is not entirely transparent.

If China chooses to follow through and become the "point person" for an assistance package, the pressure will be taken off the IMF. But, if the United

States does not support an IMF package, it will forego major geopolitical potential in the region to its main competitor, China.

Pakistan represents a litmus test of all future cases in which the IMF, United States, China, and any emerging market country are all involved. Depending on how Beijing chooses to navigate Pakistan's financial crisis, China may soon find itself responsible for rectifying the debt burdens of Zambia and many other BRI countries.

U.S. geopolitical "equities" in Pakistan

The United States is invested in Pakistan because of its significant geopolitical importance.

1. Pakistan is an important component of the balance of power in South Asia. Both India and Pakistan have nuclear weapons capabilities. Moreover, China, India, and Pakistan have been in dispute over the Kashmir region since 1947. Regional stability is in the interest of the United States.
2. Despite its ambiguous stance on militant groups, Pakistan is ostensibly an ally of the United States because of its proximity to Afghanistan. Since the War on Terror began in 2001, Pakistan has been an active partner in the elimination of core al Qaeda within Pakistan and has facilitated aspects of the U.S. military campaign in Afghanistan.
3. The United States now seeks a negotiated settlement to the conflict in Afghanistan. To accomplish this, perhaps the United States will come to Pakistan with a simple offer: "deliver the Taliban, and we will give you the IMF."
4. Whereas previous administrations may have tried to "play nice" with Pakistan, under the Trump administration, there is a chance that the U.S. government will push the IMF to adopt stricter terms for a Pakistan bailout, citing the Pakistani government's failures of the last two programs.
5. Other than strategic military importance, one of the most important national security challenges to the United States is Pakistan's demographic trends. Currently, over 64 percent of Pakistanis are under the age of 30—the largest percentage of youth in the country's history. Over the next 30 years, Pakistan's population will increase by over 100 million, jumping from 190 million to 300 million by 2050. The spike in youth population presents an opportunity for the U.S. government and private sector to increase investment in Pakistan. Pakistan's economy must generate 1 million jobs annually for the next three decades and GDP growth rates must equal 7 percent or more per year to keep up

with the population boom. Were Pakistan's economy to collapse, the world would see the first instance of a failed state with a substantial arsenal of nuclear weapons.

6. An economically healthy Pakistan could be a large market for U.S. goods and services. If the U.S.-Pakistan relationship is strained as a result of this financial crisis, it will not only harm the United States militarily but will also harm U.S. businesses and Pakistani consumers.

U.S. support an IMF package to Pakistan

Given the geostrategic importance of Pakistan for the United States, we should support a package but with stronger conditionality than in 2013 along with full transparency and disclosure of its debt obligations.

5

The Commercial Policy of Pakistan

It gives me great pleasure, Mr. Chairman, to be here this morning with you all at this you're 88th Annual General Meeting. I presume it is an accident to hold this meeting in the premises of the Karachi Cotton Association, for one can hardly dissociate Karachi from commerce and the commerce of this place from cotton. You have, Mr. Chairman, covered a very wide field in your address, from the founding of the sovereign and independent State of Pakistan to the petty usurpations of power by minor official here and there over this far-flung Dominion, from the intricacies of cotton trade to the common place of delays. You will, however, hardly expect me to follow you in every detail in my reply. I cannot, however, let an opportunity, such as you have presented to me today, pass without calling attention to certain salient points arising out of your address.

Let me, Mr. Chairman first acknowledge the tribute which you have justly paid to my Government and my people for the manner in which they faced up to the tragic events which so closely followed the establishment of Pakistan. It was inevitable that many otherwise sensible people should greet Pakistan as an unwanted and intolerable child whose birth could not long survive their displeasure. You have rightly pointed out how mistaken were the people who, because the idea of Pakistan was new and unfamiliar to them, thought Pakistan would have but only an ephemeral existence. None can now doubt, in your words, Mr. Chairman that a new Power was born among the nations of the world on August 14, 1947. The difficulties and the tribulations through which Pakistan has passed have helped to strengthen and temper the new State into steel, which is now, well and truly set upon the course on the uncharted seas of the future. The people who have made the effort which secured their separate freedom in the face of derision, disbelief and the utmost political opposition will not fail to make the additional effort necessary to consolidate their liberties, and any delusion or elusion from which some people still suffer, let me make it clear, that the sooner they bring their notion—Pakistan surrendering to India or seeking Union with Central Government—the better it will be for peace and prosperity of both the Dominions and will help a great deal to establish goodwill and neighbourly good feelings.

I am glad to note that you are disaffiliating your Chambers from the Associated Chambers of Commerce of India as a necessary corollary of the partition, and intend to form an Association of your Pakistan Chambers of Commerce.

You, Mr. Chairman, have rightly given pride of place to cotton in dealing with trade and commerce. I am glad to know that you have recognised that Pakistan's cotton policy could not have been more liberal or less restrictive than it was until the impact of India's decision to decontrol cloth and refuse it to us except in return for cotton, forced measures of regulation on us. Even so, all contracts made before 23rd January 1948 by traders in Pakistan—national or foreign—were honoured. That the cotton trade should have shown such admirable capacity to adjust itself to changing conditions is a matter for gratification. I would like to express the appreciation of the Government of Pakistan for the manner in which traders have played their part in helping to move cotton to the port and from the port to the markets of the world.

You have also referred at some length to the import policy of the Government of Pakistan and internal controls exercised within the country and have pleaded that, as few handicaps should be placed on trading as possible. Regulation and restriction with their attendant administrative evils will be imposed only where conditions compel, and any expressions of opinion you care to make from time to time will always receive my Ministry's careful thought. I can assure you on behalf of the Government of Pakistan that it is their intention and policy to let the channels of free trading flow as freely as possible. In so far as the internal controls on essential commodities are concerned, my Government have already decided to review them at a conference with the Provinces in an attempt to relax and remove as many of these as circumstances would now permit So far as overseas trade is concerned a considerable sector of imports has been released from licensing by the notification of an Open General Licence for a wide range of goods coming from Commonwealth sterling countries. This list will be kept under constant review with the object of expanding it and the question of including therein imports and other soft currency areas is now receiving the attention of the Ministry for Commerce. The situation in regard to dollar imports and other hard currencies is, of course very difficult and licensing must continue to protect the balance of payments. Even in this field, however, you can assist by bending your energies to directing and increasing our exports to dollar and hard currency countries. This, fortunately, should not be difficult in the case of the major Pakistan raw materials and I shall look forward, Gentlemen to your constant support in this matter. Anything that Government cans do to facilitate exports to these areas by removing as many restrictions as possible will be done. I have little doubt, gentlemen, that your efforts in this direction will bear fruit as we are rich in the commodities which the world so badly requires, like cotton, jute, hides, skins and wool. You have made a plea that in the interests of trade. Government should make an announcement of the import policy in good time. The Government of Pakistan fully appreciates this view and will do all they can to make as early an announcement as circumstances would permit. The uncertain factors, which delayed the announcement of their policy in the past will, Government hopes, not recur in future.

The complete breakdown of the banking and financial mechanism in the West Punjab is a matter which government action alone cannot remedy. We can make the conditions as favourable as possible but bankers alone can repair the machine. It is our unalterable determination to maintain law and order and to secure and retain public confidence in our administration of affairs. In this context and given your goodwill, the reconstruction and restoration of our commerce and trade should proceed apace. This is my appeal to you today, Gentleman, to make a steady and sustained effort to help us to help you.

There is one matter, Mr. Chairman, which you have mentioned only in passing, namely, the statement issued by my Government on the Industrial Policy of Pakistan. The statement is of such far-reaching character that I would ask of you as a business community to examine it with the care and attention which the importance of the subject and the direct bearing it has on your own well-being requires. That my Government should have taken time to consider matters carefully before formulating their policy, which must vitally, effect the future of the country, is a matter that need not cause any sense of frustration. For I am reminded in the connection of an observation of that wiseman, Francis who said—"It is good to commit the beginnings of all great actions to Argos with his hundred eyes and the ends to Briarcus with his hundred hands; first to watch and then to speed" Whilst I do not propose to recapitulate the statement here, I would like to call your particular attention to the keen desire of the Government of Pakistan to associate individual initiative and private enterprise at every stage of industrialisation.

The number of industries Government has reserved for management by themselves consists of Arms and Munitions of War, generation of Hydel Power and manufacture of Railway wagons, Telephone, Telegraph and Wireless apparatus. All other industrial activity is left open to private enterprise, which would be given every facility a Government can give for the establishment and development of industry.

Government will seek to create conditions in which industry and trade may develop and prosper by undertaking surveys of Pakistan's considerable resources of minerals, schemes for the development of country's water and power resources plans for the improvement of transport services and the establishment of the ports and an Industrial Finance Corporation. Just as Pakistan is agriculturally the most advanced country in the Continent of Asia as mentioned by you, I am confident that if it makes the fullest and the best use of its considerable agricultural wealth in the building up of her industries, it will, with the traditions of craftsmanship for which her people are so well known and with their ability to adjust themselves to new techniques, soon make its mark in the industrial field. I am glad to know that you are favourably impressed with the concessions announced by the Finance Minister to new industrial enterprises in the matter of Income Tax and depreciation that you regard the statement as holding out more encouragement to new industry than the corresponding statement of policy made by the Government of India. If you want any clarification of any aspect of the policy, my Government will be only too willing to furnish the same.

Fortunately, in the port of Karachi, we have adequate facilities to handle not only the trade of Western Pakistan but also such trade as offers for Afghanistan and the adjoining areas of the Indian Dominion. For reasons into which I need not here enter, this trade has suffered a severe setback since partition. I hope that in everybody's interest you will endeavour to restore Karachi's standing in this regard. I have no doubt that the port of Karachi has a very bright future. It is the only port, which serves this side of Pakistan, and the location of the Pakistan Naval Headquarters had added greatly to its importance. I can look with confidence to its rapid development. The scheme for remodelling the East Wharf and the provision of Naval and Commercial Dry Docks is under our active consideration and should, when completed, make Karachi one of the most modern ports. I may assure the business community that I am watching with keen interest the present and future interests of the port. The end of the period of "Standstill" and the consequent entry of India and Pakistan into normal international relations should advance and give precision to the movement of trade. Bonding facilities are being provided by my Government in Karachi port for this purpose. On the other side of the subcontinent, the Government of India has also agreed to provide bonding facilities in Calcutta so that from now on, the capacity of the port of Chittagong to handle raw jute will be supplemented by transit facilities through the port of Calcutta.

In the field of Civil Aviation, Pakistan is fortunate in having at Karachi, the best-equipped airport in the East. Its position and climate are in its favour and now that Karachi has become the Capital of Pakistan, there is no likelihood of the Airport ever losing its importance. Its pre-eminent position will be maintained, as we are alive to the need of its continued development in accordance with the international standards and to the need of facilitating in every way national and international air transport operations. Karachi will remain one of the main centres of international air traffic as most of the progressive countries of the world have approached us for bilateral air transport agreements and we already have agreements with U.S., France, Netherlands, Iraq and recently negotiated agreement with India and Ceylon. Delegations from U.K and other countries are expected in Karachi soon. For all these Karachi will remain the airport of entry and departure. The use of Bombay as the port of entry for Trans-World Airlines was provided for in Air Transport Agreement between U.S.A. and India before partition and does not indicate a subsequent tendency to transfer operation from Karachi to Bombay. On this service Karachi Airport was used, in the first instance, as a temporary measure pending the provision of health facilities at Santa Cruz. You have referred to the rise in airline operating costs occasioned by the recently increased cost of aviation spirits in Pakistan. This is question, which I have, no doubt will be considered by my Government in the light of your observations.

I am glad to hear that you have appreciated the difficulties which beset Orient Airways in establishing, at a very short notice, vital air communications within Pakistan between Eastern and Western Pakistan and between Karachi and Delhi and between Karachi and Bombay. These agreements had to be made on a temporary basis while a long-term national air transport was being formulated. The Government announced their policy on the 5th of December 1947, limiting air transport operations to two commercial airlines to be selected for the operation of all the scheduled services to be licensed by the Government. The names of these companies will be announced shortly together with the routes to be operated by them subject to finalisation of agreement recently negotiated with the Government of India. To serve these companies and to a large extent, the Royal Pakistan Air Force, it is also proposed to establish, at Karachi a company to carry out major overhaul and repair of aircraft, the training of mechanics and maintenance engineers, and such other common services as the Government and airlines may require. The Government will participate financially in this enterprise and plans for the establishment of this company are now under active consideration of the Government.

You have referred to the difficulties experienced by your members on account of the uncertainty of booking restrictions. As you are aware, booking restrictions have been rendered necessary on account of coal shortage due to spasmodic and insufficient receipt from India. The Northwestern Railway has always endeavoured to move as much traffic as possible with their available resources. The movement of refugees placed a heavy strain on the Railway's capacity at a time when coal receipts were at their lowest, but in spite of these difficulties essential goods, *e.g.* foodstuffs, kept on moving though restrictions had perforce to be imposed on the movement of goods carried under lower priorities. The Railways, however, relaxed restrictions to the extent possible whenever there was even a slight improvement in coal receipts, but whenever the coal position deteriorated restrictions were reimposed.

In spite of the manifold difficulties created by inadequate supplies of coal from India, the refugee traffic, the numerous staff problems created by partition, the Railway administration, as and when the position improved, restored the facilities which had to be curtailed from time to time. I hope that the Chamber would appreciate their efforts in keeping the rail transport going. There was some improvement in the coal position on the Northwestern Railway during February and March and as you are aware, unrestricted booking was resumed with effect from 4th March in local bookings and from 12th April in foreign bookings. Unfortunately, coal supplies from India have been inadequate during April and, although some of the coal ordered from the U.S.A. has been received, stocks are dwindling. Representations have been made to India, and it is hoped that there will be no reimposition of the previous unfortunate restrictions, except those occasionally imposed for operational reasons. As regards the complaint that the railway staffs at stations are unaware of the restrictions imposed from time to time, I am advised that all restrictions are conveyed to stations immediately on their imposition. It is possible that in the early days after partition, due to large-scale transfers of staffs, there was a certain amount of disorganisation resulting in incorrect information being furnished to merchants. The Northwestern Railway has, however, taken suitable action to ensure that correct information relating to restrictions is conveyed to merchants.

As regards preparation claims, I hope you are aware of the provisions of the Indian Independence (Rights, Property and Liabilities) Order 1947, under which the liabilities and financial obligations of the governor-general in Council, outstanding immediately before 15th August, 1947, devolved on the Dominion of India. The Pakistan Government has already made the position in this respect clear in their press note of the 25th March 1948. The matter is under correspondence with the Government of India and it is hoped that a settlement in regard to this outstanding question will be reached at an early date.

Reference has been made by you to the difficulties and anxieties, which naturally spring, from shortage of residential and office accommodation in this town. The Government of Pakistan has, subject to the approval of the Constituent Assembly, decided to locate the permanent Capital of Pakistan at Karachi. Detailed planning of the layout will take some time but this should not delay construction of some residential accommodation. In this field, as in many others, gentlemen, you have a big contribution to make. There are vast open areas where buildings could, with advantage, be constructed. Building materials such as cement and stone are available in abundance, though steel and timber are rather scarce. All the same, my Government would like to see the business community take up a programme of large-scale building construction in Karachi.

Mr. Chairman, Commerce and Trade are the very lifeblood of the nation. I can no more visualise a Pakistan without traders than I can one without cultivators or civil servants. I have no doubt that in Pakistan, traders and merchants will always be welcome and that they, in building up their own fortunes, will not forget their social responsibility for a fair and square deal to one and all, big and small. Government have for sometime been perturbed over the constantly rising spiral of prices of the necessities of life in Pakistan. They are now engaged in a study of how best the spiral could be broken and prices brought down. I have little doubt that my Government can confidently count on your full support in every measure they may decide to take to achieve this object

Commerce, Gentlemen, is more international than culture and it behaves you to behave in such a way that the power and prestige of Pakistan gain added strength from every act of yours.

I have no doubt the Commerce of Pakistan would be an effective instrument in the establishment and maintenance of high standards of business integrity and practice. If Pakistani goods are to establish for themselves a reputation all their own, a beginning must be made now and here. I assure you, Gentlemen, that anything my Government can do to achieve this end, and they shall do. I would like Pakistan to become a synonym and hallmark for standard and quality in the market places of the world. Let me, Mr. Chairman, thank you once again for the honour you have done me in asking me to be the guest of your Chamber on this occasion. I wish you and your Chamber well in the many years that lie ahead of us and may you as true Pakistanis help to reconstruct and build Pakistan to reach mighty and glorious status amongst the comity of nations of the world and that let us pray that Pakistan will make its contribution for peace, happiness and prosperity of the world.

FOREIGN TRADE, REMITTANCES, AID, AND INVESTMENT

Investment

Foreign investment had significantly declined by 2010, dropping by 54.6% due to Pakistan's political instability and weak law and order, according to the Bank of Pakistan.

Business regulations have been overhauled along liberal lines, especially since 1999. Most barriers to the flow of capital and international direct investment have been removed. Foreign investors do not face any restrictions on the inflow of capital, and investment of up to 100% of equity participation is allowed in most sectors. Unlimited remittance of profits, dividends, service fees or capital is now the rule. However, doing business has been becoming increasingly difficult over the past decade due to political instability, rising domestic insurgency and insecurity and vehement corruption. This can be confirmed by the World Bank's Ease of Doing Business Index report degrading its ratings for Pakistan each year since September 2009.

Tariffs have been reduced to an average rate of 16%, with a maximum of 25% (except for the car industry). The privatization process, which started in the early 1990s, has gained momentum, with most of the banking system privately owned, and the oil sector targeted to be the next big privatization operation.

The recent improvements in the economy and the business environment have been recognised by international rating agencies such as Moody's and Standard and Poor's (country risk upgrade at the end of 2003). 47.1% increase in Net FDI in 2014–2015 (July–October) as compared to 2013–14 (July–October).

Foreign acquisitions and mergers

With the rapid growth in Pakistan's economy, foreign investors are taking a keen interest in the corporate sector of Pakistan. In recent years, majority stakes in many corporations have been acquired by multinational groups.

- PICIC by Singapore-based Temasek Holdings for $339 million
- Union Bank by Standard Chartered Bank for $487 million
- Prime Commercial Bank by ABN Amro for $228 million
- PakTel by China Mobile for $460 million

- PTCL by Etisalat for $1.8 billion
- Additional 57.6% shares of Lakson Tobacco Company acquired by Philip Morris International for $382 million
- In 2016, Arçelik acquired Dawlance for $243 million.
- In 2016, FrieslandCampina acquired 51% stake in Engro Foods for $446.81 million.
- In 2016, The Abraaj Group sold its 66.4% stake in K-Electric to Shanghai Electric for $1.77 billion.

The foreign exchange receipts from these sales are also helping cover the current account deficit.

Foreign trade

Pakistan's external sector continued facing stress during 2016–17. But still Pakistan's merchandise trade exports grew by 0.1 percent during the fiscal year 2016–17. The imports continued to grow at a much faster rate and grew by a large percentage of 18.0 during the FY 2017 as compared to the previous year. World imports had been stagnant between 2011 and 2014 but registered significant drop since early 2015 because of weak commodity and product prices and weak global economic activity.

Economic growth was lacklustre in the OECD countries which contributed to the slowdown in China. Furthermore, the ratio between real growth in world imports and world real GDP growth substantially declined. This decline in the import content of economic activity triggered a shift in consumption worldwide from traded towards non-traded goods, import substitution, a slowdown in the pace of trade liberalization, and gave currency to protectionist measures.

A bulk of Pakistan's exports are directed to the OECD region and China. Historical data suggest strong correlation between Pakistani exports to imports in OECD and China. As per FY 2016 data, more than half of country's exports are shipped to these two destinations i.e. OECD and China. A decline in Pakistan overall exports,thus occurred in this backdrop.

Pakistan's imports are showing rising trend at a relatively faster rate (18.0 percent) due to the increased economic activity as part of China Pakistan Economic Corridor(CPEC), particularly in the Energy sector. The construction projects under CPEC require heavy machinery that has to be imported. It is also observed that the economy is currently being led both by investments as well as consumption, resulting in relatively higher levels of imports.

External imbalances

During FY 2017, the increase in imports of capital equipment and fuel significantly put pressure on the external account. A reversal in global oil prices led to increase in POL imports, accompanied by falling exports, as a result the merchandised trade deficit grew by 39.4 percent to US$26.885 billion in FY 2017. While remittances and Coalition Support Fund inflows both declined slightly over the same period last year, however, the impact was offset by an improvement in the income account, mainly due to lower profit repatriations by oil and gas firms.

Current account – The Current account deficit increased to US$12.4 billion in FY 2017, against US$3.2 billion in FY 2016.

However, the impact of high current deficit on foreign exchange reserves was not severe, as financial inflows were available to the country to partially offset the gap; these inflows helped ensure stability in the exchange rate.

Net FDI grew by 12.4 percent and reached US$1.6 billion in the nine-months period, whereas net FPI saw an inflow of US$631 million, against an outflow of US$393 million last year. Encouragingly for the country, the period saw the completion of multiple merger and acquisition deals between local and foreign companies.

Moreover, multiple foreign automakers announced their intention to enter the Pakistani market, and some also entered into joint ventures with local conglomerates.This indicates that Pakistan is clearly on foreign investors' radar, and provides a positive outlook for FDI inflows going forward. government's successful issuance of a US$1.0 billion Sukuk in the international capital market, at an extremely low rate of 5.5 percent. Besides, Pakistan continued to enjoy support from international financial institutions (IFIs) like the World Bank and Asian Development Bank, and from bilateral partners like China, in the post-EFF period: net official loan inflows of US$1.1 billion were recorded during the period. As a result, the country's FX reserve amounted to US$20.8 billion by 4 May 2017 sufficient to finance around four month of import payments.

Economic aid

Pakistan receives economic aid from several sources as loans and grants. The International Monetary Fund (IMF), World Bank (WB), Asian Development Bank (ADB), etc. provide long-term loans to Pakistan. Pakistan also receives bilateral aid from developed and oil-rich countries. Foreign aid has been one of the main sources of money for the Pakistani Economy. Collection of Foreign aid has been one of the priorities of almost every Pakistani Government with the Prime Minister himself leading delegations on a regular basis to collect Foreign aid.

The Asian Development Bank will provide close to $6 billion development assistance to Pakistan during 2006–9. The World Bank unveiled a lending programme of up to $6.5 billion for Pakistan under a new four-year, 2006–2009, aid strategy showing a significant increase in funding aimed largely at beefing up the country's infrastructure. Japan will provide $500 million annual economic aid to Pakistan. In November 2008, the International Monetary Fund (IMF) has approved a loan of 7.6 billion to Pakistan, to help stabilise and rebuild the country's economy. Between the 2008 and 2010 fiscal years, the IMF extended loans to Pakistan totalling 5.2 billion dollars. The government decided in 2011 to cut off ties with the IMF. However the government newly elected in 2013 re-established these ties, and a negotiated a three-year $6.6 billion package which would allow it to deal with on-going debt issues. In May 2019, Pakistan finalised a US $6 billion foreign aid with IMF. This is Pakistan's 22nd such bailout from the IMF.

The China–Pakistan Economic Corridor is being developed with a contribution of mainly concessionary loans from China under the Belt and Road Initiative. Much like BRI, value of CPEC investments transcends any fiat currency and is only estimated vaguely as it spans over decades of past and future industrial development and global economic influence.

Remittances

The remittances of Pakistanis living abroad has played important role in Pakistan's economy and foreign exchange reserves. The Pakistanis settled in Western Europe and North America are important sources of remittances to Pakistan. Since 1973 the Pakistani workers in the oil rich Arab states have been sources of billions of dollars of remittances.

The 9 million-strong Pakistani diaspora, contributed US$19.3 billion to the economy in FY2017. The major source countries of remittances to Pakistan include UAE, US, Saudi Arabia, GCC countries (including Bahrain, Kuwait, Qatar and Oman), Australia, Canada, Japan, Norway, Switzerland, UK and EU countries.

Remittances sent home by overseas Pakistani workers have seen a negative growth of 3.0% in the fiscal year 2017 compare to previous year when remittances reached at all-time high of 19.9 billion US dollars. This decline in remittances is mainly due to the adverse economic conditions of Arabian and gulf countries after the fall in oil prices in 2016. However, the recent development activities in the Qatar FIFA World Cup, Dubai Expo, Saudi Arabia's implementation of its Vision 2030 and particularly the recent visit of the P.M to Kuwait should all be helpful in opening new avenues for employment in these countries . Going forward one can expect improvements in the coming years.

Remittances sent home by overseas Pakistanis in the fiscal year 2016/17 are as under:

GOVERNMENT FINANCES

Fiscal budget summary (FY2017/18)

- Fiscal year: 1 July – 30 June
- Budget outlay: Rs 5,013.8 billion rupees
- Revenues collection estimated: 4,713.7 billion rupees
- Expenditures estimated: 5,103.8 billion rupees
- Bank borrowing estimated: 390.1 billion rupees

Revenues and taxation

Pakistan has a low tax/GDP ratio, which it is trying to improve. The current tax-to-GDP ratio is 12.6% (2016), which is a little less than its neighbour India 16.6% (2016) while a slight more than Sri Lanka 12.3% (2015). The pace of revenue mobilization has witnessed an upward trajectory since FY 2013. Overall revenues increased to 15.3 percent of GDP in FY 2016, compared to 13.3 percent of GDP recorded in FY 2013. Among those, tax revenues increased from 9.8 percent of GDP in FY 2013 to 12.6 percent of GDP in FY 2016.

Expenditures

Government expenditures were 4,383.6 billion rupees (FY 2016–2017 July to March). Total expenditures witnessed a downward trajectory without compromising the expenditures on development projects and social assistance. Particularly, expenditures under Public Sector Development Program (PSDP) have been raised adequately in order to meet the investment requirements. During FY 2017 the size of federal PSDP has increased to Rs 800 billion from Rs 348.3 billion during FY 2013, showing a cumulative increase of over 129 percent. During first nine months of current fiscal year, the fiscal deficit stood at 3.9 percent of GDP against 3.5 percent of GDP recorded in the same period of FY 2016 on account of higher development expenditures along with various tax incentives to promote investment and economic activity in the country and security related expenditures.

On the basis of previous estimates of GDP at Rs 33,509 billion, the fiscal deficit was recorded at 3.7 percent during first nine months of current fiscal year against 3.4 percent registered in the comparable period of FY 2016. Total revenues grew at 6.2 percent to Rs 3,145.5 billion during July–March, FY 2017 against Rs 2,961.9 in the comparable period of FY 2016.

6

Crisis of Democracy in Pakistan

Meanwhile, Benazir Bhutto lost the battle to maintain her authority over an increasingly radicalized society, and in October 1996 she was, after a protracted power struggle, dismissed by the President. It was the third time in eight years that an elected government had been dismissed less than halfway through its term. Weak democratic institutions, lack of a democratic political culture, politics of patronage, ineptitude of political leadership and the military's involvement in politics all contributed to the continuing crisis of democracy in Pakistan. In the subsequent elections, former Prime Minister Nawaz Sharif was re-elected with a large majority. Sharif was determined not to lose power again and set about undermining the role of the presidency and the judiciary. He used Islamic policies to bolster his own position. Sharif introduced an Islamic sharia bill, reinforcing the Islamization process initiated by General Zia. His exploitation of religion for political purposes strengthened the Islamic orthodoxy and religious militancy. That also led to an upsurge in religion-based violence. Sharif's preoccupation with power proved to be a fatal distraction, as the country drifted towards an economic meltdown. The fiscal indiscipline brought the country to the verge of bankruptcy. Sharif had a total disregard for institutions – he neither understood nor respected nor learnt to live with the institutions of a modern state and followed a patrimonial style of government. Editors and journalists were arrested and harassed for criticizing the government. Sharif had planned to make further amendments to the Constitution, declaring himself 'Amirul Mominin' (absolute leader of the Muslims).

While suppressing civil society and democratic institutions, Sharif increased his reliance on the army to manage everything from state-owned corporations to development work. A quarter of a million troops were mobilized to conduct a long-delayed population census. Another one hundred thousand were deployed to read electricity meters and run an almost bankrupt Water and Power Development Authority, which was responsible for electricity supply and the country's huge irrigation network. At one point, army soldiers were brought in to help kill stray dogs in Sharif's home town, Lahore. Such a large-scale induction of army personnel into civilian affairs was unprecedented even in Pakistan. The growing dependence on the army created its own predicament. Increasingly tasked with administration of civilian affairs, the army top brass wanted more political power in the state. This led to tensions between the army and Sharif, who was determined not to cede power to anyone. Sharif had picked General Pervez Musharraf ahead of two senior generals as the new army chief. He deliberately chose a man from the Mohajir minority ethnic group to head a predominantly Punjabi army, assuming that he would not be able to challenge an all-powerful Punjabi Prime Minister. But he failed to understand that the conflict with the army had a strong institutional dimension and was not simply about personalities. He erroneously assumed that the army would remain subservient to his rule once he had put in a man of his own choice at the top. For Sharif it was a game of persons. For the army it was an institutional matter.

The trigger for the eventual showdown between the army chief and the Prime Minister came in May 1999, following Sharif's peace talks with India, at which point Musharraf decided to revive the faltering campaign in Kashmir without telling the Prime Minister. The Pakistani army sent in soldiers to occupy Indian positions in the Kargil peaks, which the Indian army traditionally vacated during winter. The move led to a stand-off with India, and a terrified Sharif had almost begged President Clinton to mediate. He was forced to make a humiliating climbdown, which provoked an inevitable backlash from militants at home. By the time he tried to reassert himself by sacking Musharraf in October, it was already clear that it was, as it had always been, the radical military, not the elected government, who was in the driving seat in Pakistan.

On the morning of 11 September 2001, Lt.-General Mahmood Ahmed, the chief of the ISI, was at a breakfast meeting on Capitol Hill in Washington with Senator Bob Graham and Congressman Porter Goss, the chairmen of the Senate and House Intelligence committees. Also present there were Senator John Kyle and Pakistan's ambassador to Washington, Maleeha Lodhi.

As they talked about terrorism, specifically about bin Laden, a member of Senator Graham's staff informed them about the planes hitting the World Trade Center. The meeting continued until one plane was reported heading towards Capitol Hill and evacuation was ordered. General Mahmood expressed his deep sympathy to the people of the USA before the five hurriedly dispersed. General Mahmood had been due to return that evening after completing his week-long official visit to Washington, but his departure was delayed as all the airports were closed after the terrorist attacks. He had arrived in Washington on 4 September on the invitation of the CIA chief for routine consultations with senior US officials. The CIA and the ISI, erstwhile partners in the covert war against Soviet forces in Afghanistan in the 1980s, had maintained close contact despite the low in the relations between Washington and Islamabad that had followed the USA's nuclear-related sanctions on Pakistan in 1990.

It was General Mahmood's second visit to Washington as the ISI chief. His previous trip in April 2000 followed President Clinton's short stopover in Islamabad. The visit was arranged by the CIA with a view to cultivating Pakistan's new chief spymaster. He was hugely pampered as the CIA officials tried to win his confidence. At the General's request, the agency had arranged a private tour of Gettysburg, the venue of a crucial battle during the American Civil War in 1863. General Mahmood had a special interest in the battle of Gettysburg and had done his thesis on the subject at the National Defence College. He would talk endlessly on the tactics and other aspects of the battle. The CIA officials, however, were not sure whether all that effort won his cooperation. The trip went sour at the end when he received a dressing-down from Thomas Pickering, the US Under-Secretary of State, for helping the Taliban regime. He went back home angry and humiliated. The incident did not help improve relations between the USA and Pakistan, which had already become strained after the return of military rule and imposition of democratic sanctions. Pakistan's patronage of the orthodox Taliban regime, which had provided a base for bin Laden and thousands of other militants from different countries, was a serious concern for the Bush administration.

General Mahmood was the second-most-powerful man in the Pakistani military junta after General Musharraf. A stocky man with a long handlebar moustache, he was ruthless and highly ambitious. Because of his brashness and arrogance he was not very popular among his fellow officers. As the commander of the key 10th Corps based in Rawalpindi, he was one of the two coup-makers who brought Musharraf to power on 12 October 1999. His troops seized control of Islamabad and arrested the Prime Minister, Nawaz Sharif. He was rewarded for his loyalty when Musharraf appointed him director general of the ISI. During his tenure as head of the country's premier intelligence agency he had accelerated support for Islamic militant groups. The jihadist activities in Kashmir saw an unprecedented rise and Pakistan got much more deeply involved with the Taliban's efforts to expand their control in Afghanistan.

During his second stay in Washington, General Mahmood had met with senior CIA, Pentagon and National Security Council officials. Terrorism coming out of Afghanistan was the central issue of their discussions. He defended

Pakistan's policy of engagement with the Tailban and told George Tenet and other CIA officials that Mullah Omar was a pious and religious person, not a man of violence. The situation became tense when, on 9 September, two suicide bombers masquerading as journalists assassinated Ahmed Shah Masood, the leader of the rebel Afghan Northern Alliance. The leaders of the alliance blamed al-Qaeda and the ISI for the murder. General Mahmood was watching television coverage of the Twin Tower attacks at Ambassador Lodhi's office when he received a call at 5 pm inviting him for an emergency meeting with Richard Armitage, the US Deputy Secretary of State. At 10 am on 12 September, the General, accompanied by Ambassador Lodhi and Zamir Akram, a senior official at the Embassy, arrived at the State Department. Armitage was terse as he began saying that Pakistan faced a stark choice. 'We want to know whether you are with us or not. This is a black and white choice with no grey, 'he said. The General enquired what his country could do in that situation. 'We need your country's full support and cooperation. We will tell you tomorrow the specifics about the cooperation that is required,' said Armitage and asked the General to meet him the next day.

Returning to the Embassy, General Mahmood telephoned President Musharraf. Musharraf had been speaking to a group of local government representatives in Karachi when his Press Secretary had interrupted to tell him about the World Trade Center attacks. He immediately perceived the choice that he was about to be faced with. 'I took a fast decision,' he later told me, 'but I thought about it very carefully.' Only afterwards did he consult his aides and senior military commanders. 'I keep to Napoleon's view that two-thirds of the decision-making process is based on analysis and information and one-third is always a leap in the dark.' The shock and anger in Washington which was relayed to him by his spy chief did not surprise Musharraf. He had also received a telephone call from Secretary of State Colin Powell, who had spelled out the situation in stark terms, telling the Pakistani President: 'The American people would not understand if Pakistan was not in this fight with the United States.' Musharraf assured him of his country's full cooperation.

On 13 September, General Mahmood returned to the State Department for the second meeting. 'This is not negotiable,' said Armitage, as he handed him a single sheet of paper with a list of seven demands that the Bush administration wanted him to accept. The General, who was known for his hardline pro-Taliban position, glanced through the paper for a few seconds and passed it on to Ambassador Lodhi. Before she started reading the paper, General Mahmood replied, 'They are all acceptable to us.' The swift response took Armitage by surprise and left Pakistani officials flabbergasted. 'These are very powerful words, General. Don't you want to discuss this with your

President?' he asked. 'I know the President's mind,' replied General Mahmood. A relieved Armitage asked General Mahmood to meet with Tenet at his headquarters at Langley. 'He is waiting for you,' said Armitage. General Mahmood looked glum as he was driven to Langley for a crucial meeting with the CIA officials. He later grumbled about the high-handedness of American officials. He was not at all happy with the terms for cooperation with the USA, which he had acceded to a few minutes previously. He looked like a general who had just lost a battle. Meanwhile, Ambassador Lodhi returned to the Embassy, from where she faxed the paper to President Musharraf in Islamabad.

General Mahmood stayed in Washington until 16 September, discussing Pakistan's role in the 'war on terror' with American officials. But it was apparent that he was not keen to see that role implemented. On 13 September, Wendy Chamberlain, the newly appointed US ambassador to Islamabad, met with Musharraf and conveyed a formal message from President Bush with the same list of demands which had earlier been handed over to General Mahmood in Washington. It read:

(1) Stop al-Qaeda operations on the Pakistani border, intercept arms shipments through Pakistan and all logistical support for bin Laden.
(2) Blanket over-flight and landing rights for US planes.
(3) Access to Pakistan's naval bases, air bases and borders.
(4) Immediate intelligence and immigration information.
(5) Curb all domestic expression of support for terrorism against the United States, its friends and allies.
(6) Cut off fuel supply to the Taliban and stop Pakistani volunteers going into Afghanistan to join the Taliban.
(7) Pakistan to break diplomatic relations with the Taliban and assist the US in destroying bin Laden and his al-Qaeda network.

The same evening, General Musharraf made a statement assuring the US President of his unstinting cooperation in the fight against terrorism. He declared Pakistan would commit all of its resources in an effort coordinated with the USA to locate and punish those involved in that horrific act. President Bush responded to Musharraf's message of support by saying, 'Now we'll find out what that means. Won't we?' Pakistan's support was important for the USA. Its geographic proximity and its vast intelligence information on Afghanistan were seen as crucial for any military action against the Taliban and al-Qaeda. Pakistan was one of the three countries – the others were the United Arab Emirates and Saudi Arabia – which had formally recognized the conservative Afghan Islamic government and the only country which had maintained diplomatic relations with Kabul. The American demands, to which General

Mahmood had agreed in next to no time, required Pakistan to abandon its support for the Taliban regime and provide logistic support to the American forces. After having spent the past seven years helping the Taliban consolidate their rule, providing them with military, political and financial support, Pakistan was now being asked by the Bush administration to help the USA dislodge the Islamic fundamentalist government.

THE CONSTITUTIONAL AND LEGAL STRUCTURE OF PAKISTAN

However, the first authoritative statement made on 11 August 1947, that is only three days before independence, in the Pakistan Constituent Assembly by Jinnah deviated from the main thrust of the Muslim League's propaganda in favour of cultural nationalism. To the utter surprise of many, he made the following observation in a long address:

You are free; you are free to go to your temples, you are free to go to your mosques or to any other place of worship in this State of Pakistan. You may belong to any religion or caste or creed that has nothing to do with the business of the States. We are starting with this fundamental principle that we are all citizens and equal citizens of one States I think we should keep that in front of us as our ideal and you will find that in due course Hindus would cease to be Hindus and Muslims would cease to be Muslims, not in the religious sense, because that is the personal faith of each individual, but in the political sense as citizens of the State.

This patently secular and territorial idea of nation contradicted the rationale for the creation of Pakistan as a state for a cultural nation. The controversy that it caused has been generating ever more confusion as time goes by. While the fundamentalists usually dismiss it as irrelevant and an aberration, mainstream Muslim modernists argue that he was actually operating within an ideal Islamic framework of tolerance and justice for non-Muslims within an Islamic state. Marginalised secularists, leftists and oppressed minorities, however, raise it to the level of a sacred covenant that his successors have allegedly broken.

It seems that Jinnah's wording reflected his usual political sagacity rather than a firm ideological position. Communal violence was at its worst at that time. The Radcliffe Award was about to be announced and one could guess that it would result in population movement on a gigantic scale. The speech probably purported to discourage mass migration, uprooting and further communal violence. However, it is doubtful whether in the wake of the communal riots such a prescription enjoyed any real credibility in Muslim-Pakistani society, Jinnah's prestige and authority notwithstanding. In this regard, it is significant to bear in mind that Jinnah never again reiterated such a commitment although he lived for another year. After his death on 11 September 1948, the idea of a secular state never again received much attention in mainstream Pakistani politics. Rather, Islamic idiom became a central feature of official rhetoric.

One can even argue that once the initial euphoria was over and a framework for national identity and nation building had to be found, the Pakistani leadership felt constrained to distinguish itself from India. There were undoubtedly other issues to be dealt with by the government of Prime Minister Liaqat Ali Khan (d. 1951) but maintaining distinctiveness from Congress and secular India must have been an important consideration.

Thus the Objectives Resolution moved in the Pakistan Constituent Assembly by Prime Minister Liaqat Ali Khan on 7 March 1949 proclaimed the novel idea that sovereignty over the entire universe belonged to God. Democracy was to be practised, but within 'Islamic limits'. The minorities were assured that their legitimate interests would be safeguarded, and that provisions would be made for them in accordance with Islam freely to profess and practise their religions and cultures. Although such proclamations sounded like innocuous 'boasts', in the longer run they proved to be constraints that facilitated the politics of exclusion of different religious minorities and deviant sects from the category of nation.

Thus the first constitution of Pakistan adopted in 1956 contained a commitment to bringing all laws into conformity with Islam. In 1973 the third constitution was adopted. Unlike the first two constitutions that only required the president of the republic to be a Muslim, the third also required the prime minister to be a Muslim. It further obliged them to take an oath testifying their belief in the finality of Prophet Muhammad's mission.

The Educational System

The invention of a distinct historical past for the so-called Muslim nation of India justifying its separate existence within the boundaries of Pakistan has been felt to be necessary for conferring legitimacy and authenticity on it. Attempts to imagine such a nation have unsurprisingly resulted in distortion and exaggeration of facts on a massive scale, resulting in mythogenesis.

The main concern has been to foster a Pakistani-Islamic identity defined negatively, as a contrast to India. In his book The Murder of History a leading Pakistani educationalist and historian Prof. K.K. Aziz has scrutinised 66 textbooks used for teaching history, Pakistan studies and social studies in Pakistani schools, colleges and universities. Pakistan studies deal largely with the Muslim nationalist/separatist movement. It is a compulsory subject from 1st grade up to university and not only all students of humanities and social sciences but also scientists, doctors and engineers must gain a pass.

The author alleges that Islamisation by the government of General Zia-ul-Haq vitiated the general academic environment in Pakistan. He cites extensively factual errors, logical fallacies, inconsistencies, falsifications, mythologisations and crass propaganda from books used both in the Urdu and English-medium schools and colleges.

The military and the long military rules are presented in positive terms while hostility towards India, Hinduism and Hindus is their hallmark. For example, Congress is described as a Hindu party. That there were many Muslims among its members and that some held leading positions is not reported. India is described as the state of Hindus, although there are as many Muslims or more living in India as in Pakistan. Furthermore, a grossly exaggerated role is assigned to Muslims in the anti-colonial struggle. The Muslim League is declared as the party of the Muslim masses that successfully resisted both British colonialism and Hindu domination. Only Muslims are mentioned as victims of the partition riots and massacres, which are alleged to have been begun by Hindus and Sikhs. Any comment on the loss of lives among Hindus and Sikhs during that period is conspicuous by its absence. He sums up this approach in the following words:

It is declared that the Muslims of India made 'tremendous' sacrifices to win their freedom. The fact is that, apart from the brief years of 1858-60 and 1920-22, Muslims suffered little hardship between 1857-1947. It is forgotten by everyone that the Muslim League's search for protection and safeguards (in the early years) and its struggle for an independent state (in the later years) were strictly constitutional efforts, peaceful campaigns and political fights, conducted through parliamentary debates and negotiations No Muslim League leaders languished in prisons. No Muslim masses faced British bullets. The many people who died or suffered horribly in 1947 were running away from their homes because their life was in danger, not because they were fighting for the creation of Pakistan. They were casualties of communal riots, not of anti-British warfare.

He comments further, 'A sane educational system does not train students in hate. Whatever the justification for it or the compulsions of patriotism, hatred corrupts the mind, more so if it is still tender, and retards its healthy growth'.

Islamisation, Confessionalism and Hostility to Minorities

States founded on religious and ethnic nationalism invariably discriminate against atypical minorities. Ethnocracies can be a more apt description of such states, even when they practice democracy. Israel is a case in point. However, Pakistan has the rather unenviable distinction of extending the logic of confessionalism to its ultimate limits. In Pakistan, not only non-Muslims but also deviant sects within the broader category of Muslims who were mobilised in support of the 1945-46 elections have been alienated over time. Also, women as a whole have been victims of the so-called Islamisation process.

In 1953, violent anti-Ahmadiyya riots took place in Punjab in which several hundred lives were lost and considerable Ahmadiyya property was destroyed. The masterminds behind those riots were politicians from the ruling Muslim League seeking to challenge the ruling faction within the party. In 1974, the Islamic socialist Zulfikar Ali Bhutto played the anti-Ahmadiyya card again in the hope of extending his populist constituency into the stronghold of the doctrinal-minded Islamic parties of Pakistan. Consequently, when General Muhammad Zia-ul-Haq seized the reigns of power in July 1977 by toppling Zulfikar Ali Bhutto in a bloodless coup, a long tradition of relying on Islam to define national identity and the rights of citizens was already in place. Upon coming to power in 1977, General Zia announced an ambitious programme to Islamise Pakistan. He expressed his political philosophy in a succinct manner : 'I have a mission, given by God, to bring Islamic order to Pakistan'. His main source of inspiration for an Islamic order was the ideas of the arch fundamentalist Abul Ala Maududi. The latter had set up headquarters in Lahore after Partition, from where he had been propagating his idea of a totalitarian Islamic state. The pre-Partition tradition of exploiting Islamic slogans to rouse Muslim fears against Hindus had been converted into a Machiavellian art by Pakistani politicians that involved damning their opponents as renegades to Islam and enemies of Pakistan. The various governments used it to slur the opposition's call for democracy and elections, while the various fundamentalist parties and factions pushed all governments into a corner with allegations of insincerity in their commitment to Islam. An Islamist political discourse evolved incrementally, each addition supplanting modernistic vagaries with puritan certainty. It bore the hallmarks of Maududism.

Thus in 1979, the government announced the imposition of the Hudud Ordinance, i.e. traditional Islamic punishments for the offences of adultery, false accusation of adultery, drinking alcohol, theft, and highway robbery. In 1984, a new Law of Evidence was adopted which reduced the worth of the evidence give by a female witness in a court of law to half the value of that given by a male witness. It was also a period when Islamic scholars notorious for their misogynist views appeared on television to advocate strict segregation between men and women and the confinement of the latter to the private sphere. In subsequent years the incidence of 'honour killings' has increased sharply. The victims are wives and daughters killed by their own families for allegedly defiling the family honour by demanding divorce or refusing to marry a man chosen for them by their elders. The courts have generally been very lenient to the culprits. Also in 1984, many new restrictions were imposed on the

Ahmadiyya group. They were prohibited from using Islamic nomenclature in their religious and social activities and may no longer call their places of worship mosques. In 1985, separate electorates were reintroduced (they were abolished in 1956), whereby non-Muslims were to constitute a separate body of voters, being thus entitled only to elect non-Muslim legislators to the various assemblies. Consequently their right to take part in normal law-making is severely restricted. It was followed by the adoption of the Blasphemy Law in 1986. It reads as follows:

Use of derogatory remarks etc. in respect of the Holy Prophet: Whether by words, either spoken or written, or by visible representations, or by any imputation, innuendo or insinuation, directly or indirectly, defiles the sacred name of the Holy Prophet (peace by upon him) shall be punishable with death, or imprisonment for life, and shall be liable to fine.

General Zia died in a plane crash in August 1988. The elected governments of Benazir Bhutto (1988-90, 1994-96) and Nawaz Sharif (1990-93; 1997-99) did not dare question the validity of the laws passed during the time of General Zia. It seems that once a law has been adopted in the name of Islam no politician is willing to attempt to rescind it. In October 1997 retired Lahore High Court judge Arif Iqbal Bhatti was shot down by unidentified members of extremist religious groups. His death was believed to be linked to his role in the acquittal in 1995 of two Christians, Salamat Masih and Rehman Masih, charged with blasphemy. The Pakistan Human Rights Commission has been providing details of the increasing terrorisation of minorities. Charges of blasphemy have been framed against many Ahmadis and Christians. Forced conversions of Hindus have also been reported. The military government of General Pervez Musharraf, which came to power through a coup d'état on 12 October 1999, initially presented a progressive position on Islam, but it had quickly to withdraw from such a position under pressure from the extremists.

Shia-Sunni Terrorism and the Emergence of the Jihadis

During Gen. Zia's regime Sunni-Shia doctrinal differences erupted into open conflict. The difficulties were compounded further when in the late 1980s powerful external actors began to cultivate their lobbies in Pakistan. Thus Saudi Arabia and Iran were believed to be sending large sums of money, books, leaflets, audio and video cassette-tapes and other propaganda material to Pakistan. Such propaganda offensives were backed by the inflow of firearms and other weapons. Sunni and Shia militias began to menace and terrorise society; the assassinations of several rival Sunni and Shia ulama and regular gun battles and bomb explosions have been taking place in Pakistan in recent years.

An international Islamic guerrilla movement comprising Sunni militants, aptly described as Jihadis (holy warriors), has been establishing its headquarters in the northern Pakistani city of Peshawar in recent years. The Jihadis have declared war on India and want to liberate Kashmir through violent means.

The United States is another enemy, as are Israel, secular Turkey and the central Asian republics. In some pronouncements, all non-Muslims have been declared enemies of Islam.

The coming into power of the arch-fundamentalist Talebans in neighbouring Afghanistan has once again revived the old pan-Islamic project of Chowdhary Rahmat Ali. In a recent interview, a leading American South-Asia expert Selig Harrison claimed that General Zia's involvement in Afghanistan was meant to promote a pan-Islamic superstate in the region.

He also alleged that such a scheme has powerful backers in the Pakistani military establishment. It can be assumed that Iran (because of its deviant Shia Islam), Turkey (secular) and the central Asian republics (also secular) will have no interest in such a project. Instead what is more likely is that the totalitarian, obscurantist, anti-modernist, medieval type of state and society created in Afghanistan could envelope Pakistan.

Separatist Movements

Although the Muslim League was successful in presenting a broad Muslim unity against Congress, after Partition it quickly dissipated and the centre became a stronghold of mainly Punjabi-Urdu-speaking groups.

Recently the equation has been changed and it is a Punjabi-Pukhtun ruling axis which dominates Pakistan. Separatist movements have emerged several times.

The Pukhtun nationalists seeking to create a separate Pukhtunistan in the north-western province of Pakistan were contained by a policy of carrot and stick during the 1950s and 1960s. The people of the former East Pakistan seceded to form their independent state of Bangladesh in 1971. It cost, however, between 1.5 and 3 million lives. The Pakistan army especially targeted the Hindus. A bloody guerrilla war raged in Baluchistan during the early 1970s, which was defeated by forceful military action. However, a virulent ethnic conflict that has claimed several thousand lives has been going on in the Sindh province, mainly as a confrontation between the native Sindhi-speakers and the Urdu-speaking refugees (both primarily Sunni Muslims) who settled in the urban areas of that province after Partition. Military action has been undertaken several times to restore law and order. In addition, hundreds of thousands of Afghan refugees have settled in Karachi, where armed militias run lucrative businesses in drugs and arms smuggling.

STRATEGIC DEPTH IN PAKISTANI MILITARY

The list was clearly only the first step in testing Pakistan's resolve. Washington had also asked for a comprehensive report from the ISI about every detail it had on bin Laden, including his contacts with Pakistani and other Islamic militant organizations. Pakistan eventually negotiated with the USA that no combat missions would be carried out from its territory and, instead of blanket over-flight rights, an air corridor was assigned to US planes. Pakistan was ready to break diplomatic relations with the Taliban government immediately, but the move was delayed on American advice. The US Assistant Secretary of State, Christina Rocca, told Ambassador Lodhi that Pakistan should keep the diplomatic channel open with the Taliban until the US invasion was completed. Breaking off diplomatic relations at that point, in Washington's view, would have given a clear indication to the Taliban about the exact timing of an impending US attack.

The turnaround was met with astonishment by the military. They had been actively supporting the Pashtun Taliban regime, which, according to them, provided Pakistan with 'strategic depth' against any aggression from arch rival India. The Pakistani military feared that they would lose their strategic depth in Kabul if they withdrew support from the hardline Islamic regime. Several efforts by the USA prior to 9/11 had failed to elicit Islamabad's cooperation in the expulsion of bin Laden from Afghanistan. Musharraf's coming to power in October 1999 had reversed a secret mission plan with Washington to send a Pakistani special commando force into Afghanistan to capture bin Laden using the ISI's information.

Under the plan, which was suggested by the then Prime Minister Nawaz Sharif during his visit to Washington in July 1999, the USA had agreed to provide $25 million for training a group of ex-ISI and Pakistani army officers for the operation. The detail of the operation was worked out in subsequent meetings between the ISI's then chief, Lt.-General Ziauddin, and CIA officials in Washington in September. But before the plan could be implemented Sharif had been ousted from power. General Ziauddin, who was appointed as Chief of Army Staff by Sharif, was arrested after Musharraf's loyalists took over control of Islamabad. Pakistani military officials argued the plan was not realistic and would never have taken off. However, Washington continued to press the military regime to get bin Laden expelled from Afghanistan. In January 2000, Musharraf promised senior American officials that he would meet with the Taliban supreme leader Mullah Omar and press him on the matter of expelling bin Laden.

But the visit never materialized. In March 2000, President Clinton made a one-day stopover in Islamabad on his way back from India. It was the first time a US president had been there since 1969. Clinton made the trip despite strong opposition from members of his administration. Washington had imposed sanctions on Pakistan after the military coup and relations between the two countries had hit a new low. During his brief one-to-one meeting, Clinton asked the General for help regarding bin Laden. The US President later told his aides: 'I offered him the moon when I went to see him, in terms of better relations with the United States, if he would help us get bin Laden and deal with another issue or two.' Ambassador Lodhi, who was present at the meeting, denied that any such offer was made. 'I don't remember any moon that Pakistan was offered,' she said.

Again in May that year President Clinton reminded Musharraf to carry out his promise to visit Afghanistan and convince Mullah Omar to get rid of bin Laden. In June, CIA Director George Tenet travelled to Pakistan with the same message. Musharraf could not visit Afghanistan because of clear indications that Mullah Omar would not respond positively to any suggestion to extradite bin Laden. It was also apparent that his hardline generals, particularly General Mahmood, were not keen to push the issue too much as the Taliban prepared to launch the 'final' assault against the opposition Northern Alliance. The Arab militants were an important part of the Taliban fighting machine and their role was crucial in the coming battles.

Frustrated by the inaction, Washington became openly critical of Pakistan for supporting the Taliban offensive to complete their control over Afghanistan. In December, the United Nations Security Council imposed fresh sanctions against the Taliban regime, calling for bin Laden's expulsion and forbidding any country to provide them with arms or military assistance. The latest sanction, however, did little to stop Islamabad from continuing to supply weapons and financial aid to its ally. There was a complete stalemate in US relations with Pakistan in Clinton's final year as President.

The administration had little incentive to offer with congressional nuclear- and democracy-related sanctions against Pakistan. The US 'stick heavy' policy failed to force Pakistan to cooperate. Immediately after his inauguration, President Bush raised the terrorism issue with Pakistan's military ruler; in February 2001, he sent a letter to General Musharraf seeking his support in dealing with terrorism. He emphasized that bin Laden and al-Qaeda were a direct threat to the United States and its interests and that this threat had to be addressed. There was, however, a clear shift in the approach of the new US administration. Instead of just using the stick, Secretary of State Colin Powell recommended providing some incentives to persuade Pakistan to cooperate. To break the logjam, the US administration moved to pursue a policy of enhanced engagement with Islamabad and also considered lifting some of the sanctions against the military government. But, because of a negative view of

Pakistan on Capitol Hill, the idea of lifting sanctions could not make much headway. On 4 August, President Bush again wrote to President Musharraf registering his concern over terrorism emanating from Afghanistan and requested him to engage actively against al-Qaeda.

Although Pakistan's leverage over the Taliban had weakened over the years and relations between them had become quite testy, Musharraf was not willing to pull support completely. He snapped shut a green folder containing a letter from Mullah Omar when I and a colleague from Newsweek arrived in the first week of February 2001 for an interview at his office in the Army General Headquarters in Rawalpindi. Mullah Omar's letter was in reply to Musharraf's message that had drawn the Afghan leader's attention to the international concern over the terrorism issue.

'I told him he must address the problems of terrorism, religious extremism and the gender issue to improve the Taliban's image,' he told us, but there was no indication from him that he was going to abandon support for the conservative regime, which he believed was in Pakistan's interest. Musharraf was visibly unhappy with the UN sanctions slapped on the Taliban regime. 'We are putting them against the wall,' he said, 'They have banned poppy cultivation. The world should understand that, since we have imposed sanctions as well, that means we are telling them to commit suicide.' On the bin Laden issue, the President suggested a middle way could be found on the issue of his extradition. 'He can be sent to any third country.' But he was not sure how it could be done.

In the event, the change came astonishingly fast in the aftermath of the 9/11 terrorist attacks. The quick about-turn surprised even the American authorities. Concern for the state of Pakistan's democracy melted away and the military government was hailed by the West as 'an exemplary country in the fight against terrorism'.

Events in Washington and Islamabad during the week following 11 September provide an interesting insight into the decision-making process in Pakistan on crucial national security and foreign policy issues. Like the policy to support the Taliban regime, the decision on the about-turn was also taken by just a few people. There were no consultations at any level when President Musharraf decided to abandon support for the Taliban and gave the American forces complete access to Pakistani territory and airspace. It was all done in the best national interest, Musharraf later declared. The military leader had offered the same argument when Pakistan got into a messy situation by supporting the Taliban.

There was no discussion with the political parties on the paradigm shift in the country's strategic policy. President Musharraf took his handpicked cabinet into his confidence almost three days after he had already consented to the US demands. On 14 September, he met with his cabinet and the National Security Council in a marathon session lasting until the early hours of the morning in which he explained why he had decided to support the US. His line was that Pakistan itself was a victim of terrorism and the Taliban government was providing refuge to the religious extremists involved in sectarian killings in Pakistan.

'We had given a long list of the terrorists who we wanted to be handed over to us. At least they should have turned over the terrorists to us.' He told the ministers that the decision to cooperate with the United States was necessary to safeguard Pakistan's nuclear assets and its Kashmir policy. He gave them the details of military and logistic support he had agreed to provide to the US forces in the planned military action on Afghanistan. There were only a few feeble voices in the cabinet expressing concern over the possible public backlash. But largely it was a tame affair.

General Musharraf did not find it hard to convince his handpicked civilian cabinet, but it was not so smooth when it came to his top commanders and members of his military junta. There was a complete division over the issue. At least four top commanders, including General Mahmood who had earlier, in Washington, signed on the dotted line, showed reservations on the decision to provide unqualified support to the United States in its war on Afghanistan. Lt.-General Mohammed Aziz, Corps Commander Lahore, Lt.-General Jamshed Gulzar Kiani, Corps Commander, Rawalpindi, and Lt.-General Muzaffar Usmani, Deputy Chief of Army Staff, were among those who opposed pulling out support for the Taliban regime. They had all played key roles in the 1999 military coup. Musharraf, however, had the backing of other corps commanders. It was a precarious situation for him.

He could certainly not backtrack. He tried to persuade Washington to delay the attack on Afghanistan and give diplomacy a last chance. He thought there was still a possibility of persuading Mullah Omar to hand over bin Laden and avoid military action. He was worried about an extremist backlash against the US attack on a Muslim country and his government's support for it. General Musharraf expressed his concern about the domestic fall out to the American ambassador during his long meeting with her on 15 September. 'These decisions are not very easy and we need understanding from the United States and also support from them, so that I can take the nation along with me in our fight against terrorism,' General Musharraf recalled telling her. He was, perhaps, more concerned about the reaction within the military. Donning his military uniform, General Musharraf looked stressed as he appeared on state television on the evening of 19 September to explain why he had decided to side with the

USA in the war on terror. His tone was highly defensive as he told his countrymen how hard he had tried to defend the Taliban against all odds. He justified his decision saying it was done to save the country's strategic assets, safeguard the cause of Kashmir and prevent Pakistan from being declared a terrorist state.

He chose the occasion to warn India to 'lay off' Pakistan at that moment of crisis. The speech was aimed at defusing domestic opposition and to assure the military that by sacrificing the Taliban, he had protected Pakistan's vital interests. In a last-ditch attempt to put off a US attack on Afghanistan, and the backlash it would provoke, General Musharraf dispatched General Mamhood to Kandahar on 17 September to persuade Mullah Omar to hand bin Laden over to the USA. 'I was trying to drill home to him that he shouldn't make the people of Afghanistan suffer for a person who's not even an Afghan, but someone who's come from outside,' General Musharraf said.

When the Saudi fugitive had first settled in Afghanistan in the 1990s after his expulsion from Sudan, relations between him and Mullah Omar were not cordial. Mullah Omar would often call him 'donkey' and make fun of bin Laden among his fellows. The Taliban leader would argue that he had inherited the Saudi militant and had to treat him as a guest and protect him according to Pashtun tradition. 'He is like chicken bone stuck in our throat,' he once told a senior Pakistani diplomat. The Taliban and al-Qaeda were very different in their aims and political and religious philosophy. The Taliban represented an ultra-conservative society; their agenda was Afghan-specific. Before 11 September, the USA was not their number one enemy. Al-Qaeda, on the other hand, had a wider international agenda. Its main objective was to attack US interests wherever possible. Its cadres were not necessarily orthodox religious people.

Over the years, bin Laden had expanded his influence as the conservative Islamic forces became increasingly reliant on his financial support and foreign fighters to extend control over the rest of Afghanistan. There was a visible hardening in Mullah Omar's stance with the improvement in relations with his guest.

Islamabad seemed to be losing whatever clout it had on the Islamic fundamentalist regime. Mullah Omar was not prepared to listen to his patrons anymore. The biggest embarrassment came in early 2001 when the he snubbed Musharraf's Interior Minister, Moinuddin Haider, who sought the extradition of leaders of a Pakistani sectarian group who had taken refuge in Afghanistan. They were wanted in several cases of murder and attacks on Shia mosques. The worst snub came in March 2001, when Mullah Omar rejected Pakistan's request not to obliterate statues of Buddha in Bamiyan. Pakistan had tried to use the Taliban and al-Qaeda to promote its influence in war- torn Afghanistan – only to eventually lose control over both of them. Despite international outrage and dissent within their own ranks, hardline Taliban extremists systematically destroyed Afghanistan's pre-Islamic heritage.

Some Taliban sources later associated the decision to blow up Afghanistan's ancient Buddhist statues with the growing influence of bin Laden. The military commanders who supported the decision were believed to have strong links with the al-Qaeda leader. They had fought together against the Soviet forces and that bond was further strengthened over the years during his stay in Afghanistan. The Taliban's growing dependence on Arab fighters who, along with Pakistanis, constituted the most crucial part of its war machinery had caused an increase in bin Laden's influence. The terrorist training camp funded by him had expanded with new recruits from across the Islamic world. Many of those trained there were assigned to the 55th Brigade, a unit bin Laden had created to help the Taliban fight its Afghan opponents.

General Mahmood arrived in Kandahar on 17 September 2001 and met with Mullah Omar without any aides. A senior Pakistani foreign ministry official who accompanied the ISI chief said he was surprised when the ISI chief asked him to stay outside and insisted on meeting the Taliban supreme leader alone. No one knew what transpired in the meeting, but he reported back to General Musharraf that 'he was encouraged by Mullah Omar's response.' General Musharraf said that Mullah Omar seemed to show 'a little bit of flexibility'.. The flexibility Mullah Omar had indicated was not enough to meet the American demand of surrendering bin Laden. He had only agreed to form a court comprising Islamic religious scholars to try him, provided America was prepared to present evidence of his involvement in the terrorist attacks. But the trial never took place.

A few days later, General Mahmood sent a delegation of religious scholars to Mullah Omar. Interestingly, the delegation comprised hardline pro-Taliban clerics headed by Mufti Nizamuddin Shamzai, who later issued a fatwa (religious edict) for jihad against the American- led coalition forces. While he himself led violent protests against the Musharraf government, one of his sons went to Afghanistan to fight on behalf of the Taliban. There was a strong suspicion that the ISI chief may have been involved in deception. Some officials suggest that he had told Mullah Omar to remain steadfast and not to succumb to American pressure.

As Pakistan's desperate diplomatic efforts failed to make Mullah Omar change his mind, by the end of September American forces were making final preparations to launch an attack on Afghanistan. They had already acquired three air bases in Pakistan close to Afghanistan and set up a command post at the air force base in Jacobabad in the southern Sindh province. The American military build-up and the presence of US troops in Pakistan had fuelled public anger. Thousands of people, largely supporters of hardline Islamic organizations, poured into the streets of Pakistan's main cities.

It was a tricky situation for the USA when it decided to go for military action against bin Laden and the Taliban regime in Afghanistan. For Washington, the factors that made the ISI valuable also made it suspect. Not only had Pakistan turned a blind eye for years to the growing ties between bin Laden and the Taliban; the ISI had also relied on al-Qaeda camps for training Kashmiri militants. The agency had maintained an indirect but long-standing relationship with Osama bin Laden. The connection came to light in August 1998 when the USA launched a cruise missile attack against al-Qaeda camps near Khost in Afghanistan in response to the bombings of two US embassies in East Africa. The casualties included several members of a Pakistani-backed Islamic militant group, HuM, who were training in the camps. In some cases, ISI agents also facilitated Arab militants travelling to Afghanistan to wage jihad. It was widely suspected that bin Laden escaped the attack because of a tip-off from the ISI. However, there had not been any evidence of the agency ever being directly involved in al-Qaeda terrorist activities against the USA. In fact, the ISI cooperated with the CIA and the FBI on several counter-terrorism operations in the 1990s. The agency was instrumental in the 1995 capture in Islamabad of Ramzi Yousuf, the mastermind of the first World Trade Center bombing in 1993, and the arrest in Pakistan in 1998 of Aimal Kansi, who had shot dead two CIA employees outside the agency's headquarters in Langley, Virginia in 1993.

With its deep involvement in Afghanistan, the ISI had the most extensive intelligence data on that country and the Taliban. When Pakistan changed its course, it also brought about a reversal in the ISI's role. The ISI was back together with the CIA for a new war, very different from the one that they had fought in the 1980s. It was not the convergence of interests that fostered the alliance this time, but a forced relationship. The agency was now required to undo the politics of militancy, which it had actively promoted for almost a quarter of a century. It had never been easy for the agency to completely break its association with the Islamists.

With General Mahmood at the helm of the powerful ISI, President Musharraf would have had a difficult time pushing his new US-backed Afghan policy. There was no way Pakistan could have delivered what the Americans were demanding, with some top generals not in full agreement. General Musharraf was also not very happy with General Mahmood's arrogant style, and for not consulting him before agreeing to Armitage's seven-point demands.

Though the President would have given his consent, he did not like being bypassed. A new policy needed a new team.

On 7 October 2001, just three weeks after his decision to join the US war on terror, Musharraf sacked General Mahmood and sidelined three other top generals known for their hardline Islamic views in a major shake-up of the army top brass. Initially, Musharraf just wanted to remove General Mahmood from the ISI and offered to elevate him to the post of Chairman of the Joint Chiefs of Staff Committee, which he refused. General Aziz reluctantly accepted the job. 'I just want to know whether it is your own decision or are you doing it because America wanted it?' General Aziz asked his boss. General Musharraf replied that it was his decision. General Usmani simply resigned after being superseded by the appointment of General Mohammed Yousuf to the newly created post of Vice Chief of the Army Staff and General Gulzar Kiani as Quarter Master General. Ironically, in his new position of Chairman Joint Chiefs of Staff Committee, General Aziz coordinated with the Pentagon for logistical support for 'Operation Enduring Freedom' in Afghanistan.

The changes coincided with the launching of the joint US-British military operation in Afghanistan, and were seen as a part of General Musharraf's plan to appoint to key positions those officers who would support his pro-West policy shift. The shake-up in the army high command changed the entire composition of the junta, which had ruled the country since seizing power in October 1999 and consolidated General Musharraf's position as the sole power centre. In the past, every decision taken by the cabinet and the National Security Council had to be stamped by the powerful coterie of generals. The top brass now bore a totally new and liberal image, tailored to the requirement of the new situation with Pakistan trying to cut its umbilical cord with militant Islam and the Taliban.

With no peer, Musharraf could now operate much more freely. The removal of the hardline generals from the decision-making process came as a great relief to the USA as well. Within a few weeks of 11 September, Musharraf had swept aside five of his top 13 generals. 'The critical element of strategy are timing, space and strength,' he told me in January 2002, appearing much more relaxed and basking in his new-found international role. 'No democratically elected government could have moved so quickly,' he added. General Mahmood's removal was important, but it did not solve all the problems. Many senior officers harboured strong anti-American sentiments and obviously resented Pakistan fighting what they described as 'America's dirty war'. 'I hate to work with the Americans,' a senior ISI brigadier told me. 'I wish they get bogged down in Afghanistan.' Some of them refused to accept that al-Qaeda or Muslims were responsible for the 11 September attacks. It was going to be very difficult for them to break their associations and change their opinions after collaborating with militant Islamists for so long.

Musharraf chose Lt.-General Ehsan ul-Haq, a moderate officer with a strong intelligence background, as the new ISI chief. A Pashtun from Pakistan's North West Frontier Province, he had earlier served as head of Military Intelligence and was known for his middle-of-the-road views. One of his first jobs was to revamp the agency and to weed out those officers who had a long association with the Islamic militants. General Haq signalled a significant change in course, disbanding two major units of the ISI that had close links to Islamic militants in Afghanistan and Kashmir.

The move was seen as one of most significant shifts emerging from Musharraf's decision to align his country with the USA and to reduce ties with Islamic militants there and in Kashmir. The measure resulted in the transfer of perhaps 40 per cent of forces assigned to the ISI, which drew most of its manpower from the military. The action also served a major purpose of purging the 'Taliban cell' set up in the intelligence agency by General Mahmood. The American intelligence officials reportedly helped in compiling a list of suspect pro-Islamic officers who were to be removed from the organization. Despite the massive changes, the ISI's links with the Islamists were never successfully severed. They found it difficult to leave the old linkages behind. Nevertheless, the ISI helped tilt the balance in the battle in Afghanistan. The withdrawal of the ISI's support catalysed the swift fall of the Taliban regime. The agency, which had been deeply involved with the Taliban from its inception, guided the American forces in ousting its own creation.

Unlike his predecessor, General Haq kept a low profile, but became a key member of Musharraf's inner coterie. The ISI had assumed a much greater importance not only because of its new-found role in the US-led war on terror, but also because of its growing involvement in domestic politics. General Haq kept the Americans happy by capturing hundreds of al-Qaeda fugitives, but there was also huge scepticism over his efforts to curb home-grown Islamic militants, who continued to operate unabatedly, despite the apparent ban on their activities. Though the changes in the military hierarchy had placed General Musharraf firmly in the driving seat, his position still appeared quite tenuous as he faced a strong challenge from the country's powerful Islamic groups who were out on the streets violently protesting against his pro-US policy. This was problematic for Musharraf, as these groups had significant influence among the rank and file of the army. Musharraf hoped for a quick end to the war, but his standing became more precarious when civilian casualties from the American air raids rose. The reaction from the extremist religious parties was swift and deadly. Thousands of people took to the streets in the western city of

Quetta, close to the Afghan border, destroying and looting banks and torching UNICEF offices. The army was called out in Islamabad, the capital, and other cities to control violent demonstrations.

Armed with anything from locally made rifles to machine guns, thousands of Pakistani tribesmen streamed into Afghanistan in response to the Taliban's call for jihad. In the last week of October 2001, Sufi Mohammed, a radical Islamic cleric, crossed the border with 10,000 volunteers, including madrasa students, to fight against US-led coalition forces. Pakistani forces turned a blind eye to the hordes of volunteers crossing the border. 'They should go to Afghanistan rather than disrupting civil life here,' declared an Interior Ministry spokesman. More than 5,000 Pakistani jihadists died fighting for the Taliban. Thousands of others were taken prisoner by various Afghan warlords.

LEGAL AND CONSTITUTIONAL CCONTROL OF THE INTELLIGENCE AGENCIES IN PAKISTAN

Two legal channels are supposed to control intelligence agencies in Pakistan:

- The first is the constitution. The superior court hearing a matter must determine whether the power exercised by the agencies is within or beyond their sphere of authorization. A constitutional intervention by the superior court for redress against an intelligence agency would generally occur if the grievance is based on the grounds of excess or abuse of authority.
- The second channel is provided by statutory remedies. The statutory remedies can be ordinary judicial review by processes in existing code (related, for example, to law enforcement) or legislation that creates a special law enforcement force along with investigation-gathering machinery, which automatically includes an appellate process to the superior courts.

Note that intelligence agencies in Pakistan do not have any specific authority granting them extraordinary powers. They operate under the executive powers of the federal government. Intelligence agencies are supposed to work within the general ambit of the federal government's executive powers, contained in Article 90 of the constitution.

Moreover, neither the constitution of Pakistan nor any specific laws provide exemptions or exceptional jurisdiction to the intelligence agencies to undertake any unlawful action against the people present on Pakistan's territory. All agencies remain under the jurisdiction of regular courts and the general law of the land. In theory at least, the state cannot, even during an emergency, make laws contrary to the fundamental rights of the people as defined by

Article 4 of the constitution, which states that enjoying the protection of the law is the inalienable right of every citizen of Pakistan. It is reinforced by Article 8, which states that laws inconsistent with, or in derogation of fundamental rights, are null and void. No law that benefits intelligence work can infringe on the constitutional rights of citizens of Pakistan. The armed forces and law enforcement personnel more generally cannot be prosecuted for something that is in their domain of service.

The constitution, however, states that the passage of federal laws can be a concern of the IB. In contrast, legislation regarding the MI and ISI, which are entirely controlled by the military, is indirect. Both institutions can be affected only by laws related to defense or security and only through the decisions of the General Headquarters or the federal Interior Ministry. Similarly, the IB, being a civilian institution, is fully and directly accountable to the constitutional controls by the court. The MI and ISI are not directly accountable. Their respective apex ministries are.

Nevertheless, as government activities, intelligence agency activities must respect the law of the land. In practice, the Supreme Court has the power to make an order if it is convinced that a question of public importance with reference to the enforcement of fundamental constitutional rights is involved. Such cases can be initiated by nongovernmental organizations concerned with human rights, as occurred in the missing-persons case contested by the Human Rights Commission of Pakistan.

The missing-persons case and limits of judicial control over the intelligence agencies. In practice, the capacity of the Supreme Court to exercise the full extent of its powers is extremely limited when it comes to Pakistan's intelligence agencies. According to the Pakistani press, the kidnapping and detention of individual citizens without charges is not a new phenomenon in Pakistan; it has been practiced on an unprecedented scale in recent years.

During 2006 there were hundreds of newspaper reports of "disappearances" and dozens of accounts of nationalist leaders and activists going missing, particularly in Sindh and Balochistan. The trend continued in 2007. Many of these cases have been registered by the Human Rights Commission of Pakistan, but others are not reported. People released after illegal detention are threatened by the intelligence agencies if they discuss their abduction.

It is, moreover, important to note that the cases under consideration here all have taken place outside of any Pakistani legal framework. The term "enforced disappearance" is used to describe a practice "which implies any form of deprivation of liberty committed by agents of the State, or by anyone acting with the State's authorization, support or acquiescence, followed by a refusal to acknowledge the deprivation of liberty or the concealment of the fate or whereabouts of the person deprived of liberty, which places such a person outside the protection of the law." Since 1974, Pakistan has enacted a number of antiterrorist laws, the last one being the 1997 Anti-Terrorism Act. Their provisions have often been debated on the basis of their impact on human rights. According to the constitution, however, "No person who is arrested shall be detained in custody without being informed, as soon as may be, of the grounds for such arrest, nor shall he be denied the right to consult and be defended by a legal practitioner of his choice."

Examination of available files shows that five categories of people have been detained by the intelligence agencies: journalists, Balochi nationalists, dissidents from Sindh, suspected terrorists, and people with whom the agencies intended to settle scores.

The illegality of the abductions was raised by the political parties long before the chief justice tried to address the issue. In August 2006, the PPP denounced as a national disgrace the "increasing number of citizens of the state [who] not only vanish without a trace but [whose disappearances] are greeted with deafening silence by the agencies." According to the PPP, some 800 people had disappeared during the previous five years without any legal process being followed. Organizations differed on figures; Balochi nationalist parties claim that the number of disappearances was between 3,000 and 4,000. The exact number has, in fact, never been established with certainty. But the opposition kept reiterating the demands for release in the following months.

Cases were also regularly filed in the provincial high courts but without result. Orders of the courts could be effective only with the cooperation of the agencies. In the missing-persons cases, the agencies would simply deny both the kidnapping and any knowledge of the whereabouts of the disappeared. Having no independent means of inquiry, the judges had to content themselves with the answers of the agencies.

In October 2006, the Supreme Court directed the Ministry of Interior and the attorney general of Pakistan to inform the families of the missing persons about their whereabouts and submit a report to the court in the second week of November. Out of forty-one persons who had gone missing, the government declared it had traced nine of them. Cases continued to pile up in the Supreme Court, which kept ordering that reports be submitted to it on the missing persons. The Pakistani press kept reporting about new cases, and human rights organizations kept protesting. From time to time, the agencies discovered the whereabouts of some missing persons—enough to give credibility to their claims that they had nothing to do with the other disappearances. The crisis of the judiciary inevitably gave a new dimension to the issue. Tensions increased, as did the activism of the Supreme Court. In April 2007, the Supreme Court announced that it would prepare policy guidelines to monitor the role of the intelligence agencies until Parliament legislated on the issue. In June, the court ordered the government to formulate a policy to regulate the functions of intelligence agencies under the law and constitution. In August, it warned the director general of the Federal Investigation Agency, Tareq Pervez, that the agency had to produce the missing persons or go to jail. In October, Chief Justice Iftikhar Muhammad Chaudhry threatened to summon the heads of all intelligence agencies, but he allowed them to regularize the disappearance of the missing persons a few days later, reiterating, however, that the Supreme Court had substantial evidence that those missing were in the custody of the intelligence agencies. The hope of recovering the missing persons disappeared with the imposition of the state of emergency. After the chief justice was dismissed and placed under house arrest, all action stopped. After the February 18, 2008, elections, some of the searches resumed, but no significant results had emerged by the end of 2008.

The illegality of the cases was paradoxically proven a posteriori. In November 2007, against the backdrop of the activism shown by the Supreme Court and following the imposition of the state of emergency, the government passed the Pakistan Army (Amendment) Ordinance 2007. The ordinance, among other provisions, empowered the agencies to detain civilians without pressing any charges and to keep the detainees in custody for an indefinite period. The text was made retroactive to 2003 to cover the cases of the previous years.

In late December 2007, in an apparent attempt to avoid acknowledging the existence of an elaborate secret detention system, the government freed nearly a hundred men suspected of links to terrorism. The "disappeared" had in fact been held in military or intelligence agency cells around the country without being charged, an accusation the government denied.

Only a few from the list of missing persons reappeared. The intelligence agencies knew from the very beginning that without their cooperation with the legal system no traces of the missing would be found and no order of the court could be implemented. The chief justice could ultimately do no more than raise his voice and make a public noise about the missing persons.

Past attempts at controlling the intelligence agencies in Pakistan. Civilian attempts and failures to control the ISI invite the conclusion that no one controls the agencies—they are rogues. This is incorrect. Someone gives orders. Always a practical issue, the problem became public in Pakistan on the occasion of the "Mehran scandal." Having declared that the ISI had always supported political parties, General Aslam Beg went on to say that the so-called political wing of the ISI had been created by Zulfikar Ali Bhutto and that the ISI had become completely free from the army in 1988, being solely under the control of the chief executive. Beg was trying to hold the civilians responsible for the scandal by declaring that as COAS he had merely seen that the money from the Mehran Bank received by the ISI had been used properly. With this declaration, however, he contradicted his claim of civilian control.

General Beg's statement raises a series of questions, all directly or indirectly related to the control of the agency, and all were being asked in the Pakistani press during the Supreme Court hearings. Secret service funds are part of the public exchequer and are provided for a specific purpose. They are theoretically subject to close scrutiny and audits. The director general of the ISI enjoys great discretion in the use of these funds but remains liable to account for every transaction. There are no regulations under which an official can accept a private "donation" for deposit in a secret service account. Who then had authorized a public banker to "donate" public money to a state agency? General Beg's response implied that the civilian chief executive had done so, but then the question was put to General Beg of why the director general of the ISI had to inform the army chief of the transaction as well as of the subsequent use of the money.

The question of the control of the intelligence agencies was also raised in 2006 when six petitions were filed in the Sindh High Court against the illegal detention of political activists by the MI and ISI. The representative of the Ministry of Defence informed the court that the Ministry of Defence had only operational, not administrative control, over the MI and ISI. This does not mean that the intelligence agencies are under no control. As observed by a former brigadier:

[T]he Director-General ISI, being a serving General officer, depends on the Military Secretary Branch at the GHQ for his posting, transfer and promotion—everything that has anything to do with his service career. To that extent—and what would be more important than this single factor for the individual concerned—the DG ISI must stay in the shadow of the army chief even if not under his direct command.

The ISI's occasional noncompliance with the civilian leadership's instructions reflects the possibility of conflicting loyalties, but most of the time the service is dedicated to the military. This argument does not exclude the presence of rogue individuals in the system, responsible for occasional mischief outside state control, but it does not make the organization itself a "loose cannon." As a matter of fact, the conflict of loyalty always disappears as soon as the military takes over. The ISI therefore cannot be considered an organization distinct from the military, with a political project of its own. Musharraf himself has dismissed speculation that the ISI might be a "government within the government." ISI operations are part of a larger design, of which the ISI is only an executor. This statement also partly refutes the too-common perception that the ISI is an autonomous rogue institution, as it is sometimes described by the press.

Historically, efforts have been made to limit the powers of the intelligence agencies and bring the ISI in particular under control. Fragile democratic institutions and weak political traditions have been unable to prevent the intelligence agencies from playing an extraconstitutional role. All attempts to monitor the intelligence agencies have failed, leading to the reinforcement of military control over the intelligence apparatus. Civilian leaders have nevertheless tried; they have used essentially two options: naming loyal individuals at the head of the ISI and civilian intelligence agencies and playing on the rivalry among the agencies.

M. K. Junejo, the prime minister chosen by Zia ul-Haq, intended to contain the ISI's influence in order to negotiate a political settlement of the Afghan conflict through the then-ongoing UN-led indirect talks in Geneva. During their "co-habitation" at the head of state, Zia had the ISI spy on Junejo while Junejo had the IB reporting on Zia. Junejo tried to cleanse the IB of army officers. He also tried to replace General Akhtar Abdul Rahman with a more loyal general at the head of the ISI, but he was outmaneuvered by Zia, who imposed Hamid Gul. The first instance took place during Benazir Bhutto's first tenure as prime minister. It has been written that Shahnawaz Bhutto, son of Zulfikar and brother of Benazir, was poisoned by the ISI in 1985 to intimidate his sister and prevent her from returning to Pakistan, which she did in 1986. She returned, however, willing to rein in the activities of an organization that, according to a commission she appointed to look into its activities, "had all the makings of a de facto government."

Benazir Bhutto's ambition was to reduce the power of the ISI and reorganize the intelligence community and enhance the power of the IB. To do so, she decided to no longer appoint a lieutenant general recommended by the COAS as director general, and she chose Major General Shamsur Rahman Kallue, a retired officer who had been close to her father, to replace Lieutenant General Hamid Gul. She entrusted him with the task of winding up the internal collection role of the ISI and civilianizing both the ISI and the IB. Moreover, she tried to introduce an element of competition between the various intelligence agencies by appointing her own loyalists to the Federal Investigation Agency and the IB. Not only did ISI officials refuse to deal with the newly appointed director general, but Benazir's move also resulted in a reduction of ISI power in contradiction to the intended outcome. General Aslam Beg, then COAS, responded by isolating the ISI, whose director general was no longer invited to the corps commanders' conferences. Covert operations in Jammu and Kashmir as well as in Punjab were transferred to the MI Directorate and placed under the responsibility of the chief of general staff. A number of political assignments, including political surveillance, contacts with politicians, and "developing a strategy to deal with a government with which the Army became increasingly estranged," were also transferred to the MI.

During her second term (1993–1996), Benazir Bhutto also tried to diminish the powers of the ISI by transferring the responsibility for clandestine operations to the Ministry of Interior, then controlled by a Bhutto loyalist, General Nasrullah Babar, himself an ISI officer during her father's tenure. Benazir was careful, however, not to antagonize the army by pairing Lieutenant General Pervez Musharraf, then the director general of military operations, with Major General Babar in the handling of Afghan operations.

Benazir Bhutto's main political rival, Nawaz Sharif, was not more successful in dealing with the ISI. During his first tenure (1990–1993), he too tried to oppose the COAS, Lieutenant General Asif Nawaz Janjua, by appointing Lieutenant General Javed Nasir as director general of the ISI against the recommendation of Janjua. Nasir in turn was ostracized by the COAS and not invited to the corps commanders' conferences.

During his second tenure (1997–1999), Nawaz Sharif appointed Lieutenant General Ziauddin to be director general of the ISI, against the recommendations of COAS Pervez Musharraf. Like Aslam Beg in the past, Musharraf stopped inviting the director general of the ISI to the corps commanders' conferences. More important, however, he transferred the responsibility for covert operations to the Directorate General of Military Intelligence, then led by Lieutenant General Aziz. The director general of the ISI thus was not part of the planning and implementation of the Kargil operations. The conflict over the control of the intelligence agencies soon led to contradictions in the conduct of the Afghan operations.

All civilian efforts to control the ISI have failed. Except in one instance, however, the resistance seems to have come much less from the organization itself than from the army leadership. Although the director general of the ISI is constitutionally bound to report to the prime minister, the link to the COAS always prevails. When tempted to distance himself from the military institution, the ISI director general is immediately ostracized by the military and his power reduced in favor of the more compliant Directorate of Military Intelligence. The ISI is also immediately marginalized if it shows any loyalty to the elected prime minister. It is interesting that the competition between the various intelligence agencies, in particular the MI and ISI, has never played in favor of the civilians. It has always been the instrument through which the military itself has reasserted its control over the intelligence establishment.

The military has not been purely reactive in this process. According to Hasan-Askari Rizvi, in 1996–1997 the army authorities managed to persuade the caretaker government to induct more army personnel into the IB, giving the MI a greater role in it. The military intelligence establishment has also managed over time to inject many of its officers into civilian intelligence and police institutions. For example, Pervez Musharraf appointed a general, Ejaz Shah, as head of the IB. In addition, under Musharraf, the NAB became a favorite political instrument and was used extensively to charge civilian politicians with corruption. The NAB was, however, underfunded. General Mahmood, then director general of the ISI, proposed to give it funds in exchange for the recruitment of dozens of retired ISI officers, who were thus brought into NAB. Temptations to counterbalance ISI power were forgotten by successive prime ministers. Even Zafarullah Jamali, who, despite his own political weakness, showed some semblance of independence, took great care to name a former ISI officer acceptable to Musharraf as head of the main civilian intelligence agency, the IB.

MILITARY GOVERNMENT

In light of such dissent and with secession being voiced in different regions of the country (notably in East Pakistan and the North-West Frontier Province), on Oct. 7, 1958, Mirza proclaimed the 1956 constitution abrogated, closed the national and provincial assemblies, and banned all political party activity.

He declared that the country was under martial law and that Gen. Mohammad Ayub Khan had been made chief martial-law administrator.

Mirza claimed that it was his intention to lift martial law as soon as possible and that a new constitution would be drafted; and on October 27 he swore in a new cabinet, naming Ayub Khan prime minister, while three lieutenant generals were given ministerial posts. The eight civilian members in the cabinet included businessmen and lawyers, one being a young newcomer, Zulfikar Ali Bhutto, a powerful landlord from Sind province.

However, Ayub Khan viewed his being named prime minister as the president's attempt to end his military career and ultimately to force him into oblivion. Clearly, the country could not afford two paramount rulers at the same time. Therefore, if one had to go, Ayub Khan decided that it should be

Mirza. On the evening of October 27, Ayub Khan's senior generals presented Mirza with an ultimatum of facing permanent exile or prosecution by a military tribunal. Mirza immediately left for London, never again to return to Pakistan. Soon thereafter, Ayub Khan, who now assumed the rank of field marshal, proclaimed his assumption of the presidency.

Martial law lasted 44 months. During that time, a number of army officers took over vital civil service posts. Many politicians were excluded from public life under an Electoral Bodies (Disqualification) Order; a similar purge took place among civil servants.

Yet, Ayub Khan argued that Pakistan was not yet ready for a full-blown experiment in parliamentary democracy and that the country required a period of tutelage and honest government before a new constitutional system could be established. He therefore initiated a plan for "basic democracies," consisting of rural and urban councils directly elected by the people that would be concerned with local governance and would assist in programs of grassroots development.

Elections took place in January 1960, and the Basic Democrats, as they became known, were at once asked to endorse and thus legitimate Ayub Khan's presidency. Of the 80,000 Basic Democrats, 75,283 affirmed their support. Basic democracies was a tiered system inextricably linked to the bureaucracy, and the Basic Democrats occupied the lowest rung of a ladder that was connected to the country's administrative subdistricts (*tehsils*, or *tahsils*), districts, and divisions.

It was soon clear that the real power in the system resided in the bureaucrats who had dominated decision making since colonial times. Nevertheless, the basic democracies system was linked to a public-works program that was sponsored by the United States. The combined effort was meant to confer responsibility for village and municipal development to the local population. Self-reliance was the watchword of the overall program, and Ayub Khan and his advisers, as well as important donor countries, believed the arrangement would provide material benefits and possibly even expose people to self-governing experiences.

Ayub Khan also established a constitutional commission to advise on a form of government more appropriate to the country's political culture, and his regime introduced a number of reforms.

Not the least of these was the Muslim Family Laws Ordinance of 1961, which restricted polygamy and provided more rights and protection for women.

He also authorized the development of family-planning programs that were aimed at tackling the dilemma of Pakistan's growing population. Such actions angered the more conservative and religiously disposed members of society, who also swelled the ranks of the opposition. Under pressure to make amends and to placate the guardians of Islamic tradition, the family-planning program was eventually scrapped.

An important feature of the Ayub Khan regime was the quickening pace of economic growth. During the initial phase of independence, the annual growth rate was less than 3 percent, and that was scarcely ahead of the rate of population growth. Just prior to the military coup, the rate of growth was even smaller.

During the Ayub Khan era—with assistance from external sources, notably the United States—the country accelerated economic growth, and by 1965 it had advanced to more than 6 percent per annum.

Development was particularly vigorous in the manufacturing sector, but considerable attention was also given to agriculture. U.S. assistance was especially prominent in combating water logging and salinity problems that resulted from irrigation in the more vital growing zones. Moreover, plans were implemented that launched the "green revolution" in Pakistan, and new hybrid wheat and rice varieties were introduced with the goal of increasing yields.

Despite positive economic developments, overall, most investment was directed toward West Pakistan, and the divisions between East and West grew during this period. Ayub Khan attempted to answer Bengali fears of becoming second-class citizens when—after work was begun, at his order, on building a new Pakistan capital at Islamabad—he declared it was his intention to build a second, or legislative, capital near Dhaka, in East Pakistan.

However, the start of construction on the new second capital did not placate the Bengalis, who were angered by Ayub Khan's abrogation of the 1956 constitution, his failure to hold national elections, and the decision to sustain martial law.

East Pakistanis had many grievances, and in no instance did they genuinely believe their purposes and concerns could be served under Ayub Khan's military government.

Subsequent developments only served to enforce these beliefs. Water rights agreements signed with India and hydroelectric projects along the Indus River benefited the West, as did military agreements reached with the United States.

The Pakistani officer class was largely from West Pakistan, and all the key army and air installations were located there—even in the case of naval capability, Karachi was a far more formidable base of operations than Chittagong in East Pakistan.

In 1962 Ayub Khan promulgated another constitution. Presidential rather than parliamentary in focus, it was based on an indirectly elected president and a reinforced centralized political system that emphasized the country's viceregal tradition.

Although Ayub anticipated launching the new political system without political parties, once the National Assembly was convened and martial law was lifted, it was apparent that political parties would be reactivated. Ayub therefore formed his own party, the Convention Muslim League, but the country's political life and its troubles were little different from the days before martial law.

Ayub Khan won another formal term as president of Pakistan in January 1965, albeit in an election in which only the Basic Democrats cast ballots. Opposed by Fatima Jinnah, the sister of Mohammed Ali Jinnah, who ran on a Combined Opposition Parties ticket, the contest was closer than expected.

During the election campaign, Zulfikar Ali Bhutto—who as foreign minister was supposedly a loyal member of the Ayub Khan cabinet—promised in a public address that the conflict over Kashmir would be resolved during Ayub Khan's presidency.

Bhutto indicated that Kashmir would be released from Indian occupation by negotiation or, if that failed, by armed force, but there was little indication that Ayub Khan had sanctioned Bhutto's pronouncement. Nevertheless, the foreign minister's speech appeared to be both solace to the pro-Kashmiri interests in West Pakistan and a green light to the Pakistan army to begin making plans for a campaign in the disputed region.

A new war over Kashmir was not long in coming. Skirmishes between Indian and Pakistani forces on the line of control between the two administrated portions of the region increased in the summer of 1965, and by September major hostilities had erupted between the two neighbours.

Indian strategy confounded Pakistani plans, as New Delhi ordered its forces to strike all along the border between India and West Pakistan and to launch air raids against East Pakistan and even threaten to invade the East.

Pakistan's military stores soon were exhausted, a situation made worse by an American-imposed arms embargo on both states that affected Pakistan much more than India. Ayub Khan had to consider halting the hostilities.

Ultimately, Ayub Khan was forced to accept a United Nations-sponsored cease-fire and to give up Pakistan's quest for resolving the Kashmir problem by force of arms. Embarrassed and humiliated, Ayub Khan saw all his efforts at building a new Pakistan dashed in one failed venture, and he was compelled to attend a peace conference with the Indian prime minister, Lal Bahadur Shastri, in Tashkent, in Soviet Uzbekistan.

There the two leaders were unable to reach a satisfactory agreement of their own making, and their hosts compelled them to sign a draft prepared for them.

At that juncture, Bhutto, who had accompanied Ayub Khan to the conference, indicated a desire to separate himself from his mentor.

Ayub Khan's popularity had reached its lowest level, and, in the Pakistani game of zero-sum politics, Bhutto anticipated gaining what the president had lost. Pressed by Ayub Khan, Bhutto held up his resignation, but soon thereafter he broke with the president, joined his voice to the opposition, and in due course organized his own political party, the Pakistan People's Party (PPP).

Ayub Khan was never the same after signing the Tashkent Agreement. Confronted by rising opposition that was now led by Bhutto in West Pakistan and Mujibur Rahman in East Pakistan, Ayub Khan struck back by arresting both men.

Acknowledging that he could not manage the country without a modicum of cooperation from the politicians, Ayub Khan summoned a conference of opposition leaders and withdrew the state of emergency under which Pakistan had been governed since 1965.

These concessions, however, failed to conciliate the opposition, and in February 1969 Ayub announced that he would not contest the presidential election scheduled for 1970. In the meantime, protests mounted in the streets, and strikes paralyzed the economy. Sparked by grievances that could not be contained, especially in East Pakistan, the disorder spread to the western province, and all attempts to restore tranquility proved futile. One theme sustained the demonstrators: Ayub Khan had remained in power too long, and it was time for him to go.

In March 1969, Ayub Khan announced his retirement and named Gen. Agha Mohammad Yahya Khan to succeed him as president. Once again the country was placed under martial law. Yahya Khan, like Ayub Khan before him, assumed the role of chief martial-law administrator.

In accepting the responsibility for leading the country, Yahya Khan said he would govern Pakistan only until the national election in 1970. Yahya Khan abolished Ayub Khan's basic democracies system and abrogated the 1962 constitution. He also issued aLegal Framework Order (LFO) that broke up the single unit of West Pakistan and reconstituted the original four provinces of Pakistan—i.e., Punjab, Sind, North-West Frontier Province, and Balochistan.

The 1970 election therefore was not only meant to restore parliamentary government to the country, it was also intended to reestablish the provincial political systems. The major dilemma in the LFO, however, was that in breaking up the one-unit system, the distribution of seats in the National Assembly would be apportioned among the provinces on the basis of population. This meant that East Pakistan, with its larger population, would be allotted more seats than all the provinces of West Pakistan combined.

PAKISTAN'S MILITARY ORGANIZATIONS

The first Pakistani jihadist group emerged in 1980 when thousands of volunteers, mainly students from religious seminaries, joined the anti-Soviet resistance in Afghanistan.

By 2002, Pakistan had become home to 24 militant groups. Highly disciplined paramilitary organizations operated in every neighbourhood, pursuing their own internal and external agenda. The largest among them were LeT, JeM, Harakat-ul-Mujahideen (HuM) and Harkat-al-Jihad-al-Islami (HJI). All these paramilitary groups, originally from the same source, had similar motivations and goals, and recruited from the same kind of people (often unemployed youth from Punjab and the North West Frontier Province). The only difference was in patronage: HuM and HJI were both strongly linked with the Taliban, whilst LeT had strong links with Wahabi groups in Saudi Arabia.

These militant organizations were not clandestine nor had they sprouted surreptitiously. Their growth, if not actually sponsored, had certainly been looked upon with favour by the state.

Their activities were not secret, and found expression in graffiti, wall posters and pamphlets all over the country, inviting Muslims to join forces with them. They also carried addresses and telephone numbers to contact for training. 'Jihad is the shortest route to paradise,' declared one of the many exhortations.

'A martyr ensures salvation for the entire family.' Every jihadist organization had funds to help families of 'martyrs'. Although money was not the primary motivation of jihadists, it was essential to sustain the culture of jihad.

The state's patronage helped the jihadists to raise funds at public places. The militant groups had developed a powerful propaganda machinery. Their publications had gained a large readership and their messages were also available on video and audiotapes.

During the 1980s and 1990s, the objective of jihadist movements in Pakistan was not, like that of Arab Salafists such as bin Laden, the establishment of a global Islamic caliphate. Their objectives were more in line with the regional strategy of the Pakistani military establishment: the liberation of Kashmir from India and the installation of a Pashtun Islamist government in Afghanistan. Almost all the Islamic militant groups served as instruments of Pakistan's regional policy. The army needed them as much as they needed the army. After 9/11, Pakistan's support for the American-led war on terror pitted it against its former clients.

The Wahabi-inspired LeT, the most radical face of jihad in Pakistan, was also more amenable to the ISI than any other militant outfits. After the 2002 ban, it reduced its public visibility. Instead of challenging Musharraf's military led government, it agreed to work within new parameters and restrict its activities to a 'controlled jihad' in Kashmir while keeping a low profile inside Pakistan.

However, this tactical truce was a strained one. Islamist groups, even government-friendly ones like LeT, were becoming radicalized by the ideological currents of the region. Increasingly, their ambitions exceeded the goals of the ISI. Even in 2000, the founder of LeT, Hafiz Mohammed Saeed told me that he saw the struggle in Kashmir as 'the gateway to the liberation of Indian Muslims'.

He went on: 'We believe in a clash of civilizations and our jihad will continue until Islam becomes the dominant religion.' A former university professor, Hafiz Saeed is not a charismatic man; he comes across as shy and self-effacing, not the ingredients that militant leaders are generally made of.

Short and chubby, his long beard dyed with henna, when I met him in January 2001 he was always surrounded by his young followers. For him, killing infidels and destroying the forces of 'evil and disbelief is the obligation of every pious Muslim'.

The horrors of the partition of India in 1947, which uprooted his family from their home in Simla, left a huge imprint on Hafiz Saeed's personality. Millions of people were massacred in the communal violence that followed the creation of the new Muslim state. Thirty-six members of his family were killed while migrating to Pakistan. There his family settled in the central Punjab district of Sargodha. Farm land allotted by the government, and hard work, brought prosperity to the family.

Hafiz Saeed's parents were very religious. His mother taught the Qur'an to her seven sons. Five of them were still alive.

Hafiz Saeed received his primary education in the village. After graduating from the University of Punjab he joined the King Abdul Aziz Islamic University in Riyadh where he also taught for many years.

During his stay in Saudi Arabia he developed close links with Wahabi clerics. After returning to Pakistan, Hafiz Saeed took up a teaching job at the Department of Islamic Studies at the Lahore University of Engineering and Technology. His two brothers lived in America. One was head of an Islamic centre and the other pursued an academic career. Hafiz Saeed himself had never travelled to the USA or any other western country. In the early 1980s, Hafiz Saeed joined the mujahidin war in Afghanistan which also brought him into close contact with Abdullah Azzam and Osama bin Laden. Their 'dedication to jihad' inspired him immensely.

'Osama was a man of extraordinary qualities,' he recalled. Azzam, a Palestinian who had worked as a professor of Islamic jurisprudence at the University of Jordan in Amman had a huge influence on Hafiz Saeed.

The Palestinian scholar arrived in Pakistan soon after the invasion of Afghanistan by Soviet forces and took up a teaching position at the Islamic University of Islamabad. But his stint was short.

He shifted to Peshawar and emerged as the main jihadist ideologue. With Saudi finance he recruited volunteers for the Afghan jihad from all over the Arab world. He was assassinated in a bomb attack in Peshawar in 1989.

Azzam helped Hafiz Saeed establish Markaz Dawal al-Irshad (MDI), an organization for Islamic preaching and guidance which was ideologically affiliated with Wahabi Ahle Hadith. In the tradition of the reformist Sunni movements, the MDI sought to purify society and Islam of 'outside influences'. Its sprawling headquarters in Muridke on the outskirts of Lahore housed a university, a farm, a clothing factory and a carpentry workshop. The objective was to create a model Islamic environment removed from any state interference. In 1994, the movement set up a network of schools across the country with the objectives of promoting the Wahabi version of Islam and preparing the students for jihad. The MDI observed a strict educational philosophy that was directed towards developing a jihadist culture and to produce a reformed individual, who would be well versed not only in Islamic moral principles, but also in science and technology.

The teaching was aimed at producing an alternative model of governance and development. These schools, located in the poorer urban and rural neighbourhoods, attracted children of families who could not afford a better education. The organization encouraged its supporters to have large families, so that more volunteers were available for jihad. Hafiz Saeed founded LeT in 1990, soon after the withdrawal of Soviet forces from Afghanistan, as a military wing of the MDI to wage jihad against the Indian authorities in Kashmir. The LeT announced its arrival on the Kashmir jihad scene on 5 February 1993 with a ferocious attack on an Indian military force in Poonch district that killed at least two soldiers.

Two of the guerrillas were also killed. Since then the outfit has been responsible for hundreds of guerrilla raids in the disputed territory. Within a short span, LeT emerged as the fiercest militant organization – it possessed not only thousands of well trained and highly motivated fighters, but also a huge propaganda network. Its several publications in different languages had a circulation of hundreds of thousands. Its main publication, Al-Dawat, had more than 80,000 copies printed and sold at major bookshops across the country..

LeT had worked in close coordination with the ISI, which also provided support to launch the militants across the border. LeT was an extremely secretive organization. Except for the top leadership, the identity of its members was not disclosed. Since its inception in 1990, it has produced thousands of highly trained fighters, who have given a new dimension to the guerrilla war in Kashmir. The earliest fighters were trained in various camps in Afghanistan. But after 1992 the camps were shifted to remote regions of Azad Kashmir (Free Kashmir) and the mountainous tribal regions of the North West Frontier Province close to the border with Afghanistan.

The procedure was simple. Any jihadist aspirant could enroll himself for training at one of hundreds of LeT centres operating openly across the country. The volunteers, most of them in their teens, were then taken to various camps for military training, conducted in two stages.

At the initial level they were given basic weapons training for three weeks. The second stage of rigorous guerrilla training was restricted to those who were fully committed to jihad and were practising Muslims. At the camp, volunteers began their day with the call to morning prayers.

They were then kept busy in gruelling physical and military exercise until dusk. Part of the training, included religious instruction, Qur'anic lessons and adherence to prayers. The trainees learned to transform their lives in line with the teaching of Islam. To be in the ranks of the 'soldiers of Allah', growing a beard was mandatory, shalwar (loose trousers) had to be hiked above the ankle, and watching television and listening to music were banned. Individualism was curbed, beginning with the sharing of food and drinks from the same utensils.

After the initial training, the would-be mujahid was sent back, usually to his home town, and kept under observation by senior LeT officials for a couple of months. His conduct was closely watched as he performed routine organizational duties. He was supposed to collect funds, organize propaganda meetings and practise the preaching of Islam in his home and neighbourhood. Only a select number of volunteers were chosen for the extended programme. They returned home completely transformed after the course. They kept their hair long and stopped cutting their beards. They were identified by new names, mostly the surnames of companions of the Prophet Mohammed or of the earliest Islamic heroes. Between 10,000 and 30,000 young men were trained at LeT camps.

Combat Operations

The extended training, however, did not ensure that a volunteer would be sent for combat operations. Thousands of trained guerrillas anxiously awaited their turn to cross into Kashmir, but not everyone was given the chance. 'I pray to Allah that my turn [to go to Kashmir] comes soon, 'said Abu Mohammed, a young college student who had already completed the second level training. Hafiz Saeed often said that he would not put a weapon in the hands of any young recruit who was not secure in his faith. To be a combatant one had to be a pious person.

LeT, unlike some of the other jihadist groups, drew its recruits from universities and colleges as well as from among unemployed youth. The traditional Islamic madrasas provided only ten per cent of the volunteers. Influenced by radical Islamic literature, many university and college students joined the group. 'Those coming from educational institutions are much more motivated and conscious of what they are doing,' said Naveed Qamar, an LeT activist and graduate of the University of Engineering and Technology, Lahore. The top leadership of the group, including Hafiz Saeed, had been on the faculty of that university. A large number of LeT activists also came from the working class or were school drop-outs. In the countryside, LeT recruits were largely from families which were influenced by Wahabi Islam.

The majority of LeT recruits came from Punjab, particularly from Lahore, Gujranwala and Multan where Ahle Hadith had its strongholds. In some central Punjab district villages LeT had considerable influence because of support for the Kashmir jihad. Gondlawala, a small dusty village, is now called Pind Shaheedan (the village of martyrs) because at least one person from every family had fought or died in the Kashmir jihad, mainly as an LeT fighter. The group's increasing influence was indicated by the fact that the villagers would accept its arbitration in local and even in domestic disputes.

In recent years, LeT had started attracting an increasing number of volunteers from Pakistan's southern provinces of Sindh and Balochistan where Wahabi influence had increased. Muslims from other countries, including Britain, had also joined LeT. Shamshur Rehman, an Afghan, was the chief commander of LeT when he was killed in Badgam district in Kashmir in May 1995 in an encounter with Indian security forces. Several foreign militants were believed to have received training at LeT camps in Pakistan. Among them were Guantanamo Bay inmates David Hicks and French terrorist suspect Willie Brigitte, who were accused of planning attacks in Australia. LeT gave a new and more violent dimension to the Kashmiri struggle by launching Fidayin raids against Indian forces and military installations. The term 'Fidayin attack' was used by the LeT leadership for target operations well inside the

Indian military bases. 'A Fidayin is one who must complete his mission even in the worst circumstances,' explained Abdullah Muntazir, an LeT spokesman. He insisted that the concept of Fidayin was different from that of a suicide bomber, who blew himself up to kill others. 'We consider suicide attacks un-Islamic. Many Fidayin come back alive after completion of their missions,' said Muntazir. The Fidayin attacks had brought an unprecedented ferocity to the Kashmir jihad.

A Fidayin is chosen from among the best and most courageous fighters and not every guerrilla meets the tough criteria. An otherworldly level of devotion to the cause is required, as I discovered when I met a Fidayin recently returned from his mission. His thin frame, gentle eyes and polite manners gave not the slightest indication of his being a guerrilla fighter.

The young bearded militant, who used the nom de guerre of Abu Ukrema, had just returned from Kashmir when I met him at the LeT headquarters in Lahore in January 2001. Abu Ukrema walked with a limp because of a bullet wound, received during an encounter with the Indian troops. 'I will return to the fighting as soon as the bullet is removed and the wounds are healed,' he told me. 'It is my desire to become a martyr.' His face lit up as he narrated how he and his fellow guerrillas had destroyed an Indian army post after a fierce gun battle which lasted several hours and left many soldiers dead.

CIVILIAN "DEMOCRACY" VS MILITARY "DICTATORSHIP" DEBATE IN PAKISTAN

Asian Tigers became Asian Tigers under dictators before they became democratic. There is not a single example of a developing country that became a developed country under democratic rule since WW II. Development gap between China, a one-party state, and India, a multi-party democracy, is huge and growing. Developed countries in Europe and North America took centuries to develop under democratic systems. Asian Tigers did it much faster under dictators. China is doing so now. Asia's experience has shown that democratic processes act as speed breakers to slow pace of development and stymie efforts to reduce poverty, ignorance and disease to deliver higher living standards. Let's examine these statements and see how they apply to Pakistan.

Asian Tigers

Taiwan, Singapore and South Korea experienced a dramatic rise under authoritarian regimes from 1960s through 1990s. The dictators who led these states also showed the way to fellow Asian dictators in Indonesia, Malaysia, Thailand and China who also industrialized and prospered using the same formula that rejected the Washington Consensus of democracy and free markets as the basis for development of all nations.

1960s Pakistan

Pakistan was on a similar trajectory as the Asian Tigers during 1960s under Gen. Ayub Khan's rule. GDP growth in this decade jumped to an average annual rate of 6 percent from 3 percent in the 1950s, according to Pakistani economist Dr. Ishrat Husain. Dr. Husain says: *"The manufacturing sector expanded by 9 percent annually and various new industries were set up. Agriculture grew at a respectable rate of 4 percent with the introduction of Green Revolution technology. Governance improved with a major expansion in the government's capacity for policy analysis, design and implementation, as well as the far-reaching process of institution building.7 The Pakistani polity evolved from what political scientists called a "soft state" to a "developmental" one that had acquired the semblance of political legitimacy.*

Bangladesh

Some argue that it was Ayub Khan's rule in 1960s that resulted in the loss of Pakistan's eastern wing and the creation of Bangladesh. I strongly disagree with this view. I believe that ill-conceived general elections of 1970 gave the opportunity to Pakistani politicians to lie to mostly poor and illiterate electorate of the time to win their votes.

Shaikh Mujib exploited normal regional economic disparities that can be found in any country, including India and US, to argue that Bengalis were unfairly treated. Just look at the income data for various states in US or in India and you'll see huge gaps in incomes and standards of living.

Indian Punjab's per capita income of Rs. 88,783 is 1.4 times higher than West Bengal's Rs. 62,831. Bihar's per capita income of Rs. 28,317 is less than a quarter of Haryana's Rs. 122,660. New Jersey's per capita income of $53,628 is much higher than Mississippi's $33,073. In the end, Zulfikar Ali Bhutto refused to sit down and talk with Shaikh Mujib and forced the split. Here's how one of Bhutto's friends late Gov Salman Taseer offered his view in his book "Bhutto: A Political Biography"

"Blame can never be satisfactorily or finally apportioned to the major players in this grisly drama, but that Bhutto, Mujibur Rahman and Yahya Khan share responsibility there can be no doubt. Many, indeed, are inclined to the view that Bhutto, as the most sure-footed politician of the three and thus the best equipped to assess the consequences of his actions, must accept the lion's share of the blame. Argument on this point will remain one of the central themes of Pakistani politics, perhaps for decades." The fact is that economic gap between former East Pakistan and Pakistan has grown over the last 40 years, and the per capita income in Pakistan now stands at more than twice Bangladesh's in 2012 in nominal dollar terms, higher than 1.6X in 1971.

India

As China's share of the world's extreme poor (living below $1.25 per day per person level) has dramatically declined, India's share has significantly increased. India now contributes 33% (up from 22 % in 1981). While the extreme poor in Sub-Saharan Africa represented only 11 percent of the world's total in 1981, they now account for 34% of the world's extreme poor, and China comes next contributing 13 percent (down from 43 percent in 1981), according to the World Bank report titled State of the Poor.

The share of poverty in South Asia region excluding India has slightly increased from 7% in 1981 to 9% now, according to the report. India now has the world's largest share of the world's poor, hungry, illiterate and sick who still lack access to very basic sanitation.

In a recent book "Street Smarts", a hedge fund Manager Jim Rogers makes some important points to explain how East Asians have succeeded in rapidly developing while others have failed:

"Many Asians say that the Asian Way is first to open your economy, to bring prosperity to your country, and then, only after that, to open up your political system. They say that the reason the Russians failed is that did it the other way around. Russia opened up its political system in the absence of a sound economy, everybody bitched and complained, and chaos inevitably ensued. As an example of the Asian path to political openness, they point to South Korea and Taiwan, both of which were once vicious dictatorships supported by the United States. Japan was at one time a one-party state supported by the US military. Singapore achieved its current status under one-party, authoritarian rule. All these countries have since become more prosperous and more open.

Plato, in The Republic, says that the way societies evolve is by going from dictatorship to oligarchy to democracy to chaos and back to dictatorship. It has a certain logic, and Plato was a very smart guy. I do not know if the Asians ever read The Republic, but the Asian way seems to suggest that Plato knew whereof he spoke." Not only is the Asian model different from that of the Soviets, it stands China in marked contrast to those thirty-year dictatorships previously mentioned. Chinese leaders have put a high premium upon changing the country's economy, presumably to seek prosperity for the 1.3 people who live there."

"And yet,in 1947, when it achieved independence, India was one of the more successful countries in the world, a democratic country. But despite democracy, or maybe because of it, India has never lived up to its potential. China was a shambles as recently as 1980. India was far ahead of it. Bt since then China has left India, literally in the dust....As China rises, India continues to decline relatively. Its debt-to-GDP ratio is now 90 percent, making a strong growth rate virtually impossible."

Pakistan's Economic History

Since 1947, Pakistan has seen three periods of military rule: 1960s, 1980s and 2000s. In each of these decades, Pakistan's economy has performed significantly better than in decades under political governments. In a 10/12/1988 interview with Professor Anatol Lieven of King's College and quoted in a book "Pakistan-A Hard Country", here is how eminent Pakistani economist Dr. Mabubul Haq explained lower economic growth under "democratic" governments:

"..every time a new political government comes in they have to distribute huge amounts of state money and jobs as rewards to politicians who have supported them, and short term populist measures to try to convince the people that their election promises meant something, which leaves nothing for long-term development. As far as development is concerned, our system has all the worst features of oligarchy and democracy put together.

That is why only technocratic, non-political governments in Pakistan have ever been able to increase revenues. But they can not stay in power for long because they have no political support...For the same reason we have not been able to deregulate the economy as much as I wanted, despite seven years of trying, because the politicians and officials both like the system Bhutto (Late Prime Minister Zulfikar Ali Bhutto) put in place. It suits them both very well, because it gave them lots of lucrative state-sponsored jobs in industry and banking to take for themselves or distribute to their relatives and supporters."

Human and Economic Development under Musharraf

Pakistan saw yet another confirmation of accelerated economic and human development under military rule in years 2000-2007. Pakistan's HDI grew an average rate of 2.7% per year under President Musharraf from 2000 to 2007, and then its pace slowed to 0.7% per year in 2008 to 2012 under elected politicians, according to the 2013 Human Development Report titled "The Rise of the South: Human Progress in a Diverse World".

At 0.515, Pakistan's HDI is lower than the average HDI value of 0.558 for South Asia which is the second lowest among the various regions of the world tracked by UNDP. Between 2000 and 2012, the region registered annual growth of 1.43% in HDI value, which is the highest of the regions. Afghanistan achieved the fastest growth (3.9%), followed by Pakistan (1.7%) and India (1.5%), according to the United Nations Development Program. Overall, Pakistan's human development score rose by 18.9% during Musharraf years and increased just 3.4% under elected leadership since 2008. The news on the human development front got even worse in the last three years, with HDI growth slowing down as low as 0.59% — a paltry average annual increase of under 0.20 per cent.

Who's to blame for this dramatic slowdown in the nation's human development? Who gave it a low priority? Zardari? Peoples' Party? Sharif brothers? PML (N)? PML (Q)? Awami National Party? Muttahida Qaumi Movement? The answer is: All of them. They were all part of the government. In fact, the biggest share of the blame must be assigned to PML (N).

Sharif brothers weren't part of the ruling coalition at the center. So why should the PML (N) share the blame for falling growth in the nation's HDI? They must accept a large part of the blame because education and health, the biggest contributors to human development, are both provincial subjects and PML(N) was responsible for education and health care of more than half of Pakistan's population.

Going further back to the decade of 1990s when the civilian leadership of the country alternated between PML (N) and PPP, the increase in Pakistan's HDI was 9.3% from 1990 to 2000, less than half of the HDI gain of 18.9% on Musharraf's watch from 2000 to 2007.

Acceleration of HDI growth during Musharraf years was not an accident. Not only did Musharraf's policies accelerate economic growth, helped create 13 million new jobs, cut poverty in half and halved the country's total debt burden in the period from 2000 to 2007, his government also ensured significant investment and focus on education and health care. In 2011, a Pakistani government commission on education found that public funding for education has been cut from 2.5% of GDP in 2007 to just 1.5% - less than the annual subsidy given to the various PSUs including Pakistan Steel and PIA, both of which continue to sustain huge losses due to patronage-based hiring.

Political and Performance Legitimacy

The issue of rulers' legitimacy often raised in Pakistan is not as back and white as it appears. Polls showed that military rulers like Gen. Pervez Musharraf of Pakistan made up with performance legitimacy for lack of political legitimacy. On the other hand, civilian leaders who ascended to power did demonstrate political legitimacy but they have consistently lacked performance legitimacy. Similarly, the terms "democracy" and "dictatorship" are often vague in Pakistan's context. Pakistani "dictators" were much more "democratic" than civilian politicians in deregulating mass media and allowing lots of political debate which was absent before Musharraf's coup in 1999.

Benazir Bhutto Created Taliban

Many Pakistanis hold the military responsible for creating the Taliban who are now responsible for daily carnage in Pakistan. Few Pakistanis know that the Taliban movement was midwifed by Benazir Bhutto and her right-hand man and interior minister Naseerullah Babar during her term in office in 1993-1996. Benazir is often referred to as the Mother of the Taliban because of her role in giving birth to the Taliban movement.

Once born and nurtured by Benazir and Babar, the Taliban quickly became a force to be reckoned with. The Taliban under Mulla Omar's leadership defeated the Afghan Mujahedeen who had fought against the Soviets and quickly took control of much of Afghanistan in just a few years. The Taliban became so confident that they resisted Pakistan's pressure and refused to agree to the Durand Line as international Pak-Afghan border when they were in power in Kabul in 1990s.

7

Military Budgets and Economic Impact in Pakistan

Pakistan's defence budget for the year 2006-07 was $4.1 billion (~3% of GDP) in response to India's hike in defence budget of 2006-07 at $20.11 billion (~ 2.5% of GDP). Pakistan's hike in military budget would be partially funded by its government coffers and partially by borrowing whereas India's military spending would be entirely off its own funds. India's ambitious budget prompted Pakistan to up its own military budget, despite the country's widespread poverty and socio-political problems. Apart from its GDP, Pakistani military also gets a considerable funding from United States. Considering that India has a far larger economy overall, its military budget is also several times larger, despite being a smaller share of India's GDP.

Manpower and Ground Forces

As of 2005, India has the second largest military manpower in the world - at 3,773,300 personell, next only to China. Pakistan's manpower of 1,449,000 personell, although smaller in numbers, is proportionally higher than India in terms of their population ratios. Pakistan's ground forces are equipped with American or Chinese weapons like *FIM 92 Stinger* SAMs, *BGM-71 TOW* anti-tank missiles, *T-82* tanks and other equipments. Indian ground forces are equipped with mostly home-made and Soviet technologies like IR guided *9K35 Strela-10* SAMs, 3rd Gen IR guided *Nag* anti-tank missiles, UAVs and a large inventory of tanks and support vehicles. In terms of both numbers and equipments, Indian military dominates the Pakistani ground forces.

Comparison of Air Forces

As of 2006, Indian Air Force (IAF) has over 170,000 personnel and 3,382 aircrafts, of which 1,330 are combat aircrafts operating off 61 airbases - making it the fourth largest air force in the world. India's strike fighters consist of Russian and French aircrafts like *Mikoyan MiG-29, Dassault Mirage 2000, Sukhoi Su-30* - the last one developed under dual licensing by HAL, India's aerospace industry in Bangalore.

In addition to these, Indian Air Force also owns ground attack aircrafts, reconnaissance aircrafts, UAVs and support helicopters - a majority of them either of Soviet or French origin. Pakistan Air Force (PAF) has about 530 combat aircrafts and 65,000 active personnel, operating out of 9 airbases. Its strike fighters consist of US, Chinese and ageing French fighters like *F-16 Fighting Falcon, JF-17 Thunder* and *Dassault Mirage ROSE-III*. It also has transport aircrafts like *Lockheed Martin C-130* and *Airbus A310*, however unlike India, there are no UAVs or reconnaissance aircrafts in the Pakistani Air Force.

Naval and Sea Based Forces

After the overwhelming losses in the 1971 war against India, Pakistan rapidly increased the size of its naval fleet which doubled in the 1980s after a massive 3.2 billion dollar military and economic aid by US President *Ronald Reagan*. At present, Pakistan's navy owns over 45 vessels , most of them of US or European origin which include submarines, destroyers, frigates, patrol and mine warfare boats. It operates from its sole naval port in Karachi and sometimes from naval facilities in UK, USA and France.

It had recently been involved in various humanitarian operations during the 2005 Tsunami in South East Asia. Indian Navy on the other hand, is a three dimensional naval force consisting of missile-capable warships, an aircraft carrier, mine sweepers and a host of marine aircrafts. Most of the warships in the Indian navy are indigenously built in its own dockyards. The navy operates from its major naval bases in Visakhapatnam, Mumbai, Goa and the Andaman Islands. Indian Navy has significant capabilities of being a true blue water Navy and is experienced both in war and peacekeeping operations in the Indian Ocean.

The Nuclear Club

India tested a nuclear bomb in 1974 using materials from Canada and technical help from Soviet Union. However, the embargo on heavy water export from Canada after the test stalled India's nuclear ambitions till 1998, when it shocked the world by conducting five nuclear detonations termed as *Shakti* tests. The highest yield was by a 48 kiloton staged fusion device, which India claimed was a thermonuclear bomb but seismic data on the tests proved otherwise. In the same year 1998, Pakistan conducted a series of six nuclear detonations in a test termed as *Chagai*. The highest yield was reported to be about 25 kiloton from a two stage boosted device. At present Pakistan's nuclear stockpile is slated to be around 30-40 warheads while India possesses 70-100 warheads. The nuclearisation of India and Pakistan became a turning point in the history of conflicts between these two countries with high tensions but no war, not very much unlike the US vs USSR Cold War.

Ballistic and Cruise Missile Proliferation

In the nuclear delivery front, both India and Pakistan have a series of ballistic and cruise missiles in addition to ground attack aircrafts. The maximum range among India's operational ballistic missiles is 2000 km achieved by Agni-2. India's Agni ballistic missiles are indigenously developed by its own missile defence industry known as *IGMDP*. The maximum range among Pakistan's missiles is by *Hatf V Gauri* which is reported to do over 2200 kms. Pakistan's Hatf missiles are based on North Korean *No-Dong* series of IRBMs. Both Pakistan's *Hatf* and India's *Agni* ballistic missiles are nuclear capable. India has also developed a supersonic cruise missile *BrahMos* which is by far the fastest cruise missile at Mach 2.6 and maximum range of 290 km. It is reported to be nuclear capable but it is not confirmed yet. On the Pakistan side, its *Babur* cruise missile has a reported range of 700 km and a maximum speed of 880 km/h (Mach 0.7). As with India *BrahMos, Babur* is also reported to be nuclear capable but there is no confirmation yet.

The Final Verdict

Both Pakistan and India are almost evenly matched head to head in nuclear and missile fronts, however India has strategic and technological superiority over the conventional forces of Pakistan. Indian Navy is larger in fleet and personnel size with a more varied range of ships including an aircraft carrier while Pakistan's Navy is smaller and has no aircraft carriers. Indian's IAF is equipped with highly capable fighters like 4.5th generation *Su-30*s and 4th gen *Mirage 2000*s which are technologically superior to Pakistan PAF's *F-16*s and *Mirage III*s. Additionally Indian pilots are better trained and more capable in air combat than Pakistani forces as was demonstrated by its various wars with Pakistan or joint exercises with US and UK. In the area of conventional ground forces both the Indian as well as Pakistani Army is well equipped and highly trained to survive in extremities of topography and climate in combat conditions, like wars in the high Himalayas.

If a purely conventional war were to take place between both these countries, India would most likely overpower Pakistan owing to its superior military technology and infrastructure, larger manpower, more territorial area and a strategic advantage in its sea and air forces. It must also be noted that a war between these two countries will matter more than India's conventional superiority as both these nations are nuclear powers on an equal deadlock. India has maintained a 'no first use' nuclear policy in the lines of a similar policy by China while Pakistan does not have any such policy, considering their only hope against India is in nuclear deterrance. It would be risky for India at the present scenario to go into any aggressive war against Pakistan as the repercussions would be serious a nuclear devastation for both countries.

Unfortunately India and Pakistan had adversarial relations since sixty years. After the Mumbai carnage Pakistan is under threat of pre-emptive strikes. Fourth Indo-Pakistan war could be triggered by another terrorist attack anywhere in India. This is a dangerous scenario. India and Pakistan have fought three wars, and war drums for the fourth war are getting louder.

It is in order therefore to comprehend Indian military capabilities, and Pakistan's ability to defend itself. Defense capability is an interplay of economic and military potential. Indian economy is booming, and its GDP growth is in double digits. The global recession has impacted Indian economy, but its defense capability remains intact.

Military power and capabilities are sustained by economic and industrial potential. Geography, demography, population, oil resources and reserves, industrial capability including defense production, dollar reserves, self reliance, education, quality of manpower and leadership have a bearing on military power. Seven lakh Indian troops are tied down in Jammu and Kashmir. India has over one hundred billion dollar reserves. The West, Israel and Russia are India's weapon suppliers.

Indian Army has eighteen Corps with 34 Divisions including four Rapid Action Divisions, which would spear head ground offensives. Pakistan Army has ten Corps and twenty five divisions. Indian Army has eighteen Infantry, ten Mountain, three Armored, and two Artillery Divisions. Besides it has five Infantry, one parachute, thirteen Air Defense, and four Engineering Brigades, designated as independent formations. In addition there are two Air Defense Groups, and fourteen Army Aviation Helicopter units. This is a sizeable force, capable of launching major offensives from several fronts. The decentralized command structure will be an advantage, as compared to Pakistan's centralized Army command organization. Pakistan Army has an active force of 620,000 well trained personnel, with 528000 reservists, and 150000 para-military troops. Pakistan armed forces are seventh largest in the world. Pakistan Army's doctrine of "Offensive Defense", evolved by General Mirza Aslam Beg was put to test in 1989 in Exercise Zarb-e Momin.

The doctrine is to launch a sizeable offensive into enemy territory, rather than wait for enemy strikes or attacks. In case of Indian land offensive Pakistan Army and Air Force will respond with land and air offensives to gain and hold enemy territory. Before embarking on further offensive, gains shall be consolidated. In 1990 the Central Corps of Reserves was created to fight in the desert sectors , where enemy land offensives are expected. These dual capable formations trained for offensive and holding actions are fully mechanized.

Pakistan Army has ten Corps including the newly formed Strategic Corps. The Army has twenty six divisions (eight less than India). Two more divisions were raised as Corps reserves for V and XXXI Corps. Pakistan Army has two armored divisions, and ten independent armored brigades. Presently one hundred thousand troops are stationed on the Pak Afghan border to fight terror. Special Service Group-SSG comprises two airborne Brigades i.e. six battalions.

Pakistan Army has 360 helicopters, over two thousand heavy guns, and 3000 APC's. Its main anti-tank weapons are Tow, Tow Mk II, Bakter Shiken and FGM 148 ATGM. The Army Air Defence Command has S.A- 7 Grail, General Dynamics FIM-92 Stinger, GD FIM Red Eye, and ANZA Mk-I, Mk-II, Mk-III and HQ 2 B surface ti air missiles. Radar controlled Oerlikon is the standard Ack Ack weapon system.

The ballistic missile inventory of the Army is substantial. It comprises Ghauri III and Shaheen III IRB'S; medium range Ghauri I and II and Shaheen II, and short range Hatf I- B, Abdali, Ghaznavi, Shaheen I and M -11 missiles. All the ballistic missiles can carry nuclear war heads. Nuclear and conventional weapon capable Babur Cruise missile is the new addition to Pakistan's strategic weapon inventory. Number of ballistic missiles and war heads are almost the same as India has. So there is a parity in nuclear weapons, which is a deterrent.

Indian armor is of Russian origin. Out of 2295 Indian Army's Main Battle tanks, 2235 are of Russian origin. The main battle tanks are; 310 T-90-S Bishsma's (300 are on order), 1925 T-72M Ajeya's.. The T-90 and the T-72 have 125 mm smooth barrel guns. T-72 though old is the backbone of Indian Armor Corp's. 268 Ajeya's have been upgraded with Israeli Elbit thermal imaging systems. 1000 T-72 MBT's are awaiting up-gradation.

There have been several instances of T-72's gun barrel bursting. 124 Indian made Arjun (heavy 56 ton) MBT are on order. Sixty Arjun's are in operational service. Arjun's engine overheating problem has not been solved. Arjun has a 120 mm gun, but is unfit or desert operations. Pakistan Army is equally strong in armor, capable of giving a fitting response to any Indian military adventure.

Main Battle tanks Al-Khalid and Al-Zarrar are the backbone of Pakistan's armor Corp's. Both are Pakistan made. Pakistan's tank armory comprises :five hundred Al-Khalid MBT's; 320 Al-Zarrar type 85 II MBT's, 500 Al-Zarrar

MBT's; 450 79II AP (Chinese type 81 upgrade, and 570 T-80 UD MBT of Ukranian make. In addition Pakistan has 880 Type 59, which were procured from China in 1970.This makes a total of three thousand six hundred and twenty tanks.

All Pakistani MBT's except T-59's have 125 mm smooth barrel guns. Indian armor offensives in Kashmir, Punjab, and Sind would be effectively challenged by Pakistani armor and mechanized formations, depending on PAF's ability to keep the skies over the battle areas clear of Indian Air Force. India's modern air defense system has Israeli Arrow anti-missile missiles, and 90,000 surface to air missiles-SAM's. India has one hundred nuclear armed ballistic missiles (Agni-1 and Agni II), and Brahmos the new supersonic cruise missile. Indian Army is well trained, equipped and highly professional, and so is Pakistan Army.

Air power is likely to play a key, if not a decisive role in any future major or minor India-Pakistan armed conflict. The aim of Indian pre-emptive strikes will be maximum destruction by surprise air attacks, combined with shock commando action. A possibe scenario is; intensive bombing of the target to be followed by attacks by armed helicopters and ground assault by heliborne Commandoes. An overview of Indian Air Force and Pakistan Air Force will help comprehension of IAF's offensive capabilities, and defensive capabilities of Pakistan Air Force.

Indian Air Force has 3000 aircraft including training, transport, helicopters and 800-1000 combat air craft, which operate from sixty air bases, including Farkhor airbase in Tajikistan.. Six hundred IAF's strike and air defense fighters are expected to be operational. Pakistan Air Force has 630 aircraft, which include 530 combat aircraft, with 400 operational at any time. In 1996 India signed an agreement with Russia for the purchase of 90 Su 30 Mk-1 multi-role fighter-bombers. In 2004 a multi-billion licence was signed for building additional 140. 240 Su30-Mk-1's were ordered, 120 are already in service. With a maximum speed of Mach 2.3 and range of 8000 Km with refueling and ability to carry tons of conventional munitions and nuclear weapons, it is a lethal and menacing weapon system for the strike and interception role.

Other IAF's advanced strike and combat aircraft are: 51 Mirage-2000 (of Kargil fame), 60 Mig-29's (for air defense), 250 old Mig-21's (110 have been refurbished with Israeli help), 47 Jaguars and 70 Mig-27's for ground attack. 220 LCA Teja's under manufacture at HAL Bangalore will start entering service in 2010... IAF's fighter pilots are well trained and have out shone American pilots during joint exercises.

Pakistan Air Force has 200 rebuilt Mirage- 3's (for night air defense) and Mirage-5's for the strike role. They can carry nuclear weapons. They have been upgraded with new weapon systems, radars, and avionics. Additionally the PAF has 42 F-16's, 150 F-7's including 55 latest F-7 PG's. Manufacture of 150 JF 17 Thunder fighters (jointly designed) is underway at Pakistan Aeronautical Complex Kamra. The JF -17 Thunder is a 4th generation fly by wire multi-role fighter aircraft. Eight are already in PAF service. An order has been placed with China for the purchase of 36 JF-10, a Mach 2.3 -5th generation multi-role fighter, comparable in performance to the Su-30 Mk-1 with the Indian Air Force. PAF is on Red Alert, and is maintaining full vigil to intercept and destroy IAF intruders.

During the recent air space violation, the IAF intruders were in the sights of PAF's F-16's, but were allowed to escape unscathed to avoid a major diplomatic crisis. PAF pilots and technicians are well trained, high professionals, who will be able to prove their mettle in the future battle with India. A comparison of Indian Navy and Pakistan Navy reveals that Pakistan Navy could inflict substantial damage to the Indian Navy. Indian Navy has 16 submarines; Pakistan Navy has ten, some are brand new. Indian Navy has 27 war ships, Pakistan Navy has ten. Indian Aircraft Carrier Veerat, will be a menace, and must be sunk by submarine or air attacks, if it attempts to block Pakistan's sea lanes or ports. It is hoped that better sense prevails and India desists from invading and attacking Pakistan. If it does, the consequences will be horrible for both the countries.

ORGANIZATION, MANAGEMENT AND BUDGET

The Army Long-Range Planning System is supplanting the Army Staff Long-Range Planning System. It allows the warfighting CINCs through the Army component commands, the major Army commands, and the major subordinate commands to participate in the Army Staff's long-range planning process. Spokesmen for the nine Army Staff functional areas (manning, sustaining, equipping, managing information, facilities, structuring, training, mobilizing/deploying, and managing), planners in the three Army Staff special interest areas (space, intelligence, and health services), the Army component commands, the major Army commands, and the major subordinate commands now will develop their individual long-range plans that will combine to create the next biennial iteration of the Army Long-Range Planning Guidance. A draft AR 11-32 on the new Army Long-Range Planning System circulated among the participants during FY 88 with publication expected in early 1989.

Organization

The 1986 Defence Department Reorganization Act imposed reductions in Army headquarters personnel. Title V prescribed a maximum combined strength of military and civilian personnel permanently assigned to

Headquarters, Department of the Army, during peacetime at 3,105, or a 15 percent cut that also applied to general officers, effective 1 October 1988. Title VI called for other personnel strength changes. Section 601 (a) levied a 10 percent cut by 1 October 1988 on the Army's permanent military and civilian employees who performed management headquarters and management headquarters support duties, and also those assigned to combatant commands, based on their September 1986 strength. Section 601 (a) excluded the Secretariat, Army Staff, and the immediate headquarters staff of combatant commands. Section 601 (b) specified a 15 percent cut by 1 October 1989 for Army personnel of the same description as 601 (a) and 10 percent for those in nonmanagement headquarters who worked for Defence Department agencies and field activities. The law prohibited compliance with these headquarters personnel strength limits by redefining duties, functions, or agency organization. Congress expected the Army to relocate functions and jobs from headquarters to field activities rather than abolish them. Army compliance with these required changes proceeded on schedule during FY 88.

The TAPA became a reality as a provisional organization on 1 October 1987. The leadership of the Army's personnel systems had studied the need for TAPA for several years prior to passage of the 1986 Defence Department Reorganization Act. The Secretary of the Army and the Chief of Staff authorized creation of TAPA as a part of the Army's implementation of that legislation. Intended by its creators to integrate the execution of personnel management policy for military and civilian personnel from enlistment through separation, TAPA failed to attain fully centralized personnel management operations. The Army leadership decided that the Recruiting Command, the Community and Family Support Center, and the Safety Center, which some personnel managers hoped to integrate within TAPA, would remain separate entities. TAPA acquired five directorates-enlisted, officer, civilian, personnel service support, and mobilization and contingency operations-and four field operating agencies-Military Police Operations Agency, Military Academy Prep School, Physical Disability Agency, and the Drug and Alcohol Operations Agency. Commanded by a major general, TAPA maintains advisory relationships with the Army Reserve and National Guard personnel centers.

The Army redesignated the Army Space Agency as the Army Space Command on 7 April 1988. Located in Colorado Springs, Colorado, the Army Space Command has attained equal status with the Air Force and Navy Space Commands as components of the Space Command. The U.S. Space Command has three missions-space operations, surveillance and warning, and ballistic missile defence planning. The Army Space Command, with about 100 people including those previously assigned to the Army Space Agency and the

Defence Satellite Communications System Ground Mobile Force managers from the Army Information Systems Command, remains a field operating agency of ODCSOPS. Activation of the Army Space Command marks the first step of a plan to consolidate all Defence Satellite Communications System command and control ground functions under the Army during the next several years. The Army Space Command also has responsibility for oversight of deep space surveillance conducted at Kwajalein Atoll in support of the Space Command's worldwide space surveillance net and a detachment at Johnson Space Center.

ODCSOPS made organizational and functional changes during FY 88. In June 1984 the Chiefs of Staff of the Army and the Air Force established joint Assessment and Initiatives Offices (JAIO) to facilitate the joint Force Development Process.

It increased the number of joint warfighting initiatives from 31 to 38, resolved 44 candidate initiatives, and prompted 21 interservice agreements. In September 1988 the Army disbanded its JAIO as a functioning element within the Office of the Assistant Deputy Chief of Staff for Operations and Plans for Joint Affairs. In another area, the Strategy, Plans, and Policy Directorate created a new division, the Conventional Arms Negotiations Division. Effective 1 July 1988, it became the Army action office for all conventional arms control matters. These include acting as the Army Staff point of contact for all conventional arms control negotiations such as Mutual and Balanced Force Reductions, Conventional Stability Talks, the Conference on Security and Cooperation in Europe, and the Conference on Disarmament in Europe.

The number of federal and state environmental laws has increased dramatically in recent years. As a consequence, the Army has witnessed increased environmental violations, litigation, and curtailment of missions because of environmental considerations. The Army received 129 Notices of Violation during FY 88 from regulatory agencies. Actually, this number represented a significant reduction from FY 87, but wastewater and drinking water violations increased.

The Army's installation restoration program grew significantly as seventy-three additional installations entered the program. The Army completed a fivefold increase in preliminary assessments/site investigations, which brought the total to 3,054 sites. It also completed 55 remedial investigations/feasibility studies, which brought this total to 300, along with 99 remedial design/remedial actions. Notable among these cleanups were Cornhusker Army Ammunition Plant (incineration of explosive contaminated soil), Alabama Army Ammunition Plant (Area A Cleanup), West Virginia Ordnance Works (remediation of explosives contamination), Twin Cities Army Ammunition

Plant (installation of a ground water recovery system), and Rocky Mountain Arsenal (Basin F cleanup).

In order to streamline Army environmental management, effective 1 October 1988, the Army Environmental Office became a Headquarters, Department of the Army, staff support agency under the Assistant Chief of Engineers who serves as the Army's Program Manager for the Environment. The U.S. Army Toxic and Hazardous Materials Agency (USATHAMA), located at Aberdeen Proving Ground, Maryland, transferred from the Army Materiel Command to the Corps of Engineers as a field operating agency that also reports to the Assistant Chief of Engineers. USATHAMA has performed hazardous waste cleanup on Army properties since the mid-1970s. Its primary responsibilities have included the Installation Restoration Program, the Army equivalent to the Superfund program, and development of new technologies to abate or permanently treat hazardous waste. With its transfer to the Corps of Engineers USATHAMA assumed two new duties-providing oversight on environmental compliance at Army installations, ultimately the responsibility of installation commanders, and developing and implementing an environmental training program for the entire Army:

The issue of closing or realigning military installations received considerable attention within and without the Defence Department during FY 88. A matter of ongoing concern to the Army, it received recent investigation by the Army Long-Range Stationing Study (LRSS) established by the Chief of Staff in November 1986. He tasked the LRSS group to examine the Army's long-range stationing needs through the year 2020. It has produced a computer model for making stationing decisions and will develop a plan to transfer the model to Army Staff operational proponency. In May 1988 the Secretary of Defence chartered the Commission on Base Realignment and Closure to investigate workable methods for the Defence Department to eliminate installations and property excess to American defence needs. Composed of twelve persons-former members of Congress, retired Pentagon officials, and military and environmental specialists-commission members deliberated eight months.

Prompted by the deliberations of the Commission on Base Realignment and Closure, Congress passed PL 100-526, which President Ronald Reagan signed on 24 October 1988. The law endorsed the work of the commission and cited particulars to implement its findings. It required the Secretary of Defence to approve or disapprove the entire list of the commission for closing or realignment of American military installations. If he approved, he must forward it to Congress no later than 16 January 1989 or the action would automatically terminate. Congress could not modify the list and had forty-five working days, beginning 1 March 1989, to disapprove the complete list by a majority in both houses or the measure would become law. The commission released its findings on 29 December 1988 and recommended that the Pentagon close 86 bases (13 of them major ones), partially close 5 others, and realign another 54, which would result in either adding or losing personnel. Recommended action on Army installations included closing Fort Sheridan, Illinois, and the Presidio of San Francisco, realigning Fort Dix, New Jersey, to semiactive status, but significantly increasing personnel at Fort Belvoir, Virginia, and Fort Devens, Massachusetts. Public Law 100-526 stipulated that closings and realignments would begin 1 January 1990 and end by 30 September 1995.

GOOD PRACTICE IN THE MILITARY BUDGETARY PROCESS

From the perspectives of public policy and budgetary process, the military sector shares many of the characteristics of other sectors of government. This means that the citizens of any country will benefit from a military sector that is subject to the same broad set of rules and procedures that are applied to other sectors. It is therefore essential to give a high priority to principles such as transparency, accountability to elected civil authorities and comprehensiveness of budget coverage. In that respect, military budgeting should be no different from budgeting for other governmental sectors.

At the same time, it is often argued that the military sector is different from other parts of the public sector in at least two ways. The first is the need for confidentiality in the area of national security. The second is the highly political nature of expenditure decisions relating to the military sector, especially arms acquisition decisions.

It is clear that some degree of confidentiality is necessary in the area of national security. However, this should not be used to justify a lower level of oversight or a lack of adherence to internationally recognized standards of public expenditure management. Different forms of oversight may be necessary for some areas relating to national security. It is also important to be clear about the distinction between confidentiality and the lack of public scrutiny. It is possible to retain a high degree of confidentiality in highly sensitive areas without compromising the principle of democratic accountability. A subject may be sensitive—off-budget activities, for example—but it should not be kept secret. War plans, on the other hand, should be confidential. Even so, holding war plans in confidence does not mean an absence of democratic accountability. It simply requires appropriate systems of clearance and procedures for consulting the legislature and other oversight bodies.

All budgeting involves political decisions and trade-offs, but it is often argued that political considerations carry greater weight in defence than in other sectors. To the extent that this is true, provided that the political system is open, it should still be possible to contest the basis on which decisions are made and, in particular, to ensure that the principles of sound financial management are not violated. Thus, the highly political nature of decisions concerning the military sector should not prevent that sector from adhering to the important principles of transparency, oversight and accountability.

CONSTITUTES GOOD PRACTICE IN MILITARY BUDGETING

In order to develop an appreciation of good practice in the military budgetary process, it is important to consider: (*a*) the relevance of good practice; (*b*) the principles of sound public expenditure management; and (*c*) the key principles of democratic governance in the security sector.

The principles of sound public expenditure management

The 10 principles of public expenditure management are widely accepted as the basis for budgeting processes. It is important to understand that these are the ideals that public officials should have in front of them as a guide. No public expenditure system anywhere in the world gets top marks on all 10 principles. The point is to progressively improve adherence to them. There is no justification for the military sector to violate any of these principles. The way in which it implements some of them may be a little different from some other sectors, but the principles themselves must not be violated: they are all relevant to a well-managed budgetary process. The principles most frequently cited in relation to the military sector are transparency and accountability. The confidentiality suggest, transparency is the cornerstone on which an accountable military budgetary process is built. Transparency and accountability are crucial issues in the allocation and management of defence resources for all levels of planning, programming and budgeting. If the allocation and management of defence resources are not transparent, the military sector will never be able to achieve public support or the cooperation and support of broader government. If it is not accountable to government and the people, the military becomes a cause unto itself and will not be aligned with national interests and priorities. It will easily be corrupted and decision making will be easily diverted towards self-interest.

Civil involvement in and control of overall budget decisions, as well as careful auditing at all levels, can help ensure that resources are actually used to accomplish policy objectives. The most effective way to achieve this is to obtain at all levels a commitment to national interests and objectives and to develop clear and transparent planning, programming and budgeting processes and systems to implement them. These processes must of necessity be aligned with the national financial management framework. Transparency and accountability can be enhanced through a system of performance agreements. Such agreements rely on the definition of clear output objectives and performance standards and on agreement on the required resources. The system is also based on negotiation, ensuring better insight, understanding and cooperation. Important as transparency and accountability are, it is essential not to lose sight of the other principles of public expenditure management. In particular, attention should be given to: (*a*) the *comprehensiveness* of the budget; (*b*) the *predictability* of the level of revenues backing that budget and the macro-economic policies on which those revenues depend; (*c*) the *contestability* of the budget process; and (*d*) the *honesty* with which estimates of revenue and expenditure are developed.

The relevance of good practice

Good practice is based on adherence to principles of sound public expenditure management. One might well question the relevance of somewhat abstract principles when dealing with an issue like military spending, where actual practice diverges significantly from good practice and the conditions for achieving good practice are frequently not present, as is the case throughout much of Africa. The purpose of starting with good practice is that it provides a clear vision of the objectives of policy reform—in this case, a democratically governed military sector under civilian leadership that adheres to the principles of sound budgeting and financial management. Without such a vision, it is impossible to develop either a strategy for reaching the ultimate objectives or benchmarks to measure progress along the way. It is also impossible to determine where the problems lie with existing policy and practice.

The key principles of democratic governance in the security sector

The 10 principles of democratic governance in the security sector are increasingly widely accepted. They reflect the mutual obligations that civil authorities and security personnel have towards each other. Security forces have a responsibility to be accountable to civil authorities; to uphold the rule of law, including the protection of human and civil rights; and to carry out their professional duties to the best of their abilities. Civil authorities have the responsibility to avoid politicizing security bodies; to respect their professional prerogatives; and to provide them with a clear mandate and adequate resources and training to carry out that mandate. As in the case of the principles of public expenditure management, there is no justification for the military sector to violate these principles.

MILITARY BUDGETARY PROCESS INTO GOVERNMENT-WIDE PROCESSES

There are five crucial, interrelated components of the management of expenditure in any sector: (*a*) strategic planning; (*b*) review of the previous year's performance; (*c*) determination of what is affordable; (*d*) allocation of resources both between and within sectors; and (*e*) efficient and effective use of resources. The linkages between these components in the case of the military sector, with reference to the broader security sector.

For the budgetary process to be effective, every sector needs to follow good practices internally and to link with the broader, government-wide financial management and oversight process. All of this must occur within the framework of democratic governance and the principles of sound budgeting and financial management.

Strategic planning in the security sector

As in any other part of the public sector, military budgets should be prepared in accordance with a sectoral strategy. This involves identifying the needs and key objectives of the security sector as a whole and the specific missions that the defence forces will be asked to undertake.

The starting point for developing policies and strategies for the security sector is an understanding of the causes of insecurity and the identification of the instruments that government wants to employ to enhance security. Governments have various tools for strengthening security. Key among these are diplomacy; economic and political tools to reduce economic and social inequalities and tensions; mediation to resolve conflict domestically and regionally; and, of course, the country's security bodies. Once the broad areas of responsibility for the security forces are identified, governments should agree on the tasks that will be undertaken by the different bodies: armed forces, police, gendarmerie or paramilitary forces, and intelligence bodies. Based on these assessments, governments should develop a formal defence policy framework. This policy then informs planning, programming and budgeting. The planning and programming process, along with the linkages to the military budgetary process.

While it is true that 'policy is what government does, not what it says it wants to do', formal policies and plans to implement these policies are important. In the absence of well-thought-out and clearly articulated policies, it is impossible to manage the finances of the military sector in a rational manner. Budgeting becomes ad hoc. In the absence of a clear statement of which activities undertaken by the armed forces are included in the 'defence' function, it is impossible to develop adequate functional breakdowns of expenditure and to understand how much it costs to provide adequate military security. In addition, it is difficult to develop performance benchmarks and thus to assess the efficiency and effectiveness of expenditure in the military sector. In the absence of a strategic plan, countries risk not obtaining a level of military security commensurate with their financial outlays.

As the case studies in this volume illustrate, few governments in Africa have undertaken thorough, participatory strategic review processes of the sort outlined. What is more, defence policy and planning processes are rarely based on a broad evaluation of a country's security environment and a detailed assessment of the specific tasks that should be undertaken by the country's various security forces. A counter example is Uganda, which undertook a broad security assessment in 2002–2003. It identified 134 'threat agents', of which three were specific to the military. This result underscores the importance of not attempting to undertake defence planning in a vacuum, but of linking it with planning for the police, paramilitary forces, civilian intelligence and other state security forces, as well as with the country's economic and developmental objectives.

In highly resource-constrained countries, such as those in Africa, it is extremely important for governments and societies to use resources as efficiently and effectively as possible. The first step in this process is to engage in strategic planning. In doing so, it is important to ensure that the defence review process takes place in a manner consistent with the country's economic objectives and capacities. The demonstrates, economic considerations need to be taken into account at the beginning, the middle and the end of the review process. A defence force costs money. A country will not be secure if it develops a defence policy for which it cannot provide resources in an open, accountable and sustained manner. Thus, part of the guidance for the review process should include the financial framework for the security sector in general and the military sector in particular. Throughout the entire process, the finance minister and other key economic managers need to be informed and consulted. Options for force structures need to be developed within the context of the financial parameters and the risks associated with buying a certain level of defence. The final decisions must reflect economic realities.

Review of the previous year's performance in the security sector

While strategic reviews occur infrequently in African countries, it is important that the outcome of the previous year's financial planning and implementation period be reviewed at the beginning of the annual budget cycle. The efficient and effective management of resources in any sector, including the security sector, requires that information on performance be fed back into the budgeting process. While defining and measuring performance for the military sector is more difficult than for many other sectors, a focus on readiness or capability has been shown to be helpful for any discussion of the role, structure, performance and resource needs of the defence forces. However performance is defined, the review of the previous year's budgetary performance will be facilitated by a well-functioning financial management information system (FMIS).

Determination of what is affordable in the security sector

Government policies, whether in the security or any other sector, must be affordable. Affordable policies require a sustainable macroeconomic balance, which is critical to the long-term economic health of a country. To attain a sustainable macroeconomic balance, governments must give a high priority to exercising discipline over public expenditure.

Overall financial discipline is also critical because a ceiling on funding that can be easily raised allows governments to avoid firm decisions on priorities. At the other end of the spectrum, without a solid floor to the budget, resources become unpredictable and operational performance suffers. It is therefore extremely important to have in place institutions that can achieve long-term macroeconomic stability, determine the overall resource envelope for public expenditure and enforce government decisions on expenditure priorities and levels.

Financial discipline is weak in many African countries. While the military is by no means the only body that exceeds the agreed limits of the financial allocation in the course of the financial year, it frequently enjoys a privileged position. Government officials, military officers, and heads of state and government have intervened in the resource-allocation process with flagrant disregard for established procedures and predetermined spending priorities. Military officers have presented the treasury with invoices for expenses incurred outside the budget framework. Defence ministers have refused to share the details of defence spending with finance ministers and parliament. The full financial implications of arms-acquisition decisions, including debt incurred for military purposes, are often not reflected in budgets, which may eventually destabilize financial policy. This sort of behaviour contributes to the widespread problem in Africa of military budgets that cannot fully fund the defence function.

As far as the failure to respect lower limits on expenditure, the armed forces are less likely to have their allocations reduced during the course of a financial year than other security forces, such as the police or gendarmerie. Nonetheless, it is important to develop clear rules for any reallocation of resources during the financial year—including those occasioned by shortfalls in revenue—and to apply them across the board.

Medium-term expenditure frameworks (MTEFs) are one mechanism that can help reduce incentives to evade financial discipline. MTEFs have become popular with the development assistance agencies because they can help: (*a*) improve the linkage between policies and objectives and between inputs and outputs; (*b*) make the budgetary process more transparent, especially by improving monitoring; (*c*) focus on outputs and service delivery; and (*d*) increase ownership by sectoral ministries.

As several of the case studies in this book demonstrate, it can be difficult for African governments to develop realistic multi-year plans, given the lack of predictability in government revenues and the reliance on a strong institutional base. However, something like an MTEF is important because the military sector needs a time frame for planning and budgeting of longer than one year. As the case of South Africa demonstrates, adopting a multi-year framework is not impossible in the African context.

A specific benefit to the military sector of adopting a medium-term framework is that it encourages full costing of defence programmes, particularly outlays on arms acquisition and major construction projects. Irrespective of the difficulty in implementing an MTEF, it is still important to have a full costing of the different components of the defence programme. Full costing will help make the case for a particular level of funding. It will also clarify the sustainability of individual programmes and it will help maximize efficiency and effectiveness in those cases where budget cuts become necessary. Full costing is therefore critically necessary for the operational effectiveness of the defence forces.

ALLOCATION OF RESOURCES FOR THE MILITARY SECTOR

Once the overall resource envelope is agreed, resources must be allocated according to priorities both within the military sector and between the military sector and other sectors. Sectoral strategies and information on performance (outputs and outcomes) are critical components of the allocation process. It is important that assessments of past performance be fed into planning for the coming year (or years in the case of multi-year budgeting cycles). The key financial and economic managers plus the legislature must have the capacity to be fully involved in the resource-allocation process and the process must include all relevant actors. The central budget office should assess the appropriateness of the defence ministry's budget. The armed forces must compete fully with other sectors for funding. The legislature must have adequate time to review and comment on the proposed defence budget before the beginning of the financial year. Methods of incorporating public input into the allocation process can help build public support for the final budget.

In many African countries the conditions required for the effective allocation of resources are not present. Institutional capacity for military budgeting is weak in both the executive and legislative branches of government. Financial management and oversight within the armed forces are correspondingly inadequate. The military sector holds a highly privileged position compared with other sectors when the overall resource envelope is divided among sectors. Arms acquisition requests include neither justification nor full costing. The legislature frequently receives even less information on the defence budget than on budgets for non-security activities, and input from the public on spending priorities is actively discouraged or ignored. The challenges facing legislative oversight of the armed forces in West Africa.

While the military often enjoys a privileged position in terms of resource allocation, financial constraints have led some African governments to fail to provide the armed forces with adequate resources to carry out their assigned missions. This not only places at risk the safe and secure environment that is necessary for both economic and political development, but also creates frustration and resentment within the armed forces. Participants in a workshop on democratic governance in the security sector held in Dakar in October 2001 argued that adequate transparency in the military sector is critical so that the serious underfunding that afflicts armed forces throughout the region is clear for all to see. They suggested that there is both disdain for the military among civilians and a belief that military security is a comparatively low priority among those who control their countries' financial resources. In their view, this not only leads to inadequate defence budgets and thus inadequate external security but can also heighten internal insecurity through a threat of coups. For reasons of both financial and political stability, it is important that the military sector competes on an equal footing with other sectors and that the process of allocating resources among sectors takes place in a transparent and accountable manner.

OUTCOME BUDGET

The Department of Expenditure, Ministry of Finance on 30th December 2005, has given guidelines for preparation of an outcome budget which was introduced by the finance minister in Para 100 of his budget speech (budget 2005-06). The need for an outcome budget has arisen owing to weaknesses that have crept into the performance budget, given the absence of a clear one-to-one relationship between the financial budget and the performance budget. Though the MOD and a few other ministries/departments have been exempted from the preparation of the outcome budget, they have been asked to carry out this exercise for internal reviews and to voluntarily decide to place it in the public domain, fully or partially. The memorandum called for a tabular format which could be visualized as "vertical compression and horizontal expansion" of the budget estimates (BE) as given in Volume II. The components in the format for the outcome budget comprise financial outlays, projected physical outlooks, and projected/budgeted outcomes (intermediate/partial and final). The system of budget, as evolved by the Ministry of Finance, thus includes the outcome budget for the ensuing year and performance budget for the previous financial year. It implies that the performance budget format now includes linkage with not only the financial budget but also the outcome budget. The implication for the Ministry of Defence is that an outcome budget can be evolved for the ensuing year even within the existing structure and format of the budget without waiting for the development of a programme budget in a number of areas of activities in defence.

The key terms 'outlays', 'outputs' and 'outcome' in the budget have been defined by the Ministry of Finance as follows:

Outlays imply total financial resources deployed for achieving certain outcomes. Outputs are a measure of a physical quantity of the goods or services produced under a scheme or a programme. They are usually an intermediate stage between outlays and outcomes. Outcomes are the end products/results of various initiatives and interventions, including those in partnership with public sector undertakings, autonomous bodies, etc. They involve much more than mere output since they cover the quality of the goods or services.

The Finance Minister in his foreword to the outcome budget document on 25 August 2005, aptly stated: "I must caution that outlays do not necessarily mean outcome. People of the country are concerned with the outcomes." The Ministry of Finance has recognised that, in respect of certain ministries, the conversion of outlays into outcomes is a complex process. The Ministry of Defence and certain other departments have been exempted from preparation of outcome budget. But it is evident that the principles enunciated in regard to the outcome budget in the civil ministries such as benchmarking standards/ quality of outcome in services, standardising unit cost of delivery, capacity building for requisite efficiency at all levels in terms of equipment, technology, knowledge and skills, and to further ensure flow of appropriate funds at the right time to the right level, with neither delay nor "parking" of funds, effective monitoring, evaluation and feedback system are equally applicable to the defence setup. The introduction of outcome budget in defence will further enhance and ensure accountability at all levels. Outcome will be readily transparent to all those involved in the management of budget as well to the parliament and the tax payers.

The outcome budget, linked with performance budget, should not merely reflect results of a year but also indicate the progress in achieving certain long-term objectives, such as cumulative performance and final outcome. As an example, hypothetically if an outcome budget has been finalised reflecting the goal and vision of the self reliance plan, formulated in 1993, which aimed at 70 per cent self-reliance in certain areas of defence production over a 10-year period, it would have known by now what has been achieved and where the government has fallen short. This would have helped in taking corrective measures for the next decade to reduce imports and achieve greater self-reliance. The eleventh report on the demand for grants of the Standing Committee on Defence (April, 2006) has emphasised the need to enhance indigenisation and reduce imports. It is felt that the formulation of an outcome budget would help to monitor the results with respect to the plan. There are a number of areas in the defence sector which are amenable for introduction of outcome budget. Areas where these could be considered with definite yardsticks for measurement are:

- Maintenance and production workshops in the three services
- Ordnance factories
- Training
- Repairs and refit of certain ships under the navy
- Certain components of research and development establishments
- Capital works other than those connected with any weapon system.
- Ordnance depots (at least other than arms and ammunition), etc.
- Married accommodation project
- Ex-servicemen's health scheme.

There could also be a number of other items. A rough conservative estimate of those that are non-sensitive in nature, show that at least Rs. 15,000 crore of the defence budget could be brought under the outcome budget and placed in the public domain. This could form part I of Volume I of the outcome budget. In these areas, the public has as much right to information as in the civil sector. Many more categories, especially of equipment, can also be brought under outcome budget for purposes of internal controls. This second segment could be Volume II of the outcome budget and can be the internal document of the government, which has the right to keep information to itself in case it is of a sensitive nature. Preparation of an outcome budget would automatically imply preparation of performance budget vis-à-vis the outcomes planned. The formats of the documents are given in the Ministry of Finance office memorandum cited earlier.

Evaluation of performance indicators has a major role in providing credible information to decision-makers. Such an evaluation is not easy in intangible areas. Premchand in his book, Public Expenditure Management, 4 has identified this issue as follows: "Performance indicators should follow the objective set for the organisation. These objectives should be specific, disaggregated, and measurable in one form or the other. Indicators in such a context seek to serve as a bridge between the objectives, resources allocated and the organisation's outputs. They could indicate the following aspects:

- Throughput or volume;
- Productivity and cost; Time target;
- Demand for services;
- Availability of services; and
- Outcome".

Programme Budget

The development of programme budget is a complex task. As a first step, the Integrated Defence Staff needs to formulate elements of the programme budget after defining various programmes. Some steps have already been undertaken by them. A multi-disciplinary group, which will also comprise a cost committee, would need to complete this task.

There are several questions that could arise while considering the introduction of a programme budget. As per the knowledge and experience of the author, the issue has been under consideration at least for the past two decades. It is not clear whether all concerned in the defence set-up are keen about a programme budget. The question also arises whether the programme budget is feasible within the existing structures and systems. It is also common knowledge that in the last decade much more information was available in the media about defence matters than before. This has also motivated many defence departments to rush to the press for publicity about success of a mission, weapons system, etc. While this may be good from the point of view of morale of the citizens, quite a few achievements are being publicised though the projects may be far from achieving their ultimate outcome. Another complexity in evolving a programme budget arises when the definition of the programme cuts across the services. Even within a service, especially a large service like the Army, there could be complexities in reflecting the estimates and expenditure of different arms especially in a situation where not all transactions are cashbased and many are on the basis of documents. Jointness in the field among the three services, if achieved, could facilitate evolution of a programme budget. The IDS are in the process of experimenting and evolving some concepts in this regard. The identification of various programmes should be the starting point for spelling out the elements of a programme budget.

Development of a programme based budgeting would require a huge amount of cost accounting. Work needs to be done for each type of transaction in various units, formations, workshops, headquarters, etc., within a service and across the services. A highly automated system, with networking cutting across the boundaries of services and departments, would facilitate the task. The methodology and structure for programme based budgeting in a time-bound manner would require systematic planning and implementation in a phased manner.

In the interim, the best approach would be to enhance the financial information system and networking, and operate an outcome budget as spelt out in the preceding paragraphs, which will enable better-decision making. A danger is that even a system once created or established tends to get into disuse with poor maintenance. For instance, the initial enthusiasm for creation of websites in various institutions, especially in the government sector, was not sustained thereafter due to poor maintenance in terms of updated information. The financial system without regular and online update and with thousands of inputs coming from different units would make any budget and reporting systems incomplete and may even be misleading.

The defence budget is already of a very large magnitude. In a period of 15 years, it has grown five and a half times-from an outlay of Rs. 16,347 crore in 1991–1992 to Rs. 89,000 crore in 2006-2007. As a component of the central government budget, it continues to be the largest among all departments, some 15.78 per cent. It has very large components of expenditure that are totally non-sensitive in nature and on which information is available through various documents. But what is lacking is information on results of the large outlays and sometimes even the output. The defence budget has not had the benefit of having a performance budget component. Though the performance budget in many of the civil ministries does not always help in assessing the value of money realised out of the outlays, these aspects can be rectified through the outcome budget. Allocation of funds to the defence would soon touch Rs 1,00,000 crore and would continue to grow from year to year, especially in view of the huge costs involved in certain modern systems. Therefore, the financial information systems need to be improved and enhanced. The budget system should ensure transparency and accountability and responsibility at all levels and display that value for money has been realised. The information technology available today will facilitate tasks which were not possible earlier. A document such as an outcome budget will enable a single point reference for all concerned in place of a multiplicity of papers that need to be consulted. An outcome budget, along with a performance budget, would be a first step in this direction. These would be supplements to the existing volumes of DSE. There is also a need to make a beginning in preparing programme budget in select areas, given the manpower resources constraints and the gaps in total connectivity and network.

Financial Information System

A crucial aspect for achieving success in evolving any improved budgetary systems for evaluation of results in the defence set-up, would be the development of a total and comprehensive financial information system with a wide area network covering all the three services, the concerned defence department, the defence accounts department and the Ministry of Defence.

A report in this regard was submitted in August 2002 to the Ministry of Defence by the author who after his retirement as Secretary Defence (Finance) in February 2002 had been appointed as Adviser to the Ministry of Defence. In the Report, a number of recommendations were made to improve the existing system and to make available more information to the MoD officials.

The need to build an information system on liabilities has been felt for more than a decade and half and some progress has been achieved, especially in regard to items under 'capital'. But building an institutionalized reporting system on commitments made in contracts, supply orders and liabilities incurred thereon is a necessary adjunct to any budgetary exercise.

Once this reporting system is institutionalised and relevant information becomes part of supporting budget documents, the seriousness would be bestowed to the preparation of liabilities figuring in the report. The review of contracts, supply orders and updating of the figures would then become a continuing exercise from the point of view of ensuring outcomes as well as taking corrective action when required. There is also a need to have convergence between various services/departments on aspects like unit code and contract code to facilitate the creation of a better information system.

Uniformity in redesigned source documents needs to be enforced by the MoD in all services/departments. This has implications for the right kind of information-control the MoD would like to exercise. Network needs to be established between various services, departments, and especially between the CGDA and the Service Headquarters and other defence departments. Computerisation without a total communication network for exchange of data/information would produce less than optimum results. Adequate networking would facilitate better output in terms of content, details and availability of information on time. Quality of information would be crucial in any system and modern technology facilitates it. To evolve an improved budgetary control system, this would be a necessary prerequisite since, in the manually dominated or partially computerised system, and the manual process itself adds to the difficulties.

DEFENCE AND ECONOMIC PROCESS

The defence sector has a major share of the budget in most countries. The perceived adverse effects of higher defence spending on economic growth are due to the following:

- Purchase by the defence sector of domestic goods, or the use of foreign exchange to purchase imported goods.
- The government sector shows no measurable productivity increases. Thus, an enlargement in defence spending shifts resources from the productive sector to the non-productive sector.
- A shift of resources to defence reduces the resources available for the rest of the economy and in particular "crowds out" private investment as well as diverts skilled workers from civilian sectors.

The dominant view among economists has been that defence is a drag on economic growth. A contrary view was brought out strongly for the first time in a study of developing countries on this topic by Benoit in 1973. Of the favourable effects of defence spending, Benoit lists many, of which the following seem relevant for the Indian situation: Security effects—To the extent that the military provides security to the country, it enables an atmosphere conducive to investment and long-term planning decisions. Training effects—Military manpower receives training even at the rudimentary level and this can be beneficial if the recruits come in substantial numbers from the subsistence economy and if the military programmes introduce people to 'modern' methods and social skills and general inculcation of 'national' values.

Infrastructure effects—The military may create infrastructure, such as roads, airports, docks and communications, which can be used by the civilian sector, especially 'up country'.

Consumable effects—The services provide substantial numbers of people with food, clothing, shelter and medicines. They also engage in 'civic action' programmes and in 'hearts and minds' campaigns. The existing research by and large seems to indicate that certain groups of developing countries derive positive benefits from military spending. The sustainability of the defence budget is a function of the health of the economy. A glaring example of this in recent times has been the inability of the Soviet Union to sustain high levels of defence spending in superpower competition with the USA, in the face of a faltering economy. Defence expenditure in India has benefited from higher growth rates in the recent past. In real dollar terms, the Indian defence budget has more than doubled in the past decade. The ratio of defence expenditure to GDP is well below 3% today, which is a healthy sign. On the flip side, internal security is adversely impacted by social and economic backwardness and regional balance issues seems to be needed for the sustainability both of growth-fostering reformist economic policies as well as a stronger defence.

Military Work Force

The human resource dimension of defence economics is a relatively neglected field. US studies dominate the theoretical, empirical, and policy literature on military manpower. Two issues have been pre-eminent. First, studies of conscription versus an all-volunteer force. Second, the concern with downsizing and its implications for military manpower. In India, the structure of military manpower has changed little since British times. Reliance continues on a large, conventional force with over 1.3 million men in uniform in the armed forces and another nearly 1.7 million paramilitary personnel with about 400,000 of these in organisations directly performing a defence role. In addition, entities like the Border Roads Organization (employing about a lakh) and defence civilians (estimated to be of the order of another four lakhs) perform a support role. There probably is a case for looking at overall numbers in the context of modernization; even the Chinese People's Liberation Army has apparently made conscious manpower reductions in recent times. Putting a price to the manpower input into defence would also be instructive in taking a call on these issues.

Arms Control and Trade

Arms imports by India in the 2001-05 period are estimated at over $9 billion at constant 1990 prices. Defence markets are large, government regulated, and generally non-transparent in their functioning. Economic factors are relevant in understanding and dealing with defence markets. For example, the post-Cold War situation and disarmament in NATO and in the former Warsaw Pact countries has made their defence contractors seek export sales to compensate for declining domestic procurement. As a result, disarmament in one part of the world might actually promote arms exports, regional arms races, and possibly instability elsewhere in the world. Similarly, major technical advances result in new products and fuel demand from buyers who need to "catch up."

The Indian Context

Issues relating to arms imports are important for India, which has only a 30% rate of self-reliance in arms procurement, despite a sizable arms industry. By their very nature, arms import deals tend to involve large amounts of money, and are politically highly sensitive. It is possible to work out the costs and benefits of a procurement alternative in quantitative terms, and such exercises should be encouraged, so that better decisions are made.

The putting in place a new, more transparent Defence Procurement Procedure in India in 2006 has drawn attention to the issue of "offsets". As the arms trade takes place in a buyers' market, it follows that arms importing countries are in a dominant position to extract compensatory investment. The new procedure in India requires direct offsets of 30% of the value of the contract to be made for all defence capital contracts of over Rs 300 crores. This is expected, according to the Defence Minister, to result in gains for the country of over Rs 45,000 crores ($10 billion) in investments over the Eleventh Plan period (2007-12). The limited international research on the subject, however, tends to cast doubt on the net benefits of defence offsets to national economies. As has been pointed out in this context, "there are no free lunches."

MILITARY BUDGETING AND FISCAL MANAGEMENT

Sound fiscal management of the entire security sector is essential if a country is to have effective, efficient and professional security forces that are capable of protecting the state and its population against internal and external threats. Highly autonomous security forces that are able to act with impunity in the economic and political spheres are invariably professionally weak and highly cost-*in*effective. Because the armed forces generally absorb the majority of resources allocated to the security sector and tend to have a high degree of political autonomy, this project focuses on the process by which military budgets are developed, implemented and monitored.

A central premise of this paper is that, from a public policy and process perspective, the military sector shares many of the characteristics of other sectors and that the citizens of any country will benefit from a military sector that is subject to the same broad set of rules and procedures of other sectors. As such, gives high priority to principles such as transparency, accountability to elected civil authorities, and comprehensiveness of budget coverage. The differences between the need for confidentiality in the defense sector, on the one hand, and a lack of public scrutiny of the military sector, on the other hand. The relevance of good practice. The process of integrating the military sector into the planning, policy-making, and budgeting systems and procedures of a country in a manner consistent with democratic, civil control of the defense forces.

FINANCIAL MANAGEMENT PROCEDURES

Failure to follow sound financial management procedures in the military sector is often justified by the need for secrecy to protect national security. It is clear that some degree of confidentiality is necessary in the area of national security. However, there appears to be a tendency to conflate the concepts of "sensitivity" and "confidentiality" and to use the need for confidentiality in some areas of the military sector to reduce opportunities for scrutiny by appropriate management and oversight bodies in government and by civil society. Military-related issues – in particular, those relating to military intelligence-are sensitive in all societies. Even long-established democracies retain varying degrees of confidentiality in the realm of national security. It is important to be clear, however, about the distinction between confidentiality and the lack of public scrutiny. It is possible to retain a high degree of confidentiality in highly sensitive areas without compromising the principle of public accountability. It is also important to be clear about what is being held in confidence and why it is considered sensitive. War plans should be held in confidence. That the armed forces are regularly exceeding their budget allocations, are purchasing expensive military equipment with scant attention to need or ability to maintain this equipment, or are engaged in illegal, off-budget activities are clearly sensitive matters, but should not be held in confidence.

A highly non-transparent military sector provides the perfect cover for off-budget transactions. [It also provides the perfect cover for the diversion of resources into private hands (or pockets).] The issue of off-budget military spending is addressed in more detail in a companion article ("Off-Budget Military Expenditure and Revenue"). The point to be made here is that when a significant portion of a country's military expenditure occurs off-budget and is fed by off-budget revenues, not only are core principals of fiscal responsibility in the public sector violated. It is also highly likely that the operational capacity of the armed forces will suffer and that the military will not receive value for money. Therefore, an important component of the Sipri/ASDR project on military budgeting will be to determine the extent and nature of off-budget financing and expenditure.

GOOD PRACTICE IN MILITARY PROCUREMENT AND ACQUISITION

There should be little difference between public expenditure management in general and public expenditure management in the military sector. Defence procurement and acquisition should accordingly be carried out according to the same principles that guide public sector procurement in non-military areas: fairness, impartiality, transparency, cost-effectiveness and efficiency, and openness to competition. In addition, it is essential that there be high-level consultation and evaluation of all major projects for all forms of public sector procurement and acquisition. A generic procurement process, applicable to all sectors of government.

At the same time, with the exception of procurement of works and commodities (such as construction, clothing, food, fuel, office equipment, general vehicles and consultancy services), defence procurement does exhibit some distinctive characteristics: (*a*) the relative importance of cost in determining which bid is accepted; (*b*) the confidentiality associated with national security considerations; (*c*) the time frame for major weapons procurement; (*d*) the complexity of defence procurement; and (*e*) the existence of international arms control treaty regimes and national legislation governing arms procurement. These distinctive characteristics are deviations in scale rather than principle. There certainly should be scepticism about any claims that procurement of relatively standard works, services and commodities for the military should be subject to different rules.

Cost considerations in bidding

While standard procurement practice in non-military sectors is giving increasing emphasis to value for money, defence analysts argue that factors other than cost are more frequently the major factors in accepting a bid for weapon procurement projects in the military sector. They point out, however, that national legislation can play an important role in regulating the part that cost plays in weapon procurement processes in the military sector. In South Africa, for example, the 1998 Defence Review and the 1999 White Paper on defence-related industries spell out which technologies are considered 'strategically essential capabilities' and thus exempt from lowest-cost considerations. The South African Parliament has approved both policy documents.

Confidentiality

Transparency in defence procurement must be limited by national security interests. Confidentiality clauses will be required in the arms procurement process. This, too, can be regulated by national legislation. The South African Defence Review lists a number of reasons for confidentiality in defence procurement. These include: the protection of third-party commercial information, the national security of South Africa, prevention of harm to South Africa's ability to conduct international relations, and the protection of South Africa's economic interests and the commercial activities of government bodies.

The time frame for major weapons procurement

From inception to final acceptance of the product, procurement of major weapon systems may take as long as 15 years. Some flexibility needs to be built into the procurement process to take account of contingencies such as fluctuations in currency exchange rates. This long time frame also makes it essential that quality control takes place throughout the procurement process, rather than when the product is ready for delivery. Arms procurement projects should also take into account full life-cycle costs and support for the acquired systems. The long time frame also makes it essential to attempt to forecast spending farther into the future than in non-defence sectors. The UK, for example, has a 10-year 'long-term costing' system for defence.

The complexity of arms procurement

Because of the complexity of arms procurement, sound management of the procurement process requires interdisciplinary project teams. Such teams should have expertise on engineering, resource management, contracting, quality assurance and design assurance. In addition, because of the particular complexity of the procurement of major weapon systems, which can involve a substantial number of subcontractors, opportunities for corruption are great. These projects therefore require the highest level of management and scrutiny by governmental accountability mechanisms. For example, South Africa has three levels of approval for major arms procurement projects within its Department of Defence. For major projects, parliamentary approval may also be required.

International arms control treaty regimes and national legislation governing arms procurement Procurement in the military sector is distinct from general government procurement in being subject to international treaties and specific national legislation. Some defence

OUT-OF-BALANCE BUDGETS

The other critical obstacle to democratization and stability in Pakistan is the country's weak economic performance. The civilian government inherited a cash-strapped, highly indebted economy from the Musharraf regime and had to ask the International Monetary Fund for a $7.6 billion bailout in 2008 to avoid default. Last summer's heavy floods, which displaced some 20 million people and caused considerable damage to Pakistan's civilian infrastructure, dealt a devastating blow to the prospects of economic resurgence. Perceptions of widespread government corruption and civilian authorities' apparent unwillingness to cut spending have not helped. Moreover, Pakistan has one of the lowest tax-to-GDP ratios in the world — only two percent of the population pays any taxes at all — yet the government has not been able to agree on critical tax reforms.

Pakistan must also reckon with the need to alleviate the economic hardships faced by its poor. Skyrocketing inflation of basic commodity prices, chronic power cuts, persistently high levels of unemployment, and general lawlessness are fueling public resentment of the current government. Some observers fear that the downward economic spiral could play into the hands of Islamists, but there is no automatic link between economic woes and the influence of Islamists in public life. In Pakistan, Islamist influence has been closely tied to state patronage, not popular support. Islamist parties continue to perform poorly at the polls, never garnering more than 10-12 percent of the vote, whereas the two main moderate parties — the PPP and the PML-N — typically claim about 60 percent of the vote and 70 percent of the seats in the national parliament.

Still, Pakistan's civilian government must stabilize the economy to bolster public confidence in democratic institutions. It must invest in Pakistan's long-term economic development and create opportunities for the country's rapidly growing population. It may even need a long-term, multibillion-dollar Marshall Plan to help build civilian institutional capacity, rebuild areas hit by last year's floods, invest in public-sector and infrastructure projects, and plug the energy shortages that have all but crippled the manufacturing sector, especially its top-exporting textile industry. Of course, such a plan should come with proper controls to fight corruption and waste.

It is worth noting that Pakistan's economic difficulties are the result not just of bad luck and poor management, and therefore they cannot be fixed with development aid alone. They are rooted in fundamental structural problems as well: military expenditures dwarf spending on development. Pakistan has one of the world's largest out-of-school populations, yet it spends seven times as much on the military every year as on education, an investment with a higher national security payoff in the long run. Thus, the country must find a way to rationalize its military expenditures.

Some progress toward a resolution of the Kashmir conflict could induce Pakistan to scale back its military behemoth. It could also potentially reduce the attractiveness of using militancy as an instrument of foreign policy. As Steve Coll chronicled in *The New Yorker* in 2009, Musharraf and Indian Prime Minister Manmohan Singh were quite close to reaching a breakthrough accord on Kashmir in 2008, but it was aborted by the rapid erosion of Musharraf's authority in the face of domestic opposition to his dictatorial rule.

The point is that only a strong, stable, and legitimate elected government will be able to mobilize the public opinion necessary to clinch a lasting peace with India. Both the PPP and the PML-N favour cooperation over confrontation in the region, and each has tried to mend fences with India, through high-level diplomacy as well as backdoor talks, only to be upbraided by the generals for compromising on national security. These parties need more room to pursue peace with India while holding the military at bay. This is something the United States can help provide, by firmly supporting democratic institutions in Pakistan even as it works with the military to fight al Qaeda.

No Means No

The Obama administration came into office in 2009 with a solid commitment to supporting Pakistan's then year-old civilian democratic government as a hedge against militancy and terrorism. The Kerry-Lugar-Berman bill, which was passed into law as the Enhanced Partnership With Pakistan Act of 2009, authorized the U.S. Congress to triple civilian development assistance to Pakistan, raising it to $7.5 billion between 2010 and 2014. The aid package was designed to signal a new era in the United States' relationship with Pakistan, shifting the focus of U.S. aid from the military to civilian democratic governance and social development. Continued military aid was also tied to a yearly certification by the U.S. secretary of state that the Pakistani military has refrained from interfering in politics and is subject to civilian control over budgetary allocations, officer promotions, and strategic planning.

Not surprisingly, the Pakistani military balked at this affront even as the civilian government welcomed the aid. Joining with opposition parties, the military publicly decried the bill as a threat to Pakistani national security and mobilized right-wing sections of the media against U.S. meddling. In response, the bill's sponsors buckled and effectively defanged the conditionality measures. Even though the text of the law is intact, the United States meekly assured the Pakistani military that the intent of the conditions was misinterpreted and that the United States would keep its nose out of the generals' business. Indeed, most contact between the two countries still occurs behind closed doors between the two militaries or between the CIA and the ISI. The CIA's use of unmanned drones against militants in FATA, which are reportedly flown out of Pakistani bases, exemplifies this lack of transparency. The secrecy of the program allows both the United States and Pakistan to escape responsibility for civilian casualties.

The climb-down on the Enhanced Partnership Act indicated that even though the U.S. Congress recognizes the folly of building exclusive alliances with the Pakistani military, it still prefers engaging with Pakistan's military over its civilian leaders. This is partly pragmatism: the military is still the most powerful institution in Pakistan. But by continuing to treat the Pakistani military as a state above the state, the United States only reinforces the military's exaggerated sense of indispensability and further weakens civilian rule.

If the United States had stood its ground, the Pakistani military would have eventually backed down. It is dependent on the United States for military aid and high-tech armaments, including upgrading its aging fleet of F-16 fighters. And although the military has leverage over Washington since it controls U.S. supply routes into landlocked Afghanistan, its bargaining position has weakened over time. Although Washington generally remains reluctant to pressure the Pakistani military, appropriately using sticks has not necessarily meant losing the generals' cooperation in fighting terrorism. For example, the U.S. Congress warned that it would cut off U.S. aid in response to Pakistan's detention of a CIA contractor, Raymond Davis, who was arrested in January for fatally shooting two Pakistanis in the eastern city of Lahore. In the end, Davis was released from jail in March — the families of the victims agreed to pardon him after receiving compensation. His release would not have been possible without military complicity.

Such political and diplomatic pressure should be used to censure the military for political incursions. In this spirit, the United States should signal to the military that cracking down on terrorism is not a license for it to destabilize or overrun the government. The U.S. military should remind its Pakistani counterpart that interference in politics will not be tolerated and could have serious repercussions, including a downgrading of military ties, the suspension of nondevelopment aid, and broader diplomatic isolation. Although the United States is confronted with an economic recession of its own, more civilian aid for (and trade with) Pakistan would cost relatively little compared to the money that the United States spends fighting Afghan and Pakistani extremists. And the potential dividends could be enormous: U.S. civilian aid could help secure civilian rule in Pakistan for the long haul and diminish anti-Americanism as well. To reduce the danger of moral hazard, this aid should be tightly linked to Pakistan's economic performance, progress in combating corruption, and transparency and responsiveness in government.

One relatively easy way for the United States to boost economic productivity in Pakistan would be to grant Pakistan emergency duty-free access to the U.S. market for textiles. This concession would face opposition from politically powerful U.S. textile interests, but the Obama administration should pursue this legislation on at least a temporary basis because it could crucially improve the economic stability of a vital ally by increasing the revenue it gets from this important industry.

Although a settlement of the Kashmir conflict is unlikely in the short term, Washington should continue to push both sides to achieve that goal. Of course, there are no guarantees that peace would be sufficient to reduce Pakistan's military expenditures or restrict the military to its proper constitutional sphere. But it is worth the effort because the international community has a stake in ending the nuclearized Indian-Pakistani rivalry, which not only endangers global security but also has spilled into Afghanistan.

With over a hundred nuclear weapons, a war-prone rivalry with India, and the presence of some of the world's most dangerous terrorists on its soil,

Pakistan is too important to be left to the devices of its generals. For too long, the United States has sacrificed democracy for order. The results have been less than ideal, especially for the people of Pakistan. Pakistan urgently needs support from the international community to help stabilize its civilian democratic institutions and bolster its economy. Only such support will ensure its stability and reliability as a U.S. partner in the region.

THE ISI

By 2008, as the Taliban insurgency against Pakistan itself gathered pace and an increasing number of ISI officers and informants fell victim to it, the ISI itself began to see the need for a new and much tougher approach to some of its militant allies within Pakistan.

However, the military is genuinely concerned that if it attacks some of these groups it will drive them into joining the Pakistani Taliban – as has already occurred with Sipahi-Sabah, Lashkar-e-Janghvi and some sections of Jaish-e-Mohammed. The suspected involvement of JeM activists in the attempts to assassinate Musharraf in December 2003 (apparently with low level help from within the armed forces) led to a harsh crackdown on parts of the group by Pakistani intelligence.

The ISI's long association with the militants, first in Afghanistan and then in Kashmir, had led some ISI officers into a close personal identification with the forces that they were supposed to be controlling. This leads to a whole set of interlocking questions: How far the Pakistani High Command continues to back certain militant groups; how far the command of the ISI may be following a strategy in this regard independent from that of the military; and how far individual ISI officers may have escaped from the control of their superiors and be supporting and planning terrorist actions on their own. This in turn leads to the even more vital question of how far the Pakistani military is penetrated by Islamist extremist elements, and whether there is any possibility of these carrying out a successful military coup from below, against their own high command.

Since this whole field is obviously kept very secret by the institutions concerned (including Military Intelligence, which monitors the political and ideological allegiances of officers), there are no definitive answers to these questions. What follows is informed guess-work based on numerous discussions with experts and off-the-record talks with Pakistani officers including retired ISI officers.

Concerning the ISI, the consensus of my informants is as follows: There is considerable resentment of the ISI in the rest of the military, due to their perceived arrogance and suspected corruption. However, when it comes to overall strategy, the ISI follows the line of the high command. It is after all always headed by a senior regular general, not a professional intelligence officer, and a majority of its officers are also seconded regulars. The present Chief of Army Staff, General Ashfaq Kayani, was director of the ISI from 2004-2007, and ordered a limited crackdown on jihadi groups that the ISI had previously supported.

Concerning the Afghan Taliban, the military and the ISI are at one, and the evidence is unequivocal: The military and ISI continue to give them shelter, and there is deep unwillingness to take serious action against them on America's behalf, both because it is feared that this would increase Pathan insurgency in Pakistan, and because they are seen as the only assets Pakistan possesses in Afghanistan. The conviction in the Pakistani security establishment is that the West will quit Afghanistan leaving civil war behind, and that India will then throw its weight behind the non-Pathan forces of the former Northern Alliance in order to encircle Pakistan strategically.

Concerning the Pakistani Taliban and their allies, however, like the military as a whole, the ISI is now committed to the struggle against them, and by the end of 2009 had lost more than seventy of its officers in this fight – some ten times the number of CIA officers killed since 9/11, just as Pakistani military casualties fighting the Pakistani Taliban have greatly exceeded those of the US in Afghanistan. Equally, however, in 2007-2008 there were a great many stories of ISI officers intervening to rescue individual Taliban commanders from arrest by the police or the army – too many, and too circumstantial, for these all to have been invented.

It seems clear therefore that whether because individual ISI officers felt a personal commitment to these men, or because the institution as a whole still regarded them as potentially useful, actions were taking place that were against overall military policy – let alone that of the Pakistani government. Moreover, some of these men had at least indirect links to Al Qaeda. This does not mean that the ISI knows where Osama bin Laden (if he is indeed still alive), Aiman al-Zawahiri and other Al Qaeda leaders are hiding. It does however suggest that they could probably do a good deal more to find out.

On the crucial question of support for terrorism against India, it is obvious that not just the ISI but the military as a whole are committed to keeping Lashkar-e-Taiba (under its cover as Jamaat-ut-Dawa) at least in existence, both as a potential future weapon against India and because they are genuinely scared of driving this very powerful and popular group to revolt.

Jamaat-ut-Dawa's extensive international network in the Pakistani diaspora also leads Pakistani officers to fear that if they attempt seriously to suppress the group it will also launch successful terrorist attacks in the West, with disastrous results for Pakistan's international position. Lashkar-e-Taiba members certainly have contacts with Al Qaeda, and helped Al Qaeda operatives escape from Afghanistan after the defeat of the Taliban and helped shelter them within Pakistan. As Stephen Tankel writes:

"Ideologically, for all of its strategic restraint following 9/11 Lashkar is, after all, a jihadi organization with a long history of waging pan-Islamic irredentist campaigns. Indian-controlled Kashmir may be the group's primary ideological and strategic target, but it has never been the apotheosis of Lashkar's jihad."

PAKISTAN'S NEW MILITARY BUDGET

It should come as no surprise that the release of Pakistan's federal budget on June 5 went unremarked in Washington. Nevertheless, Pakistan's budget—particularly its defense budget— will quietly attract the attention of American officials and analysts who work this issue because important U.S. interests are engaged in Pakistan.

Pakistan is a large country with the potential to enjoy robust economic growth and attract foreign investment. It is a front-line state in the fight against violent extremism, and it is one of the world's nuclear powers. The United States, in other words, wants Pakistan to succeed. Its national budget can help or hinder success.

Pakistan's potential won't be realized until it is at peace with itself and its neighbors. Pakistan needs to be defended against internal and external threats. A strong, transparent defense budget that reflects a balanced strategy for national security would advance Pakistan's national interests. The finance ministry has yet to release the country's budget documents in full, but based on the few details that have already emerged, it appears that this defense budget will in many respects be similar to those in previous years. It may also offer some surprises.

Two elements of the budget represent continuity with the past—the military spent more in the last year than it was allocated, and this year's spending increase was similar to past increases. According to the Budget in Brief , the country spent $7 billion on defense affairs and services in FY 2014-15. This is almost $200 million more than the military was allocated. Since 2008—when the government first began releasing reasonably substantive budget documents—Pakistan's defense spending has always run over-budget. Consistently going over-budget is problematic, particularly as fiscal consolidation has been a central pillar of the current government's economic agenda. The defense budget grew from $6.1 billion (629.8 billion Pakistani rupees) in FY 2013-14 to $7 billion in FY 2014-15—a 14.7 percent increase. This is the largest year-on-year percentage increase since 2012, and it reverses a trend in which the defense budget had been growing at a slower pace over the past eight years. Although in real terms the spending increase is not as significant—a decline in global oil prices has reduced year-on-year inflation to 3.2 percent as of May 2015—it is still in keeping with long-term trends in Pakistan. The proposed budget for FY 2015-16 of $7.6 billion is $390 million less than what the Pakistan Tehreek-e-Insaf's shadow budget proposes.

There appear to be a few surprises in this year's budget. First, the military spent nearly twice its allocated development budget in FY 2014-2015. While it was allocated $22.1 million under the Public Sector Development Programme (PSDP), the military actually spent $41.9 million. While this represents less than 10 percent of total defense spending according to the government, going 100% over-budget is problematic on any scale.

Second, a recent report suggested that the development budget for the Pakistan Atomic Energy Commission (PAEC) has been cut in half from $578.9 million to $296.8 million for FY 2016. While the report has not yet been confirmed, this is noteworthy not only for the size of the cut, but the fact that there was a cut at all in a key component of Pakistan's nuclear program. According to past budget documents, the PAEC's overall budget has increased steadily since 2008.

In all likelihood, Pakistan's defense budget is higher than what the official documents indicate. First, the defense budget has not included pensions since the early 2000s. In the first years of the most recent Pakistan People's Party government, the issue of where to place military pensions became the subject of parliamentary debate. In a 2010 meeting of the Public Accounts Committee (PAC), then-parliamentarian and current defense minister Khawaja Mohammad Asif reportedly said , "Whom we are trying to fool by showing military pension budget as part of civilian budget?" The entire fund in 2010 reportedly amounted to roughly $704 million.

Second, the use of "contingent liabilities" raises important questions. According to the Pakistani government, contingent liabilities "are possible future liabilities that will only become certain on the occurrence of some future event." The finance ministry explainsthat they do not appear on the balance sheets, and "such off-balance sheet transactions cannot be overlooked in order to gain a holistic view of a country's fiscal position." According the recently-released Economic Survey , the outstanding guarantees to Public Sector Enterprises (PSEs) under the contingent liability fund exceeds $5.9 billion. While the government does not document the percentage of contingent liabilities that go to the military, it is safe to assume that some percentage does, and that this would further inflate the defense budget. It will be possible to conduct a more comprehensive analysis of defense spending once the government releases more detailed budget documents to the public in the next few weeks. Although Senate Chairman Raza Rabbani was recently quoted as saying that parliamentary debates on the specifics of the defense budget should remain secret, a more transparent budget process strengthens democracy and thereby national security. With more information, observers might be able to find answers to questions that have already emerged from the release of top-line spending figures. Perhaps most importantly, the Pakistani people will be able to debate the budgetary trade-offs necessary to enhance national, economic, and social security.

THE RISE IN PAKISTAN DEFENCE BUDGET

Pakistan's Budget was unveiled last month, as part of ruling Pakistan Muslim League-led government's last budget for its term before the elections kick-in in the coming months. Of all the allocations, the allocation to defence sector generated headlines, as defence budget rose by 19.6 percent to Rs. 1.1 trillion from previous year's allocation of 920.2 billion, and over the last five years, it was close to a two-fold increase compared to Rs. 630 billion figure of Financial Year 2013-14. During Financial Years 2016 and 2017, it rose 11 percent and 7 percent respectively. The hike does not consist of the 260 billion meant for soldiers' pensions. Moreover, the highest growth was registered in naval allocation amounting to 21.4 percent greater than army's 19.4 percent, a probable hint towards an increased outlay over the maritime commitments for the CPEC and submarine deal with China.

The quantum of hike does necessitate an inquiry into whether it could have extra-regional connotations or not, since the move comes in the backdrop of the new low bilateral ties reached post-surgical strikes, when the LoC is characterised by an exponentially rising ceasefire violations and unrest in Kashmir. Pakistan had also expressed its concern over India's rising defence spending, following which Pakistan reportedly apprised the UN Secretary General about the developments. In the larger backdrop, the increase comes amidst lukewarm, if not deteriorating, relationship with the United States amidst the pressure to bring the Taliban to the negotiating table, given the deteriorating security section in the nation.

A break up of Rs. 1.1 trillion allocation shows that:-

1. "Rs. 423 billion have been allocated for employee-related expenses", covering "salaries and allowances paid to troops in uniform and civilian employees".
2. Rs. 253.5 billion are for operating expenses, consisting of "transport, Petroleum Oil, and Lubricants, ration, medical treatment, training".

3. Rs. 282 billion for local purchases and import of arms and ammunition, and,
4. Rs. 141 billion for civil works, which consists of "funds marked for maintenance of existing infrastructure and construction of new buildings".

While some strategic developments, including operationalisation of the 15,000 troop strong Special Security Division to protect the CPEC, and post-Zarb-e-Azb security measures like fencing of the Durand Line and fortifications along it, may plausibly allude to higher spending, the hike must not be interpreted purely as a threat, given domestic political and administrative issues at play, and since several possibilities surface if one reads into this.

Given the civil-military equation in Pakistan, defence spending is an area where the military establishment has had a greater say despite the civilian administration allocating the budget. A clear discussion is yet to take place in the Pakistan Parliament where one could make out the exact procedure followed on defence spending. Until then, the budget would be open to numerous interpretations. Also, since major planned acquisitions have been kept out of this hike, much cannot be said about the military's intent on seeing these figures which appear innocuous, and given the purpose described.

The least that could be inferred from this is that the hike comes at a time when civil-military relationship in the nation is undergoing a critical phase, following Nawaz Sharif's ouster and when the establishment has cleared the ground for other political players to ensure a fractured mandate, given Sharif's desperate attempts to play victim as election draws closer. The fact that even at this critical juncture of civil-military ties, the government could allocate more for defence spending reconfirms its writ.

Keeping the speculations aside, Pakistan's rising GDP growth rates also leave excess resources for the nation to allocate towards defence spending, a phenomenon natural to any growing economy. In last two years, the economy has grown 5.4 percent and 5.8 percent respectively, and during the last five years, revenue collection, according to the federal board of revenue, has risen from Rs. 1980 billion in 2013, and is being estimated at 4888 billion by the end of this year.

In Conclusion, while the budget data does not point to any threatening developments per se, what would be of importance is to see how Pakistan's evolving defence engagements with powers like Russia and US fare over the course of time. Since some big-ticket purchases are on the cards, especially with Russia, such engagements may even impinge on India's own defence engagements with those nations.

8

Pakistan: Nuclear Stability and Diplomacy

The conceptual discourse, contributed to in the main by Western scholars, on the security and strategic stability of new nuclear weapon states like India and Pakistan seems alarmist. In reality, however, India and Pakistan have been mutually deliberating on various aspects of nuclear confidence-building measures (CBMs). This chapter is an effort to identify the issues of nuclear security concerns in two spheres-academic and policy formulations. The emphasis is more on the nuclear thinking of the two countries and the diplomatic challenges ahead particularly on the nuclear CBMs. Nuclear South Asia is a reality today. As soon as India and Pakistan conducted their nuclear weapon tests in May 1998, the debate-predominantly outside the Indian subcontinent-over nuclear security and stability assumed significant momentum. Many critics have questioned the rationale behind India and Pakistan possessing nuclear weapons.

The strategic factors, especially those related to the nuclear-deterrence concepts, are being reviewed in the context of new nuclear weapon states by many diplomats, academics and strategic planners all over the world. With the passage of time, on their part, both India and Pakistan have also been long deliberating on the security compulsions behind the development and possession of nuclear weapons at various international platforms. They are also trying, in their own ways, to cope with the international disarmament discourse dominated by the P-5 states who have refused to accord India and Pakistan de jurestatus in the elite nuclear club. At the same time, acknowledging the fact that nuclear weapons remain significant to strategic stability between the two countries, both India and Pakistan have been trying to evolve mechanisms for ensuring the long-term nuclear security of the region. Various nuclear confidence-building measures (CBMs) are being mutually discussed by the two nuclear neighbours with increasing determination.

This chapter seeks to highlight the issues emerging out of available academic and policy debates concerning the security and stability of nuclear South Asia. Accordingly, it is an effort to broaden the understanding of the challenges before India-Pakistan nuclear diplomacy.

India and Pakistan as States with NuclearWeapons: ATheoretical Perspective Maintaining its commitment to work towards global nuclear disarmament, India believes: "The end of the Cold War had provided the opportunity to reduce the salience of nuclear weapons but we saw instead that most of the world acquiesced in the manoeuvres to perpetuate forever the right of a handful of nations to retain their arsenals. ...The search for unilateral advantage has led to measures that undermine the principle of irreversibility of committed reductions. There is no move towards collective renouncing of 'first-use'. Instead there are prospects of advocacy of pre-emptive use and a move towards developing new types of arsenals justified by new rationale."

Nuclear weapons have been a central element of the security discourse among American and Western scholars and policy-makers since the beginning of the Cold War. Possession of nuclear weapons by a state beyond the P-5 club is commonly described in Western academic and strategic communities interchangeably as 'spread' or 'proliferation' of nuclear weapons and they call it 'new nuclear weapon state'. By the end of the Cold War,in the course of the last five decades, a complex theology has evolved about the extent to which nuclear deterrence preserves or endangers world peace and security. Despite lacking universal acceptance at policy-making levels, "the debate over nuclear proliferation" in the Western world is instructive for its multiple intellectual inputs.

However, there appear two significant limitations in the prevailing debate. First, a lack of universal appeal is apparent in the inherent criticism by each group of scholars. They differ mainly over mutually contested assumptions and applications of each theory. Second, academic formulations on non-proliferation do not adequately advance the comprehensive nuclear disarmament approach. They fail to acknowledge the existing discriminating non-proliferation regimes. Instead, by and large while discussing 'deterrence' in the context of 'new nuclear weapons states', most of the academic writing legitimises the nuclear weapons of P-5 states and remain suspicious of the rationale of others. And, "there is little in the literature to tell us how a country should plan to use its nuclear weapons to deter its adversaries while denying the possession of these weapons."

There are two main streams of theorisation on nuclear proliferation, namely, Optimist and Pessimist. One more competing theory is also found in the writings of international relations-Political Relativist. Some prominent Realist scholars, classified under 'Proliferation Optimists', have argued that there is virtually no risk that nuclear weapons will actually be used if more countries obtain them. They believe that proliferation would result in lesser number of wars and greater peace and stability. Afew of them (Optimist scholars) believe that except from a slight rise in the probability of nuclear accidents, the increased deterrent effects of nuclear proliferation lower the likelihood of war among nuclear-armed states. Rooted in the assumption that states behave in a self-interested and rational manner, the pioneer among Proliferation Optimists, Kenneth Waltz, argues: "More May be Better"

He suggests the following six assumptions to prove his argument:

- o International politics is a self-help system.
- o Balance of terror is indestructible.
- o 'Uncertainty' about controlling escalation is at the heart of deterrence
- o Deterrence provides a guarantee against accidents.
- o Nuclear weaponry makes miscalculation difficult due to greater awareness of possible damage and sensitivity to the cost of war.
- o New nuclear states will feel the constraints of old nuclear states (meaning new nuclear states will learn lessons from the maintenance of deterrence during the Cold War).

Related to the issue of nuclear weapons and regional stability, however, for the states sharing common borders, Waltz says: "Where states are bitter enemies one may fear that they will be unable to resist using their nuclear weapons against each other. This is a worry about the future that the past does not disclose."

But, he indicates that nuclear weapons caused China and Soviet Union to deal cautiously. Political relativists, who give primacy to the character (political structures, ideology, culture, system of governance, etc.) of the possessor state over the technicalities involved in the existence of arsenals, challenge the optimistic view. Political relativism is an approach that stresses more on the internal structure of states, rather than the international political environment in which the states act.

Political relativists believe that deterrence can fail when required the most, and that nuclear weapons are not secure in the hands of "bad states". Criticising the rationality factor in Waltz's argument, Robert Jervis, one of the 'political relativists' argues: "Proliferation among strongly dissatisfied countries would not necessarily recapitulate the Soviet-American patterns of stability."

While suggesting that mere possibility of nuclear use causes extreme caution all around the world, Waltz believes that preventive attacks are more unlikely to take place.

Instead of creating large arsenals, based on the Cold War experience, for better survivability, Kenneth Waltz says: "Though large and complex nuclear arsenals are hard to control, the relatively small and simple forces of new nuclear states are not." In contrast to Proliferation Optimists, the Pessimists believe that the spread of nuclear weapons to other states beyond P-5 will make the world more dangerous.

Opposite to Waltz's theory of 'More May Be Better', Scott D. Sagan, also known as a 'conditional pessimist', believes that 'More Will Be Worse.' Against Waltz's rational theory, pessimistic assessments of Sagan are based on the organisation theory. The organisation theory implies that whereas the government (civilian) leaders may behave rationally, the final implementation of policy decisions is influenced by powerful groups/forces within the country.

Since the military organisation of any country is finally responsible for operational requirements of nuclear weapons, Sagan assumes that it determines the behaviour of the state. He argues: "professional military organisations-because of common biases, inflexible routines, and parochial interests-display organisational behaviours that are likely to lead to deterrence failures and deliberate or accidental war." While elaborating on how the United States and the former Soviet Union faced difficulties in handling issues like deterrence, deployment, safety and security of nuclear weapons, Sagan raises doubts as to how the new nuclear weapon states will follow the necessary precautions to avoid escalation, preventive wars or accidental hazards. Sagan in his thesis 'More Will Be Worse'provides the following pessimistic assumptions:

- o Spread of nuclear weapons to new states will make the world more dangerous. Deterrence failures are more likely in the new nuclear states;
- o Military biases can lead to larger arsenals but not necessarily more survivable weapons;
- o Opaque (covert) nature of nuclear proliferation exacerbates nuclear weapons safety problems;
- o Poorly designed operating procedures can undermine survivable nuclear forces;
- o Lack of organisational and financial resources can result in inadequate mechanical safety devices;
- o Accident-prone nuclear operations will be more prevalent in states with volatile civil-military relations;

- o The most worrisome case in point is Pakistan;
- o Efforts should be made to assist the new nuclear states in making their nuclear forces safe, secure and survivable.

Describing the nature of the nuclear problem in South Asia, Sagan argues that the greater danger is the risk of nuclear war arising through deliberate escalation of a conventional war started over Kashmir. And, in addition, there is the risk of an accidental nuclear war, caused by a nuclear weapons accident, i.e., the unauthorised use of a nuclear weapon, or a false warning of an attack.

Among the Pessimists, the Abolitionists hold the view that all nuclear powers should dismantle their nuclear arsenals and put their stockpiles of military and civilian fissile materials under the control of an international agency. Developing the argument that the United Nations would not indulge in nuclear weapons production, others have proposed an operational nuclear force or static nuclear stockpile under the command of an international body like UN.

And some, who believe that wisdom derived from the revulsion of war lies only with European and the North American societies, hold the notion that the possible use of nuclear weapons exists only in other parts of the world. They believe that "weapons of mass destruction could yet become a turning point, indeed a final point, of human history in a catastrophe beyond imagination."

Both Waltz and Sagan have provided a persuasive framework to academics in terms of policy-making of states. The policy prescriptions reflect on the responsibility of states, which nuclear weapon states may acquire, by virtue of possessing such arsenals. However, no analysis can be said to be complete because of their selective interpretation of facts and events. Each has interpreted the events of the Cold War period to justify an individual theoretical formulation: "The strategic arms race after both the United States and the Soviet Union secured second-strike capabilities is a mystery to nuclear optimists." Sagan's theoretical emphasis is pointed more towards weapons seekers (so-called nuclear proliferation) and is less critical about the lack of disarmament efforts.

Peter R. Lavoy has brought out 12 specific concerns about nuclear proliferation:

- o Incomplete nuclear weapons systems invite preventive military attack;
- o Vulnerable nuclear forces invite pre-emptive military attack;
- o Primitive command and control raises the risk of nuclear accidents;
- o Unstable command and control risks the loss of control over nuclear forces, raising the possibility of unauthorised nuclear use or nuclear terrorism;

- o Nuclear arms racing is inevitable and raises the risk of war;
- o Nuclear proliferation could increase the likelihood of conventional military conflict;
- o Conventional conflict could escalate to nuclear war;
- o Nuclear forces might be used for coercion and aggression;
- o New nuclear states might assist proliferation elsewhere;
- o Successful nuclear proliferation could induce further nuclear proliferation;
- o Nuclear proliferation raises the risk of cataclysmic nuclear war; and,
- o New nuclear states could limit the political and military influence of major powers.

A preventive strike refers to an attack on the adversary to forestall acquisition of nuclear weapons facilities, implying waging a war before the adversary acquires weapons capability. Israel's attack that destroyed the Osirak reactor in Iraq in 1981 can be cited as an example of such preventive strike. The possibility of preventive military strikes has little or no relevance for India and Pakistan after both nations signed an agreement in 1988 on the 'Prohibition of Attack against Nuclear Installations and Facilities'of each other.

Pre-emption includes military action when an attack by an adversary is imminent. This attack may include targeting of the opponent's strategic arsenals or decapitate its command channels to prevent the adversary from launching a retaliatory strike. India and Pakistan have already established nuclear command authorities. However, due to lack of adequate information currently available in the public domain, there remains some scope for analysts outside the official establishment to debate on the operational issues of command and control and communications.

The willingness shown by both India and Pakistan towards nuclear confidence-building is indicative of their concern for mutual understanding to minimise threats that go with possession of nuclear weapons.

The possibility of conventional conflict escalating to the level of nuclear exchange may remain a concern for all till Pakistan comes out with a declaratory 'nuclear doctrine'. India is already committed to no-first-use (NFU) in its defined nuclear doctrine. It could be a point of discussion among strategic analysts as to why India and Pakistan would not follow the Cold War-like deterrence postures and why one should not worry that India and Pakistan too would refrain from using nuclear weapons. Both India and Pakistan have adequately expressed in respective threat concerns that impelled them to go for the nuclear choice. Pakistan's security formulations are India-centric, whereas India has a more comprehensive national security outlook that is not country specific.

Yet, in a significant assertion both the countries have recognised "that the nuclear capabilities of each other, which are based on their national security imperatives, constitute a factor for stability." The history of the development of nuclear weapons is linked with MAD-i.e., mutually assured destruction, a concept evolved during the Cold War.According to the MAD concept, the use of nuclear weapons by one against the other is apprehended in final destruction of both the attacker and the defender. The inducement aspect of proliferation, that successful nuclear proliferation could induce further nuclear proliferation, as averred by Western scholars, may be placed within the larger debate in answering two pertinent queries. First, why does a country seek nuclear weapon capability? And second, why is it so difficult to relinquish possession of nuclear weapons? Answers to these two questions remain contested in the light of progress towards global nuclear disarmament.

The Nuclear Non-Proliferation Treaty (NPT) includes a provision under Article VI: "Each of the Parties to the Treaty undertakes to pursue negotiations in good faith on effective measures relating to cessation of the nuclear arms race at an early date and to nuclear disarmament, and on a treaty on general and complete disarmament under strict and effective international control."

This provision however does not provide any time frame for achieving the disarmament objective. At the same time, P-5 states also lack any serious commitment towards making the world free from nuclear weapons. The US abrogation of the 1972 Anti-Ballistic Missile Treaty (ABM), its pursuit for National Missile Defense and Nuclear Posture Review, none of these indicate reduction in stock of missiles and elimination of nuclear weapons in the near future. Potential US nuclear policy strategies seem to be at odds with its commitment to the NPT.

ECONOMIC EMERGENCE AND POLITICAL CHANGE

Seeds of economic change have long been embedded in the liberal system that North America and Europe together constructed after the Second World War. Indeed, as more of the world adopted liberal market-oriented strategies, the club of developed countries widened, and the international system evolved as a result.

This has not always been a seamless process; shifts in the economic balance of power invariably alter relations among states, and in so doing generate no small degree of friction. China's explosive economic emergence, however, promises the greatest shake-up ever of the reigning post-war economic order. It will invariably alter international relations and, by extension, North American-European relations in profound and perhaps unanticipated ways.

China, however, is hardly a new economic power. Prior to the closing of its borders in 1500, its emperors presided over the world's largest and most sophisticated economy. Although modern Europe moved quickly to catch up and ultimately surpass China over the ensuing centuries, it still generated 32% of the world's wealth in 1820. (Hale and Hale) The forced reopening of its borders at the hands of colonial powers marked the beginning of China's return to the world stage; yet colonialism, anarchy, warlordism, nationalist reaction, world war, occupation, civil war and communist revolution rendered this an exceedingly fitful and terribly painful process.

It was only with the 1978 reforms launched by Deng Xiaoping that Communist China began to develop in a more organic fashion. Oddly enough, this reform commenced in the countryside when the state suddenly allowed peasants to adopt market structures in order to encourage production and boost income. Since 1994, however, China's economic revolution has been largely an urban and industrial phenomenon. Growth along the Eastern coast has far outstripped development in the countryside. Between 1978 and 2003, China's per capita GDP grew by 6.1% a year, registering a 337% increase over that period. (Wolf) Large swathes of China's vast hinterland have however been left behind in this process.

China has very quickly moved from a communist ownership model, in which the state possessed virtually all the means of production, to a far more complex system in which private ownership increasingly overshadows state ownership. It has also advanced rapidly up the production scale, moving from very simple assembly to ever more complex manufacturing processes.

The area for autonomous action by the individual in China generally has also been expanding, despite persistent, regrettable and ultimately counter-productive limitations on political freedom.

The Chinese people now enjoy unprecedented freedom of movement, information flows are far more developed and open today, and young Chinese possess ever-greater control over their destiny despite the real political constraints they confront. In the words of one western analyst, the Chinese at least enjoy the freedom not to engage in politics. This is hardly the same thing as democracy, but it suggests an important evolution away from the totalitarianism of the Cultural Revolution when the Chinese were compelled to live and breath politics.

Yet, within parameters defined largely by the Communist leadership, China's economic boom is providing an outlet for the country's long pent-up commercial energies and the aspirations of its people for a better life. The possibility of achieving this has certainly diverted some of the political passions that spilled onto Tiananmen Square in 1989, (Hutzler) although repression has done its part as well. China's huge student population certainly has its share of aspirant democrats, but many have simply abandoned politics to focus on their careers. Recent polls suggest that the Chinese are tremendously optimistic about the future; particularly the well educated, who are best positioned to benefit from China's economic expansion and global integration. (Giles)

China's civil society has grown more complex and articulated since 1989 and this too is shaping both the aspirations of its people and the likely manner in which future political change will unfold. Many people today recognize their growing stake in the preservation of civil order. This does not mean that democratic reform will not come, rather it points toward new modalities for pushing for these changes-strategies in which pressure comes from both within the governing elite and from an ever-more articulated civil society.

In the words of the historian Lanxin Xiang, the Chinese have embraced Perestroika (restructuring) but have no desire to push for glasnost (openness). (Meeting with Lanxin Xiang) The great threat to the current order may come not from the kind of students who were targeted during the Tiananmen crackdown, but rather from the millions of disenfranchised Chinese, many living in the country's vast interior, who have not benefited from economic reform and growth.

China's elite is aware of this and clearly hopes that by easing conditions in the vast hinterland, the regime will be better positioned to defend the political status quo and the stability needed to generate economic growth. But even this offers only a temporary solution to the longer-term problem of China's lack of democracy.

Several years ago after the high technology stock bubble, American economists were ringing their hands over the question of which country might possibly serve as the engine of a global economic recovery. Europe, it was said, was hopelessly over-regulated and increasingly uncompetitive; the United States was heading down a path of rising government and consumer debt, corporate accounting scandals and investor uncertainties; and Japan's economy remained mired in a deflationary recession. Two bright spots, India and China, it was then claimed, lacked the economic weight for their high growth rates to have any significant spillover impact on global growth. Such forecasts, it seems, were made under the old assumption that the global economy and OECD member countries, with a few important caveats, were more or less the same thing.

That assumption proved false. According to a recent Economist survey, China now accounts for 13% of world output in purchasing power parity terms (second only to America's) and will soon be the world's third largest exporter after the United States and Germany. Its domestic demand has been the single greatest factor in Asia's recent recovery, and it is a major underwriter of American deficit spending through its purchase of US treasury bills. The IMF has suggested that if China proves able to implement much needed banking reform, the country will continue growing over the coming decade at 7-8% per annum, a rate which could push the country's GDP above that of the United States by 2020 in purchasing power parity terms. (The Economist, October 2, 2004.) China is thus crossing a threshold. Its economy can no longer be judged as a mere potentiality. It is now an integral player in the global economy, and its international economic weight has grown extraordinarily consequential.

Over the last year, the world economy grew by 5%. The two engines of that growth were an American economy unleashed by loose monetary and fiscal policies, very low savings rates and a high propensity to import, and Chinese producers, who are orchestrating one of the greatest economic expansions in recent memory. Yet, China remains a developing country. This accords it a rather unique place in the world economy, one that is perhaps rendered all the more paradoxical by the fact that this ever more economically liberal society is still administered by a Communist party.

THE CHINA-PAKISTAN NUCLEAR "DEAL"

Others, such as Brad Glosserman, executive director of the Pacific Forum Centre for Strategic and International Studies, have gone further, arguing that the U.S.-India deal has in fact opened the floodgates for exactly such transactions as are now proposed by China toward Pakistan: "We all knew at the time that an agreement such as the India-U.S. one would have consequences for the non-proliferation regime and that's what you are seeing now.... The India-U.S. deal was a bad, troubling example to set, for proliferators, however justified the desire in Washington to improve ties with India." In other words, if the U.S.-India agreement had not been consummated, the currently proposed Chinese sale of new nuclear rectors to Pakistan would likely not have occurred.

These claims, however, are not persuasive. Whatever one's views of the U.S.-India civilian nuclear cooperation agreement, the accord reached between President George W. Bush and Prime Minister Manmohan Singh is fundamentally different from the proposed Chinese effort to export additional power reactors to Pakistan. *Pace* the recent claims of Maleeha Lodhi, the U.S.-Indian agreement is not "a fundamental violation of the [Nuclear Non-Proliferation] Treaty" because nothing in the treaty forbids agreements for peaceful nuclear cooperation—to include the export of reactors, other nuclear technologies, and nuclear materials—with states that are not signatories to it.

All that the NPT requires is that every nuclear transaction with any non-signatory state be solely for peaceful uses and that all transferred items be fully safeguarded by the International Atomic Energy Agency (IAEA). The U.S.-India civilian nuclear cooperation agreement meets both these conditions and, therefore, cannot be considered a violation of the NPT by any stretch of the imagination.

The bilateral agreement between Washington and New Delhi, however, was clearly in conflict with the full-scope safeguards criterion encoded in the 1978

U.S. Nuclear Nonproliferation Act (NNPA) and adopted by the NSG at its Warsaw meeting in 1992 (which enjoined its members to refrain from any significant nuclear exports to non–nuclear-weapon states that had not adopted comprehensive safeguards).

Consequently, the Bush administration expended enormous political capital in the U.S. Congress to amend the relevant components of American law, which previously had permitted nuclear cooperation agreements with non– nuclear-weapon states only after they had accepted full-scope safeguards. Thereafter, the administration, working in concert with the government of India, committed significant diplomatic resources to convince the NSG to accord India an exceptional waiver from the full-scope safeguards criterion that would have otherwise stymied international nuclear cooperation with New Delhi.

From the very beginning, President Bush always had the option of pursuing nuclear cooperation with India in the manner now pursued by China toward Pakistan. That is, the United States—after amending its own national laws—could have unilaterally begun nuclear trade with India, disregarding the sentiments of its NSG partners and abusing the normative character of the NSG's guidelines.

Because maintaining the integrity of the global nonproliferation regime, however, was always important to the United States— and was perhaps even more important because of the exceptional treatment contemplated for India—the Bush administration spent considerable energy from October 2005 until the final extraordinary plenary in September 2008— consulting with its NSG partners *during eight meetings over four years,* not to mention the bilateral discussions that occurred in national capitals—to finally secure the special waiver for India that exempted it from the constraining condition of full-scope safeguards.

The current Sino-Pakistani nuclear transaction could not be more different.

For starters, the interstate agreement governing the potential export of the two Chinese reactors to Pakistan is a secret covenant, secretly concluded.

Unlike the U.S.-India nuclear initiative, whose terms were public and vociferously debated in both countries starting with the initial announcement in July 2005, the conditions regulating the proposed Chinese sale (and any potential future transfers) are unknown to the international community.

Furthermore, the Chinese have sought to advance this transaction with Pakistan by subterfuge. By insinuating privately, but without any accompanying formal declaration, that the prospective sale of two nuclear rectors to Pakistan is grandfathered, in Maleeha Lodhi's masterfully equivocal formulation, "under the [Sino-Pakistani] agreement dating back to the 1980s that provided for an understanding in 2003 for further long-term collaboration," Beijing has sought to convey that all Chinese sales to Pakistan are *ipso facto* exempted from its obligation to uphold the NSG's requirement of full-scope safeguards because China joined the NSG only in 2004, well after the latest "understanding" reached with Pakistan.

This minor detail, however, eluded Chinese diplomats when they provided the NSG with a rendition of their outstanding commitments upon joining the organization. As Mark Hibbs has described it, "China then explained to the NSG that a longstanding framework agreement with Pakistan committed China to provide a second reactor, Chashma-2, more research reactors, plus supply of all the fuel in perpetuity for these units." Notice there is not a word about additional power reactors beyond the already contracted Chashma-2, which began construction in 2005, the year after Beijing joined the NSG. Finally, and most conspicuously, unlike the U.S.-Indian civilian nuclear initiative, China has made no effort thus far—and is unlikely to make any in the future—to seek a specific NSG exemption for its nuclear trade with Pakistan.

The Bush administration campaigned for a waiver from the NSG's full-scope condition for India on two defensible grounds: first, India's nonproliferation record justified its progressive integration into the international nuclear regime and, second, its growing technological mastery over different nuclear fuel cycles made the international regime stronger through its inclusion rather than its continued exclusion.

After long and arduous diplomatic efforts, these arguments finally carried the day—but not before the NSG wrested from New Delhi a strong reiteration of its disarmament obligations. What is most pertinent, however, is that the United States made the investment over several years to persuade the NSG and, further, that the NSG's members took their time to consider the American proposal in all its complexity. To be sure, many were torn by the nature of the U.S. initiative; some were frustrated by what was perceived as strong American pressure; others had to balance their long-standing commitment to nonproliferation with their strong ties to India and/or the United States; and all had to struggle to figure out how best to integrate India into the global nuclear regime. When the consensus finally came, it did only after all the competing interests were weighed and adjudicated in 44 national capitals—which is exactly what the process was meant to do.

China, in contrast, has chosen a different route: seeking to short-circuit the NSG rather than appeal to its judgment. Knowing full well that Pakistan's poor nonproliferation record and its continuing reluctance to come clean on the activities of A. Q. Khan and his cohort will prevent the NSG from granting Pakistan any waiver from the full-scope safeguards requirement, Beijing appears committed to persisting with the course of action it has adopted thus far: namely, to attempt consummating various nuclear trades with Pakistan secretly if it believes it can get away with such dealings because of either diffidence or contrivance on the part of the international community.

The glaring differences between the U.S.-Indian agreement and the proposed Chinese-Pakistani transaction thus say more about, in Hibbs' apt phrase, "China's growing nuclear assertiveness" than they do about any purported similarity between these two initiatives. Consequently, the United States can— and should—oppose China's current effort to sell new reactors to Pakistan without fear of "charges of hypocrisy." If duplicity is at issue on this question, it emanates only from Beijing and not Washington.

An Opening for China?

But even if American nuclear cooperation with India is in fact fundamentally different in its structural characteristics from that between China and Pakistan, is there any truth to the charge that the former has engendered the latter? Many commentators in the United States seem to think so. Commenting on the Sino-Pakistani agreement, for example, Henry Sokolski, executive director of the Nonproliferation Policy Education Centre in Washington, has argued, consistent with Brad Glosserman's remarks quoted earlier, that "two wrongs make a wrong, but it was to be expected once we made the case for an exemption [involving India]."

Not so fast. In fact, the Chinese attempt to sell Pakistan additional nuclear reactors beyond the Chashma-1 plant agreed to in 1991 goes back to the first term of the George W.

Bush administration—long before the U.S.-Indian civilian nuclear cooperation agreement was even contemplated. It is often forgotten that for over a decade now, Beijing has sought on various occasions to expand its civilian reactor sales to Pakistan. Sino-Pakistani discussions on this subject occurred even after China had joined the NSG in 2004. For most part, however, these efforts historically were stymied by Islamabad's lack of financial resources, although China's unwillingness to confront the international community through politically provocative transactions played some role as well.

In any event, whenever it appeared that a Chinese nuclear sale to Pakistan was in the offing, successive U.S. administrations reacted quite unfavorably.

During the two terms of President George W. Bush, for example, the U.S. government démarched China formally or sharply queried it informally on several occasions, warning Beijing about American concerns regarding possible Pakistani diversion of Chinese-origin technology and materials to Islamabad's weapons programs while cautioning China not to violate standing NSG regulations on this issue. Similar démarches were issued in Islamabad, admonishing Pakistani policy makers about U.S. concerns regarding the potential circumvention of NSG guidelines.

Such complaints were leveled throughout the Bush years—*before, during, and after the civil nuclear cooperation initiative with India*. In every instance, the strong American remonstrations produced the desired effect: no Chinese reactor sale to Pakistan was consummated, even though it was obvious to U.S. policy makers that both Beijing and Islamabad were constantly testing the waters, probing the strength of American opposition. The unvarying character of the conversations themselves gave the game away. Although intelligence alerts or news reports indicating a potential Chinese sale to Pakistan usually precipitated the démarches in both capitals, neither Chinese nor Pakistani officials would ever acknowledge the conclusion of any contract or confirm whether binding interstate agreements governing the contracts even existed to begin with.

Rather, they would simply recite the facts about Pakistan's unsatisfied energy needs; assure the United States that any Sino-Pakistani nuclear energy cooperation—should it occur—would always be under IAEA safeguards and hence supposedly consistent with NSG guidelines; and, in the last years of the Bush administration, clamor for parity of U.S. treatment between India and Pakistan.

Whatever China is proposing to consummate with Pakistan today in regard to reactor and other nuclear sales, thus, has a long, repetitious, and even convoluted history that bears little *causal* connection to the U.S.-Indian civilian nuclear initiative.

If nothing else, Lodhi's laconic explanation about Sino-Pakistani civil nuclear cooperation substantiates this conclusion fully. While there is no doubt that Pakistan's appeals for equal treatment with India have grown in intensity since the conclusion of the U.S.-Indian nuclear accord, the historical record equally corroborates the fact that China's desire to press forward with renewed nuclear cooperation with Pakistan predates the landmark agreement between Washington and New Delhi. As Hibbs noted—accurately— in a recent radio interview, the commercial contacts between China and Pakistan were very, very advanced indeed at the time that the United States and India made a separate nuclear deal and the Chinese were merely waiting for an opportunity to advance this project and they have that opportunity now because the U.S. has gone ahead with its project with India and the Nuclear Suppliers Group in 2008 has approved it. So China has had a few years to wait, they've waited and now the U.S.-India project is going ahead and China now sees this as their opportune moment.

The U.S.-Indian nuclear accord, then, cannot be held responsible for precipitating Sino-Pakistani civilian nuclear commerce—or its latest iteration.

What the U.S.-Indian civilian nuclear cooperation agreement possibly contributed is a change in the psycho-political environment. This change encouraged China to test the prospects for forcing further change in the global nonproliferation system by implementing its own version of "exceptionalism" for its preferred strategic partners—in the hope that other states who acquiesced to the U.S. initiative would feel obliged to extend comparable courtesies to China.

Even if that were true, it only implies that Beijing and Islamabad ought to be held *a fortiori* to the same standards of endorsement for such cooperation, namely, securing an NSG exemption by China on behalf of Pakistan.

The reasons for insisting on such a process are simple: even if the problematic character of Pakistan's nonproliferation record is discounted, the integrity of the global nonproliferation system requires an orderly and coordinated process for managing change—which the NSG currently provides—and China, as a member of that group, should be permitted to consummate its prospective deal with Pakistan only if it can first secure an NSG exemption from the current guidelines. In other words, China should be permitted to preserve its standing within the NSG only to the degree that it complies with the organization's existing rules.

U.S. Leadership Is Indispensable

Whether China chooses to respect the NSG's guidelines and follow the process adopted in the case of the U.S.-Indian nuclear accord, however, will depend greatly on the U.S. response to Beijing's prospective sales to Pakistan.

Although it is tempting to believe that the United States has few options and that the Sino-Pakistani deal could go through because China would simply disregard the NSG given its strategic interests in Pakistan, the historical record suggests otherwise.

For all of China's supposed nonchalance, Beijing is in fact quite sensitive to both American and international pressure on issues regarding proliferation, given its own past history with Pakistan, Islamabad's nonproliferation record, and the discomfiture associated with visible but awkward and undeniable transactions. Determined U.S. opposition to China's planned sales to Pakistan would engender caution in Beijing and energize resistance from other NSG members, most of whom are already apprehensive about Beijing's efforts to circumvent the existing guidelines. This is especially relevant because the dramatic expansion of China's civilian nuclear power program has already made Beijing more dependent that ever before on international cooperation for its success; China's reliance on imported fuel, new reactor technology, and alternatives to the uranium cycle, in fact make it all the more important for Beijing to stay in the good graces of key NSG member states.

As Hibbs has concluded succinctly, "... countries like Australia, the United States, Canada, countries that are in a position to support China's nuclear energy development, these countries are not powerless and would be in the position to engage China to restrain its behaviour."

In the NSG, as in any other international organization, however, a demonstration of robust U.S. leadership is indispensable.

Resolute opposition by Washington will mobilize the pervasive international discomfort that might otherwise lie recessed and, in the case of Sino-Pakistani nuclear cooperation particularly, would be the single most important factor that makes the difference to whether China's plans in current form are realized or frustrated.

Unfortunately, the Obama administration's early response on this issue was hesitant and fumbling.

T. P. Sreenivasan, formerly India's ambassador to the IAEA, has written about a closed meeting in Washington of nonproliferation experts in early June where a senior White House official despairingly remarked, "India imitates China, Pakistan imitates India.

What can we do to stop their nuclear activities?" Further noting that Washington "did not want to displease China or Pakistan at this juncture," the official argued that American priorities today apparently cannot stray from "the economy and the war on terror." Commenting acidly that such observations reflect the attitudes of "a weak state, not a superpower," Sreenivasan chastised both U.S. policy makers and his own government for not standing up to China for its disregard of NSG processes.

It is indeed regrettable that many in Washington today conclude that the American "need" for China and Pakistan at this juncture in history prevents the administration from issuing a more tough-minded riposte toward their transgressions.

This conclusion is certainly confounding because the United States arguably does not rely on China and Pakistan any more today than it has since

2001 and, consequently, has no reason to be more forgiving of their challenges today. In any case, the mark of superior American diplomacy has always been its ability to integrate cooperation and resistance—depending on the issues—vis-à-vis a given state.

Accordingly, pressing Beijing and Islamabad is by no means doomed to failure, especially since Washington *has* managed to successfully navigate complex competing pressures involving both countries in disparate issue areas during the last several years and because, at the end of the day, the United States still wields far more power than either or both of these countries combined.

Fortunately, the Obama administration is becoming more resolute than it was initially, thanks partly to the fact that the nonproliferation community within the U.S. Department of State has succeeded in slowly forcing change on this issue. As has often been the case in the past, internal divisions within the State Department have been largely responsible for the hesitant position initially adopted by Washington.

Thankfully, it appears as if the United States is gradually recovering both its wits and its fortitude. The State Department's spokesman, P. J. Crowley, for example, recently asserted publicly that the Sino-Pakistani plans regarding the Chashma-3 and -4 reactors "appear to extend beyond cooperation that was grandfathered when China was approved for membership in the Nuclear Suppliers Group," thus amplifying the position taken earlier by another State Department spokesman, Gordon Duguid, who had declared pointedly that the United States "expects Beijing to cooperate with Pakistan in ways consistent with Chinese nonproliferation obligations."

PAKISTAN REMAINS FAITHFUL PARTNER OF CHINA

In April when President Xi Jinping visited Pakistan, China and Pakistan elevated the bilateral relations to "all-weather strategic cooperation partners." China has established partnerships with a lot of countries in the world, but Pakistan is the only one that is called an "all-weather strategic cooperation partner."

For countries with different social systems and ideologies that want to collaborate with each other, the China-Pakistan relationship has become a model to follow. This type of relationship is not based on common values and systems, but on same or similar strategic and security interests. Today common security concerns still exist, and some new concerns like global terrorism and maritime security have arisen for both sides in recent years.

Since the beginning of the 21st century, the basis of China-Pakistan cooperation has expanded. The "One Belt, One Road" initiative and China-

Pakistan Economic Corridor has enlarged bilateral strategic and cooperative partnership to a more comprehensive framework.

Before, the basis of the all-weather partnership mainly included political, strategic and security cooperation, now the closer economic ties have become a part of this basis, which makes two countries form a "community of shared destiny." The two sides not only have common economic interest and common security concerns, but also share the dream of national peace, stability, and prosperity. "Shared destiny" is the solid foundation for our cooperation in international affairs.

China-Pakistan international cooperation has some key features as follows: First, China and Pakistan respect principles, value friendship, and "share weal and woe." When dealing with international affairs, both sides take the Five Principles of Peaceful Coexistence as the basic principle; when facing international affairs, both sides advocate justice and fairness, protect the common interests of developing countries, and have the courage to speak up.

In addition, China-Pakistan cooperation is always based on close communication and coordination, deep understanding of the other side's situation and interest, and full consideration of the other side's feeling. Pakistan always gives China full support on the Taiwan, Tibet, Xinjiang, and South China Sea issues. China is also a strong supporter of the independence, sovereignty, territorial integrity, and national dignity of Pakistan.

In 1972, the People's Republic of China used its veto power for the first time to support Pakistan at the UN Security Council by refusing to admit Bangladesh, the former East Pakistan, to the UN. After 1989, every time when China was blamed by the US and other Western countries at the UN Commission on Human Rights, Pakistan was always the first one to stand up and speak for China.

China and Pakistan conform to trends of the times, expand scope of cooperation, and jointly resolve challenges. After the Cold War, especially in the 21st century, the world has seen a trend toward peace, development, and cooperation.

Apart from traditional security issues, more and more non-traditional challenges arise. As a result, China-Pakistan cooperation has expanded from political and security fields to economy and trade, climate change, food and energy security. China takes the interests of Pakistan and other developing countries into careful consideration when it negotiates with Western countries.

China and Pakistan support each other in regional cooperation. Pakistan actively supports China further deepening cooperation with the South Asian Association for Regional Cooperation.

China supports Pakistan to become a full member of the Shanghai Cooperation Organization. Pakistan is one of the founding members of the China-initiated Asian Infrastructure Investment Bank, and shows solid support to the project. Pakistani scholars and diplomats actively support China's New Security Concept.

The China-Pakistan Economic Corridor will help Pakistan to advance its relationship with neighboring countries and become the hub of regional economic integration. On Afghan issues, China values Pakistan's unique role.

China and Pakistan can further strengthen bilateral policy coordination and strategic cooperation. They have a stake in each other's success. As a stronger peer, China should pay more attention to Pakistan's interest in international and regional affairs. As Pakistan makes progress in its economic development, China should support Pakistan becoming a member of APEC and RCEP.

However, people-to-people exchanges are the missing part in the foundation of China-Pakistan cooperation in international affairs. Our Pakistani friends enjoy a lot of advantages when contacting Islamic countries, so Pakistan could act as a bridge between China and Islamic countries for further cooperation and collaboration, especially in the process of building "One Belt, One Road" and realizing the Asian community of shared destiny.

DEVELOPMENT OF NUCLEAR WEAPONS

The Indo-Pakistani War of 1971 was a crushing defeat for Pakistan, which led to Pakistan losing roughly 56,000 square miles (150,000 km^2) of territory as well as losing millions of its citizens to the newly created state of Bangladesh. It was a psychological setback for Pakistanis; Pakistan had lost its geopolitical, strategic, and economic influence in South Asia. Furthermore, Pakistan had failed to gather any significant material support or assistance from its key allies, the United States and the People's Republic of China. Isolated internationally, Pakistan seemed to be in great mortal danger and felt that it could rely on no one but itself. At United Nations Security Council meeting, Prime Minister Zulfiqar Ali Bhutto drew comparisons with the Treaty of Versailles, which Germany was forced to sign in 1919. There, Bhutto vowed never to allow a repeat. Bhutto was "obsessed" with India's nuclear program, and that is why Bhutto immediately came up with the idea of obtaining nuclear weapons to prevent Pakistan from signing another 'Treaty of Versailles' as it did in 1971.

In 1969, after a long negotiation, the United Kingdom Atomic Energy Authority (UKAEA) signed a formal agreement to supply Pakistan with a nuclear fuel reprocessing plant capable of extracting 360 g of weapons-grade plutonium annually. The PAEC selected a team five senior scientists, including geophysicist Dr. Ahsan Mubarak, were sent to Sellafield to receive technical training. Later, the team under Ahsan Mubarak advised the government not to acquire the whole reprocessing plant but key parts important to building the weapons, while the plant would be built indigenously.

At the Multan meeting on 20 January 1972, Bhutto stated, "What Raziuddin Siddiqui, a Pakistani, contributed for the United States during the Manhattan Project, could also be done by scientists in Pakistan, for their own people." Raziuddin Siddiqui was a Pakistani theoretical physicist who, in the early 1940s, worked on both the British nuclear program and the U.S. nuclear program. Although a few Pakistanis who worked on the Manhattan Project were also willing to return and do the same for their native Pakistan, Prime Minister Bhutto still needed to recruit and bring in other Pakistani nuclear scientists and engineers who never worked in the United States. This is where Dr. Abdul Qadeer Khan, a German-educated metallurgical engineer, came into the picture. Some of the initial funding came from oil-rich Arab states, particularly Saudi Arabia.

In later years, some funding for the continuation of the nuclear development programme came from the large British Pakistani population. In December 1972, the science advisor to the President, Dr. Abdus Salam, had called theoretical physicists from the ICTP to report of Munir Ahmad Khan, Chairman of Pakistan Atomic Energy Commission. This marked the beginning of the "Theoretical Physics Group" (TPG). Later, Pakistani theoretical physicists at Institute of Theoretical Physics of Quaid-e-Azam University also joined the TPG headed by Salam. The TPG, which directly reported to Abdus Salam in PAEC, was assigned to do research in the development of nuclear weapon devices, and conduct mathematical calculations on complex hydrodynamical phenomenons and the fast neutron calculations. Professor Salam also had done the groundbreaking work of the "Theoretical Physics Group", which was initially headed by Salam until in 1974 when he left the country in protest. The TPG division at PAEC closely collaborated and completed its physics and mathematical calculations on fast-neutron calculations with the Mathematics Group led by Raziuddin Siddiqui and others, a division which contained the pure mathematicians.

On other side, Munir Ahmad Khan began to work on indigenous development of nuclear fuel cycle and the weapons programme. Munir Ahmad Khan, with his lifelong friend Abdus Salam, had done a groundbreaking work in the nuclear development, and after Salam's departure from Pakistan, scientists and engineers who were researching under Salam, began to report to directly to Munir Ahmad Khan. In 1974, Munir Ahmad Khan, days after

Operation Smiling Buddha, launched the extensive plutonium reprocessing and uranium enrichment programme, and the research facilities were expanded throughout the country.

In 1965, amidst skirmishes that led up to the Indo-Pakistan War of 1965, Zulfikar Ali Bhutto announced:

"If India builds the bomb, we will eat grass and leaves for a thousand years, even go hungry, but we will get one of our own. The Christians have the bomb, the Jews have the bomb and now the Hindus have the bomb. Why not the Muslims too have the bomb? "

In 1983, Khan was convicted in absentia by the Court of Amsterdam for stealing the blueprints, though the conviction was overturned on a legal technicality. A. Q. Khan then established a proliferation network through Dubai to smuggle URENCO nuclear technology to Khan Research Laboratories. He then established Pakistan's gas-centrifuge program based on the URENCO's Zippe-type centrifuge.

Through the late 1970s, Pakistan's program acquired sensitive uranium enrichment technology and expertise. The 1975 arrival of Dr. Abdul Qadeer Khan considerably advanced these efforts. Dr. Khan was a German-trained metallurgist who brought with him knowledge of gas centrifuge technologies that he had acquired through his position at the classified URENCO uranium enrichment plant in the Netherlands. He was put in charge of building, equipping and operating Pakistan's Kahuta facility, which was established in 1976. Under Khan's direction, Pakistan employed an extensive clandestine network to obtain the necessary materials and technology for its developing uranium enrichment capabilities.

"It took only two weeks and three days for Pakistan to master the field... and (detonate) the nuclear devices of our own..." —Benazir Bhutto, on first nuclear tests on May 1998,

A new directorate, known as Directorate of Technical Development (DTD) under Dr. Zaman Sheikh and Hafeez Qureshi, was established in March 1974 by Munir Ahmad Khan. The DTD was tasked to manufacture chemical explosive lenses, trigger mechanism, and tampers used in atomic weapon. The DTD was later charged with testing Pakistan's first implosion design in 1978, which was later improved and tested on 11 March 1983 when PAEC carried out Pakistan's first successful cold test of a nuclear device, codename *Kirana-I*. Between 1983 and 1990, PAEC carried out 24 more cold tests of various nuclear weapon designs. DTD had also manufactured a miniaturised weapon design by 1987 that could be delivered by all Pakistan Air Force fighter aircraft.

Dr. Ishrat Hussain Usmani's contribution to the nuclear energy programme is also fundamental to the development of atomic energy for civilian purposes as he, with efforts led by Salam, established PINSTECH, that subsequently developed into Pakistan's premier nuclear research institution. In addition to sending hundreds of young Pakistanis abroad for training, he laid the foundations of the Muslim world's first nuclear power reactor KANUPP, which was inaugurated by Munir Ahmad Khan in 1972. Thus, Usmani laid solid groundwork for the civilian nuclear programme. Scientists and engineers under Munir Ahmad Khan developed the nuclear capability for Pakistan within the early 1980s, and under his leadership the PAEC had carried a cold test of nuclear device at Kirana Hills, evidently made from non-weaponized plutonium. The former chairman of the PAEC, Munir Ahmad Khan, was credited as one of the pioneers of Pakistan's atomic bomb by a study from the International Institute for Strategic Studies (IISS), London's dossier on Pakistan's nuclear weapons program.

Policy

Pakistan acceded to the Geneva Protocol on 15 April 1960. As for its Biological warfare capability, Pakistan is not widely suspected of either producing biological weapons or having an offensive biological programme. However, the country is reported to have well developed bio-technological facilities and laboratories, devoted entirely to the medical research and applied healthcare science. In 1972, Pakistan signed and ratified the Biological and Toxin Weapons Convention (BTWC) in 1974. Since then Pakistan has been a vocal and staunch supporter for the success of the BTWC.

During the various BTWC Review Conferences, Pakistan's representatives have urged more robust participation from state signatories, invited new states to join the treaty, and, as part of the non-aligned group of countries, have made the case for guarantees for states' rights to engage in peaceful exchanges of biological and toxin materials for purposes of scientific research.

Pakistan is not known to have an offensive chemical weapons programme, and in 1993 Pakistan signed and ratified the Chemical Weapons Convention (CWC), and has committed itself to refrain from developing, manufacturing, stockpiling, or using chemical weapons.

Pakistan is not a party to the Non-Proliferation Treaty (NPT) and is not bound by any of its provisions. In 1999, Prime Ministers Nawaz Sharif of Pakistan and Atal Bihari Vajpayee of India signed the *Lahore Declaration,* agreeing to a bilateral moratorium on further nuclear testing. This initiative was taken a year after both countries had publicly tested nuclear weapons.

Since the early 1980s, Pakistan's nuclear proliferation activities have not been without controversy. However, since the arrest of Abdul Qadeer Khan, the government has taken concrete steps to ensure that Nuclear proliferation is not repeated and have assured the IAEA about the transparency of Pakistan's upcoming Chashma Nuclear Power Complex series of Nuclear Power Plants. In November 2006, The International Atomic Energy Agency Board of Governors approved an agreement with the Pakistan Atomic Energy Commission to apply safeguards to new nuclear power plants to be built in the country with Chinese assistance.

Protections

U.S. Secretary of State Hillary Rodham Clinton informed that Pakistan has dispersed its nuclear weapons throughout the country, increasing the security so that they could not fall into terrorist hands. Her comments came as new satellite images released by the ISI suggested Pakistan is increasing its capacity to produce plutonium, a fuel for atomic bombs. The institute has also claimed that Pakistan has built two more nuclear reactors at Khoshab increasing the number of plutonium producing reactors to three. In May 2009, during the anniversary of Pakistan's first nuclear weapons test, former Prime Minister of Pakistan Nawaz Sharif claimed that Pakistan's nuclear security is the strongest in the world. According to Dr. Abdul Qadeer Khan, Pakistan's nuclear safety program and nuclear security program is the strongest program in the world and there is no such capability in any other country for radical elements to steal or possess nuclear weapons.

NUCLEAR WEAPONS SECURITY SOUTH ASIA

Assistance on nuclear weapons security would be extremely limited if it were considered desirable. The objective of such measures would be to ensure that weapons could not be stolen or detonated by an unauthorized person. Again, the simplest measures are armed guards; undoubtedly both India and Pakistan are aware of the advantages of protecting their nuclear weapons. Advice or equipment to ensure no unauthorized use of nuclear weapons, such as PALs, would require access to nuclear weapons. General information on permissive action links, such as concepts or approaches, is publicly available and would not require access to weapons. In all likelihood, however, both India and Pakistan have probably exhausted public sources of information on that topic. Beyond the warheads themselves, measures to ensure that command and control systems work would also help ensure no unauthorized use, but could possibly enhance operational capabilities.

Personnel Security

The types of measures for personnel security that could be implemented absent Pakistani and Indian disarmament are limited. Obviously, if there are ongoing nuclear weapons programs, the two governments are unlikely to welcome proposals to divert their scientific expertise into civilian enterprises. However, there are clearly training programs in physical security and personnel vetting that could provide more security to those nuclear programs without enhancing their nuclear deterrents in a way that would contravene the NPT. Strictly civilian cooperation could have a positive spillover effect. On January 12, 2004, President Bush announced a new strategic partnership with India, to cooperate in three areas: civilian nuclear technology, space technology and high-technology trade. U.S. officials reportedly stated that any civilian nuclear technology must not be used in India's nuclear weapons program, although it is unclear how that would be achieved. Reportedly, cooperation has allowed for exports to safeguarded nuclear facilities.

This program might have the potential to develop relationships with Indian scientists that would benefit any future, more intrusive cooperative threat reduction program. With respect to Pakistan, assistance may be more difficult. Pakistan has denied U.S. officials direct access to AQ Khan, and although this might be an exception because of Khan's unique status, it could also become the rule. Pakistani officials, both with respect to the nuclear arsenal and nuclear scientists, appear to have taken a "hands-off" attitude.

Issues for Congress

Costs

India's and Pakistan's nuclear programs are far smaller than Russia's and unlikely to incur the kinds of costs that the CTR program has thus far incurred. On the other hand, data are scarce on the state of nuclear materials in India and Pakistan, so it is difficult to determine the scope and time frame of any such program.

At a minimum, however, such a program is likely to be incrementally implemented. Costs could be minimal if a quick-fix, low-technology, information-oriented approach is taken or they could be more substantial if a sophisticated, high-technology approach is taken that would incorporate cameras, encryption, remote monitoring, and other means.

Certifications

In 1991, the legislation that created the Nunn-Lugar program stipulated that U.S. assistance in destroying nuclear and other weapons may not be provided to the Soviet Union, any of its republics or successor entities unless the President certifies to the Congress that the proposed recipient is committed to:

- making a substantial investment of its resources for dismantling or destroying such weapons;

- forgo any military modernization that exceeds legitimate defence requirements or is designed to replace destroyed WMD;
- forgo the use of fissile materials and other components from destroyed nuclear weapons in new nuclear weapons;
- facilitate U.S. verification of weapons destruction that uses U.S. money;
- comply with all relevant arms control agreements; and
- observe internationally recognized human rights, including the protection of minorities.

Initially, Presidents George H. W. Bush and Clinton certified that the recipient nations — Russia, Ukraine, Belarus, and Kazakhstan — met those conditions. The Clinton Administration withdrew its certification of Belarus for human rights abuses in FY1998 and the George W. Bush administration withdrew its certification of Russia in 2002 for its failure to comply with arms control agreements, namely, the Chemical Weapons Convention and the Biological Weapons Convention.

The Bush Administration subsequently requested a waiver from Congress for the certification. It is not clear whether Congress would opt to apply the same certification requirements to recipient states outside the former Soviet Union. However, S. 2980, which was introduced by Senator Lugar in the 108th Congress, sought to remove the need for certifications, as well as other restrictions. The 109th Congress may consider this issue more fully if legislation is once more introduced.

NUCLEAR FACTORS IN THE MIDDLE EAST SECURITY

Middle East is heading, with an accelerating pace, for a turning point in its history that will drastically alter its internal and external power balance equilibrium as well as the prevailing security concepts, creating a powerful and lasting ideological impact on the Region.

The old security dogma of Israel will soon be tested against the reality produced by the socio-economic and ideological transformations that occurred in this country the last 25 years. This security dogma demanded the timely and effective elimination of all strategic (nuclear) threats against it within a distance from it coinciding with the strategic missile range capabilities of potential enemies. For almost 20 years Iran's nuclear ambitions were considered by far the most important strategic security problem of Israel. Evidently, the effective elimination of this threat demands not only an attack on Iran's nuclear and missile installations but a neutralization of its technological, economic and industrial power base that can produce as outputs these installations and their contents. In a country that has a population of 70 million and a regime that can unleash powerful ideological tremors all around the Region, the only way that the above task can be accomplished is through nuclear means. On the other hand, the continuous improvement of the living and educational standards of the people of Israel and the subsequent increase in their social and environmental awareness and sensitivity requires a drastic and continuous reassessment of the social, economic and environmental costs, as well as the political, associated with a nuclear attack against Iran. To make things more complex, this reassessment should occur in parallel with a continuous reassessment of Iran's capabilities to produce either the first nuclear warhead or in the worst-case scenario, a critical mass of them. In this context the effects of a series of extremely complex factors and parameters should be carefully assessed.

The impact on Israel of airborne radioactive pollutants that will be unleashed by a nuclear attack against Iran, the assessment of which is extremely difficult due to the highly complex micro-meteorological profiles of Iran. The probability that Iran possesses a given number of nuclear warheads (the number being a critical variable in impact analysis scenarios) and the conditional probability that Teheran may use them successfully in a counter-attack against Israel.

The threshold level of the impact from an Iranian nuclear counter-attack (mainly the loss of human lives) that the Israeli society can accept and its economy can withstand. The short, medium and long term impact of the reactions from the international community and especially of the Arab and Muslim World and as well as at least from some European powers and the EU. In this context, the assessment of the (true) motives and strategies of all powers that have significant interests invested in the Eastern Mediterranean Region which can exert a direct or indirect influence on it is of the outmost importance.

During the last 3000 years Iran has had a continuous, highly influential and cautious presence as an imperial power in the Middle East. It is evident that "cautiousness" is not simply a characteristic but a prerequisite for its sustainable presence in the region. Present, mainly verbal, extremism exhibited by Iran's President and by a narrow circle of decision makers around him either is allowed as a tactical diplomatic maneuver or it is manipulated by a predominantly cautious clergy. In the context of this theory, Iran may undertake an internationally provocative exhibition of its nuclear capabilities or offensive military potential only in the case that it possesses a critical mass of nuclear warheads.

Iran's efforts to develop nuclear technology extend to the times of the late Shah. These efforts are known to be fairly well coordinated and supported by the government, and what can be considered a highly politicized vocal sector of the public. In the light of the inability of the Western intelligence community to reject convincingly the nuclear capabilities of Iran not only technically but also regarding political will, it would be morally questionable for Israel to lay the cost of the doubt on the shoulders of its innocent public when assessing the worst-case scenarios of a nuclear adventure by Teheran. On the other hand the indecisiveness of Israel to act against Iran for such a long period of time cannot be explained solely on the viability of the non-nuclear scenario, i.e., that Iran's capacity is not as fearsome as it is made to sound. It is very probable that this indecisiveness is also due to an inconclusive assessment regarding Iran's possession of nuclear weapons. It may also be caused by the uncertainty associated with the operational reliability of (some of) Iran's defence systems.

The third factor in the equation deciding the security balance is the international community represented by the Quartet (U.S., E.U., U.N. and Russia) which has significant economic, political, ideological and moral interests invested in the Region. The last two years Quartet has been very active in trying to bridge differences and diffuse tensions, bargaining for time against certain promises offered by Iran. The benefits for the West and especially for Israel of "selling" time to Iran are not at all clear except for one that is very significant for the general public: to avert the crisis. On the other hand, the corresponding cost is clear: an increasing possibility that Iran will produce its first nuclear warhead or in the worst-case scenario, an increasing probability that Iran will complete the production of a critical number of nuclear warheads. In this context, one cannot exclude with certainty the contingency that certain elements of the international community are willing to bargain for time with Iran in order to circumvent Israel's intransigence in negotiating a viable regional peace and security plan with its neighbours.

Once Iran traverses the critical nuclear threshold, Israel's options and field of maneuver will be reduced to attacking Iran or being forced to negotiate under the influence of the nuclear threat. In either case, Israel will be forced to drastically change its security philosophy and policies and at least for a while until things settle, a sense of insecurity will prevail among its people. The scenario of a nuclear balance of power may have an overall positive impact only in case strategic decision makers in Israel and Iran develop a sense of mutual trust and mutual responsibility to act as guarantors of a regional security arrangement. On the other hand, a nuclear balance of terror given the current conditions of intense ideological polarization may prove extremely dangerous not only for the Region but for the world as a whole. In this context, the indecisiveness for timely and effective action will have disastrous consequences for all partners in the Middle East security balance equation

J. Karkazis in his paper "A simulation-based analysis of Iranian ballistic missiles and Israeli interceptors" (Middle East Forum, issue 5, 2005), and J. Karkazis and G. Isen in their paper "Defence analysis aspects regarding the possibility of deployment of Shahab-3 and Shahab-4 class of ballistic missiles against Israel, Turkey and Eastern Europe" (Middle East Forum, issue 6, 2007) present an appraisal of Iran's *technical* capacity and potential as an aspirant to nuclear power in the Eastern Mediterranean and Mesopotamia region. The evaluation deliberately stops short of most political, sociological and psychological commentary in detail – which we propose to do in another study. In the first paper a simulation-based analysis of Iranian ballistic missiles and Israeli interceptors is presented and concepts related to critical defence analysis (Critical Defence Range and Time) are introduced. In the second paper, certain defence aspects are analyzed in the context of a scenario regarding the deployment of Shahab class ballistic missiles against Israel, Turkey and Eastern Europe.

This almost clinical examination of a "threat" situation, however, represents no pretense to play over-the-table war games. In fact, the scarcity of the word threat itself throughout the text reflects a desire to avoid value laden concepts in a technical assessment of the conditions. Looking at the ideational side of the equation however, the prevailing situation in the Eastern Mediterranean and Mesopotamia area, it is quite easy to observe a similarity with another politico-temporal dimension of fairly recent history: the *Cold War*.

Indeed, Samuel Huntington's end-of-century vision, the (in)famous hypotheses of the "*clash of civilizations*" effectively disappears if one can simply dream Iran away from the world map. Although it is almost never so outspoken, the overall assumption is that the primary post Cold War global conflict is occurring between the modern West and Islam, a specimen of the "rest". This is a notion that has gained almost universal impetus since 9-11, in spite of politically correct denials on all quarters. Such militantly anti Western and particularly anti U.S.A. and Israeli organizations as Al Qaeda, Abu Nidal, Hamas or Hezbollah whose methodology is not aversive to violence, certainly cause hairs to rise and even intelligence agencies have a hard time keeping track of new offshoots or splinter groups that spring from such motherlodes. On a closer look, though, Al Qaeda is a criminal, rather than political organization; while Hamas is more or less where the now very legitimate Fatah used to be in the late 80's. Hezbollah has come of age defending the Lebanon after a miscalculated invasion attempt by Israeli forces. Even overlooking the fact that Hamas and Hezbollah receive considerable support from Iran, all said bodies are no more than secondary players in the "clash" with Western civilization, while the spearhead is epitomized by Iran; who, at least as far as the *superpower*, the U.S.A. is concerned, now occupies a rhetorical, psychological and even spiritual void left by the demise of the Soviet Union, known once upon a time as *"the empire of evil"*. Indeed, Ronald Reagan, who introduced that expression into world politics was also responsible for escalating the "Thirty Years' War " with radical Islam that began with Ayatollah Khomeiny's revolution in Iran. Especially after the ascension of the neo-conservatives to power with President George W. Bush, Iran and its *"mullahcracy"* assumed the status of the prime movers of war in the Middle East.

Historically, the origins of the conflict between Islam and Western civilization, does not extend as far back to the era of colonialism. On the contrary, many independent Muslim Arab states in the Eastern Mediterranean and Mesopotamia owe their existence and liberty to the intervention of "imperialist" Western powers that dispensed with the legacy of the Ottoman Empire. The post-World War II inception of Israel caused the veer in the course of relations between the Arab Middle East and the West. At the time, no collision transpired on any matter between the Muslim but *Imperial* Iran and the young Jewish state. The bonds between the West and the Islamic Middle East, though stressed, survived the Suez Crisis of 1956, Soviet ambitions in the region that surged as key Arab states as Egyp, Syria, Iraq did away with their monarchies and adopted *Baath* style "socialist" autocracies and even brooked the waves of post-1967 Palestinian terror, and after the Yom Kippur War of 1973, the crippling oil embargo. As the U.S. became more involved in the Palestine dispute and was perceived to side more with Israel, psychological alienation with especially the radical Arab countries aggravated. Eventually, an unhealthy dose of anti Americanism was added to almost indemic anti Semitism in the region and has since been one cause of chronic festering in the Region.

Although chronic tensions existed with radical countries as Qaddafy's Libya, Saddam's Iraq or Syria, America's scrimmage with the Islamic world began in earnest when Khomeiny turned *Mohammed'* s teaching into an ideological fulcrum of radical and violent religious fundamentalism and attempted to export its revolution. It furthermore discursively owned up the Palestinian crisis, asserted itself as the champion of the cause and declared *jihad* against America.

On the American front, hostility toward Islamic elements largely was and still is mostly centered on Iran and by proxy, Iran endorsed *mujaheedeen* groups. Iran's discourse obfuscated the distinction between religious and the ideological. It even shadowed the difference between Arabs and Iran. The radical Cold-War-like rhetoric influenced the negative perception of most things Moslem in America and the West in general. Consecutive terrorist attacks on American targets, many of which were attributable to Iran, resulted with Islam acquiring the psycho-political function of an immediate, made-to-order enemy to blame for all evil. Such sentiments naturally peaked after 9-11.

America's *realist* epistemology in the study of world politics is a paradigm that relies on ontological dichotomies, which in daily parlance translate to "us and them", or more simply, "the good and the bad"; *binary* oppositions that cater to the most primeval reference of mankind: in-groups and out-groups. U.S. Cold War policy, since it was inspired by George "*Mr. X*" Kennan's "*long telegram*" has made excellent use of that discrimination in putting the American hegemonic project in effect. Washington employed the *containment* policy that circumscribed the political, military and economic playing field allotted to the Soviet Empire on one hand, while it placed at least as much emphasis on keeping the "free world" rallied around America against the "red threat".

American strategy not only checked the Soviets but it also seconded the former imperial powers of Europe to its hegemony, particularly in taking over global leadership from Britain, whose colonies were already drifting apart. While the hegemonic ascendance of the U.S. continued, the *Iron Curtain* that rose surrounded its friends, as well as foes, thus helping establish American priority and preponderance in deciding and determining the rules and conditions of world politics, more often than not, in the "free world".

To certain students of history, this was a force that turned the Cold War into what John Gaddis termed "the long peace". Washington could thus speak its will unchallenged in matters pertaining to the world order, not only because of its military, economic or technological superiority but also due to the aura of *consensus* that encompassed its hegemonic leadership and constituted the ideational aspect of that very hegemony. As of the 1980s, European partners and Japan could more vocally contribute to the tone of that consensus but in many senses, they now already stood to gain more by not disturbing the aura itself.

Throughout the Cold War, the U.S. and the Soviets bear hugged each other, in a dance resembling wrestlers' grapples, nevertheless keeping their respective allies in attendance, awe and assent. The "balance of terror" that put its seal on perceptions of the world for a half century, the ogre that U.S. political discourse created of the Soviets (and vice-versa), accorded either the means to keep tight ships in their own political turf. World politics were motivated by a particular "*Cold War mentality*", an ideological instrument that by invoking the fear of the other, served to maintain American world hegemony and also legitimize it so that the Western partnership was kept in array. The

Cold War motivation that ruled American political thinking for nearly half a century, simultaneously helped consolidate the leadership of both the U.S. and the Soviets in dominating their "allies" in their respective camps.

Again, a motivation to explain the situation in Iraq and the "broader" Middle East in a language somewhat similar to that of the Cold War seems to have recently pervaded the American – and to maybe a lesser extent, Western – outlook toward Middle Eastern affairs in general, and Iran in particular. Especially, since the nuclear weapons crisis with Iran has (re-)erupted, aversions and apprehensions signifying the increasing popularity of a cognitive style with a distinct Cold War flavor, have gradually infused most perceptions and narratives involving Teheran. While the rather militarist *neo-con*-inspired world epistemology in Washington, with its new set of invented narratives, institutions, norms and other ideational factors propagated war against the mullahs in one way or another, overt comparison of the new evil with the old one, the Soviets, was not unheard of either.

Cold War motivation functioned successfully in mustering allies around the U.S. not only because it happened to be the strongest nation on earth but also because it could consolidate its hegemony within a "structure" that comprised ideas and institutions which lay at the basis of the consent which legitimated U.S. military and economic power and preponderance. Within such a structural frame, power, with reference to its psychological and communicative vectors, appears as a capability to determine, dictate or dominate the discourses and/or narratives of "truth".

In other words, power appears as a requisite of truth: *"in potestas veritas"*. Truth constitutes a system of knowledge consecutive to which, reality is arbitrated. The capability of dominating the praxes of knowledge is pragmatically tantamount to determining the discourses of "reality". Possessing the technical and psychological means that lead to such capability affords considerable influence in determining the parameters of truth that an entire society (or at least the decisive majority) of individuals or communities, including nations, adheres to. Thus, the capacity to "write truth" enables the hegemon to describe the content of socio-political reality and to establish itself with as a moral author of verity and hence, the "right" ideas. It was this phenomenon ensconsed in the "Cold War Motivation" that turned the Soviets into the evil bogey-man for half a century of Western rhetoric.

Now, America's apprehensive discourse on Iran is at least in part joined – with lots of American diplomatic prompting –by the UN Security Council as well as the IAEA, which already has expressed an "absence of confidence" that Iran's nuclear programme is exclusively for peaceful purposes. Iran's President Mahmoud Ahmadinejad's repeated iterations, inviting the destruction of Israel and decrying the Holocaust as a "myth" also caused concerns to aggravate that Teheran's nuclear intentions are oriented more toward *jihad* than economic welfare. Still, Iran has long been on America's shortlist of *rogue states* to have become an instant villain, and its nuclear ambitions are no news.

It does not escape notice that an "old" dispute resurfaced at a rather opportune time for Washington, soon enough after the invasion of Iraq, and subsequently, the bungling of that invasion which led to serious attrition of confidence and concord among main trans-Atlantic allies of America, including Germany and France. Iran's role in supporting the resistance in Iraq against America and its allies, too, can be viewed as but another front in a broader conflict. Iran specializes in fighting asymmetrical "proxy wars", using the insurgents it sponsors, to undermine the occupation forces and goad them toward a defeat before Islamic militia. Their attacks occasionally take as their war zone the cities and citizens of Western countries and then, the "asymmetrical proxy wars", as they are impassionately called in academic jargon, go down as *terrorism* in the everyday language and narrative of the U.S. and its allies and more importantly, of the public, usually accessed through the media. Thus superposed, the danger of nuclear clash and the threat of terrorism make the American voice more audible and lend it the authority to "author" the truth about the war.

Terror tends to transform into a mystique in proportion to the fear it generates. The conditions of its emergence thus turn into an instrument for managing the discourses that define truth. Managing the discourses of fear by means of manipulating the narratives and rhetoric of the terrorist threat bestows on the "communication elites", the power of *polity* they need in order to construct a "convenient" reality. Just as the Cold War and the nuclear "balance of terror" once functioned as a muster call to the "free world" to unite around America's promise of democracy and prosperity, Iran's emergence as a nuclear *threat* not alien to terrorism helped marshal the major players of the Western alliance around an America, whose reputation was otherwise somewhat tarnished by its policy and actions in Iraq.

The concept *discourse management* is used here to describe a process of setting public agendas, determining the boundaries and flow of messages, monitoring their sources and impacts; limiting or remedying their damage. It involves the selection of particular means, modes and media of debate, conducive for creating favored ways of seeing, thinking, doing and being-in-the-world. Discourse by definition, constrains communication and hence, thought and social praxis by delimiting the choices and extent of cognitive foci, the parameters of knowledge and its production. Discourse is elemental in construing whatever is adhered to in the community as "truth." Even when arguments run counter to the tenets of a favored content and language of "truth", they are still largely determined by it, acquire their meaning in reference to it, and contribute to the power commanded by it.

Iran's nuke scare altered the more or less differing outlooks on the Middle East toward a convergence with the American variant of "truth", regarding the nature of the problem. For the U.S., Iraq lay at the heart of the Middle East problematique. The main issue was settling the political tumult in Iraq; dealing with the insurgents and imponderables resisting or hampering the American occupation and war effort, and with the vagaries of the "rogues", Iran and Syria, with their non-state extensions as Hizbollah.

To the U.S., Palestine, rather than the generic issue that turned the Middle East into a global trouble area, was more of a security matter because of the threat it posed for Israel. Previously, the Europeans, including Britain, who were readier to accept that the Middle Eastern conflict or the "clash of civilizations" emanates at the core from the Israeli – Palestinian disaggreement, and that Israel's role in it is hardly always constructive, repeatedly tried to draw Washington's attention to the obvious fact that stability is impossible without or prior to a workable settlement in Palestine. Washington, in rurn, assumed that keeping the Palestinians at arm's length, in poverty and subjecting them to Israel's political whim would break their will and induce them to acquiesce to a – possibly asymmetrical – settlement; or at least keep them weak enough to cause too big problems.

The billeting of Iran as a potential nuclear threat, emphasized through proper discourse management, relegated the urgency of the Palestine dispute to secondary levels. In the meantime, subsequent to the electoral victory of pro- Iran Hamas over Fatah, the Iran issue became entangled and maybe even intrinsic to Palestine.

The civil war that seems to have culminated with an effective partition of Palestine, not only instituted Hamas in the zone, it also effectively endowed Teheran with a solid, albeit vicarious, foothold in the crisis area. The emergence of Hamas, with its consistent denial of a Jewish state, as a "legitimate" political entity, has, further than disturb Washington, probably also caused apprehension among some Arab states that seemed to have little trouble with the *pre*-Hamas status quo. Although rushed statements were uttered that Western assistance and recognition would find its way to the Fatah controlled *sector* of Palestine, the influence Iran vicariously exerted on the problem also served to bring the outlook of the entire West closer to Washington's hermeneutics of the events.

If communicative power is to help achieve the mood to serve the American ambitions in the Middle East, it is not enough that only the Europeans or other "Western" allies partake in the hegemon's version of the "truth". Whatever turn events may take, "consensus" in the region cannot be achieved without adopting a course that more or less satisfies the local countries within that critical geography. Here, too, historical and political conditions exist that allow Washington to employ the mentality and motivations of the Cold War to the situation at hand and gain the regional powers to join its chorus, singing the same narratives of truth concerning Iran and its bellicose ways. Indeed, in addition to the aggressive image projected not only on but also *by* Teheran, Iranian relationship with Arab countries is already cloaked in the straints of historical adversity. Mesopotamia and Eastern Anatolia were contended territories between the Ottomans and the Shiite Safavid Empire in the 16th and 17th centuries. This contention, exacerbated by the sectarian rift in Islam, subconsciously survived when the Turks established their ultimate superiority that lasted until the end of World War I. The motive to become a force of imperial proportions through *jihad* or revolution export links at its foundations to Iran's historical territorial ambitions in the region. The ousted Shah Reza Pahlavi once for a brief period went far enough to put this ambition in practice by declaring Bahrain as Iranian territory. The anxiety caused by Iran's expansionist aspirations did not abate during the Islamic Republic either.

Under such circumstances, it is easy to realize why Teheran boasts few friends among its Arab neighbours. A masked struggle has constantly lingered between Teheran and focal Arab powers as Saudi Arabia, Jordan, Kuwait, Gulf Emirates or Egypt, which in Teheran's eyes, are lackeys of America. Iran spent eight years in a bloody war with Iraq, where, currently, its influence over the large Shiite minority can determine not just the fate of that country but thereof, the whole region. Although particular issues with Iran may vary from country to country, generally, Arabs are mainly wary that the conflict between Israel or the United States and Iran can assume a military character and spiral outward to hurt them or their interests. Even if they may eschew hot conflict on or about their territories, Arabs are apprehensive that social turbulence resulting from Iran's strategy of exporting its revolution may spread into their precarious communities, as it did in Palestine. Considering that currently, the only viable political opposition to incumbent autocracies in especially the *sharia* ruled Arab states is administered by Islamic fundamentalism of a Sunnite version, it becomes easy to understand the aversion of those commanding power to Teheran's influence. The probability that religious extremists may not only act upon Iran's revolutionary example but may also benefit from various forms of assistance from Teheran or other players in league with it – such as Syria or Hamas –, also causes concern. Iran's real or potential sway over the Shiite minorities, not just in Iraq but also in other Arab states, mainly, Saudi Arabia, Kuwait, and Bahrain, is yet another source of alarm. Qatar has always feared Iran and now it is wary that any support it extends to America, especially regarding military action, can turn it into the mollahs' target. There are also fears that a nuclear Iran might pursue a more assertive policy in the region. Although not as worrying as all-out-nuclear-war, the ultimately more realistic misgivings that a poor, technologically unadvanced Iran, possessing any nuclear capacity at all, whether peaceful or belligerent, may give rise to Chernobyl-like disasters that can devastate the region are in the books, too. All said, however, relations being what they are, Council on Foreign Relations commentators stated that an American strike on Iran's nuclear facilities would not cause the Arab world to "shed too many tears"; although, overt support to a U.S. military campaign, given America's current unpopularity, was regarded as politically suicidal.

After the Hamas electoral victory, Iran's sudden emergence as a *Western* neighbor in the Middle East as well as a *Palestinian* power placed it deeper into the midst of Arab affairs. With this strain added, Arabs may turn to look into other possibilities to ensure their security, which may include closer ties with the U.S. and render possible a more rapid thaw in their relations with Israel. In other words, they, too, might be readier to register with the American narratives of "truth". One more factor that contributes to the spread of a Cold War feeling and motivation is the "alleged" nuclear capacity that Israel possesses. Although never acknowledged, Israel is "accepted" as the first nation in the region to have developed nuclear weapons since the late 1960s. This naturally unnerves its neighbours, while it puts Israel on the same footing as Iran in view of "official" non-proliferation considerations and may even provide Iran – and maybe some Arab countries – with an alibi, if ever proved, to acquire their own WMD not to drop too low in the emerging "scale of terror". Thus, in the Eastern Mediterranean and the Mesopotamia – Persia area, the whole *Gestalt* of Cold War mentality and motivation dosed with the standard altercative rhetoric of "*terror*" and *bellum justum*, keep being rehashed.

Turning back to Iran, another similarity with Cold War balances occurs in the area of economy. Just as the crisis stricken, centralized Soviet "command economy" of the 1980s, choked by oil production problems, archaic technology, unproductivity and the invasion of Afghanistan was forced by the U.S. to further austerity in order to keep up with the pace up of the arms race began to stumble as the decade wore on,; Iran's single export, low yield, oil dependent economy, too, may have to support an unwieldy burden. Iran's economy is totally dependent on oil and gas exports, which constitute 85 percent of its outbound foreign trade. The state is by large, the principal economic actor. Iran was one of the last five remaining countries with high inflation in 2006. Ahmadinejad offered the population a greater share of oil wealth and subsidized daily consumer items which he financed by the global rise in oil prices and export revenues also helped to ease the foreign debt. Economy was nevertheless still burdened by high unemployment, inflation, expensive subsidies, and a bloated and inefficient public sector; wit rampant corruption and respect for property rights ponderable. "The class gap" between high and low earners reached levels that attracted the attention of politicians in high office. A chronic shortage of capital existed and too little foreign investors were lured by the government's incentives, given the political situation. Real GDP consistently decreased since 2002 while the budget deficit rose. "Official" inflation lingered around 15 percent.

A portion of the oil revenue which the nuclear program will have to depend on for financing was spent to fund Ahmadinajad's populist commitments and probably went also to support "proxy wars" fought outside the country. In any case, in order to rectify economic woes, overt and indirect subsidies would have to be cut off, leading to possible discontent among a highly unemployed and rapidly growing, unskilled population. Economists warned that added international sanctions due to Teheran's nuclear policy, might lead the Iranian economy to pending crisis by increasing inflation and liquidity.

Iran's problems give the impression of being systemic rather than conjunctural. The last three presidents tried to tackle protracted symptoms as lack of transparency, lack of regulations where it counts and over regulation where it isn't needed, dosed with heavy bureaucracy, rising inflation, unemployment, underemployment and corruption with little success. Ahmadinejad's economic policies may be to blame for inflation and unemployment but ailments like factionalism, push and pull from interest groups, contraband, bad management of state enterprises, badly placed subsidies, plight of social security and health aid, lack of proper economic data and taxation were long time woes that invariably plagued the sluggish, state controlled, political command economy in Iran as anywhere else. Such societies are hard to reform without curbing the state's absolute and arbitrary power and prior to the emergence of social forces that can undertake the gargantuan task of counter-balancing the political machine. The autocratic tradition in Iran is so entrenched that it would be naïve at best to expect strong classes to emerge whose impact may curb the penetrating might of the state. On the contrary, politics is limited to the control of tha absolute power and it is the exclusive prerogative of a sanctioned élite loyal to the principles of the Islamic Revolution. The ruling elite can favor either the hardline fashion represented by Ahmadinajad or be of a more reforming kind, as used to be the previous president, Mohammad Hatami.

The regime's detractors were probably unhappier under the former's government but they had little outlet for expressing their discontent for fear of reppression. Reports indicated that as the repercussions of the internatioonal dispute over nuclearization hit, Iran was "slipping back into a more oppressive mode". The government cracked down on "imaginary", as well as real opponents. Any dissent from secular liberals, trade unionists, women's rights campaigners, disgruntled ethnic minorities or any person or group including disappointed vocal clergymen, were harassed, threatened, arrested and some way persecuted. The "authorities" went as far as establishing "morality checkpoints" across the capital, inspecting the apparel of townsfolk and punishing immodestly dressed youths and women. Harsh measures were not limited to the socio-political arena. Oil was rationed, too, incurring public protests. Just as once the Soviet machine cracked down on its dissidents, the "nuclear crisis" presented Iran's officials the pretext needed to attack and quench the opposition and slip through unpopular economic measures in the meantime. Iran was preparing for the "biggest outside threat" since the Iraq war, with arrests, suppression, intimidation and austerity.

Thus, reminiscent of the Cold War's "other" front on the East of the Iron Curtain, Iran's dictatorship made use of the international nuclear crisis to whitewash its failing domestic economic and social politics. Unthreatened, the people would demand improved standards of living from their government, which the current economic system of Iran would be unable to deliver. However, as long as the United States was perceived as a threat by the average Iranian, especially with Iraq as an abject example of what can happen in the case of a clash with America, people might be induced to complain less and accept more hardship of their own volition.

NUCLEAR POLICY, DOCTRINE AND PLANNING

Minimum Deterrence and Its Requirements

After the 1998 tests, doctrine and organization were redesigned. Prime Minister Nawaz Sharif announced a principle of "minimum credible deterrence" in May 1999.8 Pakistan claims that it is against an open-ended arms race in South Asia and does not seek an arsenal equivalent to that of India.

The policy of credible minimum deterrence has been constantly reaffirmed since then. It translates into four objectives: (1) deterrence of all forms of external aggression; (2) building to this effect an effective combination of conventional and strategic forces; (3) avoiding a pre-emptive strike through protection and the threat of nuclear retaliation; (4) stabilizing strategic deterrence in South Asia.

After the 1998 tests, Islamabad adopted a long-term development plan for its nuclear force. It is now reportedly implementing its second 10-year plan (presumably covering the years 2010-2020).

Islamabad believes in the theory of deterrence of the strong by the weak: the possibility of a smaller country to deter a larger one through the threat of damage incommensurate with the stakes of the conflict. It aims at being able to inflict "unacceptable" or "unbearable" damage to India. The difficulty of defining unacceptable damage is admitted by Pakistani planners: one quasi-official report states that "because of the difficulty in predicting unacceptable damage, overkill would by necessity be built into the response". The meaning of minimum deterrence has reportedly been precisely defined, though perhaps not in numbers. In fact, general Musharraf claimed in 2005 that it had reached this threshold; but this bold statement perhaps referred just to an initial capability to deliver a few weapons on Indian cities with some guarantee of success. Islamabad insists that the level of minimum deterrence can change over time, in light of the evolution of the threat. There have been consistent official statements since 1998 that minimum deterrence "cannot be quantified in static numbers".

Guaranteed unacceptable damage implies survivability even after a first strike by the adversary. The Pakistanis are likely to use as a planning assumption an Indian pre- emptive strike (coupled, in the future, with the deployment of missile defence by New Delhi). Pakistani concerns have been compounded by the US-India partnership. In 2006, the National Command Authority (NCA) stated that "in view of the fact that the [US- India] Agreement would enable India to produce significant quantities of fissile materials and nuclear weapons from un-safeguarded nuclear reactors, the NCA expressed firm resolve that our credible minimum deterrence requirements will be met". Meanwhile, Pakistan will probably resort to concealment and mobility (*à la* China) to ensure the survival of its force.

As an example of the type of calculations that Pakistani planners may make to that effect, a former Strategic Plans Division (SPD) officer wrote that for a set of 10 possible targets, a country may need 68-70 warheads (without taking into account the risk of a pre-emptive strike).

Even though the Pakistani military seems to base its planning on rational strategic calculations, domestic political factors will also inevitably affect nuclear policy decisions. No Pakistani leader can afford to appear weak vis-à-vis India.

A Low Nuclear Threshold?

Pakistan has consistently stated that its nuclear weapons are solely intended to deter military aggression. Officials stress that "the use of nuclear weapons as a war-fighting tool is not a contemplated doctrine in Pakistani strategic thinking." Though the SPD remains rather insulated from the rest of the armed forces, Pakistan has made efforts to think through its nuclear doctrine and to integrate the nuclear dimension into its defence strategy. In 2002, the SPD participated in a joint wargame at the National Defense College. Strategic force commanders are now invited to participate in the all-important Corps Commanders Conference.

Islamabad would use nuclear weapons in response to conventional attacks by India as a "last resort". There have been consistent statements by Pakistani officials since 1987 about the nuclear threshold: if its "national integrity was threatened" (General Musharraf, 2000); "only if the very existence of Pakistan as a state is threatened" (General Kidwai, 2001).

The circumstances that might warrant nuclear use were described by General Kidwai in late 2001: (1) *The spatial threshold*. The penetration of Indian forces on a large scale would elicit a nuclear response. The threshold could be low (some 50-100 km perhaps) in Kashmir and in Punjab. (2) *The military threshold*. The destruction of a large part of Pakistani land or air forces could lead to a nuclear response if Islamabad believed that it was losing the cohesiveness of its defence and feared imminent defeat. (3) *The economic threshold*. Economic strangulation refers primarily to a blockade of Karachi, but could also concern the stopping of the Indus water flow, or the capture of vital arteries such as the Indus and the Karakoram highway. (4) *The political threshold*. A destabilization of the country fomented by India could also be a nuclear threshold if Islamabad believed that the integrity of the country was at stake. Pakistani planners insist that these thresholds are indicative and should not be viewed in isolation one from another. They do not accept that they plan for an early use of nuclear weapons.

A few statements have referred to other WMD, suggesting that the Pakistani deterrent may have a role in discouraging chemical or biological attacks. However, Pakistan's policy is also in line with the negative security assurances given by nuclear-weapon states: it will not use or threaten to use nuclear weapons against non-nuclear countries.

Pakistan also threatens nuclear retaliation in case of a preventive or pre-emptive strike. Pakistan told India in 1998 that an attack against its nuclear installations (which are the subject of a non-aggression agreement between the two countries) would elicit "swift and massive retaliation with unforeseen consequences". More precisely, the policy is "deterrence of Pakistan's adversaries from attempting a counter-force strategy against its strategic assets by effectively securing the strategic assets and threatening nuclear retaliation should such an attempt be made".

Towards Controlled Escalation?

Islamabad will certainly want to avoid an all-or-nothing strategy, to reserve forces for a second strike and ensure deterrence credibility. It has certainly developed limited options on Indian territory (for instance on a base close to the border) or on Indian forces advancing on its territory.

A limited strike might be aimed at signalling resolve, "establish intra-war deterrence" (in the words of a SPD official), and/or perhaps to force other countries to intervene. Being in a situation of perceived conventional inferiority vis-à-vis a mortal enemy, Pakistan's conception of nuclear planning is close to NATO during the Cold war.

Pakistani interest in Western concepts of nuclear escalation can be traced back to US military training and formation given in the late 1950s. (One observer notes that Pakistani policy-makers have "internalised the US Cold War literature on nuclear weapons far more than Indian strategic elites".) Given the small size of its force, however, a more appropriate reference might be the French doctrine of a final warning followed if needed by unacceptable damage.

Due to its lack of spatial depth, Pakistan "cannot afford the luxury of distinguishing between tactical and strategic, within a nuclear context". Pakistani planners insist that all their nuclear weapons are of strategic nature. But an increasing arsenal will lead it towards a posture of controlled escalation.

Pakistani planning certainly focuses on counter-value targeting, due to the low number of warheads it is believed to have and the probably poor accuracy – despite Pakistani claims to the contrary – of most missiles currently in service. Musharraf said that Islamabad should have "enough missile capacity to reach anywhere in India and destroy a few cities, if required". Pakistani analysts regularly mention about a dozen cities. It has been suggested that threatening large populations is justifiable in religious terms as a suitable way of employing "terror" in warfare. Given the size of India, Pakistan could not destroy a large percentage of its population of industry; but targeting key cities and facilities might incur unacceptable economic and psychological costs.

It is also likely that as its nuclear force grows and evolves, Pakistan will diversify its set of potential targets, as other countries have done, and it may already have done so. In a discussion of the "pain threshold of the opponent", a former SPD official, identifies possible targets as "major population centres, industrial complexes, major military bases, and communication hubs". A diversification of targets could also make the Pakistani deterrent more credible than a crude counter-cities strategy, given that any strike on India would involve massive casualties among its Muslim population.

A Force on Low Alert

Pakistani nuclear systems are widely assumed to be kept in a low alert form. In normal times, missiles may not mated with warheads. President Musharraf referred in 2003 to a "geographical separation" between them. It is also possible that warheads are kept in a disassembled form in normal times. However, the SPD insists it has never confirmed such arrangements; general Kidwai (and other SPD officials) has stated that forces are not on a "hair trigger alert" but that "separation is more linked to time rather than space". Also, a former SPD official has denied that the warheads were kept in disassembled form.

The time required for putting weapons on launch readiness is uncertain. Kidwai said in 2002 assembly could be done "very quickly". Some accounts suggest that it would only take "minutes", other refer to "hours". A different assessment was offered by former Army Chief of Staff Mirza Aslam Beg; referring to assembly and mating he said that "there would be a gap of hours, or even days before [a weapon system] could be put together" (and weapon components are stored "many miles away" from delivery systems).

Once made operational, the forces would have to contend with three possible scenarios: "launch on warning; launch under attack; launch on orders."

Fissile Material and Warheads

Pakistan began producing Highly Enriched Uranium (HEU) in the mid-1980s. As of 2011 it was believed to have produced 2-3.5 tons of HEU. It is one of only two States (with India) known to produce HEU today. It may be producing 120-180 kg a year, enough for 10-15 warheads. The Kahuta plant is believed to have a capacity of 15-45 tSWU/year.

More recently, it has begun developing an important plutonium (Pu) production capability. At the Khushab site, two reactors are operating and two others are being built. New reprocessing facilities are also being constructed at Nilore (the current one having a capacity of 20-40 tHM/year) and probably at Chashma (with a capacity of 50-100 tHM/year), which hosts a never-completed plant of French origin. As of 2011 Pakistan had stockpiled around 100-160 kilos of Pu. Estimates of production at Khushab is difficult: the two reactors in service do not operate continuously and may not be of the same type. Khushab-1 can produce 5,7-11,5 kilos of Pu/year depending on its duration of operation, enough for 1-3 warheads.

Pakistan has increased its stockpile in recent years and probably has somewhere around 100 warheads. Estimates remain uncertain since they are based on available information and assumptions regarding the number of launchers, the amount of fissile material produced, the amount of material actually converted into weapons cores, and the amount of material Pakistan uses in each weapon. Potential production of warheads per year today is 7 to 18.

The tests carried out on May 28, 1998 were 5-20 (probably 8-12) kilotons HEU fission devices. The Pakistanis claim that five devices were tested, but seismological data showed that the real number might have been two. Questions also remain regarding the 3-11 (probably 4-6) kilotons May 30 test, conducted in a separate location and with a different setup. It may have been a plutonium or composite core. Open source analysis remains divided. In 2006, Musharraf stated: "we do not have a plutonium weapon".

Pakistan has several functional weapons designs. Two models were developed by PAEC for PAF aircraft, with reported yields of 2-10 kilotons and 10-20 kilotons. Pakistan partly based its weapons designs on a 15-25 kiloton HEU implosion Chinese warhead, which can be carried by a missile. (PAEC and KRL both worked on this design.) Islamabad claims that no less than six different warheads types were successfully tested in 1998. This is certainly an exaggeration, but there is little doubt that the tests allowed Pakistan to refine its designs. Missiles are probably armed with low-yield warheads: tentative evaluations are warheads of 15-35 kiloton, 12-20 kiloton, and 1-5 kilotons for the short-range missiles (if endowed with nuclear weapons). Inquiries of the Khan network uncovered the existence of two modern, sophisticated designs allowing for the making of warheads smaller and lighter – and also more powerful – than the Chinese one.

Whether or not Pakistan already has a proven Pu-based implosion design, it is likely that it will continue to rely for long on HEU weapons.

Means of Delivery

Pakistan initially relied on aircraft as delivery vehicles for its nuclear weapons and in the mid-1980s procured 40 F-16 aircraft from the United States that, when modified, could be used for that purpose. From 1985, passage of the Pressler Amendment made delivery of additional F-16 aircraft, as well as spare parts, dependent on US Presidential annual certification that Pakistan did not possess a nuclear explosive device. In 1990 the Pressler Amendment was finally invoked. By then, Pakistan had already begun to examine a ballistic missile alternative, prompted additionally by the development of India's own ballistic programmes.

Over the past 15 years, Islamabad has begun placing part of its deterrent on ballistic missiles, dramatically increasing the probability of success of a strike on Indian territory. However, this capability remains limited. With a range of less than 1000 km, the Shaheen-1 and Ghaznavi are more theatre than strategic missiles (though they could reach some of India's cities if placed in the eastern part of Pakistan). The Ghauri's range is longer but it is liquid-fuelled, thus less reliable and more vulnerable. Thus planners refer to the solid-fuelled, long-range Shaheen-2 as the "mainstay" of the country's future deterrent. If based in Punjab, it could reach the eastern cities of Kolkata, Bangalore and Chennai.

The limitations of Pakistani nuclear missile capability explain why Islamabad will continue to maintain an air-based component. In addition, the value of diversity in the force is well-known. Aircraft could for instance be used to target an Indian formation on Pakistani territory. Some also believe that multiplication of nuclear assets and bases make Pakistan a "target-rich" environment and lessens the possibility of a pre-emptive strike. To that effect, Pakistan equips some of its ground attack aircraft, probably part of its US F-16C/D force (one squadron) and Mirage-5 force (3 squadrons), with nuclear bombs. It is not known whether the new JF-17 Chinese fighter, which equips one squadron of the Pakistani Air Force (PAF) since 2010, has a nuclear capability.

MODERNISATION AND EXPANSION

Pakistan is increasing its capacity to produce plutonium at its Khushab nuclear facility, a Washington-based science think tank has reported. The sixth nuclear test (codename: Chagai-II) on 30 May 1998, at Kharan was a quiet successful test of a sophisticated, compact, but "powerful plutonium bomb" designed to be carried by aircraft, vessels, and missiles.

The Pakistanis are believed to be spiking their plutonium based nuclear weapons with tritium. Only a few grams of tritium can result in an increase of the explosive yield by 300% to 400%." Citing new satellite images of the facility, the Institute for Science and International Security (ISIS) said the imagery suggests construction of the second Khushab reactor is "likely finished and that the roof beams are being placed on top of the third Khushab reactor hall". A third and a fourth reactor and ancillary buildings are observed to be under construction at the Khushab site.

In an opinion published in *The Hindu*, former Indian Foreign Secretary Shyam Saran wrote that Pakistan's expanding nuclear capability is "no longer driven solely by its oft-cited fears of India" but by the "paranoia about U.S. attacks on its strategic assets. Noting recent changes in Pakistan's nuclear doctrine, Saran said "the Pakistan Military and civilian elite is convinced that the United States has also become a dangerous adversary, which seeks to disable, disarm or take forcible possession of Pakistan's nuclear arsenals and its status as nuclear power."

As of 2014, Pakistan has been reportedly developing smaller, more tactical nuclear weapons for potential use on the battlefield exclusively. This is consistent with earlier statements from a meeting of the National Command Authority (which directs nuclear policy and development) saying Pakistan is developing "a full-spectrum deterrence capability to deter all forms of aggression."

CREDIBLE NUCLEAR DETERRENCE AND DOCTRINE FOR PAKISTAN

Pakistan and India since May 11/28, 1998 have come into the atomic age, despite their status as non-weapon states under the NPT regime. There should be no doubt about this fact. In fact, the sooner this fact is realized and absorbed by both these countries and their leadership as well as the five members of the nuclear club, the better it is for all concerned individuals and states. Despite my advice, and a minority of other Pakistani origin academics that also urged the Pakistani leadership not to go nuclear, Pakistan, however, decided to match India at the nuclear level for a variety of reasons.

The nuclear genie has been unleashed; it can not be bottled back. Therefore, it is better to weaponise the respective nuclear detonations and deploy nuclear weapons with complete Command, Control, Communication, and Intelligence (C3I) systems in place for a stable nuclear deterrence between the two rival states of South Asia. This nuclear factor is needed not so much as a peace maker, which is a misnomer, but more so for pure deterrence reasons. It guarantees against misadventure by any side. Now the need of the hour is to create a credible nuclear deterrence between India and Pakistan as well as to adopt a sound nuclear doctrine for Pakistan's armed forces. In order to stabilize the nuclear situation of the subcontinent, these countries must take a number of political, strategic, diplomatic, and tactical steps simultaneously. On the political and diplomatic front, there is a need to take a number of policy initiatives on the part of Pakistan.

First, Pakistan must immediately reassure the international community that Pakistani nuclear weapons are not for sale. This seems to have been done by both the Prime Minister and even more categorically by Pakistan's top foreign affairs bureaucrat, S.A. Khan. Second, Pakistan has already offered to sit down with India to discuss confidence building measures and the Kashmir affair. However, there should be a clear timeline, let's say by the end of 1999, to resolve this issue bilaterally. In case of a deadlock, which is bound to happen, the case should be submitted automatically to the UN with reference to its resolutions to ask Kashmiris to accede to either India or Pakistan as the logical and fair culmination of the unfinished business of the partition of the subcontinent. Including a third choice at this stage will not only complicate the matter more but also insult most Kashmiris like me. It is also necessary to avoid Kashmir becoming a point of conflict between extra-regional powers and China and Russia, especially if Kashmir is used as a listening post against them.

If India comes to terms on Kashmir, then the size of the Pakistan army could immediately be reduced. In order to preserve peace, the best guarantee would still be a strong Pakistan. An increase of expenditure on naval, airforce, and the nuclear deterrence capabilities for at least a decade or so would have to be taken by Pakistan to ensure that the transition to a less hostile environment in South Asia is smooth. After that period, one could reduce all elements of hostile military posturing.

In fact, what would be the need of having large standing armed and nuclear forces, if Pakistan's main bone of contention with India had been resolved amicably. Judging from the press coverage of diplomatic activities, Kashmir is back in the limelight in multilateral fora. However, Indian diplomacy will do its utmost to reduce this issue to the back burner but Pakistani diplomats must do their best to keep England, Japan and US committed to this issue at the multilateral level. If India accedes on Kashmir, then Pakistan could reward India by nominating her for the UN Security Council's permanent seat. In fact, this offer should be made to the Indians during the Indo-Pakistani bilateral negotiations on Kashmir

Third, Pakistan must be quick to capitalize on its biggest assets; the nuclear and missile scientists. Pakistan must send her atomic scientists on goodwill missions from Indonesia and Malaysia to all the way to Western Sahara and Morocco in the same manner as the first U.S. astronauts travelled around the globe. Now that Pakistan has proven its scientific credentials, these countries will most likely want Pakistan as their friend. Most Muslim countries, with the exception of the oil rich Gulf sheikhdoms, are poor and destitute, Pakistan could accommodate a number of these countries in their need to develop in many fields, including military hardware and training. In fact, Pakistan with its nuclear prowess, despite adverse international conditions and and despite severe budgetary constraints, have proven that Third World solutions must come from within the Third World.

In the short term, this move by Pakistan will signal to the U.S. and the West to lift sanctions against Pakistan or the country might be put in a position to transfer its nuclear and missile know-how to the Middle East. The Israeli lobby in the U.S. would definitely not want this to happen. Consequently, this lobby will most probably want the U.S. administration and the Congress to repeal the Pressler amendment.

The results of this policy can be seen in the Pakistani Prime Minister's immediate visit to the UAE and Saudi Arabia and the Iranian Foreign Minister's visit to Pakistan soon after the Chagai blasts. Israelies are already rethinking their policy of transferring nuclear and missile technology to India.

In the long term, however, a host of smaller countries, especially the Middle Eastern countries, could become Pakistan's important bilateral allies and trade partners that could end their individual reliance on the industrialized North at least in some critical fields. This south to south trade route change could trigger a new era of prosperity for all and amelioration of poor and destitutes of India and Pakistan.

But Pakistan must choose its friends wisely. Three countries stand out as exceptionally important to Pakistan during its nuclear journey. These are Iran, Saudi Arabia and the United Arab Emirates. Pakistan must improve its bilateral relations with Iran and nurture them even further in all fields despite opposition by U.S. and a few religious political groups at home. Pakistan must fulfil Saudi Arabian peoples' desire to become self-sufficient in their own security. Pakistan had provided defence forces to the kindom of Saudi Arabia in the past, the time to replace the American and Western alliance forces with Pakistani forces may have come. Eventually, the Saudis could become self sufficient in their defence needs. Immediately, however, they could save billions that they are remitting to the now 'unwanted' and embarrassingly expensive American forces. Now that the threat of the Iraqi nuclear (not proven) and other weapons of mass destruction has been removed, departure of the American forces seems fair and appropriate. It also removes friction between the U.S. and Iran.

In the wake of the Indian nuclear explosions of May 11, the Saudis are also beggining to think that the rapid increases in India's defence budget and types of weaponry, e.g. nuclear, and hydrogen bombs, ballistic missiles, aircraft carriers, and long-range Russian made SU-27 bombers may not be just for increasing leverage over Pakistan. They are realizing that the depth of Indo-Israeli nuclear and military connections and cooperation is not just directed at Pakistan alone. The ultimate aim of Indo-Israeli nexus could very well be the Mid East oil for India and water for Israel. The Saudis may,therefore, be inclined to send the Indian workers packing home as the reality sinks in that the remittances of expatriate Indians do help their government in the acquisition of Isreaeli nuclear and military hardware. In turn, Pakistan could benefit from increased recruitment of Pakistani workers for Saudi oil fields. The Sultan/ President of the United Arab Emirates and his people are intelligent, progressive, and endowed with a special sense of pride as well as desire for scientific advancement. Pakistan must offer a special training wing for the UAE nationals in scientific fields of their choice.

The above three countries must remain at the base of Pakistan's Middle East policy. In turn, Pakistan's help to them will keep a steady flow of foreign exchange and oil and gas for the country's industrial advancement, on the one hand, and will make sure that Washington will listen to Islamabad's concerns due the Iranian connection, on the other.

Before the euphoria of Pakistan's scientific achievement dies down, Pakistan must immediately conclude long term energy, finance, and scientific exchange agreements with these countries. Initially, a number of proposed natural gas and oil pipelines between Central Asian Islamic states, Iran as well as Qatar and Pakistan should be built in the next few years. In return, Pakistan must pay them with training in military and other 'important' scientific and educational fields.

Fourth, Pakistan must solve the ongoing Afghan problem. It is essential to have Pakistan's western front quite now more than ever.

Fifth, despite an obvious set back to NPT since May 11, 1998, the core of the nuclear nonproliferation regime is still intact. Pakistan must strengthen this core by adhering to its principals, norms and standards as far as IAEA safeguards, technology transfer and observance of CTBT moratoriums, etc., are concerned.

There is no need for Pakistan to consider the Non-proliferation Treaty (NPT) as a dead letter. Let the Indians deal with this matter on their own and let them face the US and the nonproliferation community. Pakistan's NPT stand and her South Asian Nuclear Weapon Free Zone (NWFZ) proposals were fairly clear to the international community of nations, academics and diplomats. A concerted diplomatic effort is needed to highlight Pakistan's efforts in this regard.

Also, there is no need to sign NPT or CTBT at this stage, unless Kashmir problem is resolved and India signs as well as ratifies these treaties. Kashmir must now become corollary to Pakistan's nuclear disarmament. Pakistan should refrain from reiterating that it will sign any such treaties if India signs first and may want to reassess this strategy for two reasons. First, it could have worked against Pakistan had India signed CTBT days after detonating its nuclear devices. Tremendous pressure would have been put on Pakistan and India would have benefited from computer simulation and modelling data of nuclear detonation for future development of her nuclear weapons. Secondly, Pakistan need not insist on India to sign these treaties if she is willing to conclude an equitable agreement on Kashmir. It is cledar that Indian strategy is much more grandiose than just competing with Pakistan on the nuclear front. Obviously, this is a competition which India is bound to win if one compares Indo-Pakistani situations with the Cold war competition of the U.S.

and USSR. Moreover, India may very well concede on Kashmir, if she sees that her regional and global ambitions are jeopardized by a nuclear Pakistan.

Sixthly, Pakistan must not sign a no first use of nuclear weapons with any state, especially India, as it was offered by her Prime Minister. With the offer of no fist use of nuclear weapons, India reaps the benefit of nuclear deterrence between the two countries and continues to disregard any solution on Kashmir, on the one hand, and claims its stake as a regional and possibly international power house, on the other. Pakistan's counter offer to India should be a treaty on no use of nuclear bombs on Indo-Pakistani cities.

On the military and strategic front Pakistan needs to take a number of policy and other measures as well. The most urgent need is to avoid an accidental or unauthorized nuclear war. A hotline between the Indian and Pakistani leaders, both at the armed forces and the political level, should be established immediately to minimize such a scenario. Pakistan must immediately adopt a nuclear deterrence doctrine and incorporate it into its forces' training and strategic as well tactical outlook even if it entails massive retaliation strategy against any major threat, nuclear or conventional.

Eventually, both India and Pakistan will want to go beyond first strike deterrence (also known as "use-it-or loose-it strategy"), which seems to be their current deterrence policy, to a second strike capability or the Mutual Assured Destruction (MAD) strategy. It means that the country can take an atomic hit and still retaliate with its nuclear weapons that have survived the first strike of the enemy.

Pakistan just does not have enough depth or places to conceal all its nuclear carrying missiles or warplanes from a surprise first strike of either India or any other nuclear armed country. Submarines are uniquely qualified to provide a second strike capability due to a natural stealth cover provided by many oceans and seas around the globe. The choice of submarines is crucial. Should they be diesel, nuclear, or hybrid? Should Pakistan manufacture its own or buy off the shelf somewhere? These questions have been addressed before; however, Pakistan may need to revisit them again in light of the changed geopolitical situation of South Asia.

Fortunately, the six boat submarine fleet of Pakistan that includes four Daphne and two Agosta class submarines is missile tested. There are three more Agosta class boats on order from France. Pakistan must accelerate its acquisition of the French Agosta class submarines. Next, their local assembly and construction should be speeded up from the current plan of action.

The current choice of French diesel subs is fairly sound and fortiuous for two reasons. One, these boats are much more quieter than their Soviet and German counterparts of the Indian Navy. Two, the French nuclear missile carrying boats with nuclear power engines are modelled on the Agosta design. Indeed, diesel subs are also quieter than their nuclear counterparts. However, the nuclear or a hybrid submarine with nuclear tipped missiles is considered a better guarantor of second strike capability due to its range and longer staying power at sea. For now Pakistan must immediately equip its existing fleet of Agosta and Daphne class French submarines with nuclear ballistic and cruise missiles as well as nuclear tipped torpedoes.

Moreover, the Chinese nuclear-diesel hybrid engine submarines are rumoured to be based on the Agosta model. Both these countries have time and again have proven to be reliable suppliers of arms and technology to Pakistan. Therefore, nuclear submarines' acquisition from these countries, especially China, by Pakistan at a future date of her choice will most probably not pose a major hurdle considering China did offer these boats to Pakistan recently.

In addition to ballistic missiles, Pakistan needs to develop cruise missiles for the following reasons. It is relatively easier to hide and move these weapons closer to the Indian borders. The technology is available within Pakistan. They are extremely difficult to detect during their flight. This technology provides greater length of time between launch and abandonment; if desired, such mechanisms could be incorporated with innovative sofware solutions and satellite based homing devices. This option could provid some flexibility of time and recall almost along the same lines as a piloted airborne carrier. Some technological problems will be faced by Pakistan in the fields of computers and software but it should not be impossible to overcome this problem.

It is imperative that Pakistan must let go its military reliance on the U.S., not so much out of spite but for strategic reasons. This country has never been reliable due to its global commitments and commercial interests. Pakistan's reliance on the U.S. can tantamount to suicide during the nuclear age, especially in light of the convergence of the U.S. and Indian strategic interests in South Asia and the Middle East. China, Germany and France have proven fairly reliable and can pretty much provide everything that Pakistan needs. Pakistan can forget about becoming self-sufficient in the production of high technology weapons now or for sometimes in the near or even far future. Instead of harping on this point, Pakistan should get whatever it can and transfer as much of technology as possible

Pakistan needs to have a reliable force multiplier in its airforce. Pakistanis have been fixated on the F16s and Mirage 2000 for all the wrong reasons. Both these planes have their own unique problems. The first has problem of supply and the second is very expensive. What about the Mig-29 or Sukhoi SU-27? It seems that Russia will sell to anybody with hard currency. Failing that one could approach Ukraine or Belarus for either technology as both these cuntries have most of these technologies and have been parading their military hardware in various air shows. In the long run, China is bound to induct these systems in her drive to modernize the PRC armed forces. That alone assures Pakistan of reliable supply of critical components and spares for these weapon systems.

Above all, Pakistan must improve its quilt-work of a radar system. A substantial investment in developing or acquiring AWACS is essential after Prithvis, Agnis and Shaktis have come to the neighbourhood. A better long term approach would be to develop and launch a couple of satellites, both low orbit and geo-stationery types in the near future, through two competing nuclear development establishments and three missile development organizations of Pakistan.

Last but not least, it is hoped that neither Pakistan, nor India will ever have to use the awesome power of the atom against their own kith and kin. Let's also hope that saner elements in their leadership will prevail and not test a futile attempt to test each other's nuclear preparedness. In the meantime, the U.S. and the most advance nations of the world may consider transferring C3I systems to these countries for possible unauthorized use of these weapons of mass destruction.

NUCLEAR POWER OR NUCLEAR DEFENSE?

Three events mark the shift in India's nuclear program away from one that was entirely focused on generating energy. The first was the death of Jawaharlal Nehru. While encouraging the development of a militarily capable nuclear infrastructure, Nehru had always opposed explicit weaponization. The second was the completion of a reprocessing plant and the CIRUS research reactor, which began operating in 1960. The CIRUS, India's first heavy water reactor was originally called CIR for Canada-India-Reactor, because it was built with Canadian assistance. After the United States supplied the required heavy water for staring the reactor, it was renamed CIRUS. This gave India the ability to extract plutonium and thus to make nuclear weapons. The third event was the first Chinese nuclear test in 1964, barely two years after India lost the war with China.

Of these three, the Chinese nuclear test was the most significant. For the first time several influential individuals among the bureaucracy, political parties and intellectuals argued for India developing nuclear bombs. They were the forerunners of what became known as the "bomb lobby" in India. Over the years, the bomb lobby's influence on actual policy has varied, but they have always been a prominent part of the debate. While there were considerable differences in what they advocated, they all agreed that India had to develop nuclear weapons.

The chief arguments for developing nuclear weapons were largely based on the rationales used by the U.S. and the Soviet Union during the cold war. The bomb lobby argued that nuclear weapons are required to counter nuclear weapons, they guarantee security, and that they are relatively cheaper than conventional weapons and provide more destructive power. Many in India also identified having a nuclear bomb as a source of international prestige. One of the key supporters of the development of nuclear weapons was the founder of the Indian nuclear program, Homi Bhabha. He was a successful theoretical physicist and a good institution builder. Bhabha belonged to the wealthy Parsi community, which migrated to the West Coast of India from Iran several centuries ago. After studying and working in Cambridge University, England, he worked for a few years at the Indian Institute of Science. Bhabha then started the Tata Institute of Fundamental Research, the birth place of the Indian nuclear program, in 1945. In a radio speech a week after the Chinese nuclear test, Bhabha claimed that nuclear weapons could be produced quickly and at a relatively low cost. Given Bhabha's prestige and influence, it was hard for others to argue against him.

However, after Bhabha's death in 1966, the Department of Atomic Energy slowed down the quest for nuclear weapons. Bhabha's successor, Vikram Sarabhai, felt that developing nuclear energy was more important than the defense uses of nuclear weapons. Some analysts trace the actual timing of the decision to conduct India's first nuclear test in 1974 to a few months after his death in 1971. Nevertheless, even during his tenure, scientists and technicians working in the nuclear establishment continued developing the capability to make nuclear weapons. Chief among them was actually separating Plutonium and setting up a research reactor called Purnima to study the behaviour of fast neutrons, which was very useful in designing the 1974 device.

The negotiation of the Nuclear Non-Proliferation Treaty (NPT) in 1967 prompted another round of debate over nuclear weapons in India. After initial attempts to seek security assurances from the nuclear weapon states, India decided to vote against the treaty and argued against the its discriminatory aspects. The NPT, which seeks to prevent nuclear proliferation, divides its signatories into two categories: nuclear weapon states (NWS) and non-nuclear weapon states (NNWS). Only those states that had developed and tested nuclear weapons before the treaty was negotiated were included in the first category. These are the USA, USSR, Britain, France and China, who are also the permanent members of the UN Security Council, the so-called P-5.

India objected to this division and on more than one occasion described this as "nuclear apartheid." This emphasis on non-discrimination (i.e. treating all signatories as equal) has since come to mark the Indian position on arms control and disarmament initiatives. In 1968, when the treaty was open for signing, 61 countries joined the treaty. India was not among them. Currently it is one of three countries with nuclear facilities that have not acceded to this (or equivalent) treaty. A little over a year after the NPT went into force, India and Pakistan fought their third war. During this war the US Seventh Fleet, led by the USS Enterprise, was sent into the Bay of Bengal. Henry Kissinger, Secretary of State at the time, claimed the move was designed not only to 'assist' Pakistan, but also to 'back up the Chinese'. For the Indians, however, the 1971 intrusion was a form of "gunboat diplomacy" that was possibly nuclear. This is widely regarded as a factor in the decision to conduct India's first nuclear test.

THE "PEACEFUL NUCLEAR EXPLOSION" AND AFTER

On May 24, 1974, at the height of a nationwide railway strike (led by the current Defense Minister, George Fernandes), India conducted its first nuclear test at Pokharan in the desert in Rajasthan. The telegram sent to the Prime Minister Indira Gandhi by Raja Ramanna, the leader of the team that carried out the explosion, read "The Buddha is Smiling" – a phrase that has become the source of several article titles. The device tested is believed to have been large and heavy with a yield of about 8-12 kilotons, a little less than the weapon that was dropped on Hiroshima.

India termed the test a "Peaceful Nuclear Explosion" and launched a diplomatic offensive trying to prove that it was indeed peaceful. Part of the motivation to call the tests "peaceful," was to maintain technological ties with the U.S. and Canada.

When Canada and the US agreed to provide assistance in building and operating India's CIRUS research reactor, India pledged to use the facility and the fissile material coming out of it for purely peaceful purposes. By terming its test a peaceful nuclear explosion - which was well within the terms of nuclear discourse at that time - India maintained that it had not violated its pledge. Despite this, the test led to the withdrawal of practically all cooperation in nuclear technology with the US and Canada.

To avoid such problems in the future, India subsequently built a similar, but larger, research reactor called Dhruva. Dhruva started functioning in 1985. It has been estimated that India could have accumulated about 300-500 kgs of Plutonium from these two reactors. Judging from the sophistication of the recent tests, Indian designs probably use less than 5 kg of Plutonium for each nuclear bomb. Hence, India has sufficient stocks of fissile material for over 60 to 100 bombs. It is striking that all the leaders of the group that conducted the 1974 test went on to head the Department of Atomic Energy. The first, Raja Ramanna, is known for his hawkish views. He went on to become the science advisor to the Minister of Defense in 1977-1979 and the minister of state for Defense in 1989-91. According to recent revelations, it was during his tenure as science advisor that the manufacture of nuclear weapon components, which had been temporarily stopped after the 1974 test, was restarted.

The next of the Pokharan leaders who went on to head the Department of Atomic Energy, P. K. Iyengar, also continued to expand the infrastructure to make nuclear weapons. The third leader of the group to also become head the DAE was R. Chidambaram. In a 1994 interview, while denying reports of radioactivity releases from the 1974 test explosion, he went on to triumphantly assert, "that's how good our bomb was." This was the first time a high official within the Department of Atomic Energy had publicly called the "peaceful nuclear explosion" what it was - a bomb.

The Missile Program

The quest for nuclear capability also extended to developing vehicles for delivering nuclear weapons. In 1983, the Integrated Guided Missile Development Program (IGMDP) was set up. The guiding force behind the program, Abdul Kalam, was born in a poor family in Southern India. Inspired by an article on the British Spitfire, he took up Aeronautical Engineering at the Madras Institute of Technology (known locally as MIT!). After working as a leading scientist in India's defense related research agencies, he headed the Satellite Launch Vehicle Program in India's civilian space program, before finally leading the missile program.

Abdul Kalam brought a more open management style practiced in the Indian civilian space program to the relatively closed defense research program. This included involving academic institutions in defense research as well as subcontracting projects and the manufacture of components to private firms. He also acquired technology from the civilian space program for the military missile program. This form of integration of civilian scientific programs with national security goals was clearly a result of the 1974 test. Kalam won great acclaim for his role in successfully developing guided missiles. He was appointed to head India's main defense research agency, and was subsequently awarded India's highest civilian honor - the Bharat Ratna. The Indian guided missile program started with the development of five missile systems - the short range Prithvi (Earth), the intermediate range Agni (Fire), the surface to air missiles Akash (Sky) and Trishul (Trident), and the guided anti-tank Nag (Snake). By 1988, the results of the new program were visible - the first test of Prithvi was conducted on 25 February 1988. This was followed the next year with a test of Agni. More recently, other missile systems are under development – the Pinaka, the Sagarika and the Astra.

Round Two of the Non-Proliferation Treaty (NPT)

The indefinite extension of the NPT in 1995 was another blow to the Indian position on nuclear disarmament. Under the NPT, Non-Nuclear Weapon-States abjure nuclear weapons and in exchange Nuclear-Weapon States agreed to "pursue negotiations in good faith on effective measures relating to cessation of the nuclear arms race at an early date and to nuclear disarmament, and on a Treaty on general and complete disarmament under strict and effective international control." While the Non-Nuclear Weapon-States have almost without exception kept their end of the bargain, the Nuclear Weapon-States have failed to keep theirs. Since the NPT was signed, the Nuclear Weapon-States have conducted innumerable nuclear weapons tests and increased the size and destructive power of their arsenals.

In 1995, the NPT came up for review and a decision about extending it had to be made. Despite opposition by the Non Nuclear Weapon-States, the Nuclear Weapon-States, led by the US, forced through an indefinite extension of the NPT. This was widely interpreted in India as the permanent entrenchment of an unequal system. The indefinite extension of the NPT strengthened the position of the bomb lobby in debates over Indian nuclear policy and provided grounds for a renewed campaign for nuclear weapons.

Debating the Comprehensive Test Ban Treaty

The first effect of this campaign was that India voted against the CTBT in 1996, a treaty it had championed for forty years. This came as a big surprise since India had consistently supported non-discriminatory global arms control measures such as the CTBT and a cutoff on the production of fissile material (fissban). Even as late as 1994, it co-sponsored the CTBT at the United Nations, along with the USA. However, after the indefinite extension of the NPT, things had changed.

In the domestic debate, the Indian bomb lobby argued that the indefinite extension implied nuclear weapons were going to be around forever. Hence India should either develop nuclear weapons or settle for permanent second-class status. To develop militarily useable nuclear weapons India had to test. Therefore it had to reject the CTBT.

In international forums, as well as official circles, two main arguments were used against the CTBT. First, the CTBT did not really constrain the weapons development programs of the Nuclear Weapon-States, especially the U.S. The U. S. had started a multi-billion dollar Science Based Stockpile Stewardship Program involving the construction of several facilities that could develop new weapons designs. This was not the case when the CTBT was first proposed in the 1950s. It was the hundreds of tests conducted in the intervening period that allows the U.S. to design new weapons without nuclear testing.

Second, the CTBT was no longer a step towards disarmament as had always been envisioned. Instead, the Nuclear Weapon-States viewed it as merely a measure that would, in the words of the head of the erstwhile Arms Control and Disarmament Agency of the USA, "freeze countries on the nuclear learning curve."

The rationale for the Stockpile Stewardship Program was to ensure the US nuclear arsenal would remain functional for the foreseeable future. India demanded that the CTBT be coupled to a time-bound program for nuclear disarmament. The Nuclear Weapon-State were completely opposed to this.

A less noticed, but important, shift in India's stance was the perceived role of its nuclear weapons. While refusing to sign discriminatory agreements and continuing to build its nuclear infrastructure in the past, India had always maintained that nuclear weapons were immoral and deterrence, an abhorrent doctrine. As late as March 1996, the Indian Foreign Secretary, Salman Hyder said "We do not believe that the acquisition of nuclear weapons is essential for our national security and we have followed a conscious decision in this regard." This was in line with the traditional Indian view.

However, when the Indian Ambassador to the Conference on Disarmament, Arundhati Ghose, rejected the CTBT in the present form on 20 June 1996, she said the CTBT was not "in India's national security interest" and "our national security considerations (have) become a key factor in our decision-making." This shift points to the dangerous impact on Indian nuclear policy of arguments advanced by the bomb lobby.

THE IMPACT OF POST-9/11 ON SECURITY PERCEPTIONS

After the terrorist attacks on the US on September 11, 2001, the West has expressed serious apprehensions concerning the terrorist groups acquiring weapons of mass destruction and the nuclear-related materials, from the Indian and Pakistani nuclear facilities. But, the fact remains that the prospects of these non-state actors acquiring WMD materials from the Indian and Pakistani facilities is "extremely low since both countries keep their nuclear arsenals in an unassembled form, and because their components are stored separately." Therefore, the chances of terrorist groups acquiring nuclear-related materials from within India and Pakistan for terrorism are remote. However, according to Rizvi and Basrur, fears regarding four types of nuclear terrorism cannot be ruled out. These include the sabotage of nuclear facilities, use of a "dirty bomb" to disperse radiation, terrorist takeover of nuclear installations and a threat to blow them up, as well as clandestine transfer of nuclear material for use/assemblage somewhere else. Rizvi and Basrur have suggested eight measures, which in their viewpoint could substantially enhance the safety and security of nuclear facilities in India and Pakistan:

1. Track-down the groups and the individuals engaged in violent activities and terrorism.
2. Extensive surveillance of the borders and coastlines to contain the movement of goods and people.
3. More use of modern technology to enhance the physical protection of nuclear weapons, material and installations.
4. Thorough scrutiny of the personnel handling the nuclear programmes of the two countries.
5. Acquisition of latest technologies for the transportation of fissile and radioactive materials.
6. Highly trained manpower may be employed for the protection of nuclear facilities.
7. Extensive coordination network amongst all the set-ups dealing with the nuclear infrastructure and, in addition, there should be an independent body to ensure an oversight and accountability.
8. Finally, a disaster management body may be established to handle a security alarm systems, and the actual nuclear-terrorist incidents and emergencies.

Obviously, the US and the Western countries have a strong interest in preventing a nuclear war between India and Pakistan. The military standoff of 2001-2002 between the two countries had visibly brought the two countries much closer to a war, which then prompted the US and the European Union countries to assist them in defusing the tension. Therefore, logically, in future, US and the EU countries should be keen to strengthen the safety and security mechanisms of India and Pakistan's nuclear weapons programmes, because the threat of nuclear-terrorism is global in range and its effects cannot be contained to a single geographical region alone.

On September 17, 2002, the Bush Administration announced *National Security Strategy of the United States of America*, which laid-down a comprehensive policy to combat the WMD, and to defeat global terrorism. This significant document envisaged a proactive counter-proliferation policy to deter, and to defend against the perceived threat of terrorism before it is let loose. Secondly, to strengthen the non-proliferation regimes with a view to interdict the 'rogue states' and terrorist organisations from gaining the technologies, materials, and expertise to assemble the WMD. Thirdly, to effectively contain the effects of the WMD use, whether by the rogue states or by the terrorist networks. The main thrust of this new policy is on pre-emptive actions even in an anticipatory self-defence against such states and the terrorist groups. More significantly, this doctrine considers the Cold War era's deterrence principles (as a weapon of last resort and defence) as ineffective against the present-day deterrence postures, which is primarily premised on threat of retaliation that is not expected to work against the rogue states, and the terrorist organisations, which would tend to risk the lives of their nations.

Interestingly, this strategy has an inherent flaw because it would tend to lead to more reliance on pre-emption that would "turn force from an instrument of last resort into one of first resort," comment Ivo H. Daalder, James M. Lindsay, and James B. Steinberg. Moreover, it will accord an opportunity to other states to formulate principles and strategies in accordance with their narrow national interests to have "an unfettered right of pre-emption against its own definition of threats to its security" to act unilaterally. This doctrine instead of rooting-out the scourge of terrorism is likely to widen the gulf of alienation between the friends and allies and, at the same time fails to address the question of threat to security.

It would be appropriate to make a distinction between the state and the non-state actors' acquisition and potential to use the nuclear weapons. Since the break-up of the former Soviet Union, the West became apprehensive regarding the proliferation of nuclear materials, equipment, technology, and personnel to the 'rogue states' and terrorist outfits.

In 1992, US and Russia, to ensure that nuclear weapons and materials do not fall in the hands of the undesirable elements, established the Nunn-Lugar Cooperative Threat Reduction (CTR) programme. Additionally, in 1999, the Clinton Administration announced a policy to expand the work of CTR by the Expanded Threat Reduction Initiative (ETRI) plan to ensure that WMD-related technologies did not reach the wrong hands, including to the states sponsoring terrorism.

But, since the tragic terrorist incidents of September 11, 2001, the US perspective concerning the possibility of nuclear terrorism has undergone marked transformation. Robert Kagan, a leading scholar of US foreign policy, writes,

Europe is turning away from power, to put it a little differently, it is moving beyond power into a self-contained world of laws and rules and transnational negotiation and cooperation.

It is entering a post-historical paradise of peace and relative prosperity, the realization of Immanuel Kant's "perpetual peace." Meanwhile, the United States remains mired in history, exercising power in an anarchic Hobbesian world where international laws and rules are unreliable, and where true security and the defence and promotion of a liberal order still depend on the possession and use of military might.... Americans generally see the world divided between good and evil, between friends and enemies, while Europeans see a more complex picture. When confronting real or potential adversaries,

Americans generally favour policies of coercion rather than persuasion, emphasizing punitive sanctions over inducements to better behaviour, the stick over the carrot.

Americans tend to seek finality in international affairs: they want problems solved, threats eliminated. And, of course, Americans increasingly tend toward unilateralism in international affairs. Kagan's perspective is widely shared in the United States, including by the Bush Administration, that Washington should pursue a more proactive, rather unilaterally coercive diplomacy, to finally eliminate the scourge of terrorism and to solve the other problems of the world.

But, the fact remains that US nuclear non-proliferation policy, and international non-proliferation regimes, still form an integral part of Washington's security architecture to deal with the potential threats of WMD-related terrorism.

Therefore, in the foreseeable future, US would be less inclined on the international institutions like the United Nations in order to achieve its national objectives. In this context, the US National Security Strategy and the National Strategy to Combat Weapons of Mass Destruction (NSCWMD) would continue to guide a new strategy for the US Homeland Security, and a fundamental diversion from the traditional concept of deterrence with a view to combat the WMD threats.

Because, Bush Administration perceives that its enemies were seeking the WMD, and that the NSCWMD would proactively bolster, interdiction-oriented approach to mitigate the WMD threats. Prima facie, the document is intended to target the 'rogue states,' but it also does not rule out action against the other states as well who sponsor or harbour terrorism.

The NSCWMD also envisages bolstering of US conventional, nuclear, intelligence/surveillance, interdiction, and domestic law enforcement capabilities to improve its overall deterrent posture vis-à-vis the WMD threats. This includes capabilities to detect and destroy adversary's WMD arsenals before their use. Therefore, US would consistently endeavour to formalise new agreements, which could cater for its non-proliferation objectives. In addition, strengthen the existing non-proliferation regimes to promote its security interests. Moreover, in parallel conceive a comprehensive sanctions policy as a tool of diplomacy to support its overall strategy of NSCWMD. But rightly in the view of some experts, the question of nuclear terrorism by states is fundamentally different from the issue of the "acquisitions and use of such weapons by non-state actors." Thomas Badey writes,

It is highly unlikely that countries with a desire to acquire nuclear weapons, such as Iran, Iraq, Libya, Sudan and North Korea, would spend millions of dollars and years of research to acquire nuclear weapons, only to sell or hand them over to non-state actors, knowing that they might be held accountable for the actions of potential clients.... It is much more likely that states, particularly those targeted by export controls and economic sanctions, may use non-state actors to acquire nuclear materials for them rather than the other way around.

The use of nuclear weapons by the 'rogue states' with an inadequate backing and accompanying capabilities would be counter-productive rather than proving of any strategic gain.

Because, in the case of use of nuclear weapons by the 'rogue states' and their sponsored non-state actors, it would certainly eclipse the potential benefits and, the consequences would be more horrendous to contemplate.

Besides, it is highly improbable that any single individual could equip a group to have an access to fissionable material or even to crude a form of nuclear device without the assistance of a reliable delivery system, which is otherwise only feasible with the collaboration of a major industrial enterprise.

In the views of the former head of nuclear weapons development programme at the Los Alamos, J. Carson Mark, it requires a team of a mechanical engineer, nuclear physicist, a chemist, and explosive expert, a mathematician, and along with other auxiliary staff, and at least a year to develop a nuclear device.

Besides, it would be highly unlikely for the non-state actors to hire the services of highly qualified and experienced scientists; the requisite industrial infrastructure; the financial resources; weapons-grade uranium or plutonium; and an access to clandestine transport or to a delivery system, that too, for terrorism, appears to be incredibly implausible.

However, the security of nuclear installations, personnel, and the fissionable and radiological materials in possession of the *de jure* and the *de facto* NWS, should be made foolproof.

Secondly, the existing non-proliferation regimes can be made vibrant to ensure that nuclear technology and material does not pilfer into the possession of non-state actors and the 'rogue states,' which could jeopardise the stability of international peace and security.

Though, the non-state actors can easily assemble the chemical and biological elements for terrorist attacks, therefore, rationally the emphasis should be to check the proliferation of chemical, radiological and biological agents, which the terrorist organisations may acquire from the international black-market, and then convert the same into a 'dirty bomb'. In this connection, US President Bush in a statement on May 31, 2003, during his visit to Poland, referred to the Proliferation Security Initiative (PSI) of the US in collaboration with ten other countries, including its allies, to employ all the legal, diplomatic, economic, military channels, including searching planes and cargo ships, to interdict illegal weapons, nuclear, missiles, and radiological materials. Such measures would go long way in deterring the terrorist organisations from implementing their nefarious designs, provided PSI is reconciled within the parameters of the international law. In addition, the nuclear-related CSBMs between the *de jure* and the *de facto* NWS, and other developed countries, could also collectively evolve a strategy to seize the transfer of sensitive technologies to 'rogue states' in order to minimise, if not exclude completely, the possibility of such technologies, nuclear and radiological materials falling in the wrong hands.

Unfortunately, in the South Asian context, since the Lahore Declaration of February 1999, both India and Pakistan have not been able to start talks on nuclear-related CSBMs. In August 2003, Pakistan had offered India the resumption of a dialogue on nuclear-related CSBMs that were agreed in principle in the Memorandum of Understanding (MoU) signed by them at the time of Lahore Declaration, in order to establish the strategic restraint regime. India instead of responding positively to the Pakistani proposal accused it of foot-dragging on resumption of a dialogue and other diplomatic and peace initiatives between the two countries. In this connection, again on December 18, 2003, President Pervez Musharraf, repeated the offer to India for improving bilateral relations by resolving the Kashmir dispute:

We are for United Nations Security Council Resolutions…now we have left that aside. If we want to resolve this issue, both sides need to talk to each other with flexibility, coming beyond stated positions, meeting halfway somewhere…. We are prepared to rise to the occasion; India has to be flexible also…. We have come to a stage where there is a thaw in relations, where there is expectation on both sides in the people…. If the leadership doesn't rise to the occasion, it is a pity and I think we'll disappoint our public again…. Unfortunately, magnanimity has to come from the bigger and the stronger.

President Musharraf's realpolitik and rational diplomatic proposal placed the ball squarely in India's court. It was up to India to capitalise on Pakistan's constructive initiative to resolve the neuralgic dispute over Kashmir, and to set in motion the process of improvement of bilateral relations. During the three-day 12th South Asian Association for Regional Cooperation (SAARC) Summit in Islamabad, the Indian Prime Minister, A. B. Vajpayee, urged the member states for "bold transition" from mistrust to trust, discord to concord, and tension to peace in the region. Moreover, Indian External Affairs Minister, Yashwant Sinha, in a statement also "expressed satisfaction on the progress in bilateral relations and discussed various ways to increase this momentum."

While Pakistan's Foreign Minister, Khurshid Mahmud Kasuri, too, reiterated that, "We have developed a good relationship, which is good for the people of both countries.

Our relations with India have improved. We will continue to improve our relations." Musharraf and Vajpayee in a bilateral meeting on January 5, further agreed to "maintain the momentum" generated by the confidence-building measures and diplomacy on the sidelines of the SAARC Summit. Therefore, in the second phase, if the proposed CSBMs can take a concrete shape once both countries resume a comprehensive dialogue and initiate further confidence-building measures process with a view to ensuring peace and security of the region, it could help lay the basis to eliminate the probability of terrorists' access to their nuclear, missile, chemical, biological, and radiological materials and facilities.

If the momentum resulting out of the thaw in bilateral relations is sustained, it could enable them to find a mutually acceptable solution to all their outstanding disputes, including over Kashmir.

9

Benefits and Risks of China-Pakistan Economic Corridor

Traditionally, China and Pakistan have cooperated closely at the strategic and political levels. Now the two nations are making efforts to expand their bilateral collaboration economically as well. The construction of the China-Pakistan Economic Corridor (CPEC) is a milestone that signifies this shift. At its core, the CPEC is a large-scale initiative to build energy, highway, and port infrastructure to deepen economic connections between China and Pakistan.

This initiative has been well-received in both countries, although it is not without its problems. Nevertheless, China and Pakistan regard the CPEC as a new source of potential synergy between their respective national development strategies, which may help the two countries translate their close political cooperation into multifaceted economic cooperation, attain mutual benefits, and achieve win-win outcomes. For the economic corridor to reach its potential, however, there are security and political challenges in Pakistan that must be addressed.

China first proposed the corridor project in May 2013. Chinese President Xi Jinping then visited Pakistan in April 2015, and both sides agreed to elevate their relationship to an "all-weather strategic partnership." During Xi's visit, the two countries signed fifty-one agreements at an estimated value of $46 billion.

The CPEC is now moving into the implementation phase. On May 6, 2016, there was an opening ceremony held in the city of Sukkur in Pakistan's Sindh Province, as construction began on a section of highway between Sukkur and the city of Multan—it will be part of a network of highways that will connect the cities of Peshawar and Karachi. This network is a major component of the CPEC's plans for infrastructure expansion, which highlights the progress the two nations have achieved thus far in the area of transportation. In addition, on November 13, 2016, the first large shipment of Chinese goods went through the port of Gwadar, a flagship CPEC project in Pakistan's southwestern province of Balochistan.

China considers these development initiatives a potential source of stability and prosperity for both countries. From a Chinese perspective, cooperation in the areas of security and economics are closely intertwined, and improvements on one side can improve the other.

It is almost as though security and economics are two separate wheels on the same vehicle, and both need to be spinning to move things forward. China believes economic development can strengthen Pakistan's internal stability, thus reinvigorating the latter's economy through investment in infrastructure projects as well as the construction of oil and gas pipelines. China hopes this will create a certain level of stability within Pakistan and in turn stabilize China's western periphery, particularly the province of Xinjiang.

More broadly, the CPEC has to be understood in the context of China's strategic interests in East Asia and the way the United States has challenged them. Faced with such difficulties, China hopes it can expand its strategic space by heading west. Pakistan serves as a crucial bridge between China and Central Asia, South Asia, and the Middle East. Security and stability in Pakistan will make it possible for China to exercise greater influence in these regions and to ensure security at home. This is why China is willing to pour vast amounts of resources into the economic corridor—based on the logic of improving security through economic development.

Likewise, Pakistan has realized that no other country places such high strategic importance in its economic relationship with Pakistan as China does. Pakistan also greatly values the economic corridor and views it as mutually beneficial in terms of politics and economic development. According to *Pakistan 2025*—a blueprint for economic development published in 2014 by Pakistan's Ministry of Planning, Development, and Reform—Pakistan aims to advance from being a lower-middle-income nation to an upper-middle-income nation by 2025. To achieve this goal, Pakistan hopes to attract increasing amounts of foreign investment. The country is working to improve its overall economy by constructing energy projects and other forms of infrastructure, to create employment opportunities for its populace, and to improve its governance.

The logic behind this strategy is that fundamentally improving Pakistan's economy will help alleviate the challenges posed by political extremists, radicals, and jihadists. China and Pakistan share the belief that economic development can help stabilize Pakistan and improve its domestic security situation. However, China also recognizes that the security, political, and cultural risks and uncertainties facing the economic corridor cannot be overlooked.

The first of these risks is terrorism, which has long affected Pakistan's internal security and stability. Although Pakistan has worked hard to strike at religious extremism and terrorist activities, its problems with terrorism have not substantially improved in recent years. Because the CPEC is so important to the Pakistani government, these projects' construction sites and engineering personnel may become targets for religious as well as nationalist extremists. Indeed, there already have been numerous occasions when Chinese engineers working in Pakistan have been attacked or even lost their lives. In May 2016, for instance, engineers in Karachi were attacked by Sindh separatists. Fortunately, no Chinese personnel were wounded or killed. Then in September, Baloch rebels killed at least two Chinese engineers and injured many others. Moreover, several large-scale terrorist attacks in Balochistan have killed dozens of people, which shows that the security situation in this province where China has key projects is far from ideal.

The security threat posed by terrorism remains ongoing, despite the economic benefits that the CPEC can offer Pakistan. The corridor aims to enhance the well-being of people throughout the country and bring long-term prosperity and stability. The Pakistani authorities, meanwhile, have promised China they will do everything possible to ensure the safety of Chinese workers. This is a feasible commitment in the short term. However, over time, it will become more difficult for Pakistan to guarantee the security of the CPEC's growing transportation networks, which will require increasing investments of security personnel and material support. It will likely become uncertain in the future whether Pakistan can maintain a strong enough military presence to ensure the security of all these transportation routes.

Second, Pakistan's domestic politics is also important to the CPEC's success. The country's political system has never been particularly stable. Political power oscillates between military and civilian leaders. General Pervez Musharraf's resignation as president in 2008 ended the latest period of military rule, and from that point onward, the military has been pushed from center stage. In the 2013 election, the Pakistan People's Party lost power after the Pakistan Muslim League Nawaz defeated it. The successful completion of this election, as well as the smooth transition of power that ensued, was the first time in Pakistan's history that a civilian government was able to serve out its entire term. This was a sign of improvement for Pakistan's democracy. On the other hand, Pakistan's traditional political culture, which is almost feudal in nature, also continues to play an important role. Powerful families based in different provinces, such as the Bhuttos and the Sharifs, have typically held political power. Behind the party politics are local interests groups associated with these families.

Various parties within Pakistan have disagreed a lot about how CPEC transportation routes should be mapped out. The competing parties are primarily interested in how the cake should be divided, so to speak. To strengthen its respective standing among the electorate, each of Pakistan's political parties hopes the CPEC will pass through the region it represents, allowing its local community to enjoy the corridor's benefits. In fact, since the initiative was first presented in 2013, the debate over which route the CPEC would follow has caused substantial delays. The construction of the corridor has just begun. It is expected that competition among Pakistan's domestic political groups will continue to affect its future implementation.

Yet the CPEC will not only serve as a roadway that simply connects point A to point B—the initiative is designed to do more. The corridor also aims to facilitate multisectoral economic cooperation in finance, trade, energy, and industry.

Amid a market slowdown and high unemployment rates, Pakistani Prime Minister Nawaz Sharif came back into office in 2013 with the intent of reinvigorating the economy, and he undertook a series of measures to improve Pakistan's economic prospects. One was lowering barriers to foreign investment. As for addressing energy shortages, Pakistan has been making efforts to restructure its energy industry and increase its electricity production. At the same time, the government has worked hard to strengthen investment in infrastructure, has moved forward with tax reforms, and has focused on increasing revenue and reducing expenditures. In addition, the government has adopted other measures to develop its market economy. It has overseen reforms for state-run enterprises and encouraged market privatization.

These measures are already starting to take effect. The country's GDP is growing at a stronger rate, and the economy is improving. For the time being, however, it will still remain unclear whether these economic advances can actually alleviate Pakistan's serious security and stability problems.

Cultural considerations and public relations should be also taken into account when evaluating the CPEC's prospects for economic success. Ordinary citizens in China and Pakistan are not very familiar with each other. The countries' leaders have built an all-weather friendship and close political relationship over the years, but this is not yet true of the two societies at large.

As China and Pakistan gradually expand cooperation, there will be an increasing number of Chinese corporations investing in Pakistan. Different cultural practices and ways of thinking could cause misunderstandings, and this could negatively affect CPEC projects. For these corporations to be successful, they will need to understand local cultures, norms, and rules. Having information about and services for doing business in Pakistan is also crucial for Chinese corporations.

China should abandon its traditional way of dealing only with the Pakistani government and instead get in contact with local communities to better accommodate local interests so that more Pakistani people can benefit from the CPEC. China and Pakistan need to strengthen their cultural ties and increase people-to-people interactions. This has already begun, due to the increasing economic activity between the two countries, forcing China to become more informed about the complexities of Pakistani society. The China-Pakistan Economic Corridor Council was founded in 2015 to jointly address the challenges arising in the CPEC projects. The council has opened offices in Beijing and Islamabad respectively, and its purpose is to assist with the implementation of CPEC projects.

China and Pakistan have taken positive measures to help set up the CPEC for success. Nevertheless, Pakistan's domestic situation is still decisive. Until the country's political and security conditions turn a corner, it will be difficult to judge the corridor's future prospects. For China, this means neutrality, strategic patience, and caution are needed as the construction of this grand initiative continues.

CHINA-PAKISTAN ECONOMIC CORRIDOR

The CPEC may be a bilateral endeavour, but New Delhi cannot ignore its spillover effects on regional governance and regime creation in South Asia. Beyond sketching out the broad considerations, India's foreign policy planners are yet to study the impact of the China-Pakistan Economic Corridor (CPEC) on South Asia's politics.

Views in New Delhi to the CPEC could be divided into two groups: the first believes the CPEC serves China's singular agenda of extending its strategic footprint to Gwadar and beyond, and freeing the country of the Malacca Strait chokehold that currently serves as the lifeline for Beijing's global commerce. Another section believes, with good reason, that many CPEC projects are simply not viable enough to sustain the interest of Chinese investors in the long run. Either outcome may materialise, but the CPEC is an important enough project whose economic and strategic consequences require methodical assessment. Three aspects of the CPEC in particular stand out as relevant questions for India to consider:

- o Will economic cooperation through the CPEC lead to regional military architectures in South Asia?

- o How will the US respond to the CPEC – will the Trump administration offer counter-benefits to Pakistan or other regional actors to blunt China's overtures?
- o Will Beijing see the CPEC as a case study for regime creation in Asia? That is, use it as a template to create and influence investment and trade standards in the region?

The CPEC may be a bilateral endeavour, but New Delhi cannot ignore its spillover effects on regional governance. The inequities in the China-Pakistan relationship and the nature of proposed Chinese investment in the CPEC merit a comparison with the Marshall Plan, the most successful foreign assistance project of the 20th century. Analysts in India and Pakistan have expressed bewilderment at Pakistan borrowing from Chinese banks to pay for Chinese projects in the corridor, but Beijing is simply taking a leaf out of the US playbook. The Marshall Plan – known formally as the European Recovery Plan — involved the US extending lines of credit and assistance for Western European economies ravaged by the Second World War. Credited with restoring stability in Europe, one needs to look no further than the then US under secretary of state Dean Acheson's words to gauge the real goals of the Marshall Plan. In May 1947, Acheson laid out the objectives of the recovery project in a speech at Cleveland:

"Our [US] exports of goods and services to the world during the current year, 1947, are estimated to total 16 billion dollars [...] In return for the commodities and services which we expect to furnish the world this year, we estimate we will receive commodities and services from abroad to the value of 8 billion dollars. [...] The differences between the value of the goods and services which foreign countries must buy from the United States this year and the value of goods and services they are able to supply to us this year will therefore amount to the huge sum of about 8 billion dollars.

How are foreigners going to get the US dollars necessary to cover this huge difference? [This is one] of the most important questions in international relations today."

In 1947, the US needed to finance and create captive markets that would continue buying American goods while offering their own services (cheap labour, highly skilled professionals) to the US in return. China today is looking to move its assembly lines outside the country, create cheaper supply chains and limit its economic externalities (such as environmental pollution) at home. Then, as is the case today with the 2008 recession, the global economy had slowed down after two devastating wars. The US, like China, was facing an export glut. In many Marshall Plan projects, moreover, the strategic interests of the US government were at odds with that of its private sector. The case of oil is illustrative. Soon after the Second World War, oil prices shot through the roof.

With Russian influence over Eastern Europe limiting their access to energy resources, Western European countries turned to the US for help. The US government, which saw the Marshall Plan as critical to staving off communism in the continent, sought to ensure Europe's access to oil at low prices. US oil companies, which controlled the lion's share of global oil supply, strongly resisted this move but eventually gave in to many of their government's demands.

In that case, the situation worked itself out since recipients of Marshall Plan aid used US dollars to buy US oil-refining equipment, with an eye on cheaper crude oil. But the episode highlights the important lesson that financial viability – often used to dismiss the China Pakistan Economic Corridor – is not necessarily the sole determinant of the CPEC's future. Beijing's strategic relationship with Islamabad, and its continuing quest to underwrite strategic parity between India and Pakistan in South Asia, will certainly contribute to the CPEC's longevity.

Spillover effects of CPEC

But what of the unintended or spillover consequences of the CPEC on security in South Asia? Here too, the Marshall Plan is instructive. Two years after the Economic Recovery Plan was formally announced by secretary of state George Marshall during his 1947 commencement address at Harvard, the North Atlantic Treaty Organisation (NATO) came into effect. The trans-Atlantic military alliance had been in the making for a while and the Marshall Plan by itself did not contribute to NATO's creation. But the plan freed up European coffers for rearmament and militarisation, acting as an "indirect economic subsidy". In fact, US President Harry Truman then expressly linked military support to Europe and the Marshall Plan, adopting a no-questions-asked policy to recipient NATO countries, who could then channel national budgets for defence spending.

The lines blurred between the Marshall Plan and the strategic environment in which it operated. If the CPEC's future will be determined by China-Pakistan ties, Indian policy planners should also be wary of the corridor's impact on the bilateral relationship. If China begins to guarantee the security of major projects along the corridor, would that free up Pakistan's budget and resources to target defence spending elsewhere? Support from Iran and Afghanistan would be indispensable to the CPEC's stability – will Beijing create an informal, four-way grouping aimed at securing CPEC currently, but aimed at adopting a bigger role in the years to come?

New Delhi has just not visualised the regional impact of the CPEC, wishing it away as a bilateral enterprise. In cash-starved South and West Asia, the economic corridor will be closely tailed by smaller countries to see if similar projects can be replicated elsewhere.

China, US and Pakistan

Will the CPEC grow into a large enough project to invite the US's attention? If so, what will be the consequences for South Asia? Historians generally agree that the Marshall Plan and NATO directly contributed to the Cold War, triggering a series of alliances and counter-alliances across the globe led by the US and Russia.

During this process, smaller countries often played off the major powers against each other, using their insecurities to buy weapons and aid. No doubt, the US is keeping a close watch on the China-Pakistan Economic Corridor. But before Washington D.C. gets involved in the CPEC debate, New Delhi should modulate its entry.

India and the US should begin serious conversations on the CPEC and its role as a force multiplier for China's strategic footprint in South Asia. Pakistan is unlikely to play the US off against China – its relations with both countries have evolved somewhat independently after US President Richard Nixon's 1972 visit to Beijing – but the Trump administration may yet be convinced of stronger ties with Islamabad to ward off pervasive Chinese influence.

And finally, India should observe the potential impact that the CPEC may have on regime creation in Asia. If China is unencumbered by financial viability – at least in the short and medium term – many countries will perceive Beijing to be more interested in strategic ties than purely economic arrangements. To attract 'quick and dirty' investment, therefore, autocratic regimes in Asia will invite strategic linkages with China. Indeed, the newly announced Shanghai Cooperation Organisation Bank is a sign that China itself seems to be convinced of the interdependence between military and economic regimes. This churning in economic and strategic architectures in Asia is a natural consequence of China's rise and the US's withdrawal from the region, but CPEC will be a litmus test to see whether Beijing can balance both.

India, therefore, cannot sustain its single-minded strategy of isolating Pakistan when it has clearly not had the desired effect on China and other regional players. For now, the CPEC seems to be on course for completing some of its milestones, and India would be ill-advised to rely on the false comfort that profits alone will drive China's business with Pakistan.

Understanding the CPEC's regional impact and mitigating its negative effects will require a comprehensive strategy from New Delhi that goes beyond the India-Pakistan narrative.

CHINA'S CONTINUING SALIENCE IN PAKISTANI FOREIGN POLICY

With India's recent rise as an economic and political power of global significance, Sino-Indian ties are now at a critical juncture as India tries to find the right policy mix to deal with its most important neighbour. Meanwhile, Chinese strategists remain concerned about U.S. attempts to encircle China and the profound effect on Chinese security of an eventual integration of India into a U.S. alliance.

China, according to this view, needs to remain vigilant against the growing network running "from Japan to India" that would suffocate China. As India struggles to emerge as a global power with an ambitious foreign policy agenda, China can effectively scuttle Indian ambitions by continuing with its diplomatic and military support to Pakistan. Much to India's chagrin, China has given ample indications in the recent past that it wants to follow that path. With the civilian government of President Asif Ali Zardari under intense pressure from the United States to do more to fight terrorism emanating from Pakistani soil, there are calls in Pakistan to adopt a foreign policy that considers China and not the United States to be Pakistan's strongest ally and most significant stakeholder. China's emergence as the leading global economic power coupled with recent attempts by India and the United States to forge a closer relationship has helped this suggestion gain further credibility.

Washington has historically been accused of using Pakistan in times of need and then deserting it for a policy that favours stronger relations with India to serve the larger U.S. strategic agenda. Pakistan remains angry about U.S. indifference after the United States used it to funnel aid to Afghan mujahideen and then turned its back on Pakistan after the Soviet withdrawal. Whereas only around nine percent of Pakistanis view the United States as a partner, around 80 percent of the Pakistani population considers China a friend.

The Obama administration's July 2011 decision to suspend a portion of U.S. aid to the Pakistani military has led many in Islamabad to become even more forceful in underlining Beijing's importance for Pakistan. Reacting to the U.S. move, Islamabad's ambassador to Beijing, Masood Khan, was quick to suggest that "China will stand by us in difficult times as it has been doing for the past years." Though Beijing cannot replace Washington as an aid-provider to Pakistan, the tension in U.S.—Pakistan ties provides an opportunity for Beijing to deepen its relationship with Islamabad. As it is, China is considered a more reliable ally that has always come to Pakistan's aid when India has been on the rise, even to an extent that China has conveniently turned a blind eye to Pakistan's strategy of using terror as an instrument of policy against India. Not surprisingly, Pakistan has given China a "blank cheque" to intervene in India—Pakistan peace talks. Pakistan also seems to have allowed Chinese engineers to examine the remains of the stealth helicopter destroyed during the raid that killed Osama bin Laden despite a direct request from the United States that China not be allowed to do so.

Forecast for the "All-Weather" Relationship

With India's ascent in the global hierarchy and U.S. attempts to carve out a strong partnership with India, China's need for Pakistan is only likely to grow. As tensions rose between India and Pakistan after the November 2008 terror attacks in Mumbai, Pakistan's Chairman of the Joint Chiefs of Staff Committee went to China to seek that country's support, which was readily given. The visit resulted in the signing of a new agreement on military cooperation between the two nations, with Beijing agreeing to expedite the delivery of F-22 frigates to Pakistan's Navy.

Beijing has justified its arms sales to Pakistan on the grounds that India was buying similar weapon systems from the United States (it also is buying military hardware from the Russians). China has consistently defended Pakistan's desire for high capacity weapons systems as normal for an independent nation seeking to bolster its security. In the years preceding the attacks in Mumbai, China blocked UN sanctions against the dreaded Lashkar-e-Taiba (LeT) and Jamaat-ud-Dawa (JuD), the organizations that planned and executed the attacks, despite a broad global consensus favouring such a move. Only when tensions surfaced between Beijing and Islamabad on the issue of Chinese Uighur separatists receiving sanctuaries and training on Pakistani territory did China agree to a ban on JuD. More recently, China has refused to reconsider its objection in the United Nations to proscribing the Jaish-e-Mohammed's Maulana Masood Azhar and some prominent LeT operatives based in Pakistan, despite New Delhi's presenting detailed information on them to Beijing.

With the exception of China, other major global powers such as Britain, France, Germany, and Russia supported the U.S.—India nuclear deal as they were eager to sell nuclear fuel, reactors, and equipment to India. China, on its part, made its displeasure clear by asking India to sign the NPT and dismantle its nuclear weapons. The official Xinhua news agency of China commented that the U.S.—India nuclear agreement "will set a bad example for other countries."

Since the U.S.—India deal is in many ways a recognition of India's rising global profile, China was not very happy with the outcome and indicated that it would be willing to sell nuclear reactors to Pakistan. It was a not so subtle message to the United States that if Washington decides to play favourites, China retains the same right.

Not surprisingly, China's plans to supply two nuclear reactors to Pakistan in defiance of international rules have gathered momentum. Chinese authorities have confirmed that the China National Nuclear Cooperation has signed an agreement with Pakistan for two new nuclear reactors at the Chashma site Chashma III and Chashma IV in addition to the two that it is already working on in Pakistan.

This will be in clear violation of the Nuclear Suppliers Group (NSG) guidelines that forbid nuclear transfers to countries that are not signatories to the NPT or do not adhere to comprehensive international safeguards on their nuclear program. China has suggested that "there are compelling political reasons concerning the stability of South Asia to justify the exports," echoing Pakistan's oft-repeated compliant that the U.S.—India nuclear pact has upset stability in the region. The decision to supply reactors to Pakistan which has a record of dealing with North Korea, Iran, and Libya reflects China's growing diplomatic confidence and underscores its view of Pakistan as a prized South Asian strategic power. Recent suggestions emanating from Beijing that China is likely to set up military bases overseas to counter U.S. influence and exert pressure on India have been interpreted in certain sections in New Delhi as a veiled reference to China's interest in having a permanent military presence in Pakistan.

Even though it might not be politically possible for the Pakistani government to follow through on such threats and openly allow China to set up a military base, New Delhi fears that Islamabad might allow Beijing use of Pakistani military facilities without any public announcement. Indian concerns have also risen that China and Pakistan are coordinating their efforts in regard to border issues with India. The presence of the Chinese military in the Gilgit—Baltistan area of Pakistan Occupied Kashmir, purportedly to repair and upgrade the Karakoram Highway, has enormous implications for Indian security.

Overall, it has been rightly observed that China's policy toward Pakistan is "an object lesson in how to attain long-term national goals by calm calculation, forbearance, and diplomatic skill." Nevertheless, there are indeed limits to China—Pakistan ties.

The relationship remains fundamentally asymmetrical: Pakistan wants more out of its ties with China than China is willing to offer. Today, while

Pakistan's domestic problems are gargantuan, China will be very cautious in involving itself even more. In September 2011, China Kingho Group, one of China's largest private coal mining companies, pulled out of what was to be Pakistan's largest foreign-investment pact, citing concerns for the security of its personnel. Moreover, the closer China gets to Pakistan, the faster India would move into the U.S. orbit.

Amid worries about the potential destabilizing influence of Pakistani militants on China's Muslim minority in Xinjiang, Beijing has also taken a harder line against Pakistan. The flow of arms and terrorists from across the border in Pakistan remains a major headache for Chinese authorities, and Islamabad's inability and/or failure to curb extremism makes it difficult for the Chinese to trust Pakistan completely. If Pakistan wants to keep receiving support from China, then it needs to demonstrate progress on this issue.

As tensions rose between China and Pakistan in the aftermath of violence in the border town of Kashgar in Xinjiang in August 2011, President Zardari went to talk directly with local leaders and businessmen in Xinjiang, recognizing that if he was not able to mend fences with local leadership, Sino-Pakistani ties might be in real jeopardy.

China, at least publicly, has continued to emphasize that its relationship with Pakistan is far more important than isolated incidents of violence. To be clear, Chinese involvement in Pakistan is unlikely to match the U.S. profile in the country in the short to medium term, and it is not readily evident if China even wants to match the United States.

But flirtation with Pakistan gives China crucial space for diplomatic maneuvering vis-a'-vis India and the United States, and it will continue to utilize the relationship in pursuit of its larger strategic objectives. Pakistan is not going to be a common interest that binds China with either India or the United States any time soon.

China was the only major power that openly voiced support for Pakistan after bin Laden's assassination, defending Islamabad and emphasizing that the Pakistani government may not have known about bin Laden's presence on its territory. During Prime Minister Gilani's visit, Chinese Premier Wen Jiabao affirmed that "Pakistan has made huge sacrifices and an important contribution to the international fight against terrorism, that its independence, sovereignty, and territorial integrity must be respected, and that the international community should understand and support Pakistan's efforts to maintain domestic stability and to realize economic and social development." Wen went on to state that China would like to be an "all-weather strategic partner," and would do its best to help the Pakistani government and people get through their difficulties. To underscore its commitment, China agreed to immediately provide Pakistan with 50 new JF-17 Thunder multi-role jets under a co-production agreement, even as negotiations continued for more fighter aircrafts including those with stealth technology.

Despite this generosity, Pakistan wanted even more from China underscored by its expressed desire to have China take over the operation of Gwadar port in the Arabian Sea west of Karachi, in which Beijing has invested heavily in recent years and which serves an important role in the projection of China's naval prowess in the region. Pakistan has suggested that the port could be upgraded to a naval base for Chinese use. China, however, immediately rejected this offer, not wanting to antagonize the United States and India with the formal establishment of a base in Pakistan.

Ever since Chinese and Pakistani leaders underscored their nations' commitments to each other's core security interests at the Bandung Conference in 1955, Pakistan has occupied a unique position in China's foreign policy calculus. Their relations have been described as "arguably the most stable and durable element of China's foreign relations." India has been the main factor that has influenced China's and Pakistan's policies vis-a'-vis each other. China, viewing India as a potential challenger in the strategic landscape of Asia, has tended to use Pakistan to counter Indian power in the region, while Islamabad has gained access to civilian and military resources to balance Indian might in the sub-continent. The China—Pakistan partnership serves the interests of both by presenting India with a potential two-front theatre in the event of war with either country. Each is using the other to balance India as India's disputes with Pakistan keep India preoccupied, distracting New Delhi from the task of reaching its potential as a major regional and global player.

Although some U.S. and Indian voices are asking the Obama and Singh administrations, respectively, to partner with China to restore stability in Pakistan, Pakistan's utility for China is only likely to increase, particularly as India continues its ascent in the global inter-state hierarchy and pursues a more ambitious foreign policy posture primarily to counter China, resulting in a further tightening of the Sino-Pakistan entente cordiale.

PAKISTAN'S STRATEGIES AND GEO-POLITICAL

After the emergence of the CARs, Pakistan moved actively into Central Asia, but policy makers were clearly divided as to what Pakistan would gain out of Central Asia. While some wanted an Islamic revolution in Central Asia, others wanted open trade links through Afghanistan. The dichotomy of views revealed the limits of Pakistan's Central Asia Policy. Moreover, during this period, the Central Asian leaders were extremely wary of Pakistan because of its involvement in the Afghan war and its support to the mujahideen.

During the Pakistan-backed Taliban era in Afghanistan, bilateral relations between Pakistan and the Central Asian states touched rock bottom.

After Pakistan joined the global war against terrorism as a frontline state, bilateral relations began to be revisited. During the past few years, frequent visits by Central Asian and Pakistani officials to each other's states reflect the changing nature of their bilateral relations. A number of agreements have been signed covering such areas as trade and tourism, cultural and economic cooperation during these visits. Pakistan has developed institutionalised arrangements for this purpose. Joint Economic Commissions (JECs) have been established with all the Central Asian states. Under a Special Technical Assistance Programme (STAP) initiated in 1992-93, Pakistan provides training facilities, which are fully funded by Islamabad. The programme includes courses ranging from English language, banking and accountancy to diplomacy.

In this context President General Pervez Musharraf's visit to Uzbekistan and Kyrgyzstan in March 2005 was significant. Earlier, the two-day official visit of President Nursultan Nazarbayev of Kazakhstan in December 2003 to Islamabad was a step towards strengthening bilateral ties between the two countries. During this visit, both the leaders decided to hold annual foreign ministerial consultations. While speaking at the Pakistan-Kazakhstan Business Forum, President Nazarbayev identified three zones of technological parks of information and biotechnology where Pakistani companies could invest significantly.

It is important to note that during the Tajik Foreign Minister's visit to Islamabad in January 2004, he assured President Musharraf that Tajikistan would not allow Indian military bases on its soil. This was followed by the visit of Tajik President Emomali Rahmanov to Islamabad in May 2004. During this visit, eight agreements were inked covering abolition of visas for holders of diplomatic passports, avoidance of double taxation, cooperation between the education ministers and justice ministers, combating drug trafficking, and cooperation between official news agencies and promotion and protection of investment. Pakistan-Uzbekistan relations have also been improving over the past few years given the changed security paradigm. During Uzbek President Karimov's recent visit to Islamabad in May 2006, both sides agreed to expand trade and economic ties and coordinate anti-terrorism activities. It was also planned to extend road and rail links that would enable the CARs, particularly Uzbekistan, to make use of Pakistan's seaports to develop commerce with other regions. A joint fight against extremism and terrorism has, of late, been on top of the list for both the countries. During his March 2005 visit President Musharraf assured the Uzbek leader of his determination to wipe out terrorists, including a substantial number of Uzbek nationals, from the tribal areas. How far these promises will be fulfilled is yet to be seen. In an attempt to build strong ties with Central Asia, Pakistan has sought to use its cultural links with this region.

It is perceived that Pakistan is the cultural extension of the Central Asian region that in turn is seen to be in fusion with the South Asian social milieu. In this context, a Pakistani scholar opined, "Pakistan's political existence and emergence on the world map would not have materialised but for the primordial relationship that glues us together. The roots of our faith, undoubtedly, lie in the Arabian soil but our cultural linkages are with Central Asian civilisation, which in itself is an amalgam of diverse influence and cross-cultural fertilisation"

Cooperation in the fields of education and culture is an important aspect of Pakistan-Central Asia relations. There are number of Central Asian students studying in Pakistan and similarly Pakistani students in the CARs. The lack of information makes it difficult to provide the total number of Pakistani students studying in all CARs. However, the example of Kyrgyzstan can be cited. Kyrgyz students have been pursuing studies in Pakistani educational institutions in various fields such as engineering, business administration, information technology and the English language. Kyrgyz civil servants also attend training programmes in Pakistan. Conversely, over 350 Pakistani students are currently pursuing studies, mainly in medical colleges, in Kyrgyzstan.

Quest for "Strategic Depth"

The emergence of Central Asia was viewed as an opportunity for Pakistan to spread its sphere of influence beyond Afghanistan thus providing "strategic depth" against India. As mentioned earlier, Pakistan's desire to expand its influence in Afghanistan has been very central to Islamabad's strategic thinking. In the view of Gen. Mirza Aslam Beg, "...Afghanistan will be a great source of strength to Pakistan to face any crisis and danger that it may encounter. In fact, the security of Pakistan, Iran and Afghanistan is interlinked and is indivisible..."

While examining Pakistan's Afghan policy, it has been argued that its defence planning has been handicapped by the lack of territorial depth to absorb an attack by India and then to retaliate. This elusive quest for strategic depth has guided Pakistan in its ambitious involvement in Afghanistan in spite of the multiple implications for its social fabric and political culture. Thus, Pakistan's Afghan policy was constructed with an objective to create a subservient government in Afghanistan that would be friendly to Pakistan, militarily too weak to question the Durand line and unstable to raise the Pushtunistan issue. In addition to this, the military strategists argued that a friendly Afghanistan would give Kashmiri militants a base from where they could be trained, funded and armed. The Central Asian region was seen as an extension of Pakistan's strategic space.

The end of the Taliban regime in Afghanistan has not brought any fundamental change in Pakistan's Afghan policy. Afghanistan is still very central to Pakistan's strategic thinking, and is akin to being Pakistan's backwaters. Wary about how the current situation would unfold in Afghanistan, Islamabad is trying to cement its ties with the current regime in Kabul while supporting Taliban elements and has not given up its grand strategy of establishing a friendly government in Kabul. It is believed that Pakistan's new proxy war in Afghanistan is slowly unravelling itself. There is the resurgence of Taliban in Afghanistan. The Taliban are supported by the Pakistani establishment itself – from low-level military officers and some ministers to religious parties and their jihadi infrastructure. The ISI too has been proactively working to bring the Taliban back to its life. There has been constant accusation by Afghanistan of Pakistan's interference and its support to the Taliban and Al Qaida elements to create trouble for Kabul. Afghan President Hamid Karzai during his visit in February 2006 provided evidence to President Musharraf implicating Pakistan in the recruitment, training and equipping of Islamic radical suicide bombers. The senior Afghan official who accompanied President Karzai said, "In places like Karachi, Pakistani extremist groups working on behalf of the Taliban for a fee, carry out the recruitment and then bring them to safe houses in Balochistan for training and equipping with vests." In a recent visit to Islamabad, Gen. Johan Abizaid, the head of the US Central Command reportedly showed the Pakistanis, intelligence photographs of Taliban training camps at an undisclosed location and asked for them to be shut down.

Three years ago, Dr. Timothy D. Hoyt, Associate Professor of Strategy and policy at the US Naval War College, in a hearing before the House Committee on International relations in October 2003 accused Pakistan of providing sanctuary to terrorist groups, that enjoy strong support among active and retired Army officers and intelligence officials. He said: "So long as Pakistan relies on terrorism to achieve its political objectives, it will be impossible to eliminate terrorism and the Al Qaeda presence in the region."

Regional Organisations

Apart from using its Islamic card to tie the CARs in its strategic fold against India, Islamabad also sought to use multilateral bodies in the region. Its desire to balance India through regional organisations got manifested in their wooing neighbouring Iran, Turkey, Afghanistan, and the CARs into the Economic Co-operation Organisation (ECO). Under this forum, states are expected to develop closer economic interaction.

In November 1992, Pakistan, Iran, Turkey, Afghanistan and the five former Soviet republics of Kazakhstan, Azerbaijan, Kyrgyzstan, Turkmenistan, and Uzbekistan created an extended Muslim economic bloc linking Asia and Europe.

Former Prime Minister Nawaz Sharif noted in a speech marking the occasion that the ECO "now corresponds to the boundaries of the ancient area, which brought prosperity and civilisation through fruitful exchanges along the historic silk route. The people of these lands have a shared history and common spiritual and cultural values."

Nawaz Sharif added his belief that extensive investment in infrastructure and encouragement of the private sector were the most important immediate objectives. He noted that Pakistan was building a major highway network to link Central Asia to the Arabian Sea and that its railroads were "poised to link not only member-states but also ECO with Europe, Russia, and South Asia." He added: "peace in Afghanistan is essential for political harmony and fruitful cooperation in our entire region."

Speaking about the achievements of ECO, Pakistani foreign minister Khursheed Mahmood Kasuri stated that it had made considerable progress in the trade, transport and energy sectors. The second ECO Commerce Ministers' Meeting held in Islamabad in July 2003 approved the ECO Trade Agreement (ECOTA). The agreement envisages reduction of tariffs up to 15 per cent over a period of eight years (15 years in case of Afghanistan) on at least 80 per cent of goods on tariff lines. Para-tariff and non-tariff barriers would be eliminated within a period of two years. He further stated that the implementation of ECOTA would pave the way for economic integration of the region. New strategies and plans are expected to be adopted to make the organisation more effective.

Despite claims made by Pakistan's ministers about ECO's progress, it has so far been a non-starter. The establishment of a free trade zone is difficult when basic infrastructure necessary in this regard is lacking. Moreover, the competing interests of Iran, Pakistan and Turkey limit the role ECO can play in the region. Instability in Afghanistan remains a major obstruction for expanding the area of cooperation.

Islamabad also sponsored the membership of the newly independent Central Asian countries in the Organisation of Islamic Countries (OIC). This was yet another drive to bring the CARs into the Ummah. Pakistan has also been keen to join the SCO. In early 2001, Pakistan applied for observer status but the Central Asian members of the organisation blocked its entry. A major stumbling block was Pakistan's support for the Taliban government in Afghanistan.

Though China supported Pakistan's membership, Russia wanted India to simultaneously join SCO. It was only in June 2005 that the applications of Pakistan, Iran and India were simultaneously considered and approved with consensus for granting observer status in the SCO at the Council of Heads of States Meeting in Astana on July 5, 2005. Pakistan is also a member of Conference on Interaction and Confidence-Building Measures in Asia (CICA). Much to the chagrin of Pakistan, India is included in both these organisations.

GEO-ECONOMIC

Transport Corridors and Access to Warm Waters: Many Pakistani leaders refer to their country as the gateway to Central Asia and strongly believe that good relations with the region would not only enhance its security but also provide enormous economic opportunities. In the post-Cold War period, Islamabad tried to revive its fortunes with the West by selling its new geo-strategic importance.

This brings us to the question, is Pakistan the gateway to Central Asia? Geographically, Pakistan provides a gateway to Central Asia from south/southeast; but it is not the only gateway to the seas of the south. This is the impression that Pakistani leaders have tried to create in an attempt to identify themselves with Central Asia, further their co-operation with the region and make Pakistan more relevant not only to the CARs and its neighbouring states but also to the West. In fact, Iran provides another gateway to Central Asia and has done a great deal to develop good communication systems with the region. Yet another gateway is via Turkey in the southwest.

Pakistan has been trying to make itself more relevant to Central Asia by offering the states several proposals for creating trade and transport corridors and access to ports. President General Pervez Musharraf has emphasised this time and again.

He said, "...our geo-strategic significance can't be reduced. We need to realise that we have understood that and therefore we have constructed a new port at Gwadar which is at the mouth of the Gulf almost." In March 2005, he stated again: "we are fully focused on making use of our central location and constructing ports and putting in place a network of infrastructure." Recently, he has approved a railways reconstruction programme, which would link Gwadar with the other countries via rail. It is believed that this could make Pakistan the economic and trade hub for the CARs, Gulf, Western China and South Asia.

Pakistan's geo-strategic location admittedly makes it difficult for Central Asia to ignore it. For Turkmenistan and southern Uzbekistan, the shortest route to the sea lies through Iran, but for all other states, the shortest route is through Afghanistan and Pakistan. Karachi is the nearest port city for Central Asia and by air Islamabad is closer to Tashkent than it is to Karachi.

Dushanbe is only an hour's flight from Islamabad, and by road through Afghanistan the distance from Dushanbe to Karachi is 2,720 km. In contrast, the port of Bandar Abbas is 3,400 km, Vladivostok 9,500 km and Rostov on the Don 4,200 km away. This makes Pakistan important for the CARs. Despite little success so far, Pakistan is trying to improve its connectivity to the CARs through Afghanistan and China.

In this respect, the ADB has offered $2 billion to the Pakistan railway network, which will enable Pakistan to become one of the most attractive international trade routes to the CARs, Iran and China. Pakistan and Afghanistan have already agreed to lay a 103-km railway track between Chaman and Kandahar, which would be extended to Turkmenistan and other CARs. The feasibility study of the Quetta-Kandahar railway track has been completed and Pakistan would construct the 10-12 km railway track to the Afghan border. The track from the Afghan border to Kandahar would be the responsibility of the Afghan government. The World Bank has agreed to provide $1.8 billion to Pakistan for its $6 billion National Trade Corridor (NTC) improvement programme to meet domestic transportation requirements and provide transit facilities to Central Asia, Western China, Afghanistan and Iran.

Pakistan has also proposed to construct a $90-million road through the Boroghil Pass in the Yarkhun valley to link it with the CARs. Of the 13 passes, which lead to Afghanistan from Chitral district, the Boroghil Pass is the easiest and lowest in altitude. This pass remains closed for a very short period late in winter. The road will extend to Wakhan, 13-65 km wide strategic strip in northeast Afghanistan. The area links Afghanistan with Pakistan in the south, Tajikistan in the north and China in the east. The Wakhan-Boroghil route has been preferred against the one passing through the central parts of Afghanistan due to the security situation. This road will connect the 12,484-foot-high Boroghil pass at the northwest of the Yarkhum valley in Chitral with Sarhad-i-Langar in Wakhan at a distance of about 95 km and move on to Iskashim in Tajikistan leading to the Tajik capital Dushanbe via the Korung-Kalai Chumb and Kulob areas. From the Boroghil Pass, the road will traverse over 300 km long valley and reach Peshawar. The distance from Tajikistan to Peshawar via the Wakhan-Chitral route is estimated to be 700 km. This road will also branch off to the northern areas via the 10,500-foot-high Shandur Pass and merge into the Karakoram Highway. The Pakistan government has already sanctioned a number of road projects to interlink the northern areas and Chitral.

The quadrilateral agreement signed by Pakistan, China, Kyrgyzstan, and Kazakhstan is expected to give a boost to trading activities among member-nations through the Karakoram Highway. On October 10, 2006 a road connection along the Karakorum route, Islamabad-Kashgar-Bishkek-Almaty, was opened by Pakistan. Pakistan has also offered use of the Gwadar deep-sea port to the CARs. This port would serve as a mother port at the strategic location opposite to the Strait of Hormuz and at the mouth of the Persian Gulf. The first phase of this project is already over. The completion of the Gwadar Port would be a milestone for Pakistan in this context. When it comes online alongside Karachi, it will provide the shortest access to the Arabian Sea for large parts of Central Asia. On December 31, 2005, a meeting of Pakistan-Uzbekistan Joint Ministerial Commission was held in Tashkent, where the two sides agreed to enter into a trilateral transit trade agreement with Afghanistan to benefit from land routes and the Gwadar port facility.

During Kyrgyz President Askar Akaev's two-day visit to Pakistan on January 17-18, 2005, it was agreed that Pakistan would import electricity from Kyrgyzstan and both countries would build roads to improve trade. It was decided to strengthen links through Kashgar in China and on to Bishkek and also through the Karakoram Highway.

The road being constructed on the Karakoram Highway to link the two countries completed by 2006, promoting Pak-Kyrgzy trade. Establishment of a railway link from Gwadar to Taftan in Iran via Saindak is also being planned. A road from Gwadar to Sandak, running parallel to the Iran-Pakistan border, will make it the shortest route to reach Central Asia from the warm waters of the Arabian Sea. Another 515-km long highway connecting Gwadar via Pangur, Khaan, Chaghi and Rabat up to the heart of Western Afghanistan is being planned. This would link Pakistan by road directly with the CARs.

Pakistan is also giving priority to road and rail links and related facilities for more effective and mutually beneficial access to Central Asia. Air services to Tashkent and Almaty have already been resumed. Similar services to other parts of the region are under active consideration. The laying of railway tracks from Turkmenistan to Pakistan via Afghanistan is an important part of this programme. Pakistan's Ministry of Railways has completed a feasibility study for a Chaman-Kandahar rail project.

The quadrilateral agreement is also gradually being implemented. The completion of the Murghab-Kulma road from Tajikistan to China linking the Karakoram Highway to Pakistan is also a significant development. Once operational, it will boost transit trade between Pakistan and Central Asia.

Energy and Pipeline Politics: Pakistan is also looking at the huge energy resources of Central Asia. It wants to make Pakistan the energy-transit corridor in South Asia and the Asia-Pacific region, which will bring huge economic gains for the country. Pakistan is most likely to face a energy crisis in natural gas, power and oil in the next 3-4 that could choke its economic growth for many years to come. It is estimated that Pakistan's total energy requirement would increase by about 48 per cent to 80 million tonnes of oil equivalent (MTOE) in 2010 from about 54 MTOE currently.

According to official energy demand forecast, the demand for natural gas, having about 50 per cent share in the country's energy consumption would increase by 44 per cent to the 39 MTOE currently. The power shortage is expected to be little over 5,250 MW by 2010. Oil demand would also increase by over 23 per cent to about 21 million tonnes in 2010 from the current demand of 16.8 million tonnes. Therefore, Central Asia could be a future source of energy for Pakistan.

Pakistan's importance for Central Asian countries needs to be viewed in the context of the entire pipeline politics in the region. As a transit country, Pakistan provides these states with an outlet of their energy resources. In view of the instability in Afghanistan and Balochistan, the success of these pipelines from Central Asia however remains a big question mark. Despite these uncertainties Pakistan wants to keep the Central Asian states engaged with the hope of providing a transit route for their energy resources. In pursuit of its strategy to control the pipelines and gain greater influence, it is trying to sign various agreements with these Republics. Pakistan has signed 21 agreements and MoUs in oil, gas, energy, trade, science and culture with Turkmenistan. In the energy sector, Turkmenistan, Afghanistan and Pakistan (TAP) signed an agreement in December 2002 for a gas pipeline from Turkmenistan via Afghanistan to Pakistan, whose estimated cost is $2.5 billion. The ADB is the lead coordinating partner. It has, in addition to financial and technical assistance, played an important role in integrating efforts to realise the project. Several sessions of the Steering Committee on the TAP Gas Pipeline Project have been held so far. During a ministerial level TAP meeting on February 16, 2006, in Ashkabad, Turkmenistan agreed to provide sovereign guarantees to Pakistan to supply 3.2 billion cubic feet gas per day for 30 years. This assurance was restated during Pakistan Foreign Minister Khursheed Kasuri's visit to Turkmenistan in May 2006. However, a major hurdle to the project remains the volatile situation in Afghanistan.

While Turkmenistan can provide gas to Pakistan, Tajikistan and Kyrgyzstan have the potential to be substantial producers of hydroelectric power.

Being geographically closest to Tajikistan, Pakistan stands to benefit from its hydroelectric potential. An inter-governmental agreement to that effect has already been signed. Pakistan's Water and Power Minister Liaquat Ali Jatoi has recently said, "the government is considering importing electricity from CARs via Afghanistan as an option to meet its demand and has signed an MoU with Tajikstan to import 1000 MW as well as initiated transmission routing assessment to bring such power to Pakistan."

An advisor to Kyrgyz Prime Minister Omarov said that his government was also considering a transmission line from China to Pakistan with an estimated cost of $1.4 billion. Pakistan has also signed an agreement to import electricity from Kyrgyzstan through Tajikistan and Afghanistan. Indubitably, terrain and weather conditions are clear impediments to this project, yet both states appear determined to pursue it.

Trade

With the emergence of the newly independent Central Asian States, the business elite group in Pakistan viewed this region as offering immense economic opportunities. Central Asia was seen not only as a source of needed raw materials but also as a potential export market. Some estimates even suggested that the region had a potential market of $80 billion and if Pakistan secures even 5 per cent of this market, it could earn up to $4 billion a year.

In December 1991, a 23-member delegation was send to Central Asia headed by the then Minister of Commerce Sardar Asif Ahmed Ali. A $30-million credit facility was given to Uzbekistan and $10 million to all other Central Asian Republics. These credit lines were not utilised by the Central Asian countries and Pakistan was unable to keep its commitment to provide the credit lines in future. The effort to open a fullfledged National Bank of Pakistan (NBP) met with complete failure. The NBP representative office was set up in 1995 in Tashkent but it could not facilitate the opening of a branch till 2002.

Despite high hopes, the trade between Pakistan and Central Asia remains limited. During 1992-93 Pakistani exports to the region amounted to $5.6 m and imports were $0.51 m. The figures for 1993-1995 indicate an increase as compared to 1992-93. During 1997-98 Pakistan's total trade with Kazakhstan accounted for $19.9 m.; for Kyrgyzstan 07.91m; Tajikistan $10.29m; Turkmenistan $07.75m; and Uzbekistan $35.34m. However, in subsequent years the trade figures do not indicate any major increase.

Pakistan's recent initiatives in Central Asia involve strengthening economic ties with the CARs. As mentioned earlier, Pakistan has established JECs with all the CARs. In its trade policy for 2006-07, Pakistan seeked to focus on export growth in regional Muslim countries, particularly Iran, Afghanistan and the CARs. It has been decided to establish export centres and warehouses at Peshawar and Quetta and an export centre in Islamabad. In this context the visit of Kyrgyzstan President Askar Akaev on January 17, 2005 is of significance. Both countries signed a MoU on cooperation between the foreign ministries of the two countries on different regional and international issues.

Two agreements were signed on cooperation and mutual assistance in customs related matters and avoidance of double taxation. President Akaev also offered to provide electricity to Pakistan.

This was his third visit, earlier ones being in 1994 and 1995. Kyrgyzstan and Pakistan are signatories to the Quadrilateral Agreement along with China and Kazakhstan, effective since May 2004, which aims at promoting regional trade through Pakistan's Karakoram Highway. During the first meeting of the Pakistan-Kyrgyz Joint Ministerial Commission (JMC) in Islamabad, both sides negotiated on issues of taxation, culture, and visa restrictions for enhancing the volume of bilateral ties. Pakistan is also exploring the possibility of investing in the pharmaceutical sector in Turkmenistan.

The ECO provides another common platform to generate economic activity in the region. Within the framework of the ECO the volume of trade has not increased significantly. In fact, the ECO has failed to bring about great economic or commercial results.

Competition among the member-states has been the major limitation for the success of this organisation. As Pakistan's Prime Minister Shaukat Aziz recently emphasised, the organisation needs to be used for making result-oriented policies instead of offering mere lip service. ECO can be an effective organisation if the ECO Trade Agreement, Transit Transport Agreement and the Trade and Development Bank become operational. So far, Pakistan has not been able to achieve much in terms of building economic and trade ties with the CARs. Their efforts to set up banks and hotels have received severe setbacks in Central Asia.

ECONOMIC INTERESTS OF FOREIGN NATIONS IN BALOCHISTAN

Balochistan has always been influential on local, national, and international politics. As Balochistan borders two very significant strategic countries Afghanistan and Iran, and having majority of Baloch residents in Afghan and Iranian areas, any type of unrest or violent insurgency in Pakistani Balochistan would disturb regional instability affecting the neighboring countries and consequently become a regional dispute. Baloch insurgency may create large problems in Iran and Afghanistan due to the strong demand for greater Balochistan which includes Baloch areas of Iran and Afghanistan. (Javaid, 2010:116). Being located in the middle of the Central, Western Southern and South-western Asia, Balochistan is always under the effects of global geo-politics.

The maritime significance and potential of port Gwadar to connect the landlocked, Afghanistan and the Central Asian states to the Indian Ocean as an international trade route and an energy transit corridor, and mineral resources have heightened geo-political competition among global powers, in the Eurasian region Balochistan provides an ideal profitable aim for global powers.. Plenty of energy resources, trade routes and maritime choke points, Balochistan has attained not only its national interest but can be more important than on international level too.

This unique and valuable situation provides golden opportunity to the global powers to instigate their regional play. The world is increasingly moving towards multi-polarity and economic and military powers are growing in the Asian regions. United States has been at a powerful position exclusively since the disintegration of the Soviet Union. The objectives of Asian states like China and India are to become economically more powerful to get global hegemony by controlling the major portion of world's energy resources.

Demand for energy supply of China, India, and other Asian countries is quickly increasing, so it is the biggest requirement of time to spread their influence over world energy resources, energy transit corridors, major land and maritime trade links. For this purpose, Balochistan has become the focus of global geopolitical manipulation in this region. The resettlement of borders in the name of Greater Balochistan would definitely affect the economic development of China, Iran, India and Pakistan. United States have many times highlighted the geostrategic and geo-political significance of Balochistan and they have presented and supported the idea of free Balochistan which could serve best to secure US geopolitical and geo strategic benefits.

In order to counter Iran, the land of Balochistan is of much importance for America. The natural resources of China and oil of the Arab world are going to eliminate in coming 30 to 40 years (Mazhar, et al. 2012: 120) and then the US will have to rely upon Central Asia, Iran and Afghanistan; and for this purpose, US would have to cross Balochistan and its Coast, due to the interference of China in Balochistan, it would not be possible for US to attain an influential position. America would not be able to extend its economic hegemony for a long time, it will be substituted by China which is going to be influential over Gwadar Port and coastal line of Balochistan. That is the main reason behind US displeasure with the construction of Gwadar Port in collaboration with China.

When the Taliban administration ended in Kabul and rebellious groups of Taliban crossed the Pak-Afghan border to enter into Balochistan and organized revolutionary struggle against the aliened forces in Afghanistan. Moreover, the re emergence of the Baloch nationalist insurgency also complicated the internal situation of Pakistan's security; Balochistan obtained a new geo-strategic significance and became focus of US as a Trans border energy route.

The Baloch insurgency was recharged with the development of Gwadar sea port and their demand to share the benefits of Gwadar Project attracted strong US interest in Balochistan because it has the capacity to convert Balochistan in a main corridor of energy transportation from Central Asia and Iran to other parts of the region in minimum time. The US has to maintain a crucial and essential role in the new great game of resource development in Balochistan and in other parts of Asia. Therefore, all the three prominent factors; the Taliban militancy, Baloch insurgency and future significance of Balochistan as an energy transit route, played a very strong role in attaining and developing serious attention of US to Balochistan. (Aazar, 2010:164) Prior to that, Balochistan due to its defensive proximity with Afghanistan had a significant hand in the early triumph of US war on terror post 9/11. Pakistan provided US the access to airspace and airfields in Balochistan for US aerial bombing on Kabul to destroy the Taliban regime and their network in Afghanistan. (Aazar, 2010:165) Balochistan has been playing a central role in the geo strategic development of South and West Asia long before the US war on terror post 9/11 but during war, Balochistan's territorial proximity to Afghanistan was a great strategic advantage which was fully exploited by US forces.

American involvement in Balochistan is somehow blamed for supporting Baloch insurgents in order to deal with the Chinese influence in Balochistan. It is believed that CIA agents in Afghanistan provide financial support to the Baloch insurgents. it is discovered that the US spy agency CIA is involved in recruitment of local agents in Balochistan to locate the members of Quetta based Taliban Shura. The Quetta Shura is a term used by the Americans for the Mullah Omar-led Taliban commanders. (Waheed, 2011, Apr.27) The incident of the arrest of a CIA Spy Raymond Davis in a murder case of two Pakistani in January 2011 increased the tension in Pakistan-US relationship and also exposed the CIA immoral activities in Balochistan. Above all, CIA's activities in Balochistan are clear sign of US growing interest in this region. In fact, Creation of "Greater Balochistan" is the top most agenda of US, India and Israel cooperation. (Hassan, 2011, May.04) Apparently, US propagate her concerns for the stabilization of Pakistan, but at the same time, she does have a deep interest in delaying projects that would enable China to be strategically present in this region and establish herself as an emerging economic power particularly at the Port of Gwadar. Americans are also interested in increasing their influence in Gwadar and other parts of Balochistan. Therefore, the any harm caused to China-Pakistan joint venture of development of Gwadar port is one of the main US interest in Balochistan. Thus, any type of violence in

Balochistan protects US interests in the region because it is helpful in delaying the development projects between China and Pakistan.

The basic objective is to control the increasing Chinese existence in Balochistan. China is an economic rival to US and its presence in Balochistan is not beneficial for the strategic and economic future of US. The Gwadar port can serve as the marine base for Chinese forces which is a matter of great anxiety for US. The Indian Ocean, near the Strait of Hormuz, a route for the export of oil from the Gulf States, will definitely come under the observation and influence of China will create serious problems for US in maintaining its monopoly in the region. The divergence of interests of various powers is also worsening the situation in Balochistan. Under the unstable and insecure circumstances in Balochistan, China will not move forward to provide any further technical or financial assistance to Pakistan for the development and progress of any economic project. (Mazari, 2005, Feb.2)

The clear objectives of US are to deteriorate Pakistan, Iran and Afghanistan to establish a strong hold in Central Asian Region and harming Chinese economic interests in African and Middle East through creating obstacles in the Gwadar project. This can be possible only by supporting Balochistan Nationalist Movement to disturb the situation and creating unfavorable environment for any economic investment by China. "CIA supported elements are using America, United Kingdom, India and Afghanistan as their platforms for organizing, planning and operational bases for execution of the plan of Independent Balochistan. Moreover, some militarily supported political lobbies of America and UK are facilitating anti Pakistan elements to carryout nefarious activities against Pakistan". (Hassan, 2011, May.04) US interests are also intended to counter Iran, The United Sates is not happy with the expansion of Chinese energy and military assets, particularly so close to Iran and the Gulf region. An instable Balochistan is far more preferable to US than a stable and economically flourishing Balochistan. Any disturbance in Balochistan reduces the possibility of development of the IranPakistan oil pipeline. The US has openly shown her discomfort with the proposed pipeline project. (Bansal, 2008:182).

The US is not only interested in Balochistan, but also has strong concerns about the massive resources of Central Asian States and Balochistan is the most convenient available path to these resources. US is much anxious to get control over the whole region for their future security plans and eliminate the influence of their only rival and competitor China.

US interest in Balochistan highlights two long term objectives, firstly, US has to create a secure and reliable route to all the energy resources of Central Asia to USA, and secondly to contain China. Balochistan provides the shortest passage between the Indian Ocean and Central Asia outside of the Gulf. Therefore any unrest in Balochistan directly affects and effectively discourages Trans-Afghan pipeline project that is planned for transferring Central Asian resources to South Asia as the control of economically strong and established states of South Asia over this region will not allow US to flourish economic hegemony.

US and Russia have always focused their interest on Balochistan to exploit the land as a tool to make Pakistan a weaker state. Russia has encouraged the "Secessionist Movement of Sindhu Desh, Pakhtonistan or (Independent) or Greater Balochistan" (Najmuddin, 1984: 60). With the Soviet occupation of Afghanistan in 1979, it was predicted that the Soviet would try to take possession of deep-sea-water port on the Indian Ocean, and the Baloch insurgents and their rebellious activities would be significantly helpful to Soviet attempt. (Harrison, 1981:173) Having controlled Afghanistan, Russia tried hard to convince the Baloch to revolt against central government of Pakistan and the Baloch insurgents were assured by Russia that they would be given autonomy over Balochistan after the Soviet completely conquers Afghanistan. (Ismail, 2014:184) The Russian strategy was to establish full control in Kabul as their base and to raise the issues of Pakhtunistan and Greater Balochistan from the land of Kabul, and try to separate and disconnect Balochistan from Pakistan and to either merge it with Afghanistan or to create a new independent country that should be under full control of Moscow. "Whether Russian loose their interest in Afghanistan, yet in Balochistan and Indian Ocean its interest would not die down" (Ahmad, 1992: 253).

Russia also needs a suitable corridor to the warm waters of the Indian Oceans. Like USA, Russia also wants to preserve its monopoly over all the energy resources of Central Asia. At present all the Central Asian States (CAS) are entirely dependent on Russia for export of their energy projects. Soviet Interests in Balochistan have various aspects which are not much different than that of US. Russia wants to control the Gulf oil, which constitute almost 60 percent of world's known reserves. Any trouble in Balochistan gives Russia a hope to discourage Trans-Afhgan pipeline or any other similar projects.

A Russian influenced Balochistan would bring the natural resources of the Indian Ocean and Antarctica under direct control and pressure of Russia. Fish catch from Indian Ocean and particularly from Arabian Sea, which constitutes almost 1/3rd of total fish catch, will be transported to Central Asia Republics over lands, without any trouble, in less time, thus will be more economical. (Ahmad,1992: 256) Balochistan will provide Russia the shortest route to the world's largest untapped mineral resources which are located at Antarctica. (Mazhar et al. 2012:119). All these future probabilities which can provide economical stability to Russia are related to Balochistan.

Balochistan is the only Province of Pakistan which shares direct border with Iran. The geographical location of Balochistan plays a very significant role in shaping the relations between Pakistan and Iran in the socio-cultural and economic perspectives. Balochistan is the only factor which can directly influence Pak-Iran relations both negatively and positively. Unfortunately, there are certain disappointing and inadequate factors which are creating confusions, doubts and stress and making Balochistan a weakening factor in Pak-Iran relations. Balochistan plays a key role in Pak-Iran economic and social integration. The close relation between the people of both countries on the basis of many religious and cultural similarities significantly increases the economic, cultural and social communication between the people of Iran and Pakistan. Infrastructure projects of roads and railways networks can make possible easy trade within the region and cross border.

The proposed venture of oil refinery in Hub will do a lot for the promotion and betterment of economic cooperation between Pakistan and Iran, which has been going through a tensed situation in the past few years because of political misunderstanding over Afghanistan issue. (Khan, 2012:137)

The project will provide an economic momentum to this least developed province Balochistan and will help to meet the increasing demand of high speed diesel. It will also make possible the exploration of oil and gas in Baloch region. The construction of gas pipeline between Iran-Pakistan is the most positive aspect of economic relationship. The proposed gas pipeline project would bring economic and political profit to both the countries equally.

The ongoing insurgency in Balochistan has badly affected the friendly relations of the two countries as the Iranian government blame Pakistan's involvement in the Balochistan based Jandullah Organization which is a group of Baloch nationalist militants which is also creating political disturbances in Iranian areas with the active support and cooperation of USA. (Khan, 2012:137) Moreover, the growing competition between the Pakistani sea port at Gwadar and the Iranian Port Chabahar, and strong rivalry between India, China and Pakistan to increase their influence in Central Asia through these ports, have already disturbed economic and political relations of Iran and Pakistan.

Chabahar seaport is situated at about 70 kilometer distance from Pakistani seaport of Gwadar, developed with Chinese assistance. Both these ports are great competitors as both are constructed with the same objectives in a same region. The difference between the two lies in the fact that Gwadar port is facing many issues like the bad security situation in Balochistan and lack of proper infrastructure of connecting links to main highways. The project is not making progress due to slow and process of development. While there is no such situation at Chabahar which is being developed rapidly and also has gained attention and interest of China successfully. Not only China but also Iran, Afghanistan and India are equally emphasizing at Chabahar Port ahead of Gwadar as regional trade and commerce center.

The Chabahar seaport is located outside the Strait of Hormuz, in Iran's Free Economic and Industrial Zone. This port is away from the passage of heavy seatraffic in the Persian Gulf waters and provides more easy entrance to ships besides connecting it to Afghanistan and Central Asia. A road and rail communication system is also being constructed between Chabahar and Herat to connect with Central Asian States. India is seriously interested in the development of this seaport just to avoid Pakistani route to Iran, Afghanistan and Central Asian States. (Hussain, 2015:146)

Chabahar is somehow is an Indian financed Port and a part of the Indian plan to develop another mean of transportation in eastern Iran to counter and reduce the emerging influence of Pakistani port of Gwadar. India intends to connect Chabahar port with Central Asian countries through roads and railway to avoid Pakistan, and to reduce the dependency of Central Asian countries on the port of Gwadar. (Khan, 2012:135) As Gwadar port is expected to improve not only Pakistan's but also Chinese influence in Central Asia and beyond. Gwadar can be a potential trade route for the landlocked Central Asian States and this new trade route would have tremendous economic impetus to Pakistan in the form of new and great investments as the CARs will rely upon Pakistan for their trade and commerce.

Chabahar is providing India with an easy access to Afghanistan through the Indian Ocean. An agreement between India, Iran and Afghanistan has been signed according to that, Central Asia and Afghanistan are bound to give special preference and tariff reduction to Indian trade goods. (Khan, 2012:135) Therefore, Gwadar port is a threatening factor to Indian trade through Indian Ocean. Being so close to the Straits of Hormuz, Gwadar would create negative impact on India's commercial interest by enabling Pakistan to implement vast control over entire energy routes. Gwadar will also enable China to observe and examine Indian naval activity in the Persian Gulf and Arabian Sea and any future maritime cooperation between India and Iran will be easily monitored by China. Similarly, Iran has clear apprehensions about the use of Gwadar port by the United States as a base to monitor activities inside Iran. (Asia Times, 2005,April.29).

India also is trying to secure energy routes to counter the growing Chinese influence in the Arabian Sea, Persian Gulf, and the Indian Ocean. So India chose Iran as her economic and strategic ally. India has spent huge amount on the construction and development of Iranian Port of Chahbahar. Iran is already working on Chahbahar port in sistan Baluchistan, which will facilitate Indian trade activities to Afghanistan and Central Asia through roads and rail links. The Chinese involvement in Pakistani Gwadar and Indian influence on Iranian Chahbahar has resulted not only in economic competition and strategic rivalry between India, Pakistan and China but also has increased risk of controversy for the economic and natural resources of Central Asia.

The growing competition between China and India has an unfavorable impact on the Pak-Iran relations. Gwadar and Chahbahar are the main causes of geostrategic and economic competition. China is largely alarmed by the growing Indian growth in the Indian Ocean and the Arabian Sea. Moreover, the progress and warmth in Indo-US relations since the conclusion of US-India civilian nuclear cooperation and mutual aid between India and Iran in Afghanistan and Central Asia became a matter of serious concern for China's long-standing strategic and economic objectives in the region. (Khan, 2013: 79-80)

India is establishing good relations with Pakistani neighbors; Iran and Afghanistan just to contain Pakistan and to counterbalance Chinese emerging power, because China is the only power which is quite capable of competing and suppress Indian hegemony and supremacy in the region. As Indian navy is greater than that of Pakistan, therefore to surpass India, Pakistan needs Chinese support and cooperation in the Port of Gwadar which is in the best welfare of both China and Pakistan. Through the Gwadar, China can keep a strict watch on Indian approach and emergence in the Indian Ocean, the Arabian Sea, and Persian Gulf. (Khan, 2013: 79-80). So far as Afghanistan is concerned, she has historically been remained a dispute between major powers. Mostly, Afghanistan remains in state of war and process of nation building, so there is no functional type of economy in Afghanistan and mostly depends on limited agriculture which is not meeting the basic food requirements of Afghans and they have to depend upon foreign donated food for survival. (Shah, 2007:65) The Turkmenistan-Afghanistan-Pakistan-Iran (TAPI) pipeline project is a big hope to help restore the Afghan economy as the project could bring in over 300 million dollars royalty to the country and other foreign investments in the project may do a lot to stabilize and revive Afghan economy with the renovation of other infrastructure. Afghan transit trade was earlier handled through the Karachi port, but now the Gwadar port will serve this purpose well. Afghanistan has admitted the significance of Gwadar as a gateway to wealth for Afghanistan and also has offered support for the development of the Gwadar port. (The Dawn, 2003, Aug.5)

CHINA'S SOUTH ASIAN INTERESTS AND POLICIES

China's broad objective in South Asia is to expand multi-dimensional cooperative relations with all the countries of that region. "Multi-dimensional" signifies military ties as well as more innocuous political and economic cooperation. "All" means both India and India's smaller neighbors: Pakistan, Myanmar, Nepal, Sri Lanka, Bangladesh, Bhutan, and the Maldives. India has sometimes objected to China's relations — especially military-security ties — with these countries. Beijing views South Asian countries as "neighbors" with whom it is especially important to have friendly, cooperative ties both to increase China's own economic and political influence and to lessen the ability of potentially hostile powers (currently the U.S.) to injure China's interests.

Economically, China seeks to draw South Asia's resources into China's development drive. India with its fast-growing, industrialized, and relatively affluent economy has become China's strongest economic partner in South Asia. Two-way Sino-Indian trade in 2003 was $7.6 billion, compared to $2.4 billion for Sino-Pakistan, $1.4 billion for Sino-Bangladesh, and $1.1 billion for Sino-Myanmar trade. During their April 2005 meeting, Wen Jiabao and Manmohan Singh agreed to increase trade to $20 billion by 2008. While that amount is paltry compared to China's trade with countries like Japan, Germany, South Korea, or the United States, it leads China's South Asian trade by far.

The simple fact is that India produces much more that Chinese firms want to purchase than do Pakistan, Bangladesh, or Myanmar — let alone the small countries like Nepal, Bhutan, or the Maldives. In 2003, China imported $1 billion more from India than it exported to it, while Chinese exports to Pakistan were three times the value of China's imports, exports to Bangladesh were forty times the value of China's imports, and exports to Myanmar were over five times the volume of imports. While these figures are based on official statistics and do not reflect smuggling (which is substantial in the case of Myanmar), the broader point is that India simply has more to offer China. From India China imports a wide array of mining and industrial products: steel and iron ore, zinc, aluminum and aluminum products, copper and copper products, acids and alkalines, dyes, colouring, alcohol and other chemical products, rubber, plastics, cotton, wool, thread and yarn, leather, and machinery and machine parts. From Pakistan, in contrast, China buys largely cotton, yarn, and leather.

Bibliography

Allana, G.: *Pakistan Movement: Historic Documents,* Karachi, Department of International Relations, University of Karachi, 1967.

Allen Carlson, *Unifying China, Integrating with the World: Securing Chinese Sovereignty in the Reform Era,* Stanford: Stanford University Press, 2005.

Anil, K.C.: *Military and Democracy in South Asia : Challenges, Politics and Power,* Sumit Enterprises, Delhi, 2009.

Arend, A.: *International Law and the Use of Force,* London, Routledge, 1993.

Backman, Jules. *War and Defense Economics.* New York: Rinehart, 1952.

Barber B.R.: *Strong Democracy. Participatory Politics for a New Age.* Berkeley, University of California Press, 1984.

Benoit, E.: *Defence and Economic Growth in Developing Countries,* Lexington MA: Lexington Books, 1973.

Bhat, T.P. : *India and China : Trade Complementarities and Competitiveness,* Bookwell, Delhi, 2008.

Bort, E.: *Boundaries and Identities: The Eastern Frontier of the Asia,* Edinburgh: International Social Sciences Institute, University of Edinburgh, 1996.

Brian Cloughley: *War, Coups, and Terror: Pakistan's Army in Years of Turmoil,* New York: Skyhorse, 2008.

Budge I: *The New Challenge of Direct Democracy,* Oxford, Polity Press, 1996.

Buzan, Barry : *Security: A New Framework for Analysis.* Boulder: Lynne-Rienner Publishers, 1998.

Cathy Solheim: *Military Economics: Issues, Policies, and Solutions,* Washington, D.C., Island Press, 1995.

Cheema, Pervaiz Iqbal: *Pakistan's Defence Policy: 1947-58,* MacMillan Press, 1990.

Chitkara, M.G. : *China-Pak Relations Challenges Before New Millennium,* APH, Delhi, 2001.

Choudhury, Golam W: *Pakistan: Transition from Military to Civilian Rule,* Scorpion, 1988.

Dashti, Naseer: *The Baloch and Balochistan: A Historical Account from the Beginning to the Fall of the Baloch State,* Trafford Publishing, 2012.

Digumarti Bhaskara Rao: *Military Conversion : Impact on Science and Technology,* Discovery, Delhi, 2003.

Dixit, J.N. : *India and Regional Developments : Through the Prism of Indo-Pak Relations,* Gyan, Delhi, 2004.

Dixit, Prabla: *Defence Budget: A Struggle for Power,* New Delhi, Orient Longman, 1981.

Donnan, H. and Wilson, T. M.: *Borders: Frontiers of Identity, Nation and State,* Oxford: Berg, 1999.

Dudley, Williams: *India and Pakistan: Opposing Viewpoints,* London: Greenhaven Press, 2003.

Duncan, Francis. *Rickover and the Nuclear Navy: The Discipline of Technology.* Annapolis: Naval Institute Press, 1990.

Dunne, J. P. and Brauer, J.: *Arms Trade and Economic Development: Theory, Policy,* Routledge, London, 2004.

Duscha, Julius. *Arms, Money and Politics.* New York, 1965.

Evelyn Goh, *Meeting the China Challenge: The Russia in Southeast Asian Regional Security Strategies,* DC: East-West Center, 2005.

Fatima, T. : *Islamic Law and Judiciary,* Deep & Deep Publications, New Delhi, 2001.

Fernlund, Kevin J. *The Cold War American West, 1945–1989.* Albuquerque: University of New Mexico Press, 1998.

Francis, Eric Vernon. *The Battle for Supplies.* London: J. Cape, 1942.

Friedman, G.: *The Future of War: Power, Technology and American World Dominance in the 21st Century,* N.Y., Random House, 1996.

Gao, Mobo: *The Battle for China's Past: Mao and the Cultural Revolution,* London, Pluto Press, 2008.

Ghosh, Ajoy : *China-Pak Conflict : Threat to South Asian Security,* Reference Press, Delhi, 2003.

Gilbertson, George W.: *The Balochi language. A grammar and manual.* Hertford: Stephen Austin & Sons, 1923.

Gottlieb, Thomas M.: *Chinese Foreign Policy Factionalism and the Origins of the Strategic Triangle.* Santa Monica, CA: RAND Corporation, 1977.

Herken, Gregg. *The Winning Weapon: The Atomic Bomb in the Cold War, 1945-1950.* Princeton: Princeton University Press, 1988.

Hoffman, Bruce, *Inside Terrorism,* New York: Columbia University Press, 1998.

Huntington, S.P.: *The China Defence Modernisation Military and the State,* N.Y., Vintage Books, 1964.

Hussain Mushahid: *Pakistan: Problems of Governance,* Vanguard 1993.

Imtiaz, A.: *State and Foreign Policy: India's Role in South Asia,* New Delhi, Vikas, 1993.

Jagannath P. Panda: *China's Path to Power : Party, Military and the Politics of State Transition*, Pentagon, Delhi, 2010.

James Campbell: *Excursions, Adventures and Field-Sports in Ceylon : Its Commercial and Military Importance*, AES, Delhi, 2006.

James R Blaker: *Transforming Military Force : The Legacy of Arthur Cebrowski and Network Centric Warfare*, Pentagon Press, Delhi, 2008.

Jha, Prem Shankar : *India and China : The Battle Between Soft and Hard Power*, Penguin Books India, Delhi, 2010.

Juvale, R.P. : *Military Strategy and Diplomacy*, Cyber Tech Publications, Delhi, 2010.

Kapur, Ashok: *Pakistan's Nuclear Development*, New York: Croom Helm, 1987.

Kapur, Ashok: *Pokhran and Beyond: India's Nuclear Behaviour*, Oxford: Oxford University Press, 2001.

Keane J.: *Democracy and Civil Liberty in Afghanistan*, London, Verso, 1988.

Kumar, Yukteshwar : *A History of Sino-Pak Relations*, APH, Delhi, 2005.

Laquer, Walter, *The New Terrorism: Fanaticism and the Arms of Mass Destruction*, Oxford: Oxford University Press, 1999.

Leena Parmar: *Military Budgeting: Global Perspectives*, Rawat, Delhi, 1999.

Lifton, Robert Jay and Mitchell, Greg. *Hiroshima in America: A Half Century of Denial*. New York: Avon Books, 1995.

Mary, W.: *Asian Power and Politics: the Cultural Dimensions of Authority*, Cambridge, Belknap Press, 1985.

Mazhar Aziz: *Military Control in Pakistan: The Parallel State*, London: Routledge, 2008.

Nayyar, K K : *National Security : Military Aspects*, Rupa, Delhi, 2003.

Nevile, P.: *Lahore: A Sentimental Journey*. New Delhi: Penguin, 1993.

Oudha, Abdul Qadir : *Criminal Law of Islam*, Kitab Bhavan, New Delhi, 1999.

Pash, Boris T. *The Alsos Mission*. New York: Award House, 1969.

Pierre, Andrew J. *The Global Politics of Arms Sales*. Princeton, N.J., 1982.

Posen, B.R.: *The Sources of Indian Military Doctrine*, Ithaca, 1984, Cornell Univ. Press.

Prabir De: *Pak and China in an Era of Globalisation : Essays on Economic Cooperation*, Bookwell, Delhi, 2005.

Prabla, Dixit: *Communalism: A Struggle for Power*, New Delhi, Orient Longman, 1981.

Prasad, Lal Bahadur : *Indian Political System and Law*, New Delhi, Shree, 2005.

Rhodes, Richard, *The Making of the Atomic Bomb*, New York: Simon and Schuster, 1988.

Rizvi, Hassan Askari: *The Military and Politics in Pakistan: 1947 - 86*, Progressive Publishers 1986.

Rosen, P.: *Societies and Military Power: India and its Armies*, Ithaca, Cornell University Press, 1996.

Samuel P. Huntington: *The Soldier and the State : The Theory and Politics of Civil-Military Relations,* Natraj Pub, Delhi, 2005.

Smith, C.: *The Diffusion of Small Arms and Light Weapons in Pakistan and Northern India,* Centre for Defence Studies, Brassey's, London, 1993.

Sutton, J., *Technology and Defence Market Structure,* MIT Press, Delhi, 1998.

Thampi, Madhavi : *India and China in the Colonial World,* Social Science Press, Delhi, 2010.

Thompson, William R.: *The Grievances of Military Coup-makers,* Beverly Hills: Sage Publications, 1973.

Veena Kukreja: *Civil-Military Relations in South Asia: Pakistan, Bangladesh, and India.* New Delhi: Sage, 1991

Weber, Katja: *Hierarchy amidst Anarchy: Transaction Costs and Institutional Choice.* Albany, NY: State University of New York Press, 2000.

William R. Thompson: *The Grievances of Military Coup-makers,* Beverly Hills: Sage Publications, 1973.

Wishnick, Elizabeth: *Mending Fences: The Evolution of Moscow's China Policy from Brezhnev to Yeltsin.* Seattle: University of Washington Press, 2001.

Index

L

M

N

O

P

S

T

U

W

❑❑❑